Praise for A Passion for Society

"*A Passion for Society* is a stirring rejection of the cult of dispassion in modern anthropology and sociology and a brisk rehabilitation of attempts to link fellow-feeling to pragmatic (and, yes, humanitarian) efforts to lessen the suffering of others. This defense of caring and caregiving revives old lessons and offers new ones, burnishing the example of great social theorists and of almost-forgotten ones. Iain Wilkinson and Arthur Kleinman are not trying to win an argument, although they do, but rather to offer a hopeful and humane intellectual basis for what is, fundamentally and unapologetically, a moral stance: against indifference and cynicism and inaction, and for their opposites. This fierce book is both balm and compass."

—Paul Farmer, MD, PhD, Harvard Medical School, Partners In Health, The Brigham and Women's Hospital

"The world is stuffed full of unbearable human misery. Every day billions of people in the world find themselves living in tragic desperation. What is to be done? How can a social science deal with this best? In this challenging, committed, and original study, Wilkinson and Kleinman provide a history and appreciation of the study of social suffering and urge us to place this at the heart of understanding society by putting compassion and practical care at its core. Critical of the formalism, distance, and coldness of both academic life and social science, the book creates new dialogues. It deserves to become a landmark in redirecting social science to work more passionately to make the world a kinder place."

—Ken Plummer, Emeritus Professor of Sociology, Essex University

"In their analysis of 'the problem of suffering,' Wilkinson and Kleinman provide a thoroughly convincing argument for a new approach to social theory and social research practice—one that is compassionate, interventionist, and globally oriented, and thus better able to address the pressing issues that define our age."

—Alan Petersen, Professor of Sociology, Monash University

CALIFORNIA SERIES IN PUBLIC ANTHROPOLOGY

The California Series in Public Anthropology emphasizes the anthropologist's role as an engaged intellectual. It continues anthropology's commitment to being an ethnographic witness, to describing, in human terms, how life is lived beyond the borders of many readers' experiences. But it also adds a commitment, through ethnography, to reframing the terms of public debate—transforming received, accepted understandings of social issues with new insights, new framings.

Series Editor: Robert Borofsky (Hawaii Pacific University)

Contributing Editors: Philippe Bourgois (University of Pennsylvania), Paul Farmer (Partners In Health), Alex Hinton (Rutgers University), Carolyn Nordstrom (University of Notre Dame), and Nancy Scheper-Hughes (UC Berkeley)

University of California Press Editor: Naomi Schneider

A Passion for Society

A Passion for Society

HOW WE THINK ABOUT
HUMAN SUFFERING

Iain Wilkinson and
Arthur Kleinman

UNIVERSITY OF CALIFORNIA PRESS

University of California Press, one of the most distinguished university presses in the United States, enriches lives around the world by advancing scholarship in the humanities, social sciences, and natural sciences. Its activities are supported by the UC Press Foundation and by philanthropic contributions from individuals and institutions. For more information, visit www.ucpress.edu.

University of California Press
Oakland, California

Library of Congress Cataloging-in-Publication Data

Wilkinson, Iain, 1969– author.
   A passion for society : how we think about human suffering / Iain Wilkinson and Arthur Kleinman.
        pages   cm. — (California series in public anthropology ; 35)
   Includes bibliographical references and index.
   ISBN 978-0-520-28722-8 (cloth : alk. paper)
   ISBN 978-0-520-28723-5 (pbk. : alk. paper)
   ISBN 978-0-520-96240-8 (ebook)
   1. Suffering—Social aspects.   I. Kleinman, Arthur, author.   II. Title.   III. Series: California series in public anthropology ; 35.
   BF789.s8w476 2016
   155.9′3—dc23   2015035014

Manufactured in the United States of America

24   23   22   21   20   19   18   17   16   15
10   9   8   7   6   5   4   3   2   1

Contents

Preface

He wept as he spoke, making his words sound choked and broken. An elderly Shanghainese now, he had come from a desperately poor, tiny village in Anhui Province. A friend of a friend, he was telling me how the Great Leap famine of 1960 had destroyed his family: one death from starvation following another. And how he himself had run away with two cousins to a Shanghai suburban town, where he had survived only to be caught up half a decade later in the mass violence of the Cultural Revolution. "My life was bitter," he said. "I had to endure great hardship. This was not a problem just for me: many, many fared the same. We felt, in our bodies, we saw terrible, horrible things. When I think back, I wonder how I survived. Even now, all these years later, I am carrying with me this grief." (Interview with Arthur Kleinman, Shanghai, 2006)

A small, elderly American woman now, with lively eyes and a charming but constrained expression, she quickly became solemn as she read from the books she had written about her experience in the Auschwitz death camp: bare, unadorned prose and saddening poetry conveyed the systematic brutality and inhuman horror of her Holocaust life. (Arthur Kleinman, conversation with Judith Sherman, Harvard University, 2013)

Both of these witnesses lived through now iconic times of mass violence. Their painful memories conjure not just their own, but widespread social suffering. If that collective experience of death, starvation, injury, forced displacement, and despair sounds like history, then read today's newspaper, watch the nightly news, or better yet speak with refugees in your community who came from one of the dozens of wars, civil conflicts, floods, earthquakes, or epidemics that are devastating human communities in the Middle East, Asia, Africa, and Latin America. And then speak to the poor, marginal, and broken families in Europe and America who are living the effects of structural violence in unemployment, inadequate schooling, substance abuse, mental illness, and chronic stress-related physical conditions. They too are experiencing social suffering—what Hannah Arendt referred to as "the social problem."

This modern sensibility that human misery, no matter how deeply interior in the individual, is often a collective experience resulting from large-scale societal forces that in turn break neighborhoods, villages, networks, and families emerged out of the concern of eighteenth- and nineteenth-century European and American thinkers with what human beings have had to endure. These early pioneers of social inquiry were, as we still are today, moved to witness and respond by doing something to assist not just individuals caught in desperate conditions, but whole populations, communities, and society at large. They understood that the sources and consequences of what was the matter were part of society itself, so that the interventions also had to be social.

These humanitarian witnesses and critics, who exposed social suffering in order to remedy human conditions were philosophers, novelists, poets, journalists, and reformers. Out of their efforts to question, understand, change, improve, and heal social worlds come what we now call social science, whose origins, then, are to be found in a shared conviction that the root causes of human misery lie in social conditions and that social theories, research, and policy are needed for societal reform to improve human futures.

The tendrils transmitting the founders' passion for practices of care to transform society influence medical anthropologists like Jim Yong Kim, currently president of the World Bank, and Paul Farmer, a leading figure in global health, who together developed a community-based model of accompaniment for treating AIDS and multi-drug-resistant tuberculosis among the poor in Haiti, Rwanda, Lesotho, Peru, and Siberia and who struggled to control the 2014 Ebola epidemic in West Africa by means of such society-building strategies as strengthening health services, developing community health workers, and insisting that high-quality caregiving is central to disease control. Their model of partnerships in care with the poor and marginal is based in a deep reading of social theory and the social history of colonial and postcolonial society, as well as extensive experience in the local worlds of the poorest members of society. Global public health practiced this way is a return to the passion for society that gave rise to the social sciences in the first place. The history of social medicine in South Africa in the 1940s and 1950s, which gave rise to early efforts to combine social science and medicine, as well as later developments in medical anthropology, medical history, and medical sociology—all suggest that the health arena may be an especially important social space for the building of social science projects and programs that meet the standard set by social science's founders. The fields of environmental, educational, and welfare reform provide other salient examples of where social science can build social care.

Social inquiry was originally taken up as a vital matter with human interests at its heart; and by this standard it made no sense to argue that the study of society should be undertaken for the production of knowledge for its own sake and that its practitioners should operate from a position of moral detachment. In its founding vision, in utter contrast, social inquiry was passionately committed to building knowledge, developing programs, and forging practices in order to make things better for real people facing the devastating effects of real, terrible problems: deep, grinding poverty, forced displacement, homelessness, overcrowding in sordid slums, violent alcohol-jogged lives, vicious workplace conditions, destroyed families, and early disablement and death. The clear interests of the early students of society were to document, to disguise, to improve, to prevent, and to care.

Over time, the professionalization of social inquiry and its institutionalization within the academy took it away from these meliorative and caring interests. Society was transformed from blood, guts, and anguish to an abstracted object of social inquiry. Professional research lost its human edge. It made itself into a "science" that aspired to the objectivity and reductions of the science of inanimate, unentangled entities. It lost or, in other words, diminished its human interest. Periodically, important figures—Jane Addams, Max Weber, Ferdinand Tönnies, W. H. R. Rivers,

Franz Boas and his students, C. Wright Mills, Robert Bellah, Renee Fox, a generation of American medical anthropologists and historians—protested against this development and spoke out on behalf of its originating passion. But until the past few decades, the tide was running in the opposite direction. Today, faced with an ever more pronounced crisis of relevance, social scientists are once again committing themselves to the study of social suffering and social care. Disturbing forces are pushing them to do so. Universities are turning away from humanities and social sciences to an emphasis on applied sciences, engineering, and the possibilities for basic science and technology to contribute to the economy, the environment, and health and health care. And students are voting with their feet as they rush toward preprofessional and business courses that offer better job prospects. The global revolution in information technology has added further pressure with its emphasis on the management of packaged knowledge stripped of its lived context, meaning, and interpretation.

On the more positive side, a renewed recognition of the potential contributions the social sciences can make to the downside of social change— structured violence, substance abuse, human trafficking, refugee trauma, sexually transmitted diseases, environmental health crises, epidemics of emerging diseases, broken communities, the unintended consequences of policies and programs, the increasing need for elder care—pulls social scientists toward interventions. As the ideology of value-neutral social science gives way to the practical knowledge commitments of social justice, humanitarianism, and social care, new possibilities for theory as well as empirical study are provided. This book tells this story. It seeks to show how deeper and more original knowledge of social suffering is crucial both for understanding where sociology and anthropology have come from and where they may now be headed. In that sense, it is a manifesto for a way of doing social science that the authors regard as liberating and redeeming. This is an approach to the study of society that begins and ends with the question of how to respond to social suffering.

This book is designed both as a resource for thinking about human social conditions and as a means to promote social science as an ameliorative social practice. It documents the origins and development of social suffering as a public, analytical, and critical concern. It charts the potential for problems of social suffering to awaken social consciousness and for this to inspire the pursuit of social understanding out of a commitment to initiate practical healing and progressive social change in people's lives. Our writing is informed by the conviction that a great deal of what now passes as social science is in thrall to technocratic procedures and structures of career that leave it critically sterile, cynical, and devoid of passion. By contrast, we aim to promote social inquiry as the enactment of substantive human values and as a moral commitment to building humane forms of society. On our account, it requires the cultivation of a "humanitarian social imaginary" and a commitment to humanitarian social reform. Our frame of analysis is set out in opposition to the production of social theory as mere academic discourse and against critique as an end in itself. It approaches the task of theoretical thinking with sights set on problem solving, particularly in contexts that bring great harm and damage to human life. Each chapter is designed to equip readers with resources to question the cultural character, operational conditions, and ethical value of social theory and research. By involving readers in many of the intellectual difficulties and moral tensions that are a necessary component of research and writing on social suffering, we aim to disclose the potential for this matter to reform the critical thinking and practice of social science.

This book can also be read as a further contribution to the development of a "care perspective" in social science. This notion already holds a great deal of resonance for many concerned with investigating the value placed on care in society and in understanding better the social conditions that make it possible for us to care effectively for others. Here we share in the conviction that while giving and receiving care is essential for our human flourishing as such, all too often this matter is cast to the margins of public debate and political concern. By exposing deficits in the quality of care provided to vulnerable and socially disadvantaged groups, moreover, the human costs of contemporary power relationships and social organization in terms of the corporeal and moral experience of suffering are laid bare. We understand research and writing on problems of social suffering to necessarily involve a commitment to understanding how the moral imperative to care for others is met, experienced, and negotiated under real-life conditions and is thereby either left frustrated or provided with a social space to nurture humanity. We are committed to the project of promoting care as a means to positively transform society and conditions of democracy. We would add, however, that we also see this as a fundamental requirement for the invigoration of human-social understanding. We not only argue that the value of social science should be sought in its involvement in the promotion of real acts of care in society, but also that it is through the act of caring for others that we stand to grasp how social life is made possible and sustained, most particularly in terms of what matters for people. We take the provocation of social suffering as a spur toward the alignment of social inquiry with the pedagogy of caregiving.

Acknowledgments

We owe a great debt of gratitude to many people who have helped in the creation of this book. We are grateful for the grant from the British Academy and support from Harvard's Michael Crichton Fund that bought us the space and time to start the work. At various points we were encouraged to keep writing by Gillian Bendelow, John Brewer, Keith Hayward, Gabe Mythen, and Chris Shilling in the United Kingdom; by Alan Petersen in Australia; by Ron Anderson, Paul Farmer, Anne Becker, Salmaan Keshavjee, Michael Jackson, Veena Das, João Biehl, Peter Benson, Clara Han, Angela Garcia, Yan Yunxiang, Everett Zhang, Allan Brandt, David Carrasco, Charles Rosenberg, Renée Fox, and David Mechanic in the United States; by Margaret Lock in Canada and New Zealand; and by Jing Jun, Xiao Shuiyuan, Pan Tianshu, Wu Fei, and Guo Jinhua in China. The ideas developed in these pages were presented at a seminar at Johns Hopkins University, where the thoughtful responses of Veena Das, Clara Han, William Connolly, Jane Bennett, and their colleagues were greatly appreciated. The argument presented in the book also benefited from discussion when it was presented at the University of Lisbon's Institute of Social Sciences. We are grateful to David Redmon for access to the documentary and ethnographic materials that informed the writing of the introduction and also for his encouragement. Special thanks are due to Janice Reid and Tim Strangleman, who spent time reading through drafts of chapters and offered valuable critical comments on the form and content of the text. We also wish to thank Annikki Herranen for her editorial work and proofreading. Administrative and research support from Linda Thomas, Marilyn Goodrich, Emily Harrison, Bridget Hanna, Maria Stalford, Andrew McDowell, Lindsay Alexander, and Andrew Ong is also greatly appreciated. There have been many occasions over the past few years when we have been sustained by the love of family, and without this, it is very doubtful we would have found the resolve to keep working through the most difficult times, which included most notably the death of Joan Kleinman, who helped develop the way social suffering is applied in medical anthropology and China studies. We are especially grateful to Janice Reid, Anne Kleinman, Peter Kleinman, Thomas Wong, Kelly Kleinman, Gabriel Wong, Kendall Kleinman, Allegra Wong, Clayton Kleinman, Laura Sloate, Marcia Kleinman, Anna Taylor, and Felix Wilkinson for their love, care, and understanding.

Introduction

The girl cannot spare the time to break away from her work. With urgent dexterity she carries on preparing the machine for melting and blending polystyrene with polyethylene to produce another string of plastic beads as she explains:

> We work for such a long time every day, but we only get a little salary . . . too little. It's incredibly little. Take me as an example. The most I've made this year is 500 yuan ($62) per month and not yet 600 yuan ($75). . . . Because I have come to earth I have to make a living. There are different ways to make a living. Those of us who are not well educated and don't have a good family background have no choice but to work and support ourselves. . . . When I was studying at school I dreamed of becoming an outstanding actress. But this dream will never be realized. . . . [Now I think] about how to help my parents financially and support my younger brother although I cannot realize my dreams. I still have hope in my brother. I believe he can achieve his dreams. I put all my hopes and dreams on my brother. . . . He's studying in school now. He's 12 almost 13. I suppose he has just entered middle school. . . . It's because we are poor. If I go to school, then my brother cannot go to school. Only one of us can go to school. . . . Unfairness is irrelevant. I am willing to sacrifice for my brother.[1]

Anxious to avoid the punishment of having her pay docked for not producing her daily quota of beads, she returns to her work. The air is heavy
with acrid fumes from melted polystyrene, fumes that when inhaled are
known to cause cancer and that also contain chemicals linked to hormo-
nal disruptions and birth defects.[2] The temperature inside the factory is
close to 40°C. All around her there is frenzied activity as her fellow laborers work as fast as they can to paint, polish, and solder strings of beads for
export to the New Orleans Mardi Gras Carnival, where in a glut of hedon-
istic excess they will be traded between revelers in exchanges for kisses
and sexual acts. Those riding high on the thrill of Carnival will know nothing of the many "wasted lives"[3] invested in the production of the pounds
of glittering beads hanging round their necks—all soon to be discarded as
cheap trash, flung to the street gutters for refuse collection destined for a
toxic landfill.

The vast majority of the Chinese factory laborers are girls between the
ages of fourteen and eighteen. They work with heads bowed in intense
concentration. There is no time to waste on talk; and aside from this, talk
risks further punishment of a cut in pay. Their hands are permanently
stained from handling various chemicals, dyes, and paints. Many are swol-
len and scarred from the cuts, burns, and pin prick wounds accumulated
through each working day, a day that lasts on average fourteen hours and
can rise to eighteen hours through the busiest times of the year. Between
shifts the girls live, eat, and sleep in the factory compound fenced off from
the outside world by high walls topped with lines of barbed wire in dorms
where beds are shared one between two. They only leave the compound on
their day off, which, so long as they are not required to work overtime to
meet the deadline for an order from America, comes once every two weeks.

The Tai Kuen Bead Factory is located in the "special economic zone" of
Fuzhou in the province of Fujian in Southeast China. Here "state capitalism" operates at full throttle, and nothing—least of all any concerns raised
over the health, safety, and welfare of migrant laborers—is permitted to
obstruct the frenetic pace at which consumer durables are manufactured
for export around the globe. Such zones are the powerhouses of the
Chinese economy and are the destination sought by many of the "floating"
(*liudon renkou*) rural migrant workers now caught up in the greatest
internal migration in human history.[4] In their desperate attempts to

escape rural poverty, these people are prepared to risk a marginal exist-ence outside the national *hukou* household registration system.[5] This requires them to endure brutal working and housing conditions beyond the reach of state social security and excluded from work safety legislation and basic health care provision. More often than not they are made to live and work in hazardous environments where a combination of exhausting toil, pollution, unsanitary conditions, and poor nutrition make them par-ticularly vulnerable to life-threatening disease.[6] The numbers of desper-ate "floating" people seeking work far exceeds the supply of jobs. Under these circumstances they inevitably find that as individual human beings they are treated by those in positions of power and authority as readily expendable if not little more than superfluous.[7]

This is a context of social suffering. Here the day-to-day experience of life is socially configured to involve large numbers of people in consider-able and often excessive amounts of physical discomfort and emotional distress. Social life is met and made in pronounced states of anguish and through grinding misery. People's living and working conditions are embodied in chronic fatigue, ritualized humiliations, and social shame. The high incidence of depressive symptoms and bodily disease among these populations serves as documentary evidence for social conditions that deliver harm to large numbers of people.[8] The situations in the textile industry in Bangladesh, in the mines of Burma and Congo, in the houses of Mumbai's slum dwellers where piecework is done night and day, in the garbage collecting in the northeastern Brazilian favelas, and in the broth-els of Cambodia and Lagos are the same if not worse: upending lives, breaking bodies, and vexing minds. Add violence to this destructive mix, because it is common in many places, and the resulting picture is brutal, cruel, and inhuman.

Such conditions are a key concern in this book. This places the problem of social suffering at the center of the attempt to unmask the moral char-acter of human societies. Social suffering is a critical issue that brings moral debate to the human costs exacted by our social arrangements, eco-nomic organization, cultural values, and modes of governance. The docu-mentation and analysis of this experience is taken up as a necessary part of the pursuit of social justice and as a vital matter for any who would see "care for the human" as a social priority.

This also draws the conduct and purpose of social science into debate. Here our interest lies not only in the capacity of social research to reveal how social suffering takes place and what it does to people but also with the manner of its contribution to the cultivation of bonds of social recognition and in its potential to inspire real acts of care. We are committed to exploring how social theory and research might operate in the service of social care and as a component of humanitarian endeavor. We contend, moreover, that it is through our participation in caregiving and by our involvement in humanitarian action, however difficult, frustrated, and compromised, that it is possible to attain a better grasp of what is socially at stake for people in the contexts in which they are made to live. The practice of care for others we take to be a necessary part of the pursuit of understanding of how social life takes place through enactments of substantive human values. Coming to terms with society means making sense of social suffering, and that in turn enjoins us to act in the social world on behalf of human lives.

This is another reason that we have featured the experience of a young woman working in the Tai Kuen Bead Factory as a means to introduce our text. It is drawn from a study that attempts to advance a new approach to documenting social life on a global scale by methods of visual ethnography. In his documentary film *Mardi Gras: Made in China*, David Redmon works not only to draw social attention to a chain of global relationships in the production, consumption, and disposal of Mardi Gras beads but also to provide us with an encounter with this as a matter of "sensual life." At one level his film is a study of how the sensual life of the beads, both in their manufacture and in their exchange, bind strangers across continents in a dense web of associations and interpersonal relations, many of which are exploitative, morally troubling, and destructive of human values. At another level, in addition to providing us with information on what is being done by and to people in these contexts, his aim is to have us affected by the human drama of social life. At the same time that we are invited to join with him in the shocking discovery of social arrangements that are designed to divest individuals of their humanity on one side of the globe so as to fuel the bacchanalia of consumption on the other, we are presented with material to enable us to *feel for* what is happening to people. Redmon's film is designed both to cultivate the sociological imagination and to provide a viscerally charged encounter with the brute facts of social life as moral experience in order to provoke in us a response to act to critique, unmake, and remake life.

This book further explores the role played by humanitarian feeling in the acquisition and development of our social understanding. We approach films such as *Mardi Gras: Made in China,* as well as many other sentiment-fired documents of social life, as representative of a long-standing tradition of social inquiry that aims to advance social consciousness by having us feel for people in their day-to-day challenges, perplexities, and struggles. We investigate the forms of inquiry, documentation, and methodology that are suited to make known conditions of social suffering. We set these within a history of critical debate over the category of the social as a component of human experience and as an object of "science," with an aim to question the moral values incorporated in favored terms of social understanding, especially where these are accorded a privileged place in the production of "authoritative" knowledge of social life. Our plan is to provoke debate over the human value of social science, and, further, over how it might be best equipped to advance care for the human as its prime concern.

We could have emphasized man-made and natural catastrophes, wars, epidemics, and other extraordinary forms of human misery. But instead we seek to privilege the ordinary, everyday forms of structural violence, because this is what social life is like for many people in the world who are poor and desperate, every day.

THE PROBLEM OF SUFFERING

In modern times, the problem of suffering has acquired an unprecedented capacity to confound our moral sensibilities and powers of reason. There are many occasions when it seems that the brute force of human affliction reduces the meaning of life to a worthless absurdity. Suffering is encountered not only as an assault upon our sensibilities and social understanding but also in forms and at intensities that exceed our powers of cultural representation and collective sensibility. The potential for the experience of suffering to bring us into painful confrontation with the cultural deficits of modernity and our inability to reconcile aspirations of social justice with global inequality and its profoundly human toll feature as a major provocation to philosophical and theological debate and as a principal theme of our narrative fiction.[9] The problem of suffering resides not so much in the lack of symbolic resources to give formal expression to our experience, but rather in the burden of the conviction that, in struggling to make known the human values at stake in the event of suffering, our efforts are always set to end in failure.[10] There is no form of culture that appears adequate to the task. Human suffering has inspired some of our most celebrated works of art, music, and literature. Yet more often than not it is the difficulty of understanding what suffering does to people and the torments borne through this perplexity on account of the sheer burden of experience that are featured. Our presiding concerns are how to understand and what to do.

How should we relate to a social world in which there is, quite plainly, far too much suffering? For example, how should we venture to account for the experience of the many millions of people whose lives have been, and continue to be, ravaged and drastically cut short by starvation and diseases of poverty? How should we depict the condition and fate of vast populations immersed in a constant struggle for physical survival? What form of language is suited to convey the "violence" that is done to more than a billion people who are born into the rapidly expanding slum districts of the megacities of the developing world and who are largely abandoned to work at surviving in diseased environments overflowing with industrial detritus and foul human waste?[11] How do we represent the losses and ungrounded lives of the world's 50 million refugees? And how do we use the language and understanding we do possess in order to respond?

How should we, moreover, venture to understand the great forces of destruction that have been unleashed upon the world through modern warfare and the scale of the human horror inflicted upon populations by powerful states intent on their annihilation? What kind of narrative script is adequate to capture the moral meaning of the many atrocities of war visited upon people in the mass slaughter of the Somme, the ruthless ferocity of Operation Barbarossa, the 20 million killed and 250 million displaced by Japan's war on the Chinese people, the bombing of Hiroshima and Nagasaki, the napalming of villages in Cambodia and Vietnam or the consequences of the destruction of Iraq?[12] Can anything in our culture serve to adequately account for the harm that is done to people made victims of the Shoah and other genocides or the trauma that is visited upon generations thereafter burdened by the knowledge of how the lives of those they love have been treated as no more than a superfluous irrelevance? Mass violence forces us to confront past horror and present brutality as the persistent "cruelty of the social."[13] What can be our response to such structural ferocity, such regular savagery? And doesn't that response also need to account for how memories of social suffering can fuel acts of vengeance, create vicious cycles of violence, and ruin lives of those unable to master histories of trauma?

When confronting these agonizing questions, some are inclined to take agony itself as a key to understanding how such extremes of suffering are borne within our culture. For example, Emmanuel Levinas advises that there may well be an essential part of the experience of human suffering that imposes itself on consciousness, yet must always remain somehow unacceptable to consciousness. He holds, "Taken as an experience the denial and refusal of meaning which is imposed as a sensible quality is the way in which the unbearable is precisely borne by consciousness, the way this not-being-borne is, paradoxically, a sensation or a given."[14] Levinas argues that it may well be by attending to the experience of failing to bestow sufficient meaning on suffering that we stand to gather some insight into the torment by which it is constituted in experience.

In a similar vein, others argue that we should approach suffering as a phenomenon that we literally "cannot come to grips with" and, further, hold that in acknowledging what suffering does to a person we should not flinch from declaring it "unspeakable."[15] Indeed, such a stance finds support from George Steiner when he argues that as a matter of ethical propriety we should stand opposed to the attempt to render extreme forms of human suffering amenable to representation in language, for words are always bound to trivialize such experiences to a point that is morally objectionable.[16]

A contrasting view holds that it is often through the adoption of an attitude of silence that we "mystify something we dare not understand."[17] On this account, the witness of silence is portrayed not so much as a form of empathy or moral understanding but rather as a device by which people work to remove themselves from the tensions borne in the face of the suffering of others.[18] It is argued that when struck by the difficulty of understanding what suffering does to people, our quiescence serves as a means to relinquish the effort to make sense of the brute facts of their situation. This is not only recognized as a matter of intellectual bad faith but also and more worryingly as a stance that some in positions of power and authority use to suppress wider questions of social justice and responsibility. Here many share in Hannah Arendt's concern to expose the capacity for official double-talk to silence the authentic voice of human affliction, and in this context it is claimed that it is likely that silence "degrades" the moral status of human suffering to a point where it can be treated as no more than a "meaningless triviality."[19]

A further layer of complexity is brought to these matters by Arthur Schopenhauer, who in a shift of emphasis notes that it is frequently the case that the experience of suffering is "powerfully intensified by thinking about absent and future things."[20] From this perspective, a great deal of the problem of suffering resides not so much in a lack of meaning but rather in the extent to which it acquires power to torment us through an elaborate use of meaning. Indeed, John Hick goes so far as to refer to suffering as "a function of meaning,"[21] for some terrible part of the trauma of the experience appears to consist in our capacity to imagine ourselves without suffering. On this account, it is vitally important to recognize the pain borne by people who are brought under the compulsion to reflect upon the overwhelming significance of adversity and loss. For instance, Primo Levi testifies that, contrary to what one might expect, his experience of Auschwitz was made all the more unbearable when, for a brief period, he was made to work in the relative comfort of a chemical laboratory, for here there was time and space in which to reflect upon the life he had lost and the miserable state to which he had been reduced. It was the "pain of remembering" that made his suffering even more "ferocious."[22]

At this point, while it is clear that suffering takes place within the most intimate dramas of personal life, at the same time it almost always encompasses attitudes and commitments that comprise our wider social being. As Eric Cassell observes, "[People] suffer from what they have lost of themselves in relation to the world of objects, events and relationships. Such suffering occurs because our intactness as persons, our coherence and integrity come not only from intactness of the body but also from the wholeness of the web of relationships with self and others. . . . [It incorporates] all the aspects of personhood." [23] It is almost always the case that the most grievous components of human suffering take place in the experience of broken relationships and lost connections to those individuals and contexts that bestow on our lives positive meaning. In the problem of suffering, the social constitution of our humanity is at stake. The most terrible and disabling events of suffering tend to involve us in the experience of losing our roles and identities as husbands, wives, children, friends, colleagues, and citizens; and thus we are made lost to ourselves. The social fabric of our world is torn, and may well be left beyond repair. We find ourselves enduring the unendurable. This experience of loss of a moral world is a kind of social bereavement connected to both man-made and natural disasters and registered in the individual and collective body as a sadness, disorientation, anomie, and unfulfillable longing.

Accordingly, we should not be surprised to find that the radical introspection that takes place when we are shaken by suffering cannot be withheld from a wider questioning of the social and cultural circumstances in which we are made to live. The difficulty of making adequate sense of suffering makes critics of us all. Indeed, it may well be the case that it is according to the force of our encounters with and proximity to experiences of human pain and misery that we revisit the original urgency of the drive to make "the social" component of our lives an explicit object of critical inquiry and moral concern. In this regard, the brute fact of suffering works on us so that we attend with heightened alertness and alarm to the ways in which our lives are marked by social circumstance; yet from here, many are also readily made to appreciate how difficult it is to make social life amenable to understanding, or to return to an unthinking acceptance of things as they are.

It is often suggested that under conditions of modernity—with the intensification of individual experience—the social experience of suffering has acquired a distinctive pitch and force. In part, this appears to be related to the peculiarity of the ways in which people are now socially disposed to feel, interpret, and respond to the tribulations of self and others. Accordingly, it may be addressed as a component of a series of modifications in shared ethical standpoints and cultural worldviews. At the same time, many have understood themselves to be witness to the development of social structures and material circumstances that are bound to increase the incidence and scale of human misery. Albeit with different frames of analysis in mind, the major classical social theorists tend to share in the understanding that processes of modernization give rise to institutional arrangements and cultural conditions that are experienced as deeply alienating and antihuman and that here the problem of suffering is set to grow in proportion and significance.[24]

Certainly, it is now widely recognized that it is largely due to the magnitude and force of critical events of human suffering that the past century is marked out above any other as "an age of extremes."[25] In recent history more people have been murdered or have been allowed to die as a direct result of human decisions than ever before.[26] At the same time, modern technologies of violence have greatly increased in power, range, and destructive force. It is only under conditions of modernity that it has become possible for nation-states to adopt strategies of warfare that involve the mass bombing of civilian populations. It is only here that social systems and industrial processes have been designed for the purposes of administering genocide and that we have witnessed the development of institutional practices that enable individuals to function with bureaucratic indifference and to morally disassociate themselves from the organizational behaviors that empower totalitarian regimes to perpetrate such horror.[27]

For many years social analysts have noted that modern societies are comprised by institutional arrangements that position individuals at a moral distance from the plight of others. A great deal of life is conducted according to social conventions and media of exchange that require us to deal with people in purely abstract and instrumental terms, and in this regard, it is argued that our ethical situation is quite unlike that of any other period of history.[28] Through the adoption of commonsense attitudes and routine behaviors we are thoughtlessly caught up in social processes and economic transactions that bring great suffering to distant strangers. Indeed, on this account, the problem of suffering has changed not only in relation to the scale and destructive force of catastrophes that break apart societies but also in accordance with the extent to which these are held to result as the unintended consequence of social practices that at their point of origin may well be viewed as ordinary and benign.[29] Modernity has given rise to social conditions in which the maintenance of "lifestyle" and the pursuit of "consumer aspiration" at one end of the globe are structurally implicated in the intensification of forces of destruction, violence, and oppression at the other.[30] We inhabit a global society where practices of everyday life are bound at some point to involve us in perpetuating social and cultural arrangements that deliver great harm to remote populations. Never before has social life been so thoroughly organized and regulated through institutions that remove us from the immediate task of thinking about, or rather, the stress of feeling for, the pains borne by abstract others. Here it seems all too easy for us to relate to the suffering of large numbers of people with an attitude of moral indifference, even to the point that it is possible to approach this situation as a "banal" fact of life.[31]

At the same time, however, under conditions of modernity it is possible to point to many social arenas and cultural contexts where the experience of human suffering attracts an unprecedented amount of moral attention and public concern. One of the more perplexing aspects of modern social life lies in the fact that while spending large amounts of time in institutional arrangements that dispose us to think and act without feeling for others, we are also brought into social settings where we are made to be emotionally preoccupied with the welfare of strangers. As Emile Durkheim observed, we appear to embody a social paradox in which at the same time that we might be inclined toward egoism we can also be possessed by a "sympathy for all that is human" and "a broader pity for all sufferings."[32] Indeed, some hold that it is by working to make clear the social conditions under which people acquire a heightened sensitivity to the spectacle of human misery that we begin to touch upon matters that make the modern problem of suffering quite different from any form in which it was recognized or experienced in any other time.[33]

There is a wealth of historical evidence to suggest that in the middle decades of the eighteenth century new structures of feeling and forms of sensibility took shape and gathered force in Western European societies and that these were accompanied by a major reorientation of attitudes toward human suffering.[34] This period witnessed the rapid rise of public campaigns against the use of torture in criminal proceedings, and it was also the point at which movements for the abolition of slavery gathered social momentum and political support. It is argued that at this time moral sentiment became a powerful force in our political culture; and further, that this was, and to this day remains, a vital component of humanitarian politics and the social appeal of human rights.[35]

The politics of sensibility have always been riven with controversy. At its origins many were inclined to question the authenticity of expressions of fellow feeling and moved to pour scorn upon any suggestion that there is virtue in moral sentiment.[36] More often than not, in the history of Western social science writers have worked more with a mind to question the social and political legitimacy of moral feeling than to explore the possible ways in which this might be cultivated as a means to further social understanding or pursue matters of social justice.[37] It is only in recent years that there has been a concerted movement to reappraise the cultural histories of sentiments such as pity, sympathy, and compassion, on one side, and forgiveness, remorse, and regret, on the other, so as to chart their wider social significance and contribution to public affairs.[38]

On many accounts, the renewed vigor with which social scientists now attend to the cultural and political dynamics of varieties of moral feeling is intimately connected to the spread of modern communication media, especially where this serves to make visible multiple and extreme forms of human suffering that would otherwise remain hidden and remote from our day-to-day fields of experience. John Thompson contends that via television and the Internet, we are regularly brought into contact with extreme forms of death and destruction that would have been unknown (or at least unseen) to previous generations.[39] Similarly, when highlighting the peculiarity of the cultural and moral landscapes we occupy, Michael Ignatieff observes that such technologies have made us routine "voyeurs of the suffering of others, tourists amid their landscapes of anguish."[40] In this context, it is generally held that the task of fashioning an appropriate moral response to such experience is made inordinately difficult.

It is very likely that the moral and political contradictions that arise for people in connection with the experience of being positioned as remote witnesses of other people's suffering are without precedent. Luc Boltanski contends that the widely shared experience of being a "detached observer" of human affliction intensifies a shared sense of political powerlessness and moral inadequacy,[41] for we routinely find that we have no adequate means to answer the imperative of action—to do something, anything to respond—that the brute facts of suffering impress upon us. On a more critical footing, it is suggested that when repeated over time such experience serves to erode our capacities for moral feeling and thereby makes it all too easy for us to dissociate ourselves from ties of responsibility toward others. Indeed, some are inclined to argue that the mass dissemination of the imagery of suffering via commercial forms of cultural reproduction and exchange is effecting a major transformation in the experience of social subjectivity, particularly insofar as this "normalizes" a vivid awareness of others' suffering in contexts that foreclose possibilities for participation in public debate and withhold the option of a compassionate engagement with human needs.[42] This transformation of the self holds broad significance for understanding, as well as for pursuing, how suffering is experienced and how that embodied experience is changing in distinctive cultural periods.

Throughout history and across all cultures, human suffering has been identified as a "limit condition" through which we stand to apprehend some of the most basic truths about our state of being and place in the world.[43] In this respect, it appears that the vulnerability of the human condition is such that we are always bound to take the impossibility of retreat from suffering as a bitter guide to self and social wisdom. In the record of human suffering, we repeatedly come across the extreme paradox that through experiences that entail the most terrible uprooting of life, we are brought under the compulsion to reach out for what really matters in our lives.[44] That makes suffering an intensively moral experience, one laden with value and reflective of value conflicts.

Human beings are continually set to the task of making the brute facts of suffering productive for thought and action; but on many accounts, the scale of this task now readily exhausts our capacities for thinking and makes the greater part of our actions appear useless. The dimensions and complexity of this problem are overwhelming. In venturing to make the problem of suffering a matter for social inquiry and understanding, it may well be the case that we do no more than embark on an ill-advised and foolhardy quest to carry "the weight of the world."[45] Failure seems inevitable; yet it may still be possible to fail forward toward better ways of taking account of ourselves and relating to others. This is the character of our commitment and hope. And for knowledge useful for the art of living, there is no likely alternative.

SOCIAL SUFFERING

Social suffering is a concept developed to understand how people's suffering is caused and conditioned by society. It is designed to document forms of social experience and lived conditions that determine how suffering takes place and what this does to people. In the study of social suffering, people's pains and miseries are taken as grounds on which to make our social state of being a matter for critical and moral inquiry. The labeling of problems under this heading is intended to bring critical scrutiny to the ways in which the character of society is exposed through the incidence of suffering. Research and writing on social suffering incorporates an analytical practice that aims to have us attend to the ways in which cultures and societies develop in response to the uprooting of life that suffering visits upon people. Social experiences of suffering and social responses to what suffering does to people are treated as significant forces shaping interpersonal behaviors and the directions taken by institutional arrangements. Accordingly, the experience of suffering per se is treated as a dynamic element within wider processes of social and cultural change and as a circumstance in which these might be apprehended through their human effects.

There is the potential for social suffering to take place at all levels of society and in every social event and process. While most obviously taking place in the context of critical events that involve people in experiences of sudden destruction and loss, both man-made and acts of nature, it is also a component of the structural conditions and formative processes that govern the course of our lives from cradle to grave. At the same time, as a focus on social suffering incorporates an attempt to understand the moral calamity of human catastrophe, it is also a moral register of political and economic processes that leave people materially disadvantaged, culturally undernourished, and socially deprived. Social suffering takes place wherever harm is done to human life.

As a field of inquiry, research and writing on social suffering may be located in a wider movement within current sociology and anthropology that understands bodily experience and expressions as not only the product of individual behavior but also as instances where social worlds are seen, touched, and felt. Embodied experience is held up as a mirror to society and as primary material for sociological and anthropological investigation. Social suffering draws a focus to how bodily experiences of pain and distress are conditioned and moderated by social context. This often serves to expose how "structural violence" plays a part in the social distribution of many forms of bodily disease and mental illness, and for this to be made materially evident in the limits set for people's health.[46] Bodily afflictions—from TB to AIDS, from depression to eating disorders—are analyzed in terms of what they reveal about a person's social and material conditions of existence and are treated as a platform from which to initiate critical inquiries into the structural formation of societies and the institutional exercise of power. Privations of health and health care, such as malnutrition, neonatal and maternal mortality, and untreated chronic noncommunicable diseases, are taken as instances of the violation of people's social, economic, and civil rights. Biological processes are seen as biosocial interactions that give rise to local biologies such as drug resistance, stress and placebo responses, and medicalization.

To analyze the social meaning and bounds of human suffering requires that we recognize from the outset that we are dealing with a profoundly moral experience. Suffering takes place as an intensely violent and harmful assault on human personhood. It is an overwhelmingly and, very often, alarmingly negative experience. The pain of suffering signals that something very bad is taking place and that there is something terribly wrong with our world. As such, it not only issues a demand for critical scrutiny, but also for ameliorative actions to oppose the harms that it does to people. Even though a great deal of the torment of suffering resides in the struggle to make adequate moral sense of it as an experience, an even greater part of it lies in the urgency that is brought to the imperative to reduce its effects and to remove people from harm's way. It brings brute force and volume to the fact that social life takes place in enactments of substantive human values in settings of real danger and serious uncertainties. A great deal is at stake for persons. Within the analytical frame of social suffering, the task of social understanding requires that we work at being particularly attentive to the dilemmas of moral experience and the great tensions that are borne by people under the struggle to lead a moral life, including using understanding to forge more adequate responses to suffering and, more generally, to create social care. Social suffering requires a response of care and caregiving practices, action on and in the world. This needs repeating. Social suffering cannot be studied in the absence of committing to social interventions. Such interventions, however, not only may relieve suffering; they can increase it (intentionally or unintentionally), and they also can fail. This landscape of implementation of programs and services is also the landscape of social suffering; it is fraught with moral difficulty and almost inevitably courts opposition and conflict.

FOR A NEW SOCIAL SCIENCE

We contend that under the attempt to engage with problems of social suffering, the practice of social science is brought to new ground. Here the task of understanding social life involves open expressions of moral worth and political aspiration. Empirical social research is valued both as a means to bring the evidence of lived experience to bear upon theoretical terms of analysis and public debate and as a "reflexive" process whereby practitioners are sensitized to the moral values and political investments that shape their professional conduct and genres of action. As fields of social practice and as spaces of knowledge production, the social sciences are placed under moral and political scrutiny. In addressing problems of social suffering, we are called to question the social meaning and moral worth of academic work and the formal processes whereby problems of human life are adopted as scholarly concerns.

To work at addressing problems of social suffering involves more than a drive to expose the social causes and distribution of the harms that are done to people.[47] In the commitment to the task of devising forms of social theory and research that are relevant to understanding how suffering takes place and what can be done to limit its deleterious effects on human life and to respond with care, a focus on problems of social suffering demands a thoroughgoing examination of past and current conventions of social science. It requires an effort to make explicit the social, cultural, and political conditions under which knowledge of society is produced and sanctioned as a legitimate basis for public debate and policy concern. It involves us in critically reappraising the methods and techniques that are deployed under the effort to extend the boundaries of human insight and social care. On this view, social work and social policy, including the social sciences in health and health care, are as central as sociology, anthropology, political science, history, social psychology, and social theory.

A key matter for analysis and debate concerns the involvement of lived experience in our research and thinking. This involves an examination of traditions of ontology and epistemology, and in particular, the relative importance placed on the contribution of human experiences of social life to the conceptualization and analysis of public affairs.[48] It requires that we investigate the forms of transaction that take place under the effort to document social experience, and that we make explicit the interpretive practices and expository techniques that come into play as this is disciplined to the strictures of sociological and anthropological understanding. It also calls on us to declare a standpoint with regard to claims that we are witness to, and to a greater or lesser extent contributing to cultural and political processes that impoverish people's experiences of the world and their outlooks on life.

In all this a focus is brought to the ways people experience, express, and struggle against the presence of suffering in their lives. At one level, this engages us with the task of bringing anthropological and sociological meaning to the experience of critical events and social upheavals that shock our sense of reality and overturn our normative expectations for the world. It involves attempts at understanding how personal and social worlds are suddenly and radically altered under the brute force of experiences that bring violence and destruction to those things that hold prime value and meaning for life. At another level, it incorporates the analysis of cultural processes, institutional formations, and structural conditions that either increase or diminish the negative force of suffering over extended periods. Human suffering takes place both in the experience of disruptive events that crash into our lives and as a contingent product of cultural worldviews and social conventions that are rooted in historical and material circumstance. Accordingly, we need to understand how current problems of suffering contribute to the dynamics of contemporary social and interpersonal change, but we also have the task of recognizing the extent to which past experience leaves its marks upon the forms of culture and social practices through which we deal with the present. Indeed, here the door is opened on to debates concerning the ways in which social suffering has had, and continues to have, an incisive bearing upon the trajectories set for modern processes of rationalization, from the categorization of emerging illness to the way we conceive of serious environmental problems, and how these might be more effectively managed for the benefit of humanity.

In these contexts, questions of human value are always liable to be raised in relation to the conduct of research and the tenor of thinking on display. By engaging with problems of social suffering, social scientists are frequently brought to debate with the legacy of humanism in their respective fields of practice and to answer for the damage and injury that have taken place under this name. Here social science is placed under a moral demand to make clear the ways in which it might be construed, or indeed misconstrued, as a site of learning that aims to advance the bounds of human empathy and understanding. It is brought under pressure to examine the extent to which its practices might be associated with humanitarian ideals and interventions. It is made to assess its contribution to the development of humane forms of society. On some accounts, this calls for an appraisal of the possibility that social science might be repositioned and reformed as a project of "critical humanism," that is, as an arena of study where practitioners stand opposed to forms of essentialism and reductionism that diminish our appreciation for the great variety of human conditions but united in a commitment to understand how our capacity to recognize the suffering borne by others can be nurtured as the common ground on which to establish principles of human rights and practices of care.[49]

In these quarters, the issue of social suffering has a tendency to preoccupy social scientists with further questions relating to the global relevance of their work. Researchers stand to acquire a heightened awareness of the extent to which traditions of Western social science amount to only a minority report on what is at stake for humanity within present conditions of modernity. When the incidence, severity, and distribution of human suffering is brought to the fore as a key matter for social understanding, then attention is readily drawn toward the biases set within American and Western European conventions of analysis and narrative representation. The brute fact is that many of the more extreme forms of human suffering take place in poor and often non-Western sectors of the globe, that is, those parts of the world that Western social science often treats as standing "outside" or as "lagging behind" the core experience of social life in the modern world (i.e., that which takes place within the borders of the most industrially "advanced" nations).

The focus on social suffering brings urgency to demands for a radical realignment of the poles of world understanding, particularly where it is made all too painfully clear that the majority experience of modernity takes place amidst wastelands of material deprivation and violent disorder. Here the importance accorded to matters of health not only marks an attempt to document some of the most widely prevalent and existentially decisive contexts of social suffering, but also a move to devise analytical practices and terms of critical inquiry that are suited to account for planetary human conditions, conditions shaped by social injustices and inequality. In this context, it is understood that a focus on health disparities serves to present the sociosomatic condition of humanity—the registration of social forces in the body—both as an issue of utmost importance for global social research and as the foundation for debates on social justice. And engagement with a wider world of theories of suffering, including local understandings and non-Western traditions, offers a promising alternative to the limits of established and increasingly conventional understandings in what might be called a new global social theory.[50]

This all involves a strong commitment to the development of social science as a field of social care and caring practice. There has to be more than an expression of intellectual interest and emotional concern here; there must also be an application to "work that sustains life."[51] While there are occasions when this involves an immediate attempt to disrupt social conventions and to break down moral boundaries that obstruct possibilities for human engagement, elsewhere it calls for concerted political actions to oppose social conditions and policy decisions that bring harm to populations. Under the effort to promote social possibilities for people's recovery, regeneration, and healing, it challenges us to forge alliances and working partnerships with colleagues outside our immediate spheres of expertise and nationhood. It highlights a pressing need for a critical reflexivity that aims not only to make explicit the values that shape our practice but also to take action to change the institutions that govern the way we work. It requires an active engagement with the task of reordering institutional priorities and redesigning occupational practices so that these are made more responsive to pressing human and social needs. It aims to make social science transformative in aspiration: both a caregiving and world changing activity.

CHAPTERS IN OUTLINE

Our text is designed to court many intellectual tensions and moral perplexities in the hope that these will be productive for further thinking. At the same time as we venture to mark out a distinctive position on how research and writing on problems of social suffering might be adopted as a core concern in contemporary sociology and anthropology (the areas of social science with which we are most familiar), we also aim to equip readers with some of the critical questions with which they might respond to our work. Each chapter is written as an invitation to dialogue and debate. We invite and welcome dispute, for we understand this serves as a means to involve readers in questions of human value and social purpose. Indeed, we hold that this is necessary for thinking about the human condition in contexts of social suffering.

The first three chapters trace the origins and development of social suffering as a form of human experience and as a matter for social inquiry and analysis. In this we aim to provoke debate over how we should engage with and account for "the social" in human experience. We also explore the potential for the moral experience of being positioned as a witness to human suffering to serve as a spur for the development of social consciousness and as a provocation to engage in the pursuit of social understanding. The first chapter is largely devoted to the attempt to explain how the creation of social suffering as a means to categorize human experience marks a revolution in modern terms of cultural understanding. To this end, a spotlight is focused on the earliest references to social suffering in the late eighteenth century; and here we analyze the involvement of this term in Enlightenment cultures of critical debate relating to the forms of social understanding that are made possible through moral feelings aroused by the spectacle of human misery. In chapter 2 we trace the development of these debates through the nineteenth century and examine their reception within, as well as their influence upon, nascent forms of social science. Here we also review some of the ways in which matters of moral sentiment have often been cast as anathema to conventions of social science, albeit with a concern to outline an opposing point of view. In this context we underline the particular potential for problems of social suffering to arouse dispute over the forms of social inquiry and practices of social investigation that are best suited to convey the human experience of social life. Chapter 3 further develops this theme via a critical analysis and appraisal of the ethical and methodological problems left in the wake of C. Wright Mills's celebrated account, *The Sociological Imagination* (1959). We use this as a means to frame and review some of the main developments in contemporary research and writing on social suffering. Here we begin to argue in favor of an approach to social inquiry that, while attending to the causes of human suffering and its lived consequences, takes steps to move beyond a position of critique so as to engage in the practical delivery of care and progressive social reform.[52] Accordingly, we declare an interest in redeveloping Mills's sociological ambition beyond the limits of "imagination" to a point where it holds practical value and relevance for people in lived experience. We look forward to a possible reconfiguration of social science as a critical practice of accompanying and caring, protecting and liberating.

Chapter 4 offers a broader framework of analysis for historically situating and critically appraising this endeavor by reviewing the components of Max Weber's theorization of the problem of suffering and its development as a distinct form of experience within modern culture. We hold that there is still much to learn from Weber for understanding the cultural limitations of social science and how these are exacerbated through the practice of social inquiry, and particularly where this is applied to the attempt to explain the causes and consequences of human suffering. We commend Weber's thinking on these matters for the extent to which it enables us to better recognize and endure the considerable "antinomies of existence" that we encounter when we attempt to make our research and writing hold relevance for making sense of what suffering does to people. Our interest in Weber lies not only in how he can help us to theorize the cultural context in which we operate but also in the extent to which his work might inspire us with the resolve to endure the task of living through the experience of this in practice. We see Weber's view of the tragedy of history, and especially where he engages in an attempt to understand the peculiarity of our modern social condition in terms of an experience of pronounced value conflicts and considerable antinomies of existence, as one deep reading of life that holds the potential to alter the way we live.

In chapters 5 and 6 we dwell more directly on issues of application and practice. Both these chapters review and analyze some of the modifications that are set to take place in the conduct of social research as this is fashioned to address and respond to problems of social suffering. We explore some of the strategies that may be used as a means to feature experiences of social suffering within the cultural scripts of sociology and anthropology. We promote the pedagogy of caregiving as a means to acquire social understanding and to give full rein to a passion for society.

Chapter 5 critically appraises the praxis that informs some of the methods used to render the experience of human suffering as a "text" for social understanding. We argue that a "humanitarian social imaginary" is heavily involved in the attempt to provoke social consciousness and bring moral urgency to the quest for knowledge of people in social terms in order to respond to social suffering. We also outline arguments to support this, and further, move to defend our standpoint against some of the objections that may be leveled against the incorporation of "humanitarian reason" in documents of social life.[53]

Through a review of Jane Addams's manner of "doing sociology," we turn in chapter 6 to the task of assessing possibilities for the conduct of social research to be both engaged with and to draw inspiration from practices of caregiving. We argue that, in the final analysis, it is in its potential to serve as a means to promote social care and caring social relations that research and writing on social suffering should be held up for moral and critical judgment. Our interest lies not so much in the currency of care as an ethical principle or moral ideal but rather in the ways in which real acts of caregiving, while committed to helping people live through, endure, and recover from real-life situations of adversity, also serve as a guide to social understanding. With this emphasis we declare a commitment to a social research practice that is sustained not so much by a quest for academic recognition but more by a moral concern to be actively involved in the creation of humane forms of society.

In conclusion, we provide a summary outline of the key arguments developed through the book. We also take steps to make clear the scale and character of the challenge set for social science when problems of social suffering are taken up as a core concern. This most certainly requires that we arm ourselves, as Weber might put it, "with a steadfastness of heart which can brave even the crumbling of all hopes,"[54] for there is no doubt that this must involve us in attending to social conditions that destroy both human life and the possibility of it holding positive meaning. At the same time, we take this as necessary for the cultivation of sociologies and anthropologies to inspire genuine hope for humanity, and above all, the passion to sustain the care required to deliver this in lived experience.

1 The Origins of Social Suffering

The concept of social suffering originates in the late eighteenth century. It first features as a point of reference in poetry documenting the transformation of country life in the early period of the Industrial Revolution.[1] In this context social suffering as either a manifest condition or a quality of experience is not taken up as a matter for formal analytical scrutiny; rather it is adopted as a point of reference for writers moved to document scenes of rural deprivation that make a mockery of romantic notions of the pastoral idyll. In his *Descriptive Sketches*, written in 1792–93 in recollection of a summer spent traveling around postrevolutionary France and the Swiss Alps, William Wordsworth refers to social suffering in a passage that records his encounter with destitute and sick peasants living in the forest along the banks of the upper reaches of the Rhine. He writes:

> The indignant waters of the infant Rhine,
> Hang o'er the abyss, whose else impervious gloom
> His burning eyes with fearful light illume.
> The mind condemned, without reprieve, to go
> O'er life's long deserts with its charge of woe,
> With sad congratulation joins the train
> Where beasts and men together o'er the plain

Move on a mighty caravan of pain:
Hope, strength, and courage, social suffering brings,
Freshening the wilderness with shades and springs.

In this instance, Wordsworth's encounter with social suffering draws him to reflect upon the stoic attitudes adopted by people struggling to survive in conditions of extreme adversity; and despite all he has seen, he draws hope for humanity and for himself from this. Commentators understand this poem to mark the early signs of a political awakening that led Wordsworth to an interest in the prospects for revolutionary social reform and also to the attempt to fashion his poetry as a means to raise the moral and material conditions of society as matters for public debate.[2]

The possibility of making reference to social suffering as a distinct form of moral experience signals a major revision in the terms of human understanding. It attests to the arrival of structures of feeling, intellectual convictions, and moral dispositions that are without precedent. Before the second half of the eighteenth century no reference is made to social consciousness per se, and there is no record of people moving to directly identify suffering as an intrinsic component of the social realm. The possibility of thinking about individuals as shaped by social worlds or as subject to social conditions was acquired through a large-scale transformation in popular attitudes and cultural worldviews. This involved a definitive break with traditional approaches to documenting and making sense of experiences of pain and misery. It involved a radical revision of the cultural frames of reference by which human suffering was cast as a problem for humanity.

The adoption of the concept of social suffering in writing and public debate signals the arrival of an approach to interpreting the meaning of human suffering as an explicitly *social* condition. Here the spectacle of human misery is taken as a cue to reflect critically upon prevailing social attitudes and social relations. Experiences of "fellow feeling" that take place through the witnessing of human affliction are understood to hold the potential to operate as a form of social disclosure. People's moral feelings about human suffering are taken as social bonds that imply an obligation to acknowledge, respond to, and care for the pain and distress of others. At the same time, however, it is clear that from this point on many questions remained with regard to how one should interpret, express, and manage these emotional ties, and for that matter, at its origins, the possibility of setting the bounds for social responsibility or devising conceptually adequate terms for thinking about how this should take place courts much dispute.

The early realization of social suffering as a component of human experience is accompanied by a series of intellectual difficulties and moral tensions that are often allied to the conviction that there is no sufficient means to account for, or respond to, people's suffering. At the same time that certain types of pain and distress are experienced and/or represented for the first time as matters issuing a moral demand for *social* reform, there is little agreement as to how this should be interpreted, evaluated, and set into action. The concern to understand human suffering in social terms brings critical debate both to the moral meaning of suffering and to the category of "the social." In this context, the forms of consciousness acquired by the encounter with social suffering tend to be deeply troubled and perplexed. From the outset they involve people in a struggle to articulate the insight and in an agitated search for greater clarity of understanding.

When attending to problems of social suffering, social science is set to investigate forms of experience that are constituted by many complex exchanges between meaning, feeling, thought, and action. There are three analytical concerns that feature in the discussion that follows. The first of these aims to understand the cultural circumstances under which human suffering is encountered as a radical challenge to our cultural capacities for sense-making and as a torment that brings us under the compulsion to question how we should live and what we should do. This involves an effort to document the sociohistorical conditions under which individuals are most likely to relate to the spectacle of other people's suffering and/or interpret their own experience of affliction as matters for which there is a distinct deficit of moral meaning. The second attends to the social origins and dynamics of "moral individualism," the cultural disposition that Emile Durkheim identified as giving rise to "sympathy for all that is human" and "a broader pity for all sufferings."[3] Here there is a particular concern to understand the part played by the experience of human suffering in the history of emotions and how, in turn, the response to human suffering is conditioned by social structures of feeling and behaviors that are always open to change. The third concern involves the possibility of understanding how these new problems and dimensions of human suffering are implicated in the generation of social consciousness and the moral impulse to ameliorate the social conditions in which people are made to live. In this context, a focus is brought to occasions where individuals are moved by their encounters with suffering to think about themselves and others as intrinsically *social* beings and how by acting to change prevailing qualities of social experience and reform society, they might better care for those made subject to extreme conditions of suffering.

This chapter is organized around three short essays. Each is designed to advance distinct points of view on the putative origins, likely consequences, and supposed qualities of the social and cultural changes that first made possible the categorization of human experience in terms of social suffering. The first of these offers an explanation for the lost "art of suffering" and ventures to trace some of the ways in which this is implicated in the founding and development of modern humanitarianism. The second develops some of the interests raised in the first essay but with a greater focus on the extent to which transformations in the cultural portrayal and humanitarian response to suffering are coordinated by shifts in moral feeling. The third essay examines some of the ways in which moral feelings about human suffering came to be openly recognized as social bonds, and further, bonds that implied a responsibility to care for and to take actions to alleviate the suffering of others. In each instance, emphasis is placed upon the many difficulties of understanding and moral tensions that accompany these developments. We hold that many of these continue to infuse encounters with social suffering to this day.

We aim to draw readers into debate over the ways in which the documentation of human experience as social suffering bears testimony to a series of revolutionary transformations in popular beliefs about the moral meaning of pain, the causes of human misery, and how we should care for the afflictions of others. We contend that, at its origins, the conjunction of "the social" with "suffering" marks a radical recasting of popular conceptions of the relationship between God and society, and in particular, a considerable waning of belief in so-called special providence (the conviction that God is inclined to regularly intervene in extraordinary ways in people's lives). In this setting, "the social" as a distinct realm of moral experience and action is rendered conscionable as the scale and frequency of experiences of human suffering serve to make providentialism appear both morally objectionable and intellectually implausible. Somewhat ironically, the ground is cleared for understanding human life in social terms as an unintended consequence of a strong commitment to providentialism; it is conceived under the burden of pain and distress encountered through many sustained and frustrated attempts to marry belief with experience. Here we also work to highlight how this shift in theological understanding and allied dawning of social consciousness was augmented through the acquisition and cultivation of new forms of emotionality. In this context, "the social" is first encountered not only as a provocation to forge a more "secular" (or rather, imminently rational) meaning and response to experiences of pain and suffering but also as a matter that holds the potential to affect us morally. To fully appreciate the critical issues at stake in the categorization of human experience in terms of social suffering requires us to engage with the ongoing attempt to understand how these changes were first made possible, and further, how these continue to be realized, acknowledged, and made morally forceful in our lives today.

THE LOST "ART OF SUFFERING"

"The art of suffering" is a phrase first used by the Puritan divine Richard Baxter (1615–91) when advising fellow believers on how they should relate to the pains suffered at the hands of others.[4] As a matter of Christian calling and duty, Baxter exhorts his readers to learn the "art of suffering." On this understanding, all afflictions are sent by God either as punishment for sin or as tests designed to draw believers toward a closer relationship with him. All earthly events and the conditions set for human relationships are brought about by God's will and shaped by his hand. Providence may work as much through the momentary discomforts of trivial incidents as through the trauma of great catastrophe; and for those practicing the "art of suffering," all hardships and adversities must be patiently endured in the knowledge that God is at work in all things. Comfort is drawn from the knowledge that a divine purpose lies behind apparently random events of suffering, and under this conviction the Bible is consulted as an authoritative guide to the types of actions that should take place as a means to remedy the situation.

Surveys of Christian writings and sermons through the European Middle Ages and early modern period reveal a remarkable consensus of opinion as to the meaning of human suffering. A considerable amount of dispute always surrounds the correct way to understand and interpret the mechanics of the interrelationship between God's will, human actions, and natural events, but there is no doubting the providential design of creation.[5] The Bible teaches that suffering is not only sent by God as a punishment for wrongdoing, but also that it is used by him as a means to redeem his creation from sin. God can choose to make the sun stand still, and when angered, he sends earthquakes, floods, hails of fire and brimstone, famine, and epidemic disease to destroy populations. When working to chastise people for their sin, God might well contrive to set events in place so that societies are made subject to defeat in war and suffer enslavement under their enemies. In order to fulfill his greater purpose he even chooses to treat some people as "vessels of wrath fitted to destruction."[6] Theologies of divine retribution are set alongside theologies of redemption that cast suffering as an instrument of sanctification (as supremely demonstrated in the sacrificial torture and death of Christ) and as an experience that is given to the saints, so that through their submission to God's will they may be commended to others as an example of faith. In the New Testament, Christians are advised to treat physical hardships and persecutions as blessings from God and to rejoice that he considers them worthy to partake in Christ's sufferings and, of course, to draw comfort from the knowledge that ultimately their reward will be in heaven.[7]

Marc Bloch maintains that such beliefs tended to give rise to forms of emotion and behavior that hardly enter into the motivations and experience of most modern people.[8] The conviction that God was directly involved in all things made people "morbidly attentive" to his messages as revealed through natural signs and wonders. Comets, unusual colors and patterns in the sky, floods, and unnatural births were widely held to be warnings of judgments to come. It was widely thought that God's wrath was made manifest in storm damage, disastrous fires, failed harvests, and epidemic disease. Within this worldview, it was assumed that every pain and adversity that broke into the capricious flow of bodily experience was thoroughly invested with both moral and divine meaning. Frequent and persistent encounters with devastating outbreaks of disease, sudden and untimely deaths, and periods of famine were accompanied by many "despairs," "impulsive acts," and "sudden revulsions of feeling" as people earnestly struggled to make sense of God's will and moral instruction.[9] Similarly, Alexandra Walsham contends:

> The struggle to discern some pattern behind one's violently swinging fortunes could induce an obsession, not to say neurosis, revolving around the unintelligibility of God's predestinarian scheme. Predicated upon a causal connection between affliction and guilt, this was a philosophy with a distinct tendency to deflate the self-esteem of the sufferer and foster a masochistic internalization of blame. When combined with the ingrained convictions about human depravity, a paranoid reading of providential events was liable to intensify mental stress over to a 'reprobate sense'. Direful apprehensions of divine victimization, whether in the guise of objectively verifiable experience or inner anguish and torment, encouraged an unhealthy degree of introspection.[10]

Such beliefs lent weight to the understanding that every calamity and misfortune that befell a person was a sign of his or her sinfulness or a direct result of the sins committed by persons within his or her family or community; and further, that God intended the person to "profit from affliction." For example, on the death of his infant son from diphtheria, Ralph Josselin (1616–83) was moved to reason that this was a punishment sent by God for his vanity as well as his tendency to spend too much time playing chess. He held that the pain of his grief was a call to repentance.[11] Some of the most devout Puritans were also inclined to express anxieties over not having been made to suffer enough. For example, insofar as affliction served to sanctify the believer, the English clergyman and theologian John Downame (1571–1652) proclaimed suffering to be a sign of God's "affection."[12] Similarly, there are records of the Church of Ireland archbishop, James Ussher (1581–1656), worrying over the possibility that God no longer loved him because he was not experiencing any obvious hardship or pressing matter of conscience.[13] Accordingly, the elasticity of doctrines of providence was such that, in theory, a meaning could be found for every experience of suffering; and indeed, being made to suffer was taken by many as a necessary and even desirable part of their Christian calling.[14]

Historians note that it was particularly in societies where cultures of Protestantism took hold that doctrines of providence tended to have the greatest impact upon public and personal affairs.[15] Generally speaking, it appears that in most cultures of medieval Christianity there was a greater willingness to acknowledge the roles played by chance, accident, misfortune, and misadventure in human affairs than would have been possible in the later Middle Ages and early modern period.[16] The more pronounced credulity bestowed upon popular accounts of miraculous prodigies and the firm subscription to the belief that divine providence is at work in every event and circumstance are components of a post-Reformation worldview. The volume of publications dedicated to explaining providential doctrines, the documentation of God's judgments through history, and the announcement of portentous signs and wonders testifies to the extent to which the sixteenth and seventeenth centuries mark the high point of Christian providentialism.[17]

Walsham holds that the Protestant preoccupation with providence was a direct result of theological convictions that placed heavy emphasis on doctrines of predestination and the attainment of salvation through the exclusive act of God's grace. On this account, the effort to discern "dispensations of providence" was fueled by anxieties experienced in connection with the "enigma of predestination."[18] The concern to elaborate and refine an understanding of how God worked out his purposes through nature, history, and bodily process grew along with the extent to which an "uncompromising insistence" was placed upon the need for each individual to examine his conscience, motivations, and actions in light of biblical teachings on the means to, and anticipated fruits of, salvation.[19]

A number of writers also underline the extent to which popular enthusiasm for providentialism intensified during periods of social unrest and political instability.[20] As far as England is concerned, the English Civil War and Interregnum (1642–60) stand out as the period when the currency of providential thought was inflated to the extreme.[21] Never before or since has the Bible, and particularly Old Testament sections detailing God's miraculous and cataclysmic interventions throughout the history of Israel, been so passionately studied as a source of inspiration and authority in political and military affairs.[22] At this time parliamentary speeches and political discourse in general took the form of theological exposition. Blair Worden notes that "Cromwell did not merely invoke providence as a sanction of his rule" but that "he lectured parliament at length about the workings of providence on his soul."[23] On all sides of the conflict, biblical prophecies, histories, commandments, and teachings were taken as the primary means to justify legal decisions and the infliction of violence on others. They were also the main point of reference when it came to interpreting political events, the experience of military campaigns, and the shifting fortunes of competing religious and social factions. The overall effect was "the engulfment of providence in factional strife and sectarian struggle" to a point where its credibility was undermined.[24]

At least as far as Britain is concerned, by the end of the 1650s providence was being made subject to a sustained crisis of legitimacy. As Christopher Hill notes, to many, "the infinity of reversal and changes" that followed the outbreak of the English Civil War made abundantly clear that providential theory was by no means sufficiently equipped to cast light on God's purposes.[25] Not only had it been repeatedly exposed as an unreliable and confused guide to understanding the world, but having experienced so many crushing disappointments and humiliating failures of judgment, many were now inclined to identify the bold assuredness with which they once presumed to know the will of God as a cause of civil strife. For example, the onetime "enthusiast," Richard Baxter, now cautioned against biblical literalism and blamed "the misunderstanding of providence" for the ways in which his friend Major General Berry was seduced by Cromwell into the vanity of believing that God had called him to take up arms so as to "look after the government of the land."[26] Indeed, Hill notes that Baxter grew to be wary of religious fanaticism for the extent to which it had all too often proven itself to be a spur to bloody rebellion against civility and the law.[27]

During the second half of the seventeenth century providentialism underwent a rapid process of "cultural marginalization" and, generally speaking, was no longer considered to have a legitimate role in mainstream intellectual and political affairs.[28] In educated circles it became increasingly unfashionable to explain natural events as God's interventions in history or portentous signs of his impending judgment; natural philosophy had ascendancy over providential piety.[29] As far as most of those connected to the work of government were concerned, prolonged experiences of civil unrest as well as many wars of religion and bloody persecutions across Europe made all too clear the propensity for providentialism to breed ideological fanaticism and violent intent.[30] In part the official dismissal of providentialism is explained as a result of the ways in which it was forcefully exposed as a source of unmitigated intellectual disagreement and violent social conflict.[31] There is also no doubt that its intellectual appeal was eroded as a consequence of concerted political campaigns to stigmatize providential claims as forms of superstition that marked people as "lower class," "uneducated," and prone to "fanaticism."[32] In addition to this, Keith Thomas contends that insofar as the large majority of people tended to be cast by the evidence of their material poverty and many bodily afflictions as living under the heavy hand of God's judgment, once the enthusiasm for providentialism was drained from elite and upwardly mobile social groups, it was never likely to be sustained among the mass ranks of the poor. For most of those living under extreme conditions of material poverty there was never much comfort or consolation to be drawn from the charge to learn the "art of suffering." In conclusion Thomas writes:

> It was a gloomy philosophy, teaching men how to suffer, and stressing the impenetrability of God's will. At its most optimistic it promised that those who bore patiently with the evils of this world would have a chance of being rewarded in the next. But, as a contemporary remarked, 'the poor man lies under a great temptation to doubt of God's providence and care'. It is not surprising that many should have turned away to non-religious modes of thought which offered a more direct prospect of relief and a more immediate explanation of why it was that some men prospered while others literally perished by the wayside.[33]

It is important to understand, however, that by no means did the cultural marginalization of providentialism in intellectual and public life lead to it being wholly renounced as a popular way to account for suffering.[34] For the following two hundred years or so, and particularly in the aftermath of large-scale disasters or outbreaks of epidemic disease, providentialism continued to be adopted by many people as an explanatory theory for misfortune, though in societies undergoing rapid experiences of industrialization it is possible to trace a marked decline in its cultural appeal through the second half of the nineteenth century.[35] It may still be possible to find committed Christians who venture to make sense of worldly events in terms of the workings of providence; however, it is generally held that, following the many events of mass violence and atrocity that took place through the twentieth century, it would never enter the minds of most people to identify God as the immediate cause of a person's suffering, or for that matter, to express enthusiasm for the sanctifying power of personal affliction.

In an extensive survey of sermons and Christian writings through the seventeenth century, Ann Thompson charts a major transformation in cultural attitudes toward suffering. It appears that by the turn of the eighteenth century the Puritan art of suffering was largely abandoned in favor of an approach that stressed the extent to which God's ways are beyond human understanding. At least in the writings of church leaders, human suffering was no longer taken as the cue for an anguished search for the wickedness that had angered God to the point where he moves against his people. From this point on, it was far more commonplace for the experience of suffering to be regarded as a matter for which no satisfactory explanation can be found in this world. On Thompson's account, "the fear of freedom which builds up in the spaces created by the loss of confidence in the revealed (the written) will of God is alleviated by unquestioning submission to the secret will of God."[36] Similarly, Hill notes that in many Christian writings there was a discernible shift away from using the Bible as a guide to the political actions that might realize his kingdom on earth toward an emphasis on the comfort to be drawn from the promise that this will be delivered to the faithful in the world to come.[37]

The struggle to reevaluate received tradition brought debate to the possibility that, up to that point, most theologians had seriously misunderstood the character of God and his relationship to humanity. Some commentators are now inclined to identify the second half of the seventeenth century with the introduction of a new theological emphasis on the extent to which God feels sympathy for those in affliction, and even suffers along with them. For example, Jennifer Herdt notes that at this time the Cambridge Platonist Ralph Cudworth (1617–88) set in motion a theological movement that by the second half of the twentieth century was embraced by many Christian scholars as providing a more morally palatable account of the divine character.[38] Here an emphasis was brought to the extent to which, by the example of his incarnation in the figure of Christ, God has solidarity with those who suffer and demonstrates an overwhelming disposition to relate to people with compassion.

Herdt is further inclined to identify this rejection of the immaterial, supremely transcendent, and impassible God of received tradition as a cultural shift that advanced new forces of secularization. The unintended consequence of attempting to "humanize" the Christian God was to portray him as less equipped to offer an immediate explanation for why suffering takes place or as exercising direct control over the conditions under which people are made to exist. Herdt argues that the vision of God as living alongside and suffering with us serves to compromise the possibility of understanding him as existing over and acting above us. Paradoxically, while transforming God into a personable being who has solidarity with those who suffer, his presence as a being who exercises supreme powers of control and judgment over a person's fate is diminished. All at once, God is made more responsive to and yet less responsible for the brute facts of lived experience. On these grounds, Herdt contends that the works of Cudworth and other Latitudinarian divines mark a transitional phase in Western intellectual culture that made it increasingly possible for people to regard the transcendent God of providence as practically remote and functionally detached from public secular affairs. She holds that by promoting a new image of God as sympathetically oriented to those who suffer, they made it considerably easier for more atheistic representatives of the culture of Enlightenment to treat as intellectually implausible the idea of God as the orchestrator of a great chain of being, or at least to regard this as giving rise to a worldview that is deserving of moral contempt.[39]

For example, in his poem criticizing Alexander Pope's maxim, "whatever is, is right," written in the aftermath of the Lisbon earthquake of 1755, which is estimated to have killed as many as one hundred thousand people, Voltaire urges us to question the goodness and to doubt the powers of any God who would create a world in which such events are possible or desirable by design. In one particularly angry passage he writes:

Approach in crowds, and meditate a while
Yon shattered walls, and view each ruined pile.
Women and children heaped up mountain high,
Limbs crushed which under ponderous marble lie;
Wretches mangled, torn, and panting for breath,
Buried beneath their sinking roofs expire,
And end their wretched lives in torments dire.
Say, when you hear their piteous, half-formed cries,
Or from their ashes see the smoke arise,
Say, will you then eternal laws maintain,
Which God to cruelties like these constrain?
Whilst you these facts replete with horror view,
Will you maintain death to their crimes was due?

And can you then impute a sinful deed
To babes who on their mother's bosom's bleed?
Was then more vice in fallen Lisbon found,
Than Paris, where voluptuous joys abound?
Was less debauchery to London known,
Where opulence luxurious holds her throne?
Earth Lisbon swallows; the light sons of France
Protract the feast, or lead the sprightly dance.
Spectators who undaunted courage show,
While you behold your dying brethren's woe;
With stoical tranquillity of mind
You seek the causes of these ills to find;
But when like us Fate's rigours you have felt,
Become humane, like us you'll learn to melt.[40]

Similarly, in *Candide*,[41] it seems that Voltaire has resolved that all he need do is appeal to the evidence of multiple extreme, apparently random, and evidently purposeless experiences of human suffering to convince his readers that the metaphysical "optimism" of Leibniz, as caricatured in the figure of Dr. Pangloss, is both morally bankrupt and irredeemably vexed. Here the conclusion that we should work at cultivating our own garden rather than wait for God to restore some lost state of Eden is arrived at by Candide and his companions through their painful resignation to the evident fact that most are not born to an easy life and that, such as it is, existence is made "bearable" only by human effort.[42] Indeed, Peter Gay contends that the writing of this morality tale served as a spur for Voltaire's conversion into "an aggressive social reformer."[43] On many accounts, as traditional Christian doctrines of divine providence were rendered more implausible and morally suspect, more were persuaded to the view that no good or sufficient reason could be found for human suffering. It became increasingly difficult to understand how extreme experiences of pain were related to God's interventions in people's lives. Yet here it is important to understand that for many of those who were most forthright in their denunciation of providence, it was far better to resign oneself to this great difficulty of understanding than to endure the apparent cruelty and evident irrationality of a doctrine that charged people with the task of learning the "art of suffering." Some, and sometimes many, were moved to devote themselves to a new image of God as sympathetically oriented to, but ultimately less responsible for, the suffering of humanity. Others, no doubt far fewer, were cautioned by the writings of figures such as Pierre Bayle (1647–1706) to conclude that it was better to test the probity of moral action by "the passions in the heart" than by "knowledge of a God" and, further, to share Bayle's conviction that it was better to respond to the problem of suffering with a radical questioning of the world than to seek solace in the assurances of providence.[44]

The condition and experience of social suffering became conscionable as a pressing human concern only where the workings of providence became radically questionable or otherwise fell into disrepute. Where social suffering features as a scholarly point of reference through the course of the nineteenth century, for the most part, both theists and atheists are united in the view that adverse social conditions and painful qualities of social experience should be met with concerted efforts at social reform and, indeed, in "the moral sense of responsibility or conscience" that they should move to "save human life" and "assuage pain."[45] In this regard, social suffering is as much an immediate problem for clergymen and theologians as it is for social scientists and political theorists.[46]

Through a protracted experience of intellectual frustration and moral anguish over the workings of providence that frequently reached critical proportions, by the second half of the nineteenth century most held that it was no longer possible to see the hand of God at work in suffering. To many by the turn of the eighteenth century it was already clear that, while we might draw some comfort from the thought that God shares in our suffering, we should not take human affliction as a matter fit for his purpose; and in this regard there was divine sanction behind the urgency to engage with the task of thinking how social worlds can be made more bearable. Some had no need for studied reflection on the character of God in order to find the inspiration to channel their energies in this direction, particularly insofar as they were already enveloped by a newfound passion to protest against the suffering of humanity.

BY FORCE OF FELLOW FEELING

The eighteenth century witnessed a revolution in the emotional constitution of humanity and a radical transformation of subjectivity. In particular, from 1750 on the common cultural experience and account of life is distinguished by a new sensibility concerned to express and respond to moral feelings about human and animal suffering.[47] By the turn of the nineteenth century, it seems that majority opinion holds that much that takes place in the experience of pain is wholly undesirable, and insofar as it is technically possible to eliminate the suffering of pain, its occurrence is morally unacceptable. The spectacle of human suffering is increasingly met with an attitude of revulsion and is depicted as a matter to which one should respond with moral outrage.[48] From this time on it is often the case that the distress people experience when confronted with the sight of suffering is taken as an expression of natural instinct.

Cultural historians and historical anthropologists now contend that, while frequently explained as facets of "common sense" or "human nature," these emotional dispositions and cultural attitudes are peculiarly modern traits. It is also suggested that they are among the components of modern identity that are most poorly understood and which all too often remain beyond the purview of critical self-reflection. Throughout history and across cultures there are considerable variations in the social conventions that govern the expression of emotion as well as marked contrasts in the cultural meanings bestowed upon particular types of emotional experience. In many instances it appears that societies comprise distinct "structures of feeling" that are quite different from those met under conditions of Western modernity.[49]

For example, Esther Cohen notes that during the European Middle Ages the widespread understanding that physical pain was "a function of the soul" was accompanied by expressive norms that involved social sanctions upon facial or bodily contortions, groaning, and crying,[50] for it was widely held that these visibly betrayed the extent to which a person was living under the heavy hand of God's judgment. There are many records of Christian martyrs appearing to be largely unaffected by physical tortures; or at least that is how they are portrayed within the conventions of medieval art. It is only those damned to hell who are depicted as suffering, their bodies contorted and their faces anguished.[51] Cohen maintains that such was the association of pain with mortal sin that it was only in the context of ritual visits to confessional shrines that some ventured to make a public display of their feelings about the physical torments they suffered.

Forms of emotional expression both reflect and constitute the moral experience of culture and society. As we work to understand the ways in which people relate to their feelings we are also brought to reflect upon the habits of thought, custom, and practice by which they conduct and evaluate their relationships to self and others. Each society involves its members in a cultural training of emotions, and within this, some emotions are valued while others are discouraged and even condemned. "Feeling rules" express the social dynamics of power relations and serve to delineate shifting landscapes of social opportunity and moral responsibility.[52] On this view, the sudden "flowering of sentimentalism" that takes place through the eighteenth century not only marks the introduction of a new "emotional regime" in civil affairs but also designates the arrival of distinctively new forms of sociality and moral conduct.[53]

Considerable dispute surrounds the possibility of arriving at a satisfactory explanation for how this was made possible. In part this is due to the problem of assessing the relative degree to which moral feelings are moderated, modified, or reformed as the result of processes of intellectual and public debate. It is certainly the case that many presume to explain changes in feeling as the product of transformations governed by the relative standing of cultural ideas. In particular, it is often assumed that the heightened value that is placed on expressions of fellow feeling in eighteenth-century society has its origins in a theological movement that was subsequently adopted by philosophers of the Enlightenment as part of a new ethics of human civility.

Intellectual historians tend to locate the origins of the English "cult of sensibility" in the ideological campaigns mounted by Cambridge Platonists and Latitudinarian divines in opposition to the doctrines of Calvinism and the political philosophy of Thomas Hobbes. Convention holds that in the period of the restoration of the English monarchy (1660–ca. 1700), philosophical theologians such as Henry More (1614–87), Ralph Cudworth (1617–88), Benjamin Wichcote (1609–83), Samuel Parker (1640–88), John Tillotson (1630–94), Gilbert Burnet (1643–1715), Richard Cumberland (1631–1718), and Samuel Clarke (1675–1729) moved to emphasize the positive role played by passion and affection in people's capacities for moral action and Christian understanding. Their views are explained by one of their followers, Joseph Glanvill (1636–80), as follows:

[Their aim was] to assert and vindicate the Divine Goodness and love of Men in its freedom and extent, against those Doctrines, that made his love, fondness; and his justice, cruelty, and represented God, as the Eternal Hater of the far greatest part of his reasonable creatures, and the designer of their ruin, for their exaltation of mere power, and arbitrary will. . . . They showed continually how impossible it was the infinite goodness should design or delight in the misery of his creatures. . . . Their main design was to make Men good, not notional, and knowing; and therefore, though they concealed no practical verities that were proper or seasonable, yet they were sparing in their speculations.[54]

Here the virtues of "universal charity and union"[55] were privileged above any doctrinal matter that gave rise to sectarian prejudice. Fellow feeling was encouraged as a means to vanquish the pain of factional strife and internecine dispute. Accordingly, when tracing the "genealogy of the man of feeling," some are inclined to regard this as the product of an ideological movement that, at its origins, was largely inspired by a reading of Christian theology that brought emphasis to humanitarian concerns.

From here it is argued that in the first half of the eighteenth century Latitudinarian fellow feeling underwent a process of secularization and naturalization. Philosophers such as Anthony Ashley-Cooper, third earl of Shaftsbury (1671–1713), and Francis Hutcheson (1694–1746) are commonly identified as the progenitors of the notion that humanity is distinguished by an instinctive capacity for moral feeling. They by no means shared the same understanding of how sympathy works or how bonds of fellow feeling are forged and sustained, yet both cleared the way for the "sense of common rights of mankind" or impulse toward "benevolence" to be treated as the elemental grounds for human sociability.[56]

Through the second half of the eighteenth century it became increasingly common for social commentators to recognize fellow feeling as an influence upon the course of legal and political affairs and, indeed, to declare this an essential component of civic virtue. Most notably, in the doctrines of civic humanism developed by members of the Scottish Enlightenment "moral sense" is treated as a social disposition that, when properly nurtured, might be relied upon as a means to constrain selfishness and cruelty. In this respect, Thomas Paine is already writing within a tradition of received wisdom when he holds human sympathy to be among the components of "common sense" without which "we should be incapable for discharging in the social duties of life."[57] Similarly, when Thomas Jefferson takes it as self-evident that we possess a "moral instinct" that prompts us "irresistibly to feel and to succor" the distress of others, he is voicing a point of view that was already widely shared across learned society.[58]

Perhaps it was because of such positive appraisals of human sympathy that increasing numbers of people were inclined to identify themselves as cultured by humane feelings. Indeed, it is argued that through the second half of the eighteenth and first half of the nineteenth century, the popular enthusiasm for sentimental literature was in part due to the extent to which people understood that they should actively cultivate the moral feelings that inspire benevolent social actions.[59] On the other hand, it might well be the case that a considerable part of the cultural turn toward sentimentality was fueled by the discovery of feelings that created a shared hunger for new terms of social understanding. Insofar as reason operates as a "slave of the passions," we might well turn the intellectual history of sympathy on its head.

An alternative view holds that we should not so much understand the discovery of fellow feeling as the ancillary accompaniment to debates over the moral ideals we should live by; but rather, we should dwell upon the extent to which it was primarily due to the dispersal and intensity of newly acquired qualities of emotion that moved people to reformulate their ideas about human nature and the goals of politics. Thomas notes that prior to any considered ethical reformulation of attitudes toward the cruel treatment of animals there were many outbreaks of "spontaneous tender-heartedness." The philosophical support for animal rights followed in the wake of people first being moved by compassionate feelings to alleviate the unnecessary suffering of pets and farm animals.[60] From the beginning of the seventeenth century, and with increasing frequency through the second half of the eighteenth century, there are reports of people being overtaken by sympathetic feelings that at first were as much a surprise to them as to others.

This is particularly noticeable in relation to the initiation of campaigns to abolish the use of torture in criminal proceedings. From the early seventeenth century there are records of crowds subverting convention and reacting with outbursts of sympathy to the spectacle of public execution.[61] Lynn Hunt, however, argues that the 1760s are distinguished by a marked increase in the discovery of feelings for the humanity of those subjected to cruel punishments. She notes that even though Voltaire was moved in 1762–63 to protest against the trial of Jean Calas on the grounds that it took place as an act of religious bigotry, by 1766 his principal concerns had shifted to the morally outrageous ways in which the court had attempted to use the method of "breaking on the wheel" to make Calas confess to the murder of his son. Where previously such forms of torture "had long seemed acceptable to him," ultimately, it was due to a sudden upwelling of "natural compassion" that Voltaire was brought under the compulsion to change his views.[62] Similarly, Randall McGowen notes that overwhelmingly it was the case that those campaigning against public floggings and spectacles of execution in the early nineteenth century did so by sheer strength of moral feeling.[63] Early humanitarian reformers had little need for elaborate arguments based on reasoned principle; rather, it was generally held that by direct appeal to the "sympathies of mankind," criminal law would be exposed as unjust and inhumane.

Where social theorists venture to account for this seemingly spontaneous acquisition of human sympathy, they either point to the increased integration of people within a more rationally disciplined process of "civilization" or, alternatively, claim that a sympathetic social orientation was the accompaniment to a new experience of individualization made possible by the rise of modern capitalism. Many are inclined to follow Norbert Elias in identifying the upwelling of sympathy as the corollary to a "civilizing process" that eventually succeeded in socializing people into restraining lewd and aggressive impulses. On Elias's account, the emotional makeup of large sections of Western European societies was transformed as the culture of manners that comprised medieval courtly society was gradually elaborated, adapted to, and incorporated in the construction of a new public culture of civility in the eighteenth century.[64] Drawing on a Freudian model of the human psyche, human sentimentality is explained as the by-product of sublimated feelings that are rooted in the renunciation of instinctual gratifications. The flight from the spectacle of suffering and the desire to eliminate the distress of pain are understood to result from a wider state-coordinated movement to instill a social psychology of rational order and control in society. Moreover, in looking for evidence to support this view, it is certainly the case that many of those protesting against the public use of torture were as much appalled by the moral degeneracy of drunken mobs that drew pleasure from the sight of cruelty as they were moved by compassion for the suffering of prisoners.[65]

Within an Elisian framework of analysis, attention might also be drawn to the ways in which the "civilizing process" was augmented by, and conducive to, the development of early modern capitalism, though some are inclined to attribute much more to capitalism here. For example, Natan Sznaider maintains that "by defining a universal field of others with whom contracts and exchanges can be made, market perspectives extend the sphere of moral concern as well, however unintentionally."[66] Similarly, Thomas Haskell argues that the involvement of people in market relations encouraged the reconfiguration of the bounds of moral responsibility so that they were more likely to take an interest in the needs of strangers as well as to revise their understandings of causal attribution.[67] On this account, it was only under the individualizing force of the capitalist marketplace that it became possible for people to extend shared notions of sympathy to the human condition as such.

G. J. Barker-Benfield further underlines the extent to which the "culture of sensibility" grew along with the living standards of a new middle class.[68] He argues that it was generally among relatively affluent families recently freed from traditional experiences of physical hardship and social misery that a humanitarian outlook tended to be extended to society at large. Along with many other historians of this period, Barker-Benfield also notes that, aside from experiencing any seemingly "natural" upwelling of human sensibility, a large segment of the eighteenth-century middle class took an active interest in "sentimentalism" as a form of mass entertainment. The rapid creation of a new market for sentimental literature, theater, and concerts testifies to the extent to which a capitalist industry stood to gain from the cultural manufacture of fellow feeling. It was quickly realised that many would pay to partake in the pleasure of tears. For this reason Colin Campbell is inclined to argue that, from its origins, the capitalist "spirit of modern consumerism" has always devoted a considerable amount of energy to the cultural appropriation of humanitarian sensibility, for this has proven to be a highly effective means to accrue profit.[69]

When reflecting on the ways in which religious rituals and cultural pursuits might be used to court states of feeling, some historians now argue that any structural account of the rise of humanitarian sensibility needs to be carefully moderated by an acknowledgment of the ways in which individuals consciously involve themselves in the cultural production and reproduction of emotions. From this perspective, a simple "hydraulic" conception of emotion as propounded by Elias falls considerably short of conveying the extent to which human passions are functionally interrelated with exercises of moral judgment and cultural taste.[70] At the same time that it is clear that people acquire emotional states through being made subject to many external pressures and constraints on their lives, it is also the case that many take thoughtful actions so as to produce emotions for themselves and to affect others. For this reason Reddy advises that we attend to the ways in which individuals are always to be found working to "navigate" their feelings via the creation of social spaces and cultural artifacts that either increase or diminish the possibility of entering into various forms of emotional experience.[71] On this account, the history of emotions is best explained in terms of the rise and fall of multiple "emotional regimes" in which relative degrees of "emotional suffering" or opportunities for "emotional refuge" have important roles to play within the varieties of emotional life that constitute societies. He also urges social scientists and historians to study records of emotional language and emotional claims on the understanding that, as much as any other considerations, these exemplify the force and experience of power relations within and between societies. While still acknowledging the potential for emotional conditions to be structured by the disciplinary cultures and regimes of state civility or the rise of modern capitalism, Reddy argues that understanding the emotional force of social life requires that we also attend to the ways in which individuals consciously work to fashion symbolic forms of culture as a means to gain entry into states of emotion. He holds that individuals and communities are party to the emotive ordering of their social relationships and that emotions are a necessary part of the cultural currency of movements for social change.

In light of these arguments we might reflect on the extent to which the creation of concepts such as social suffering not only document the arrival of a new compassionate orientation toward human affliction but also serve as part of the process whereby such fellow feeling is culturally constituted. There is no doubt that it is frequently the case that references to social suffering occur in the context of emotively laden discourse on experiences of misery and pain; or rather, the term is often used to draw attention to circumstances in which people are emotionally preoccupied by adverse social conditions. At the very least, social suffering is always recognized as a form of experience that is liable to involve people in negative emotions; and very often it serves to inspire an impassioned plea for the social alleviation of the conditions under which people are made to suffer.

THE BOUNDS OF SOCIAL SYMPATHY

The word *social* derives from the Latin *socius,* meaning "companion" or "partner." A new understanding of human sociality is acquired during the eighteenth century. Here references to "social" aspects of life are accompanied by inquiries into the character of moral conscience and the potential for human beings to think and act for the good of others. Social questions are adapted to, and brought within, a new domain of literary and scholarly debate. These are chiefly concerned with understanding the substance of the moral bonds that unite us, and how moral dispositions are expressed through our attitudes and behaviors. Social life is emphatically portrayed as *moral experience;* and it is further assumed that by moral feeling we stand to acquire a vital part of our knowledge of society. On these grounds, it is widely accepted that social dispositions are manifested in the moral outrage experienced in the face of human suffering and that when touched by the miseries of others we are made consciously alert to social bonds. At its origins, the critical impulse that brings debate to the human social condition as such is allied to the conviction that social life is animated by our capacity to sympathize morally with the suffering of others.

This direct association of social life with moral experience also tends to court a great deal of critical and political debate. From the outset, many scholars are inclined to doubt the power of fellow feeling to deliver adequate social understanding, and certainly, there is always a considerable amount of opposition to the view that by force of moral sympathy people can be motivated to think and act on behalf of the welfare of others. In spite of being alert to the fact that we have a propensity to be moved by social sympathy, many are inclined to dwell upon the difficulty of bringing this to bear on the exercise of moral judgment. For this reason, Sean Gaston argues that one might well characterize the eighteenth century as "a century of extended mourning for the loss of fellow feeling";[72] for even among those setting out to extol and defend the "enlightenment of sympathy," there is a tendency to draw critical attention to its evident weaknesses and excesses.[73] Many express a deep ambivalence with regard to the extent to which this operates for the overall benefit of society. At this time social life is often portrayed as inherently inconstant, unstable, and precarious. It may well consist in our sympathetic and sentimental attachments to others; but for this very reason, we are often advised that there may be good cause to worry about the degree to which our social capacities are left morally stunted and underdeveloped.

At the level of philosophical discourse Francis Hutcheson is the first to make direct reference to the phenomenon of "social sympathy,"[74] though he is not so much concerned to analyze the character of social life as to refute the propositions and arguments raised by Bernard Mandeville (1670–1733) in *The Fable of the Bees* (1723). Mandeville famously argues that human beings are fundamentally selfish. He further claims that those who advocate benevolence as a public virtue, or consider it possible for people to selflessly devote themselves to the care of others, are either ignorant of their true condition or deluded by hypocrisy.[75] By contrast, Hutcheson aims to develop a more elaborate conception of human beings as possessing "sociable instincts," "benevolent impulses," and a "moral sense."[76] Here "moral sense" refers to an instinctive capacity to experience and respond to moral events and situations, but it does not provide us with ideas as to what is morally desirable or good. Moral ideas are acquired through our experience of society and culture, and in this regard, it is unlikely that there will ever be complete agreement as to what constitutes appropriate moral action. Hutcheson is merely concerned to defend the possibility that human beings can be motivated by benevolence to act for the good of society and that we possess the potential to discern the moral good "without regard to self-interest."[77]

David Hume (1711–76), in *A Treatise of Human Nature* (1739–40), provides the first analytically refined study of "sympathy" as a social virtue. Having accepted that humans possess a sympathetic disposition that on occasion gives rise to fellow feeling, he aims in this work to make clear the ways in which sympathy serves to produce society.[78] Hume further considers the possibility that it is by the power of our sympathetic attachments to others that social solidarities are forged and maintained. He moves from an account of sympathy as a mechanism for sharing in the "passions" of others to consider the possible ways in which it also serves to fashion "an extensive concern for society";[79] however, in noting "the partiality of our affections," he also starts to question the extent to which our social sympathies can serve as an adequate guide to the exercise of moral judgment in social affairs. It appears to Hume, "[I]n the original frame of our mind, our strongest attention is confined to ourselves; our next is extended to our relations and acquaintances; and it is only the weakest which reaches to strangers and indifferent persons. This partiality, then, and unequal affection, must not only have an influence on our behaviour and conduct in society, but even on our ideas of vice and virtue; so as to make us regard any remarkable transgression of such a degree of partiality, either by too great an enlargement, or contraction of the affections, as vicious and immoral."[80] Indeed, it seems that in the years between writing his *Treatise* and the publication of *An Enquiry Concerning the Principles of Morals* (1751), Hume was increasingly inclined to dwell upon the limitations and inconsistencies of sympathy when brought to arenas of moral decision, particularly insofar as these concern the overall welfare of society. Although considerable dispute still surrounds the correct way to interpret Hume's account of sympathy, commentators note that, while retaining an understanding of sympathy as a forceful component of human sociability, in later works he appears more reluctant to invest it with the potential to corral moral opinion for the social good.[81] In this respect, Hume is more prepared to argue for the importance of allowing a social intercourse on "utility" to serve as the primary means to decide what constitutes morally appropriate behavior with regard to the general social interest.[82]

In *The Theory of Moral Sentiments* (1759) Adam Smith returns to the concerns raised by Hume's *Treatise* but develops a more sophisticated account of the role played by a social imagination in the conversion of sympathy to moral sentiment. A number of commentators are still inclined to treat this as offering some of the subtlest reflections on how people are liable to apply and moderate their feelings in the context of moral judgment.[83] On Smith's account, we are endowed both with an imaginative capacity to empathize with the painful predicaments of others and with an ability to imagine how others standing at a distance might expect us to behave. He portrays people as always caught up in a complex struggle to moderate their sympathy so as to identify with the needs of individuals in suffering and at the same time have this conform to prevailing opinion on what constitutes morally appropriate feeling and behavior. Social behavior is portrayed as akin to a dramatic public performance; and in this we always act as though under surveillance.[84] All at once, in the exercise of fellow feeling we also imagine ourselves in the position of being the spectator of our conduct. Smith observes:

> We suppose ourselves the spectators of our own behaviour, and endeavour to imagine what effect it would, in this light produce upon us. This is the only looking-glass by which we can, in some measure, with the eyes of other people, scrutinize the propriety of our own conduct. If in this view it pleases us, we are tolerably satisfied. We can be more indifferent about the applause, and, in some measure, despise the censure of the world; secure that, however, misunderstood and misrepresented, we are the natural and proper objects of appropriation. On the contrary, if we are doubtful about it, we are often, upon that very account, more anxious to gain their appropriation, and, provided we have not already, as they say, shaken hands with infamy, we are altogether distracted at the thoughts of their censure, which then strikes us with double severity.[85]

This emphasis on the extent to which moral sentiments and social behaviors are conditioned by anxieties relating to the thought of how we appear to others leads Smith to note a number of ways in which human sympathies are liable to appear strained, fickle, and fleeting. While remaining committed to the view that fellow feeling for the misery of others is an elemental component of our capacity to embrace principles of social justice, he devotes a considerable portion of his thesis to listing common tendencies and behaviors that betray the weaknesses of social sympathy.

Smith shares Hume's concerns about the partiality of our affections and claims that while it is naturally the case that our strongest sympathies are directed toward family members and friends, we also tend to be more benevolently disposed toward the rich and powerful than those living in wretched conditions of poverty. He notes that most of the subjects of tragic and romantic stories belong to the most prosperous and highest-ranking segments of society and on this evidence contends that "the grief that we

[feel] for their distress, the joy which we feel for their prosperity, seem to combine together in enhancing that partial admiration which we naturally conceive both for the station and the character."[86] In the final analysis, when advocating the cultivation of a stoical "self-command" as a means to curb the excesses and inconstancies of our passions, Smith appears to operate with a highly skeptical regard for the ways in which sympathy promotes social virtue. Indeed, insofar as his thesis culminates in advice on how to regulate and chasten our passions and feelings, it seems that he does not believe that our "sociability" works in the best interests of society.[87]

Through the second half of the eighteenth century "social sympathy" is the object of an unprecedented amount of moral controversy and political dispute. The "cool" considerations of moral philosophy are transformed into "heated" matters of public debate. While philosophers such as Hume and Smith quietly worried about the extent to which the "partiality" of our affections might detract from our abilities to think and act for the welfare of strangers, by the 1790s it is commonplace for critics to vociferously complain about the social damage caused by the popular indulgence of morbid sensibility.[88] At least as far as Britain is concerned, the tenor of debate moves from a concern to understand the conditions under which moral sympathy serves to produce the good society to the conviction that by the cultivation of sentimental feelings people may acquire immoral attitudes and engage in acts of political violence.

The 1780s witnessed a hostile literary response to the popularity of sentimental novels.[89] Here "sentimental" values were condemned on both moral and political grounds. Essayists such as Henry Mackenzie (1745–1831) campaigned against the ways in which the "enthusiasm" for sentimentalism among the "the young and the indolent" contributed to their moral degeneracy by encouraging an "alliance with voluptuousness and vice."[90] On Mackenzie's account, it was now all too clear that in their reading of novels many were inclined to separate conscience from feeling so as to enjoy the latter without any "incitement to virtue." Such arguments were also repeated by those advancing disparaging views of women and feminine culture. For example, Richard Cumberland argued that one of the serious failings of Samuel Richardson's *Clarissa* (1748) lies in the extent to which it serves to "lead young female readers into affectation and false character."[91] Indeed, for this reason, some early campaigners for women's rights moved to distance themselves from any association with the enthu-siasm for sentimentalism. Most notably, Mary Wollstonecraft (1759–97) expressed grave concerns about the extent to which the portrayal of senti-mentalism as "feminine" was used to promote an ideologically motivated conception of women as irrational and incapable of participating in rea-soned dispute.[92]

By 1790 a large number of British journalists and social commentators had joined in the public condemnation of the incitement of moral feeling for social concerns. There is no doubt, however, that the French Revolution of 1789 and subsequent years of war between Britain and France (1793–1815) served to greatly consolidate this critical movement. Through the 1790s there was a marked flight from the advocacy of sentimentality as a virtue, especially in matters of political and philosophical deliberation.[93] Many held that the French Revolution had grown out of a culture of "unreg-ulated sentimentality" that was subsequently exploited by Robespierre to initiate the Reign of Terror.[94] In this regard, when almost two hundred years later Hannah Arendt portrays "the passion of compassion" as "the driving force of revolutionaries" and warns her readers about the propensity for "boundless" sentiments to create an "emotion-laden insensitivity to real-ity," she is advancing a point of view that by the turn of the nineteenth cen-tury had already settled into political orthodoxy.[95]

The critical debates that were first raised in connection with "social sympathy" might serve as civic virtue were extremely moderate when com-pared to those provoked by later encounters with sentimentality as an inherently volatile force. The association of the "cult of sensibility" with revolutionary violence seems to be the main cause for its subsequent eras-ure from ethical discourse and political philosophy. It is important to note, however, that while sentimentalism had fallen out of favor in many literary and intellectual circles, this did not mark the demise of sentimental feeling or the waning powers of social sympathy in lived experience. Quite to the contrary; the problem with sensibility was that it had been revealed as all too inclined to provoke moral dispute, social disquiet, and political unrest.[96] By no means could "social sympathy" simply be dismissed as a social irrelevance or as holding only negligible human effects; rather, it had been revealed as holding the potential to command the course of events in public affairs. The understanding of humanity as comprising new social attributes and sentiment-fired humanitarian concerns gave way to further anxieties about the virulence of moral feeling. It was primarily out of a fear that large numbers of people might be persuaded by sheer force of emotion to transgress the bounds of civil society that many sought to disparage the enlightenment of sympathy.

For this reason, early references to experiences of social suffering can be construed as issuing a provocation. Insofar as a motion is made toward our gut response to and moral feelings about the spectacle of human misery, writers such as William Wordsworth are deliberately evoking a popular enthusiasm for matters of social justice and human rights. Wordsworth at one point joins in the moral condemnation of the "degrading thirst after outrageous stimulation" that he witnesses in the popular enjoyment of sentimentalism, but he still works to evoke social sympathy for the plight of the destitute and poor.[97] Unlike many others, Wordsworth does not renounce the attempt to draw us by force of compassion to "the social question," and in this regard, he is prepared to take a risk that Arendt deems both futile and dangerous. Wordsworth would yet have us listen to "the still, sad music of humanity," for he considers it still possible to draw the wit and guile of a sympathetic enlightenment to the task of building more egalitarian and humane forms of society.[98] Here it is still very much the case that the quest for social understanding remains allied to a cultivation of moral sentiment and, further, to a passion for humanitarian social reform.

CONCLUDING REMARKS

By exploring the social and cultural conditions that first made social suffering a conscious concern, we are drawn into debates that, largely speaking, do not feature in mainstream accounts of the rise of social science. It is commonly held that the origins of Western social science lie in a critical response to the cultural and social upheavals wrought by processes of industrialization and the rise of the modern urban experience. With a focus brought to the origins of social suffering, however, attention is drawn to the extent to which the acquisition of social consciousness is rooted in a transformation of worldviews and moral sensibilities that began some time before the experience of the Industrial Revolution.

We hold that when accounting for the origins of social thought and the earliest articulations of a distinct politics of social life we should be especially concerned to acquaint ourselves with the intellectual culture of the seventeenth and eighteenth centuries, and in particular, with the ways in which this documents and reflects changes in popular interpretations of, responses to, and feelings for human suffering. In order to gather an appreciation for the full scale and range of the issues at stake here we must (once again) work at understanding how the possibility of thinking about ourselves in social terms was made plausible and gathered legitimacy in relation to transformations in theological conviction. We must also cultivate a historical sensitivity to the ways in which our social constitution and the cultural awareness of ourselves as social beings are rooted in the acquisition of forms of moral experience and fellow feeling in which the spectacle of extreme human misery is met as an occasion for questioning the social responsibilities we bear to care for and alleviate the suffering of others.

A new humanitarian social imaginary is at work in the awakening of the impulse to make social life an object for rational inquiry and critical debate; and there is still much that remains to be explained here in terms of the sociological and historical account of its cultural formation, moral appeal, and political consequences. Some of these issues are explored in more detail in the chapters that follow. Our overriding interest, however, is the implications this holds for the practice of social inquiry. Indeed, we contend that in recognizing the extent to which social understanding is acquired and shaped through our moral feelings about human suffering, it is very likely that we shall be made to question the meaning and value of the "the social" anew and how this is rendered as an object for research.

With a focus brought to problems of social suffering, we are involved in a critical reappraisal of what passes for "social understanding." In this perspective, social life is understood to take place in enactments of substantive human values and to consist in moral experience. By working to understand its constitution as such, those invested in social inquiry are set to attend to how and why social life matters so much *for people*. When documenting instances of social suffering, the problem of understanding how people are made to experience the social conditions they embody is an issue of paramount concern.

Here social research in practice operates from the recognition that social understanding is acquired and sustained through human empathy and moral encounter. This requires us to be involved in, and court connections to, real-life human-social concerns that are often highly distressing. It requires that we involve ourselves in many of the moral anxieties, intellectual tensions, and political conflicts that accompany such circumstances under the conviction that, thereby, it is made possible for us to acquire a better understanding of people in human-social terms. It is only when we venture into the fray of social life as moral experience that the possibility of social understanding is brought within our reach. In this regard, the practice of social research is inherently moral; it involves us in ties of social responsibility in which we bear a duty of care for others. It is also bound to be political. Where this is denied or hidden from view, it is not only the case that a veil is cast over the human experience of social life, but also that "the social" is obscured as a pressing human concern.

Such convictions and points of emphasis are bound to court dispute with much that presents itself as good "social science." It is certainly the case, moreover, that they involve us in a radical questioning of the conventional ways in which the history of social inquiry is recorded, accounted for, and appraised. By setting problems of social suffering as a core concern for research, we are made to reflect on the ideological bearings of favored approaches to documenting and writing about social life. By bringing a focus to the harms done to people and the hurts we inflict on one another, it is very likely that we shall be made attentive to the extent to which social life takes place as an enactment of asymmetrical power relations; and here postures of value-neutrality and/or standpoints of "professional distance" are set to be exposed as more than mere instances of bad faith; they are also counted as potential forms of violence. In this regard, both in its history and in its contemporary developments, the conduct of social science is made an urgent matter for moral inquiry and political debate.

2 In Division and Denial

Uncle Tom's Cabin (1852) was the best-selling novel of the nineteenth century. In the year following its publication over 300,000 copies were sold in America, along with approximately two and a half million copies in English and translated editions throughout the rest of the world.[1] It quickly made Harriet Beecher Stowe "the most famous writer in the world."[2] Her book had mass appeal and was enthusiastically read by all social classes. A feature in the *Westminster Review* of January 1853 commented, "Probably no literary performance, fiction or other, ever in so short a time became such a fact. A few months ago it was appearing in the feuilleton of a weekly newspaper in the States. . . . [N]ow it is part of the history of two mighty nations, influencing their feelings, and through them surely, though indirectly their actions."[3] On many accounts, the power of this work to awaken sympathy and direct moral feeling toward the plight of slaves was "decisive to the antislavery cause."[4] By the outbreak of the American Civil War on April 12, 1861, four and a half million copies had been sold. It is widely reported that on meeting Stowe in 1862 Abraham Lincoln exclaimed, "So you are the little woman who wrote the book that started this great war."[5] Even before this conflict, however, the power of *Uncle Tom's Cabin* to shock sensibility and incite outrage over the injustices of slavery led many to regard it as the work that set the example for how to transform humanitarianism into a mass concern. Frank Klingberg notes that as she toured England in the 1850s, Stowe was frequently challenged to comment on the parallels that might be drawn between the plight of American slaves and the "wage slavery" of the English working classes and that, more generally, there was a widespread movement among social reform campaigners to attach their interests to the antislavery cause.[6] Jane Tompkins suggests that in the popular imagination of the time *Uncle Tom's Cabin* occupied a cultural position akin to Thomas Aquinas's *Summa Theologica;* for more than any other work, it served to give formal expression to the social sentiments and moral convictions of society at large. She contends that it remains "the most dazzling exemplar" of the power of literary sentimentalism to influence the course of history.[7]

It was only in the late twentieth century that cultural historians started to research the popular reaction to Stowe's work and the conditions that made it possible. There is now a considerable industry of scholarship committed to the attempt to explain how *Uncle Tom's Cabin* was able to occupy such a forceful presence within the collective conscience of its time. Accordingly, the form of language, terms of appeal to Christian metaphor, and carefully stylized portrayals of emotional distress and bodily suffering that Stowe deploys are studied in order to try to understand its power to incite moral feeling.[8]

In a pioneering work of literary criticism Edmund Wilson was the first to wonder at how, after it had such a forceful social and political impact, it became possible to forget "Uncle Tom."[9] By the beginning of the twentieth century the book was out of print and for more than a generation was only available in secondhand copies. Wilson claims that in the early decades of the twentieth century very few Americans would have known anything about the contents of *Uncle Tom's Cabin* and that most would never have come across a copy of the book. Writing in the 1960s, he confesses to having had "a startling experience" of its "eruptive force" when reading it for the first time, along with the discovery that "it is a much more impressive work than one has ever been allowed to suspect."[10] On this account, the collective forgetting and shared effort to eclipse Stowe's achievement demands an explanation as much as the novel's great popularity.

Wilson speculates that it may well have been the case that after years of bloody civil war it was too painful for most Americans to dwell any further on the sins of their forefathers and that most were ready to disregard Stowe's intervention.[11] He also notes that for many years cultural commentators were inclined to dismiss the novel as "mere propaganda" and as wholly lacking in literary merit. Indeed, in most of the more recent attempts to reappraise the cultural significance of *Uncle Tom's Cabin*, it is not so much the silent forgetting of the work but the shared view among the cognoscenti that it should be wholly dismissed as unworthy of consideration as a serious piece of fiction or as an artistic achievement that is taken up as a matter for analysis and debate.[12]

Such opinions were voiced among members of educated and literary circles from its moment of publication. As Ted Hovet Jr. notes, throughout the 1850s many reviewers sought to publicly condemn *Uncle Tom's Cabin* for its overly contrived and inaccurate portrayal of slavery and at the same time moved to claim that Stowe reveled in her notoriety as a means to promote her career as a best-selling author.[13] Tompkins further observes that through most of the twentieth century, in the field of American literary criticism, nineteenth-century sentimental literature tended to be summarily dismissed as morally degenerate, anti-intellectual, narcissistic, and naively duplicitous. For example, in one of the more scathing dismissals of Stowe's work, James Baldwin claimed that *Uncle Tom's Cabin* actually worked to "activate" and "reinforce" the very oppression it set out to decry. He writes, "*Uncle Tom's Cabin* is a very bad novel, having, in its self-righteous, virtuous sentimentality, much in common with *Little Women*. Sentimentality, the ostentatious parading of excessive and spurious emotion, is the mark of dishonesty, the inability to feel; the wet eyes of the sentimentalist betray his aversion to experience, his fear of life, his arid heart; and it is always, therefore, the signal of secret and violent inhumanity, the mask of cruelty."[14] On this account, Stowe should be condemned both for propagating racial stereotypes and for the sensational tone of her writing. For Baldwin, *Uncle Tom's Cabin* represents no more than a crude outburst of moral panic. He contended that Stowe's display of "virtuous rage" and anguished dwelling on acts of cruelty leaves no space for the development of critical thinking. Baldwin claimed that the possibility of questioning society is denied by the passion of protest and thereby held that Stowe unwittingly colludes in the maintenance of social structures and cultural attitudes that are implicated in the conditions that give rise to the violation of people's human rights.

By contrast, while remaining highly critical of the racialism of *Uncle Tom's Cabin*, contemporary scholarship is far more circumspect in assessing the role of sentimentalism in the shaping of social conscience. Attention is now brought to the extent to which nineteenth-century humanitarian social reformers were alert to the many conflicts of interpretation and range of political reactions that might take place in response to their sentimental framing of social problems.[15] For example, Elizabeth Spelman contends that by the early nineteenth century it was widely recognized that there are many dimensions to "the economy of attention to suffering," and that many antislavery novelists and feminist pamphleteers were consciously working to craft texts that not so much evoked the condescension of pity but, rather, facilitated the education of compassion.[16] Accordingly, she urges us to attend to the varied contexts of sentimentalism, the conscious risks that are taken by writers in their portrayals of human suffering, and the moral meanings acquired by texts in distinct arenas of moral and political dispute.

On this view, it is the complete absence of recognition of the potential for sentimentalism to serve as a means to acquire human understanding that stands out as a matter for investigation. It is the blind attitude that holds that an appeal to emotion is always liable to cloud moral judgment that should be held up for forensic examination. It is the absence of critical inquiry into the ideology of rationalism and the unquestioned assumption that matters of moral feeling have no legitimacy within realms of reasoned debate that need to be explained; for the attitude that holds that sentiment should be divorced from critical thinking is now (once again) held to extinguish some vital components of human experience and social understanding.

In this chapter, we approach such events as the eclipsing of *Uncle Tom's Cabin* as an invitation to question the moral and political values that have informed the history of social science; for in this, it is generally the case that social scientists are to be found operating, with a few notable exceptions, with no sympathy for cultures of sentiment. Indeed, on many accounts, the drive to "professionalize" social science involved its practitioners in a movement to sterilize the force of fellow feeling so that it was expunged from their work. It is as though, from the outset, moral sentiment was cast as an intellectual pollutant. In this regard, moreover, the founding and institutionalization of social science frequently entailed either a divorce or a distancing from popular movements of humanitarian social reform; for these were heavily identified with an attempt to raise the human-social condition for debate by the arousal of moral feeling. Instead, in America and Britain, sociology separated itself from social work, and early anthropologists largely avoided advocacy for reform in pursuit of a scientistic vision.

We chart the rise of the concept of the social as an object for rational inquiry and policy legislation. We also note some of the key cultural developments and institutional processes that served to fashion "social science" as a professional domain of rationalization dedicated to the search for statistical laws governing the health and well-being of populations. In this context, we underline the ways in which the "social science" of the nineteenth century was conceived as a matter divorced from "social sympathy." We also attend to the founding of a countermovement of social inquiry that was expelled from the corridors of professional social science, yet aimed to uphold and develop a sentiment-fired approach to human-social understanding. In it we recognize a continued concern for problems of social suffering. It appears that, in its founding orientations and practices, Western social science was configured so as to deny this countermovement a space within the official script of social life.

WITHOUT SYMPATHY

It is only over the past twenty years or so that cultural historians of the eighteenth century have dwelled in detail on the force of sentiment within the intellectual developments and political culture of the Enlightenment.[17] In this context, it is now deemed wholly unacceptable to portray the culture of the Enlightenment as devoid of sentiment or as exclusively rationalist. It is widely acknowledged that most Enlightenment thinkers regarded the exploration of inner feelings as a companion component of the attempt to apply reason to the task of understanding the workings of nature and society. The majority held that there was an indissoluble link between passion and reason and that moral feelings were embedded in processes of scientific inquiry and political deliberation. Accordingly, intellectual historians now underline the extent to which the "age of reason" was also the "age of feeling" and on these grounds share in the understanding that the rationalism of the Enlightenment was shaped in dialectical tension with its sentimentalism.[18]

The somewhat troubling discovery that over the past two centuries most social commentators have propagated the myth of Enlightenment culture as excessively rational has further unsettled many conventional narratives of modernity. For example, the casting of Romanticism as a component of a counter-Enlightenment revolt against rationalism now appears implausible;[19] in fact, it now seems Romanticism has much more in common with the culture of the Enlightenment than the cultures of "rational science" that took root during the first half of the nineteenth century. Indeed, on some accounts, we are now only just beginning to piece together the history of how it became possible for the knowledge of science to be portrayed as value-free "objective" fact.[20] Here it is the epistemological revolution whereby it became possible to treat scientific knowledge, and particularly its representation in the form of numbers, as offering "a view from nowhere" that most demands an explanation.[21] It is the possibility of charting the events and processes that combined to effect a marked break with sentimentalism in "official" and "authoritative" accounts of human experience and social life that is identified as the key to understanding the distinctive character of the intellectual culture of modernity and its adopted role within public life.

In the previous chapter we noted the increased level of philosophical and literary criticism that was directed at sentimentalism in the aftermath of the French Revolution. Following the Reign of Terror (1793–94) it was widely held that sentimentalism had been exposed as a malign influence on public affairs and that the "passion of compassion" could all too easily be used to justify acts of violent oppression.[22] In this respect, Reddy claims that from 1797 to 1814 it is possible to discern the rise of a movement to erase sentimentalism from the record of the Enlightenment.[23] He also suggests that it was at this time that wider currency was given to the notion that sentimentalism was a feminine weakness that should be confined to the domestic sphere. Likewise, in noting the popularity of works such as René de Chateaubriand's *Essai sur les Révolutions* (1797) and the censoring of Germaine De Staël's attempts to uphold the legacy of Enlightenment sentimentalism, Reddy holds that the twin myths of Enlightenment as a culture of strict rationalism and of Romanticism as a counterculture of human feeling were born.

It is now possible, however, to recognize these early revisions of the record and history of the Enlightenment as just the beginning of a more sustained, more coordinated, and inherently more hostile movement to expunge matters of moral feeling from public affairs. Historians of the culture of the British middle classes during the first half of the nineteenth century are inclined to identify the rise of a new Panglossian faith in "political economy" as a decisive factor in this regard.[24] On this account, writers such as Adam Smith (1723–90), Jeremy Bentham (1748–1832), Thomas Malthus (1766–1834), James Mill (1773–1836), and David Ricardo (1772–1823) tend to be grouped together as evangelists for the promotion of industrialism as an economic doctrine and the advancement of industry as the object of politics. In a review of British parliamentary speeches during the 1840s, David Roberts reports that "few dogmas ran deeper than the conviction that government interference in the economy was unwise" and that it was generally agreed that an ethic of "self-reliance" should be promoted as a paramount social ideal.[25]

In this context, the politics of compassion was taken to a distinctly new terrain by the shock troops of British middle-class reform, for in the most extreme expressions of this ideology it was assumed that under the "natural" force of laissez-faire capitalism there should be hardly any need for people to rely on the benevolence of others.[26] Insofar as it served to encourage idleness and discourage individual enterprise, charity was even portrayed by some not only as working to the detriment of the common good but also as a morally misguided activity that was liable to keep the poor in poverty[27]. For example, Michael Brown reports that in September 1833, while under the "inspiration" of political economy, a group of medical practitioners withdrew their voluntary labor and financial support for the Aldersgate-Street Dispensary, a medical charity founded in 1770 by the reforming Quaker physician John Coakley Lettsom, on the grounds that it reduced the income of their private practice and served as an encouragement to "pauperism."[28] On Brown's account, the debate that erupted in medical journals in the wake of the Aldersgate-Street Dispensary incident "marked an essential and irreparable split in medical and lay conceptions of institutional health care" and that from this point on, large sections of the British medical profession were inclined to hold that as a matter of principle they should be guided far more by a rational concern for "sanitas" than by the sentiment of "caritas."

Mary Poovey has perhaps done more than any other writer to expose the peculiar ways in which the "the social" tended to be conceptualized and exchanged as a moral ideal within the culture of political economy.[29] She argues that the key to understanding the emergence of the social domain as a measurable object for political debate and policy making lies in an appreciation of the extent to which it was involved in a movement to promote a moral point of view on the increasingly visible material poverty and poor health of large sections of the British working class. Following Michel Foucault,[30] she further contends that this was wedded to a project to instill a form of "disciplinary individualism" within society, so that people were made to "voluntarily" comply with new strictures of rational conduct. On Poovey's account, such shifts in social attitudes and behavior were made possible in relation to the extent to which it became accepted practice to treat human relationships as a quantifiable abstraction. She holds that by this form of "representational technology" it was possible to divest favored accounts of social reality from matters of moral commitment and political interest.[31] Accordingly, the attempt to establish "objective" conditions of society and measurable regularities of social life was intimately related to the effort to silence critical debate over the moral and political values that hereby stood to be represented as immutable laws of nature.

Thomas Malthus stands out as a key figure in the movement to bestow authority upon the artifice of numbers as the means to produce an 'impartial' account of the workings of society. In the second edition (1803) and third edition (1806) of his *Essay on the Principle of Population* (1798), he makes no mention of the providential theology that in the first edition is featured as an explicit component of the logic that informs his calculations.[32] While Romantic critics such as Robert Southey (1774–1843), Samuel Taylor Coleridge (1772–1834), William Wordsworth (1785–1859), Thomas de Quincy (1785–1859), and William Hazlitt (1778–1830) joined forces to bring critical debate to the ways in which Malthus used statistics to obscure his moral presuppositions, their objections found little sympathy within official realms of government. Indeed, on this score they found themselves standing against the tide of their times. Poovey notes that by the passing of the 1834 new Poor Law, "the machinery of government in Britain was indissolubly tied to the collection of numerical information."[33] The many philosophical and moral disputes that still surrounded the values enshrined within the production of statistics and the ideological means whereby they arrived at the point of being adopted as "facts" were disregarded by most members of the political class who held that, when brought to the task of legislating on behalf of the welfare of society, government should be conducted by the rule of numbers.[34]

As far as Britain is concerned, Edwin Chadwick is identified as among those who had the greatest influence over this development. Chadwick was chiefly responsible for the implementation of the new Poor Law of 1834 and had designed it in the belief that by introducing a strict workhouse system he would be setting up an effective deterrent against the "allure" of pauperism. Along with other enthusiasts of political economy, Chadwick held that it was largely due to the waste and idleness of large segments of the population that they were apt to fall into poverty. Having discovered that the new system was failing to deter people from pauperism and that additional infirmaries were being built at the public expense as a means to accommodate the large numbers of chronically sick, mentally ill, and disabled people who occupied workhouses, he was made to revise his explanation for the primary causes of poverty. Chadwick came to the view that much of the poverty he witnessed was not so much a consequence of fecklessness as disease. From this point on, his primary concern was to explain the condition of the sick poor.

Chadwick's quest to understand the sicknesses that bred poverty coincided with the founding of the Royal Statistical Society in 1834 and the creation of the General Register Office in 1837, and for the most part, in their early years Chadwick's cause was uppermost among their concerns.[35] Many of those who were first commissioned with the task of gathering statistics for the purposes of "social science" were drawn from the ranks of the medical profession. In this respect, the earliest attempts to render "the social body" statistically classifiable were intimately connected with a project to administer the nation's health.[36] Indeed, on many accounts, the attempt to validate a new type of medical knowledge for the promotion of public health was a prime motive for the early collection of social statistics; it was only in the twentieth century that it became accepted custom to retrospectively account for this in terms of the origins of British sociology.[37]

Historians of the rise of "public health" as a governmental concern report that when compiling data for his *Report on the Sanitary Condition of the Labouring Population* (1842), Chadwick made considerable efforts to ensure that the doctors he commissioned to map the prevalence of disease and poverty were sympathetic to the cause of sanitary reform.[38] As Christopher Hamlin notes, "Chadwick's reasons [were] plain. He was seeking to represent public sanitary improvement—water and sewers—as a means of social betterment that was consistent with the laws of political economy because it did not interfere with the play of the market in food or in labor. He based his case on the claim that diseases ranging from fever to tuberculosis, and social problems ranging from intemperance to revolutionary agitation, had one 'all pervading cause': concentrated emanations of decomposing matter, whose effects could be prevented by flushing the matter down the drain."[39] Chadwick sought to justify his approach by recourse to miasmatic theory. At this point, germ theory had yet to revolutionize the practice of medicine, so from the point of view of modern medicine his understanding of the causes of infectious disease was scientifically underdeveloped to say the least.[40] Indeed, in this respect, Hamlin notes that Chadwick went to considerable lengths in his report to place strict limits on the conception and account of the causes of infectious disease. He holds that in his concern to steer medicine away from any involvement in a political critique of industrialization or from any move to cast suspicion on the virtue of political economy, Chadwick promoted a "gratuitous rejection" of an older "constitutional medicine" that was primed to explain illness in terms of living conditions and cumulative events in a person's life history.[41] Hamlin claims that, for political reasons, Chadwick and his followers worked to emasculate any aspects of medical theory that promoted an understanding of the etiology of disease as being comprised by economic conditions or by multiple corrosive experiences of social deprivation. He suggests that this is powerfully illustrated in Chadwick's move to block William Farr's attempt to have "starvation" listed among the official classifications in the Registrar General's data on causes of death.[42] While Farr, having been trained within the older tradition of medicine, was concerned to make clear that the prolonged experience of malnutrition was heavily involved "in the production of diseases of various kinds'"and therefore should be identified among the causes of death, by contrast, Chadwick argued that this amounted to pure speculation and that Farr should limit his range of explanations to the incidence of disease alone. Hamlin contends that, as far as Chadwick was concerned, "starvation was too irrevocably a social and political issue" and to admit that this was a contributing factor to the spread of diseases of poverty would involve a threat to the credibility of his own much "cherished" point of view.[43]

Chadwick's use of statistical data to make visible public health as a problem for social policy entailed a deliberate attempt to impose strict limits on the domain of social understanding. At the very point at which the category of the social acquired the official currency to serve as a means to present aggregated populations as an object for policy debate, it also worked to disaggregate the production of knowledge about the lived conditions of social life. Poovey argues that by deploying representational technologies that served to make social conditions appear as though they were "objectively" removed from any matters of moral or political interest, Chadwick succeeded in creating a naturalized institutional and cultural space in which, henceforth, it was possible to analyze "social facts" as though they could be held apart from morality and politics. In other words, he made it possible for the social act of producing knowledge about social life to appear as though it was divorced from any enactment of moral value or expression of political preference. His "scientific" practice enabled him to portray "the social body" in a posture of moral and political neutrality that served to obscure the values shaping the construction of "laws" and "fact."

Poovey observes that beyond the accomplishment of garnering "scientific," moral, and political support for his project of sanitary reform, Chadwick's report set the protocol for subsequent government reports. She claims that his achievement established the practice of using statistical tables, expert eyewitness accounts, and formal policy recommendations as a customary means to frame social problems for rational debate and institutional regulation. More important, Chadwick's work helped constitute the cultural norms for what subsequently came to be counted as an objectively valid portrayal of social life, particularly where this was the object for government legislation. In this regard, even though many social statisticians might have taken issue with the logics at work in the design of Chadwick's statistical tables, they were unlikely to defer from adopting the technical forms of representation that he pioneered in his report.[44]

From this point on, at least as far as Britain is concerned, it seems there was an increasingly hostile and more politically pronounced division between those advocating a sentiment-fired approach to social understanding and those holding to the view that sentiment should have no part in the production of social knowledge.[45] Among purveyors of the virtue of political economy, sentiment tended to be cast not only as an anathema to clear sighted rationality, but also, as a principle cause of the failures of social policy. For example, in a study of the impact of economic depression on Southampton in 1875, Ruth Hutchinson Crocker notes that on discovering that larger than anticipated numbers of widows were receiving poor relief, a local Poor Law medical officer gave voice to the widely shared view that "it was to be regretted that sentimentality was allowed to erode sound policy."[46] By contrast, in some quarters sentimentality was ever more firmly embraced as a primary means to protest against social policies and practices that opposed the rights of humanity and the deep-felt concerns of humanitarian reform.

THE REBELLION OF SENTIMENT

In 1844 the *Spectator* magazine called for the creation of a new political party to oppose "laissez faire" by the "rebellion of sentiment."[47] David Roberts notes that this reflected the concerns of a wider London-based literary and artistic movement that made "the dictates of humanity" their primary concern. Publications such as the *Spectator, Punch,* the *Morning Herald,* the *Morning Chronicle,* the *Daily News,* and the *Illustrated London News* tended to feature the work of journalists and engravers whose accounts of social problems had a sentimental cast. Many of those associated with the humanitarian campaigns featured in such publications were recognized poets, novelists, and painters in their day.[48]

Among this group, the novelist, political journalist, and newspaper editor Charles Dickens (1812–70) was a figure of considerable influence. Indeed, most scholars studying the role of sentimentality in midcentury Victorian culture tend to regard Dickens's work as the exemplar of the genre.[49] It is widely understood that in his opposition to the cold and calculating statistical representation of social problems, Dickens sought to fashion a style of writing that evoked moral feeling and thereby a greater awareness of the moral values enacted in economic transactions and everyday social behaviors. In his satirical report on the annual meeting of the British Association for the Advancement of Science and in *Hard Times* (1854), in his caricature of Thomas Gradgrind, "the man of facts and calculations," he makes clear his opposition to any form of symbolic representation that works to obscure the moral texture of social life as it is encountered in experience.[50] As Poovey notes, he decried the "frightful empiricism" that holds that it is only in the contexts of its representation in the form of statistical laws that "society" should be held up as an object for policy debate, for in this move individual human beings are all too easily obliterated by numerical averages.[51] In his journalism and novels, by contrast, Dickens made it his mission to have his readers experience the sentiments stimulating compassion, resistance, and social care so as to raise the volume of public debate over the forms of moral experience that they were subject to, showing how, in turn, their actions were morally implicated in either the discord or the recuperation of society.[52]

A considerable amount of literary criticism is now directed at the ways in which, in works such as *Oliver Twist* (1838), *A Christmas Carol* (1843), *The Pickwick Papers* (1852), *Bleak House* (1853), and *Our Mutual Friend* (1865), he sought to fashion his social satires around "spectacularized" portrayals of suffering and sympathy.[53] Accordingly, it is argued that Dickens aimed to make his texts visually evocative so as to teach a supposedly disinterested and morally detached observer of society how to feel and what to desire. Such devices may have served to inspire a popular radical imagination, but from their publication through to the present day, it is questioned if such writing has the capacity to serve as an effective guide to moral or political action.

In a famously scathing review of *Our Mutual Friend*, Henry James argued that the characters in Dickens's books were too disconnected from real humanity.[54] James claimed that insofar as Dickens tended to compose his stories around characters exhibiting a "bundle of eccentricities," they were rendered too incredible to serve as guides to understanding real human conditions and relationships. On James's account, Dickens's infatuation with the exceptionally grotesque may have offered a macabre form of entertainment, but it did not serve to "enlarge our knowledge of the world."

More recently, David Roberts has argued that in spite of the fact that Dickens and his associates succeeded in popularizing a diffuse "spirit of humanity" complemented by an "uninhibited sympathy with and pity for the neglected, outcast and suffering," for the most part they failed to inspire any effective movements of social and political reform. Roberts claims that the efforts taken here to enrich the genre of satire and the culture of pathos were not matched by a design for remedial action. Indeed, he argues that it may well be the case that the historian William Lecky (1838–1903) was quite right to declare that, at least in relation to its incorporation in popular novels and works in public art galleries, sentimentality all too often served as "an indulgence of a hard heart that is actually indifferent."[55]

Such criticisms, however, insofar as they draw on evidence drawn from a limited range of contexts, are by no means equipped to provide grounds for an outright condemnation of sentimentality as a whole. There are multiple forms of sentimentalism and many social settings in which sentiment has influence. In this respect, in an attempt to survey the dimensions and development of visual cultures of sentimentality in Victorian times, Sonia Solicari argues that, given the enormous range of sentimental imagery and the numerous outlets for its airing in public, there can be no "single-driven motivation for emotional matter."[56] Quite simply, there are too many contrasting contexts in which sentimental cultures are in evidence, and while it may sometimes be appropriate to question the moral virtue and integrity of the feelings that are hereby generated among people, we should not presume that they are always liable to be gratuitous, false, or misleading; rather, we should be working to attend to the wide range of possible ways in which these feelings serve to reflect and shape people's moral outlooks and behaviors.

Considerable evidence suggests that already by the middle decades of the nineteenth century some of those who aimed to portray humanity in a sentimental vein were alert to the dangers of what William James was apt to refer to as the "sentimentalist fallacy," which is "to shed tears over abstract justice and generosity, beauty, etc., and never to know these qualities when you meet them in the street, because there the circumstances make them vulgar."[57]. For example, in the case of Henry Mayhew's letters to the *Morning Chronicle* (1849–50) and his later book *London Labour and the London Poor* (1861–62), we have a writer who appears to be alert

to the "pragmatic conception of truth" that holds it is in the "muddy par-
ticulars of experience" that we ought to try to apprehend the condition of
humanity and that this should also involve us in an effort to attend to the
"practical interests" and "personal reasons" with which people are disposed to account for their lives. In many instances it appears that Mayhew
is writing to have us attend to the "genuine reality" of people struggling to
live in social settings of uncertainty and danger that involve them in the
moral turmoil of conflicting feelings and values.

Robert Douglas-Fairhurst notes that Mayhew tended to criticize
Dickens for his overly sentimental depictions of working-class life and by
contrast held that an ethnographic encounter with humanity would hold
more moral meaning than any fiction could aspire to contain.[58] Mayhew
claimed that his craft was designed to provide "a literal description of [the
people's] labor, their earnings, their trials, and their sufferings, in their
own 'unvarnished' language"; and further, about many of his fellow journalists and authors he complained, "This disposition to cant, and varnish
matters over with a sickly sentimentality, angelizing or canonizing the
whole body of operatives of this country, instead of speaking to them as
possessing the ordinary vices and virtues of human nature[,] . . . is the
besetting sin of the age."[59] Yet even in the minds of his sternest critics,
there is no doubting that Mayhew was inclined to portray his respondents
in a sympathetic light and that in many instances he sought to educate his
readers in compassion.[60] A key and vital distinction in Mayhew's work is
his evident willingness to be shocked and unsettled by the experiences of
social life he uncovered and in his concern to have this made known
through the voice of working-class people. For example, the emotive
power of his account of the tragic life and death of the blind street musi-
cian Old Sarah relies for the most part on an unedited and uninterrupted
story of her life as she relays it to him in her own words.[61] We are invited
to acquaint ourselves with how Sarah feels and thinks about her life and
disability from her own point of view before he moves to shock us with a
matter-of-fact description of her brutally abrupt and painful death, as well
as that of her sighted guide and companion, Liza, in a mundane traffic
accident. More generally, in his letters to the *Morning Chronicle*, alongside any statistical information that Mayhew provides on wage levels and
conditions of employment, considerable space is devoted to detailing how

in their own words people are inclined to account for the experiences of toil and deprivation that they are subject to.[62]

E. P. Thompson observes that Mayhew appeared to be driven by a concern to draw attention to the "moral acclimatization" of human nature. He aimed to make his readers feel for the poor as fellow human beings. In this respect there are also reports of him demonstrating a remarkable degree of self-reflexivity as a component of his craft. Mayhew made considerable efforts to set his respondents at ease and sometimes worked to win their trust by ridiculing "middle-class" moralism and the condescension of "manners" that served to portray poor people as less than human. It is recorded that at a public meeting with London's East End tailors on their pay and working conditions he openly declared, "It is easy to be moral after a good dinner beside a snug sea-coal fire, and with our hearts well warmed with fine old port. It is easy for those that can enjoy these things daily to pay their poor's rates, rent their pew, and love their neighbors as themselves: but place the same 'highly respectable' people on a raft without sup or bite on the high seas, *and they would toss up who should eat their fellows*. Morality on £5000 a year in Belgrave Square is a very different thing to morality on slop-wages in Bethnal green."[63] It might be argued that, particularly for the brief period (1849–50) when he was metropolitan correspondent for the *Morning Chronicle,* Mayhew's work represented the high point of London's literary "rebellion of sentiment." It seems that more than any other work at the time, his letters held the power to shock middle-class sensibilities and expose the human costs of a nation riven by gross material, social, and health inequalities. For example, Ann Humphreys notes that Mayhew's work was "lauded" by most of the established journals of the time, was taken up as a key concern for debate among clergymen and philanthropists, and also briefly turned the *Morning Chronicle* into a vehicle for fund-raising for the relief of the poor.[64] She further brings emphasis to the extent to which this appears to have been primarily due to the unrivaled capacity of his interviews, sometimes supplemented with engravings of daguerreotypes of his respondents in their living and working environments, to magnify the facts of life stories so that individuals were powerfully revealed as "full-size" human beings.[65] Indeed, a reviewer for *Fraser's Magazine for Town and Country* echoed the sentiments expressed by many others at the time when he was moved to conclude, "The pictures which these Metropolitan letters exhibit draw from God's own storehouse of Fact [and are] stranger, sadder, terribler [*sic*] than all fiction."[66]

THE DISCIPLINE AND DISCONNECTION OF SOCIOLOGY

In his investigations for the *Morning Chronicle*, Henry Mayhew's critical concerns and manner of writing stand out as prototypes for later studies of social suffering published in the late twentieth century (see chap. 3). It is now possible, however, to recognize this as a highly exceptional and short-lived event in the history of social investigation in Britain. Following the publication of *London Labour and the London Poor* (1861–62), which was put together as part of a final angry rebuke to his detractors and critics, Mayhew experienced a radical decline in his public standing. By his death in 1887, both he and his work were largely forgotten. The possible forces behind and reasons for the forgetting of Mayhew are highly instructive for taking stock of the politics of sentiment and its relationship to social science. They also have the potential to serve as a valuable point of entry into debates over the aims, scope, and strategies of research and writing on the problems of social suffering.

Following the rediscovery of Mayhew's work in the late 1940s, considerable effort was directed to the task of understanding why it had been neglected for so long[67]. Such concerns were fueled by more than an attempt to recover the history of the making of the English working class; they were also driven by a newfound recognition of the uniqueness of Mayhew's approach to researching conditions of social life. As Raymond Williams notes, on reading Mayhew's work anew, it became clear that his records of conversations were not only "incomparable" as an account of the everyday language and experience of working-class Londoners in the mid-nineteenth century but also remarkable in terms of their power to expose the extent to which twentieth-century social commentary and sociological research were inclined to stand at a moral distance from their objects of study.[68] Indeed, Williams confesses that reading Mayhew brought him to a new awareness of himself as party to a style of cultural production that was disposed to strain out issues relating to the moral quality of interpersonal relations and problems raised by ties of human sympathy so as to privilege matters of abstract generality and authorial commentary on social conditions from afar.

Among the immediate reasons for Mayhew's retreat from public life and the decline of his career as a writer and journalist was the fact that during the brief period of his correspondence for the *Morning Chronicle* he made many enemies. As Thompson records, by the summer of 1850 it appears that the editors of the *Morning Chronicle* and the *Economist*, along with a host of journalists, philanthropists, and London business-men, had joined forces to discredit Mayhew's reports on the relationship between low wages and poverty. There is also evidence here to suggest that a considerable portion of the animosity that was directed to his work was fueled by objections to his manner of writing about, and expressions of solidarity with, the plight of the poor. For example, following Mayhew's break from the *Morning Chronicle* in the summer of 1850 over the edito-rial censoring of his criticisms of "free trade" and arguments in favor of protective tariffs, a fellow journalist, Angus Bethune Reach, reported on the incident by declaring, "I am disposed to think . . . that the editor of the Chronicle would have done well had he struck his pen through at least four of every eight columns of the disjointed lucubrations and melodramatic ravings of Mr Mayhew's sentimental draymen and poor artisans. Ever since Mr Mayhew's communications on the state of the poor attracted any attention, their author has kept summoning together public meetings of the classes among whom he had been mingling, apparently for no other purpose than to puff his own benevolent spirit."[69] Humphreys notes that aside from the success of the campaign to discredit Mayhew, there is evi-dence to suggest that he was both physically and mentally exhausted by his work. It seems that his spirit was broken and that, though still angry and embittered by the attacks on his virtue and integrity as a social researcher, he was already searching for a means to retreat from public life.[70]

Beyond this, it appears that it has only been possible to reflect upon some of the general conditions that contributed to the forgetting of Mayhew's work since attempts have been made to chart the early history of contrasting approaches to methods of social investigation.[71] In marked contrast to Mayhew's practice of entering into the homes and workplaces of the poor in an effort to make their acquaintance, most of those ventur-ing to study conditions of poverty did so from the standpoint of a member of the middle class traveling through an alien country.[72] Some were still inclined to motion with sympathy to the plight of the poor, yet it appears that little effort was made to privilege the points of view of those living in poverty. Mayhew operated with the understanding that he needed "to absorb from his informants new ideas and perceptions almost for their own sake" and thereby challenge and unsettle his own moral and intellectual prejudices.[73] By contrast, following the "rediscovery" of poverty in the 1880s, it seems that such considerations were seldom raised as a point of ethical concern or an issue of good research practice. In this respect, it appears that after Mayhew, with the notable exception of Jane Addams and her associates at Hull House (see chapter 6), very few people were prepared to give much thought to the importance of creating cultural spaces for the poor to be actively involved in shaping public understandings of the conditions affecting the experience of their lives.

Brian Harrison argues that, in part, the reluctance to follow Mayhew's example was due to the health risks involved in staying for any length of time in slum districts. He notes that it was well known that many of those venturing to gather firsthand information on unsanitary living conditions fell prey to infections causing dysentery, vomiting, and other threatening symptoms, so most social researchers were not inclined to dwell for any length of time in the poorest quarters of industrial cities.[74] At the same time, however, he suggests that the more important reason for the subsequent rejection of the type of ethnographic practice pioneered by Mayhew should be sought in the ethics of "professionalism" adopted by late nineteenth- and early twentieth-century social science. Harrison, along with other historians of social science, notes that by the late 1880s it was widely held that the most intellectually credible forms of social research were those addressed to the scale and complexity of social problems in language of abstraction.[75] From this point on, it appears to have been generally accepted that, for the sake of arriving at an authoritative account of common experience, it was necessary for social investigators to expunge matters of personal feeling and perspective from their reports on the workings of society.

On a number of accounts, this is made particularly apparent in the contrasts that can be drawn between Mayhew's letters and Charles Booth's later studies of poverty. For example, David Englander notes that during the course of his research Booth became deeply aware of the diversity and richness of working-class culture, yet he confined the record of his attention to this matter to his unpublished notebooks. Englander observes:

> There is undeniably a disjuncture between the buttoned-up Booth of the printed survey—very grave and very eminent—and the more approachable Booth of the unpublished notebooks. Booth's rejections of the structures and strategies in *London Labour and the London Poor* served to differentiate his survey from that of Mayhew, and to impress the reader with its scientific detachment, system and rigor. The curiosity and commitment, enthusiasm and energy, sympathy and humanity, so evident in the manuscripts, were all concealed within a set of literary devices that distanced the author and acted as a barrier against reader involvement with the subject of the text.[76]

In an effort to explain this, Harrison argues that Booth's manner of writing reflects the commonly held view at the time that it was only possible to mount a credible case for government to take up the reins of responsibility for public welfare by marshaling evidence untainted by personal feeling or moral interest. At one level this was a strategy designed to appeal to a political culture in thrall to the discourse of political economy. It was also fashioned as a result of mounting frustration with the perceived inefficiencies and ineffectiveness of Victorian philanthropy. It was the product of a widespread belief that actions founded on moral feelings for the subjects of philanthropy had proven themselves incapable of developing a sufficiently rational and united front for large-scale social reform. In this respect both writers on the political left and factions on the right tended to agree that sentiment should play no part in the task of social understanding.[77] While those seeking to discourage "pauperism" were inclined to hold moral feeling responsible for indiscriminate acts of charity that indulged the "undeserving' poor, by contrast, most left-leaning social reformers had arrived at the view that it was necessary to inject a strong dose of social scientific realism into their accounts of social problems so as to make a persuasive argument in favor of the state taking more responsibility for the health and welfare of populations.

In both Great Britain and the United States, the Charity Organization Society (COS) is understood to have exerted considerable influence on the cultural shaping and institutionalization of a professional form of sociology that was stridently opposed to the incorporation of sentiment in the conduct of social research. On both sides of the Atlantic, the COS worked

to introduce a "scientizing" movement in the culture and practice of philanthropy. At its foundation a great deal of COS activity appears to have
been chiefly directed to the introduction of more effective measures to
police the "undeserving" poor. In its later years, by pioneering a casework
method approach to the study of social problems, it served as a means to
bestow legitimacy on "social work" as an occupation dedicated to solving
"problems of poverty."[78] More often than not, the founding of the first COS
School of Sociology in 1903 tends to be portrayed as a largely positive
advance toward a more professionally administered approach to safe-
guarding the welfare of vulnerable populations.[79]

It was not until the middle decades of the twentieth century that British
social commentators started to offer critical reflections on the extent to
which, for the sake of presenting itself as dispassionate science, sociology
frequently served as a means to "dehumanize" the record of social life.
Arguably, it was not until figures such as Raymond Williams and E. P.
Thompson sought to advance a more humanistic form of Marxist cultural
history that a sustained level of critical reflection was brought to the extent
to which the classifications and generalizations of social science were deficient in their capacity to expose the moral experience of individuals in
their social context. It seems that it was only following the entry of working-class men and women into British universities that relations of power
and vested interest in the practice of social science were understood to
cast a veil of ignorance over the lived experience of socially marginalized
and structurally disadvantaged groups.[80]

By contrast, it seems that at the origins of American sociology a number
of pioneering researchers were more alert to the extent to which the adoption of standards of "professionalism" "officially" validating their practices
of knowledge production also closed down possibilities for attending to
large portions of human experience. For example, Ted Hovet Jr. records
that Harriet Martineau publicly defended Harriet Beecher Stowe's sentimentalism on the grounds that it was able to convey elements of the "truth"
about human experience that were beyond the reach of formal calculation
and arguments based on the discipline of reason. He observes that
Martineau argued that there was a potential within American social science for an "exceptionalism" that made space for a broad range of mutually
complementary approaches to social understanding.[81] In a similar vein, in

a largely forgotten article published in 1884, Lester Frank Ward, the first president of the American Sociological Association, advises his colleagues that they should be wary of adopting the British sociological tendency that dismisses "the sentiment of humanity" as a matter of no importance and suggests that they reject the narrowly conceived intellectualism that treats humanitarianism as no more than a "fanaticism" for social reform. Instead, Ward holds, American sociology should venture to make humanitarian sentiments "the object of deep study" so as to better understand how society might prove itself "capable of caring for the most unfortunate of its members in a manner that shall not work demoralization."[82]

Contemporary historical accounts of the founding of American sociology are now inclined to draw critical attention to the extent to which, at least until the first quarter of the twentieth century, the culture of the discipline tended to be more openly divided between those aiming to tailor their knowledge for social reform and those seeking to legitimize sociology as an "objective" and "value-free" science of society.[83] In this context, those working to develop sociology as a reformist praxis, although still alert to some of the dangers of sentimentality, tended to acknowledge an important role for sympathy as a means to make known the lived conditions of society.[84] For example, Jane Addams (1860–1935) was inclined to advocate the practical cultivation of fellow feeling as a way to acquire social understanding and, further, took this as a motive force of ethics and politics.[85] It is also clear, however, that in some quarters the more sentimentally disposed sociology of Addams was regarded as anathema that should be expelled from the academy, at least, that is, as far as any formal association with the "science" of sociology is concerned.

It is only in recent years that intellectual historians have sought to bring attention to the bitter rivalries and acrimonious dispute that accompanied the movement to establish sociology as a credible science within the American academy. For example, a number of academic papers profile Robert E. Park's contempt for Addams and her advocacy of sociology as both a sympathetic and morally committed practice.[86] Park (1864–1944), along with positivistic sociologists such as Luther Lee Bernard (1881–1951), William Fielding Ogburn (1886–1959), and Francis Stuart Chapin (1888–1974), successfully divorced social science from a pragmatic movement of social reform and also practiced a politics of erasure that aimed to obscure the achievements of those associated with earlier settlement sociology and other practically engaged forms of sociological work. In effect, as critics such as Mary Jo Deegan now point out, this involved both a move to exclude women and black men from a large portion of academic sociology and a concerted drive to devalue the intellectual standing of their work.[87]

At the time they wrote and as they occupied newly available posts at universities, most of the white metropolitan middle-class men of social science were not alert to the full force of their symbolic violence, and in many cases it appears that this was hardly made conscionable as a matter for concern. Certainly, they were not aware of the extent to which their recorded words and accompanying actions would serve to wound and offend future generations. It is now possible, however, to regard these as a spur to contemporary movements of critique. Ironically, it is by attention being drawn to the hostility displayed by mid-twentieth-century social science toward traditions of intellectual pragmatism and accompanying movements of sociological reform that researchers are now inspired to question whether there may still be a good deal of unfinished business to be drawn from cultures of sentimentality.[88] The frequently gendered and racial hurt left by the drive to remove moral feeling from the work of sociology has contributed to a new movement to question how social bonds of sympathy may once again be studied both as an elemental part of the constitution of society and as a vital component of the attempt to research the human social condition as such.

IN SUMMARY

In this chapter we have offered a brief narrative on the history of the conceptualization of "the social" components and conditions of life. We have been particularly concerned to dwell upon the extent to which methods of social inquiry allow for critical attendance to how people experience the moral force and discipline of society, particularly where this serves to dehumanize the conditions under which they are made to live. By highlighting some of the intellectual, moral, and political tensions aggravated by the attempt to make space for a more sentiment-oriented or sympathetic approach to social understanding, we aim to draw critical debate to the conditions under which documents of social life work to effect an encounter with human experience.

By no means should this be taken as a wholesale and uncritical endorsement of sentiment-fired social inquiry. We are certainly prepared to acknowledge that there are many circumstances where literary attempts to mobilize a sympathetic identification with others serve as a form of ideological abuse.[89] Let us be clear: we have no interest whatsoever in drawing critical attention away from the potential for emotive forms of social expression to work as a means to establish and sustain unequal power relations. We also recognize that there may be many occasions where emotions are indulged to the cost of the effort to engage with critical thinking and real practices of social care. At the same time, however, we are concerned to understand how sympathy is a necessary part of social understanding and, in particular, the potential for this to serve as a means to convey important matters of moral practice and personal meaning. Insofar as moral experience is strained out of the record of social life, it is rendered sterile as a means to attend to the ways in which people encounter and relate to their lives as an enactment of substantive human values. That is to say, moral emotions play a vital role in stimulating and directing the uses of research.

It is also important to note here the extent to which a substantial portion of the critical concerns raised in this chapter are echoed in contemporary scholarship on the history of ideas, and all the more so where this draws to a focus on the political conditions and institutional constraints that govern the social production of human science. In this light, we suggest that twenty years ago it would not have been possible to compile the resources to write a chapter such as this. To a large degree, the concerns raised here, directed though they are to the history of social science, are very much drawn from the present. They are inspired and informed by an interdisciplinary movement to revise the conduct of social inquiry as well as the symbolic means by which it is made possible for us to attend to the record of social life. It is in the new creative spaces provided by feminist scholarship, American literary criticism, working-class (or subaltern) studies, colonial and postcolonial research, and the medical humanities that we have found our inspiration.

There is also no doubt that these ethical and cultural movements have contributed a great deal to a newfound critical concern with problems of social suffering. They license a "hermeneutics of suspicion" with regard to the conduct of social science. They also serve to alert researchers to the potential for their outlook and practice to be transformed in the struggle to fashion an adequate moral response to what suffering does to people. It is to this matter in particular that we now turn.

3 A Broken Recovery

C. Wright Mills's *The Sociological Imagination* (1959) may well be the most influential account of sociology produced since the Second World War. In an attempt to assess the relative standing of disciplinary-defining texts of the twentieth century, following Max Weber's posthumously collected essays published as *Economy and Society* ([1920–21] 1978), it was voted by members of the International Sociological Association as the greatest source of inspiration for their work. Most of the main textbook introductions to sociology now make approving references to Mills's account of the "task" and "promise" of the sociological imagination as a means to convey the founding vision for their enterprise and to underscore its human value.

In the much-celebrated opening chapter, Mills declares that sociology concerns the attempt to understand the bearing of large-scale public issues on many personal troubles of everyday life. He portrays modern individuals as anxiously preoccupied by deep-rooted problems of moral meaning and social purpose, and in this setting, he advocates the cultivation of a "sociological imagination" as the means by which they might "grasp history and biography and the relations between the two within society."[1] Mills contends that by attending to the ways people experience "various and specific milieux," sociology is fitted to equip them with the intellectual resources to reflect critically on the social structures and cultural values that govern their lives. On his account, it is a distinct "quality of mind" that is animated by a search for progressive social and personal change. Mills championed a critical sociology that promises more than enlightened self-understanding; beyond this, it is committed to oppose and reform the "structural contradictions" that do harm to people. It aims both to inspire and to be actively involved in the creation of humane forms of society.

At the same time, however, Mills emphasized that there is a considerable amount of debate to be had with regard to existing possibilities for putting into practice the type of sociology he advocates. *The Sociological Imagination* is filled with a sentiment of disappointment. The larger part of the book is taken up with an angry denunciation of the major "tendencies" within academic sociology that Mills held responsible for leading his discipline to a point where it had become myopically obsessed with its academic standing and methodological status as "social science." He decries the "arid formalism" of sociological theories where "the splitting of concepts and their endless rearrangement becomes the central endeavour."[2] He further expresses his contempt for a culture of "abstracted empiricism" that appears to be governed by purely administrative and economic considerations. Mills portrays empirical sociology as "methodologically inhibited" and contends that its contemporary representatives are largely unconcerned with substantive questions relating to fundamental conditions of historical formation and the moral experience of social life. Most of his text is devoted to making clear his opposition to any type of sociology that does not deal with critical questions of human value, and by this standard, he advises that we regard most of what passes for sociological research as next to useless.

One of the great ironies of its subsequent canonization as a founding text of sociology, and in particular its casting as a celebratory introduction to the field, lies in the fact that *The Sociological Imagination* is largely devoted to detailing Mills's antipathy to most sociologists and their work. Those who inquire into the motives behind his writing share in the understanding that Mills intended the book to serve as a cry from the wilderness and that in this epic scene he was moving to cast himself as a lost prophet in a hostile land.[3] In addition to this, some argue that Mills hankered after greatness and while striving for recognition revealed a bullying and abrasive character. During his brief career he made many enemies, and on some readings, *The Sociological Imagination* essentially amounts to a climactic work of rancorous ressentiment.[4]

A contrasting view holds that, even if Mills reveled in his status as a radical outsider, nevertheless, through *The Sociological Imagination* he managed to clear a space for the emergence of a more critically motivated, ethically charged, and openly political brand of sociology. In most appraisals of his life and work, it is for his critical style that he is lauded as a figure of lasting significance. Arguably, however, his sociological legacy has worked far more to advance a critical attitude than to inspire an emancipatory practice. Indeed, as Craig Calhoun and Jonathan VanAntwerpen observe, while many are inclined to celebrate Mills as a maverick critic of "the mainstream," few have ventured to conduct sustained inquiries into how his sociology is best applied to the task of delivering progressive social and personal change.[5] On this account, an infatuation with the myth of Mills-the-rebel has all too often served to divert critical attention from the methodological problems raised by his work and example.

By entering into debate over the existing possibilities for realizing Mills's vision for sociology, we clear valuable analytical ground for appraising current practices of research and writing on problems of social suffering. Here the very fact that social research is asked to attend and respond to human suffering has a tendency to raise the volume of critical debate over its value as a means to document human life experience as well as over its practical purpose in movements of social care and efforts at progressive social reform. From this direction, a particular urgency is brought to the difficulty of assessing Mills's vision, motives, and methods, particularly insofar as these can be taken to be informed by a crisis of vocation and as connected to a frustration of purpose that run through academic sociology as a whole.

When engaged with the task of documenting social suffering, researchers are frequently made to examine the moral adequacy of their methods of understanding social experience and, further, are left preoccupied by the limitations of the cultural conventions of academic discourse. In almost every instance, by venturing to understand how people's lives are damaged by social suffering, those involved in the documentation of this experience are moved to critically question established practices of knowledge production. Researchers operate in circumstances riven by moral disquiet, contexts of great distress, where people are afflicted with many painful problems of embodied meaning. Many researchers are left struggling to set this within forms of cultural representation that are adequate to convey what happens to people in such difficult lived experience, and they tend to operate in a vexed relationship with the conventions of social science.

The burden of failure can be overwhelming; and it is important to recognize that this tends to move beyond the frustration of failing to provide an adequate frame of reference for the brute fact of suffering so as to make adopted methods of research and approaches to theorizing society appear lacking in human relevance and value. If, as Zygmunt Bauman contends, the practice of sociological thinking serves to "defamiliarize the familiar,"[6] thus assimilating a truism in ethnography, then in the context of research and writing on social suffering this is taken to an extreme point where, more often than not, practitioners are made to critically question fundamental components of their training, practice, and thinking. Moreover, many are left estranged from their adopted traditions of social inquiry, methods of social investigation, and means of social communication.

A major issue of concern that runs through this chapter and those that follow relates to the positions that might be occupied as well as the actions that might result from this experience. We argue that the moral and intellectual tensions borne under the attempt to acknowledge and make known what suffering does to people hold the potential to be highly productive for the acquisition of social understanding. Both here and in later chapters we also contend that whatever is hereby achieved by way of social understanding holds value only insofar as it serves to promote the value and practice of caregiving. Our interest is twofold. At one level, it lies in the development of a critical praxis that aims to involve audiences and/or readers in the aggravated tensions between, on the one hand, social suffering as a conflicted realm of moral experience and, on the other, the struggle to make this amenable to sociological and anthropological understanding. At another level, it concerns the potential for the pursuit of social understanding to be allied to practices of caregiving and indeed for these to be taken up as a necessary part of the attempt to understand the human social condition as such.

In part, the title of this chapter is intended to convey recognition of the fact that much of the new research and writing on problems of social suffering falls short of meeting our aims. In contrast to much of the work conducted with reference to this matter, we aim to advance more than a position of protest or the development of critique. In our review we are particularly concerned to advocate an approach to research and writing on social suffering that moves beyond the task of documenting and analyzing what is wrong with the world so as to engage in the practice of making it an object of care. We are opposed to the view that social inquiry should operate purely for the sake of critique (as in anthropology as critique writings); rather, we contend that it must also be committed to the discovery of better ways of living with others and to the advancement of more humane conditions of society. We further hold that its practitioners should preoccupy themselves with demonstrating such commitment in action.

The title of the chapter is also intended to indicate that, on our understanding, there is much taking place in recent research and writing on social suffering that is either informed by or stumbling toward recovering the interests featured within classical traditions of pragmatism as exemplified in the works of figures such as William James, John Dewey, and Jane Addams. At the same time that the first section of this chapter locates Mills's sociology as an attempt to marry social inquiry with a renewed critical pragmatism, it is also intended to make clear the intellectual and political lineage that frames our understanding and account of research and writing on social suffering. This tradition informs our analysis of the practices, values, and relative achievements of current movements in the field. In the second section the pragmatic concern with "experience" is reviewed as a means to set the stage for our analysis of contemporary work on social suffering. Following a review of some of the key concerns, developments, and running debates within this interdisciplinary domain, in conclusion, we return to the challenges set by Mills for social analysis and research and offer some further reflections on how these might be addressed in the context of research and writing on social suffering.

ON MILLS'S "SOCIOLOGIZED PRAGMATISM"

It is frequently noted that Mills drew a great deal of inspiration from the "classic" problem-focused social theories of Karl Marx and Max Weber, but for the most part, it is only those acquainted with his early body of work who bring emphasis to his aim to develop a "sociologized pragmatism."[7] Mills was heavily influenced by the philosophy as well as the social and political thought of the classical period of American pragmatism and, above all, John Dewey.[8] Like Dewey, he believed that we should take conflicts met in experience as the ground for social inquiry, and further, he was committed to the view that knowledge developed on this basis should be evaluated for its power to inform action. At the same time, however, Mills held that Dewey was naive when it came to understanding the workings of political and economic power in society.[9] On this account, it is important to appreciate the extent to which Mills's interest in sociology was rooted in an attempt to address "a crisis in American pragmatism," which he diagnosed as a failure to pay adequate attention to the corrosive force of capitalist interests, bourgeois consumer culture, and impersonal bureaucratic procedure on the pursuit of democratic freedoms, individual creativity, and social justice.[10] Accordingly, Mills was convinced that if pragmatism was to recover its vitality and relevance to public life, it needed to operate with a more theoretically sophisticated and critical account of presiding structures of power and inequality in society.

When approached from this direction, it may well be argued that in his concern to build a bridge from American pragmatism to the critical traditions of European social theory, Mills went too far. One of the most striking features of *The Sociological Imagination* is the mere lip service it pays to the methodological practices associated with pragmatism while it advances a form of critical commentary in a wholly abstract vein. Mills encouraged sociologists to build their inquiries from the conflicted experience of personal troubles, but he made no reference to the practices (and praxis) that social researchers operating within these traditions deem necessary as a means to uncover and respond to the lived realities of local social worlds. Among other things, he displayed no interest in engaging with the attempt to document the personal and expressed standpoints of individuals in day-to-day life. As Norman Denzin complains:

> Little men (and women, elsewhere called 'darling little slaves' and 'suburban queens') are Mills's foil. He purportedly speaks to their existential traps; the lack of meaning in their lives; their failed marriages; their unemployment; the woman's nun-like, low paying job in white collar offices; their robot like work; their drug and alcohol abuse; the fraudulent inspiration literature

and popular films they watch; and the horrible, ugly cities where they live. . . . But nowhere in the pages of his work(s) do these little people and their personal troubles speak. Mills speaks for them; or he quotes others who have written about them.[11]

Denzin argues that neither Mills nor those who followed in his wake have provided an adequate demonstration of how a politically productive and practically relevant engagement might be fashioned between the critical discourse of sociology and personal upheavals met in social context. Where some have followed Mills's "hypocritical" practice of only venturing to broker with experience through the language of theory or the discourse of cultural elites, others (like Denzin) have been inclined to retreat from the attempt to theorize the world sociologically as a consequence of being immersed in the practice of ethnography. In this regard, Denzin is morally alarmed by what he perceives to be an inherent mismatch between the cultural grammar of conventional sociological theory and the particularities of people's experience in everyday life. He shares in Arendt's suspicion that when brought to the level of public debate too much of the lived reality of social injustice and real-life conditions of despair is "explained away" by "highly efficient talk."[12]

On this account, the enduring value of Mills's work lies in the extent to which its shortcomings serve as a means to expose the scale of the task that is set for those who would yet venture to fashion a form of critical practice that is both sociologically enlightening and practically relevant. Where is "the sociological imagination" that can deliver on its "promise"? How might social understanding be fashioned as a means to inspire the practices that sustain life and enable people to relate to one another on humane terms? How might it be possible to bear moral witness to the suffering endured through experience, and also set this within a sociologically meaningful framework that equips people with the knowledge to take actions to transform the conditions of their existence?

THE EXPERIENCE OF SUFFERING

It is widely recognized that within classical traditions of American pragmatism, "experience" is a paramount concern.[13] Both William James and John

Dewey hold that human beings are thoroughly enmeshed in and subject to their experience of the world. They further emphasize that experience involves far more than a mental capacity to be consciously aware of an external environment; rather, it is constituted within human relationships and social interactions that involve the entire person in his or her corporeal being.[14] Experience takes place in the active production of social life. It involves people "knowing how" to respond to situations and taking actions coordinated by moral commitments and investments of moral feeling.

Via an appeal to and under the guidance of experience, the early pragmatists aimed to improvise an approach to thinking that is involved with real-life events and pressing human concerns. In this respect, they understood themselves to be working outside mainstream traditions of Western philosophy and social science. They rejected the Cartesian and Lockean dualisms that divide thinkers into camps of rationalists and empiricists. Writers such as James, Dewey, and Addams were also highly critical of the academic complacency of those who confine their pursuit of knowledge to the ivory tower. By contrast, they stressed the importance of acquiring understanding through direct association with individuals in real-life contexts; and in this regard, they advised that we should always be prepared for experience to boil over, to be more than that which we describe, to reach beyond itself and to disclose new understandings of, and ways of relating to, ourselves and others.[15]

In recent times, following the much-vaunted "linguistic turn" in Western philosophy, academic debates over the role of experience in social inquiry have been mired in epistemological dispute. In this context, the pragmatic appeal to experience is often portrayed as no more than a methodological strategy, and further, one that conveys a great deal of hermeneutical naïveté as well as a failure to grasp the full extent to which experience is made in and through language.[16] Notwithstanding the fact that critics often fail to acknowledge that figures such as Dewey aim to attend to the ways in which language serves as a means to convey and shape experience, they are inclined to portray the focus on experience as a purely scholastic consideration, as though it were a mere intellectual quibble or matter of academic fashion.[17] What tends to be lost here is recognition of both the passions that drive pragmatists to engage with experience and the pains that insistently demand this of them. The category of experience is thinned out and washed clean of all issues of human value and commitment; and more important, it tends to be disassociated from the sufferings borne by people in real-life situations.

It is striking to note the extent to which the founding texts of pragmatism, when underlining their concern for experience, also recognize this as a matter conceived under the trial of suffering. Ralph Waldo Emerson's famous essay *Experience* (1842) is a reflection on the grief he suffers following the death of his five-year-old son, and in particular his utter despair over the numbing emptiness of feeling that besets him. In this context, it is while under the torment of experiencing the need to be touched more deeply by his son's loss that he is made to reflect on his broken state of humanity and the seeming impossibility of being reconciled to much of the experience that that he is made subject to.[18] In a similar vein, Martin Jay notes that it is while mourning the loss of family ties and friendships, and suffering a series of personal crises that are "almost suicidal in intensity," that William James is driven to make the task of attending to "experience" the key to understanding the human condition as such.[19]

There is no doubt in the minds of many commentators that the great burden of grief carried by James, along with that of many of his associates, was gathered through the experience of the American Civil War.[20] Indeed, Louis Menand observes that the origins of pragmatism are rooted in traumatic experiences of violence, internecine conflict, and civil strife. In its classical forms, pragmatism marks an attempt to secure an alternative vision for social and political life in the aftermath of a series of social upheavals that signaled "not just the failure of democracy, but a failure of culture and of ideas."[21] It is part of a desperate attempt to devise, propagate, and enact a way of life in which people can relate to one another on humane terms. In their shared concern for the practicality of ideas, the early pragmatists were all engaged in a painful struggle to devise an approach to critical thinking that makes a vital difference to how people live together in society.

In a famous essay, *The Need for a Recovery of Philosophy* (1917), written at a point when the First World War appeared to be dragging modern societies into a terminal state of conflict and decline, John Dewey was particularly concerned to underline the extent to which the pragmatic engagement with experience necessarily involves a struggle with and through human suffering. He wrote:

What experience suggests about itself is a genuinely objective world which enters into the actions and sufferings of men and undergoes modifications through their responses. . . . Experience is primarily a process of undergoing: a process of standing something; of suffering and passion, of affection, in the literal sense of these words. . . . [It is] a matter of simultaneous doings and sufferings. . . . Philosophy recovers itself when it ceases to be a device for dealing with the problems of philosophers and becomes a method, cultivated by philosophers, for dealing with the problems of men. . . . To enforce the fact that the emergence of imagination and thought is relative to the connection of the sufferings of men with their doings is of itself to illuminate those sufferings and to instruct those doings.[22]

With this emphasis to the fore, perhaps it is not surprising to note that both Dewey and James were inclined to regard Jane Addams's book, *Democracy and Social Ethics* (1902), as a seminal contribution to their critical cause, particularly insofar as it documents the potential for pragmatism to serve as a practical way of life.[23] Here Addams treats the seemingly inexorable "perplexities" of people living in some of the poorest districts of Chicago as both the grounds for moral deliberation and a resource for social understanding. In this regard, she makes clear that within communities suffering conditions of material scarcity, broken family relationships, and pronounced experiences of political alienation, the struggle to forge ties of social sympathy is fraught with intellectual frustration and more often than not involves participants in a great deal of emotional distress. Emphasis is brought to the large difficulties of knowing how to live and what to do in social encounters where individuals are deeply divided by structures of class, "race," gender, and age. Insofar as it is left purely as a matter for dry intellectual debate, it is assumed that the meaning of social life can never be grasped in terms of its human consequences; rather, this requires a deliberate courting of fellow feeling and an active concern for the plight of others. Addams works under the conviction that social experience is inherently moral in form and consequence and to deny this is tantamount to forsaking the task of engaging with the most elemental facts of human life. She holds that it is only by our attendance to and participation in the moral dilemmas of social life that we may venture to understand its effects on people. Social insight is acquired by the quality of our association with and acts of caring for others in real-life situations (see chapter 6). In this respect, it is always highly contingent, partial, and caught in process. We should also anticipate that it is often the case that it can only be apprehended at a personal cost.

As a basic point of departure, it is important to recognize the extent to which the more recent turn to problems of social suffering marks the recovery of a form of inquiry that takes the experience of human affliction as a guide to the process of social understanding. Indeed, some are readily prepared to acknowledge a strong affinity between the passions that fire their work and those of classical traditions of pragmatism.[24] The focus on social suffering is linked with a move to devise a critical praxis that attends to social life as an intrinsically *moral experience*. At the same time that this attends to the harms done to people, it is involved in exposing how social life takes place as an enactment of substantive values with great human consequence.[25] In this context, a particular emphasis is also placed on the pursuit of social knowledge as a practical means to improve and care for the social conditions of human life. As Loïc Wacquant puts it, such work marks a deliberate attempt to fashion a mode of social exploration that "falls at the intersection of social science, politics and civic ethics."[26] The actions and forms of experience that result as a consequence of this endeavor are a key concern, and the grounds on which to judge its worth.

The focus on problems of social suffering also incorporates the understanding that it is when people are faced with extreme conditions of adversity and are made to experience events of great personal distress that their (broken) humanity and basic human needs are exposed to view. The brute force of suffering in social life can be overwhelming, and it takes place as an assault on the core elements of an individual's subjectivity and personhood. Here researchers operate on the understanding that, to make their work relevant to the experiences that painfully inhabit and cause harm to a person, they must be prepared to engage with the struggle to make sense of the ways social life contributes to and takes its course from many vexed problems of suffering.

IN CONFLICT AND DISLOCATION

The concept of social suffering has been used for over two hundred years as a means to underline the social causes of human misery, but it is only since the final decade of the twentieth century that it has featured as a headline issue of concern for projects of social science.[27] In this setting, *social suffering* is used as a generic term of reference for the lived experience of deprivation, misery, pain, and loss. An experience of social suffering is wholly negative and is part of any social event, social condition, or social process that delivers harm to people's lives. Where problems of social suffering are identified as a major cause of a person's injury and distress, researchers aim to show the ways in which their suffering is constituted through an embodied experience of societal and cultural violence. A focus is brought to the extent to which social worlds are not only inscribed on the bodily experience of pain, but are structural causes of that pain.[28] Attention is given to the moderating force of cultural meanings and the dynamics of social interaction on physiological symptoms of distress but also to the ways institutions created to control and manage suffering may worsen it out of unintended consequences or bureaucratic indifference.[29]

The gathering of interest around the topic of social suffering has come from a number of directions and is invested with a considerable range of disciplinary, analytical, political, and practical concerns. It is striking to note, however, the extent to which researchers share in the conviction that in working to document and categorize this experience, they are made to operate at the limits of their technical capacity for understanding.[30] It is widely held that when set to the task of charting the parameters of social suffering, conventional practices of knowledge production and academic writing are placed under an inordinate strain and are frequently found wanting.

Some venture to explain such difficulties as resulting from the fact that they concern problems that are at once physical, interpersonal, political, legal, and cultural. It is argued that highly technical categories operating within narrow fields of specialist inquiry are unsuited to give expression to the combined force of the multiple conditions that give rise to social suffering.[31] For the sake of arriving at a technically precise account of discrete aspects of a person's complaint, the overall quality and consequences of the person's experience tends to be strained away or lost from view. For example, in the case of many debilitating health problems, a great deal of suffering takes place not only in the struggle to endure the physical burden of deterioration, injury, and disease but also in the loss of social roles and identities that individuals experience as they are immersed in the process of adapting to their reduced state. It involves both the immediate experience of bodily affliction and the painful work of recovering (or discovering) new terms on which to relate to oneself and others. Here a considerable part of the problem of giving due acknowledgment to or providing an adequate redress for the social experience of suffering resides in the extent to which it always transgresses the bounds of formal representation. As experience, it is made in the damage done to an entire person in his corporeal and social being, and where this is disaggregated for refined professional analysis into discrete medical or social problems, too much of its reality is obscured.[32]

In addition to these problems of categorization, frustrations occur in the attempt to convey the brute force of social suffering as moral experience. By its orientation to abstraction and in its pursuit of clear-cut points of principle, academic discourse fails to capture an adequate sense of the anguish borne by people as they struggle to navigate a course through real-life conditions of adversity. Following the attempt to record how individuals in desperate circumstances both embody and give voice to their pains and distress, researchers are left troubled by the extent to which their dedicated frames of reference and forensic terms of expression fail to capture the overwhelming significance of experiences that visit torment and destruction on people's lives.[33] Pierre Bourdieu goes so far as to argue that the cultural "distortion" that takes place here amounts to a form of "symbolic violence";[34] for by this, it often appears that yet more harm is done to individuals by languages that serve to deflect attention away from the most excruciating facts of their condition and its control over them.[35]

Researchers have a moral obligation to expose the painful contradictions, exacerbated frustrations, and confounded meanings of social suffering as met in experience.[36] The emphasis placed on the experience of social suffering as intrinsically *moral* is intended to underline the extent to which it involves people in limit situations or borderline experiences from which there is no escape. Here the very possibility of knowing how to live and what to do is radically called into question, and people are made to think and act in conditions of tormenting perplexity. Individuals are brought under a painful compulsion to think beyond and act against what is happening to them; but what holds them "in suffering" is the terrifying absence of an adequate means to do this. In the most extreme forms of suffering, all that is good, rightful, purposeful, and conducive to humanity is withheld from people.[37] As raw experience, suffering exposes people to an over-whelming need for moral direction and purpose. A great part of human suffering is constituted in a desperate and often deeply injurious search to find a positive means to live through or beyond that which is experienced as wholly, and most painfully, negative in life.

Under this emphasis, research and writing on social suffering not only aims to expose the multiple ways in which suffering is constituted as a sociocultural and profoundly moral experience in people's lives but also thereby to question how social life is documented and treated as an "object" for public debate. Considerable efforts are made to expose the reality of society both as an enactment of substantive values and in terms of its human effects. Attention is brought to how people are made to embody their society and culture. Bodily experiences and people's health conditions in every sense are approached as data that expose the moral character and force of social life.[38] Here the sociological positivism that treats matters of moral standpoint and human feeling as "pollutants" that corrupt the possibility that we may arrive at an "objective" view on "the way things are" is held to impose unnecessary and potentially harmful limits on the bounds of social understanding and social action. In studies of social suffering, the human situation is a paramount concern, and most researchers aim to do all they can to allow this to be seen and heard.

The search for symbolic forms of culture to make known the pains borne by people in lived experience is also part of a project to refashion the instru-ments of social inquiry. Researchers are brought into debate with the trou-bled history and politics of modern humanitarianism and its role in the awakening of social conscience (see chapter 5). With the recognition that an active imagination for the suffering of others and the cultivation of sym-pathy are essential to the process of social understanding, a critical focus is brought to the occasions where public debates over the bounds of social justice and conditions of social life are initiated and sustained via attempts to document, describe, and visualize people's distress and pain. In this con-text, it is readily acknowledged that humanitarian culture may be appro-priated for ideological ends and that "the passion of compassion" may serve to cloud political debate.[39] At the same time, however, it is held that court-ing such hazards remains a necessary and unavoidable part of the struggle to expose the human social condition as such, and to do something positive by way of taking actions to care for people. The disavowal of social life that takes place under the attempt to deny passion a place within the bounds of social inquiry is identified as the greater danger here. It should also be recognized, however, that this tends to leave researchers immersed in the difficulty of understanding how moral sentiment can (or should) be allied to social enlightenment. When a focus is brought to problems of social suffering, the terms of social investigation are made laden with risk. Not least of these risks is the emphasis on aiding others and acting in the world based on social and other knowledge to repair, treat, and prevent. Not surprisingly, much of this work occurs in global health settings (see chapter 6).

It is generally the case that when brought to focus on social suffering we find researchers working in great tension, and sometimes in open conflict, with received traditions of inquiry and cultures of representation. Reports on the experience of social suffering tend to be accompanied by a move to critically question the cultural and political conditions under which it is made possible for us to relate to one another as social beings and, further, to realize more humane conditions of society in broken worlds. There are (at least) four domains of social research, discussed below, where such issues are now treated as a priority concern.

Health and the Social Body

A great deal of contemporary research and writing on social suffering has been developed in relation to attempts to define the field and practice of medical anthropology. Here the attendance to problems of social suffering is taken up as part of a critique of biomedicine and related processes of medicalization. Researchers work in opposition to any system of categorization, method of diagnosis, or mode of practice that obscures the social origins and determinants of people's health conditions. Medical anthropologists argue that overall qualities of health and the prevalence of disease are largely dependent on the social and economic circumstances in which individuals are made to live. A person's experience of health and their vulnerability to particular types of disease are explained more by social conditions and material constraints than individual lifestyle choice or pure physiology.

By drawing public attention to problems of social suffering, researchers aim to explain how matters of economic organization, social arrangement, and political design are implicated in the prevalence, virulence, and distribution of adverse health conditions. In this context, the extent to which populations exhibit so-called diseases of poverty such as AIDS, malaria, measles, tuberculosis, and cholera is held to expose a portion of the "global structures of violence" that do great harm to societies.[40] Emphasis is placed on the syndemic character of many diseases, that is, the extent to which they result from a clustering of deleterious social conditions. For example, social epidemiologists point to the "dangerous synergism" that takes place between poverty, childhood malnutrition, and a huge range of physical diseases and mental health problems through the life course.[41] The clustering of violence on the streets and in the family, substance abuse, depression, suicide, and traumatic injury in predatory inner-city neighborhoods and periurban shantytowns is seen not as co-morbidity but as vicious sociosomatic cycles.[42] It is argued that problems of social suffering expose "the need for a biosocial reconception of disease," both in terms of how it is caused and how it is addressed for "treatment."[43]

In addition to this, medical anthropologists attend to social suffering as a distinct form of bodily experience and/or performance. Here researchers aim to document the cultural idioms and social conventions by which individuals manifest symptoms of physical disease and mental distress. Medical anthropologists argue that social-cultural categories of meaning as well as political-economic forces are heavily implicated in the extent to which health problems are manifested by and documented among populations.[44] They observe that there are considerable cultural variations in the definition and response to particular types of disease and that these are shaped both by tradition and by the force of government policy and economic pressures.[45]

A wide range of studies are devoted to explaining how socially marginal and institutionally disadvantaged groups are more inclined to suffer chronic physical disease and mental health problems as a consequence of the ways in which epidemiological knowledge and diagnostic processes are made subject to processes of ideological manipulation and structural constraint.[46] Social suffering is identified as taking place in the bodily expression of illnesses and distress, and a particular focus is brought to the ways in which the force of social stigma, material deprivation, and conditions of political injustice greatly intensify and exacerbate the experience of affliction.[47]

People are held to socially embody conditions of material disadvantage as well as protracted experiences of shame, humiliation, and hopelessness. For example, at the same time that Paul Farmer analyzes the macroeconomic and political forces that obstruct the delivery of effective health care in Haiti, he documents the ways in which, at the local level, people struggle to make sense of their desperation through rituals of blame that often lead to terrible acts of vengeful discrimination perpetrated by the poor among themselves.[48] Similarly, in drawing attention to the connections between conditions of poverty and catastrophic rates of childhood mortality (primarily due to hunger and dehydration) among populations living in the favela of Bom Jesus da Mata in northeastern Brazil, Nancy Scheper-Hughes also explains how the "violence of everyday life" and the "routinization of human suffering" are inclined to make them inured to the horror in which they live.[49] She not only exposes the conditions that make infants vulnerable to starvation and disease but also documents how the local world's ethics of care are liable to be compromised or suspended in an economic and political context of extreme austerity and oppression.[50]

From their experience of working in such contexts, many are inclined to follow Farmer, Scheper-Hughes, and others in advocating a critical anthropology that aims to challenge and unsettle conventional biomedical premises and epistemologies.[51] Biomedicine is accused of being wedded to a reductionist ideology of individualism that, by its reticence to engage with the task of understanding health in social terms, colludes in the maintenance of power relations that cast the poor as primarily responsible for their illness and disease. This hegemony is reflected in, and further consolidated by, the ways in which medical knowledge is symbolically packaged and authorized.[52] Biomedicine operates with a form of knowledge that is materialist and makes universalist claims; by contrast, anthropology promotes a type of historically grounded social understanding that is local, conceptual, processual, and experiential.[53] Accordingly, biomedicine is criticized not only for its failure to acknowledge the reality and power of social forces in people's lives but also for being wedded to an expert discourse that is disposed to make it culturally and socially ham-fisted.

It should be acknowledged, however, that there is now a huge amount of medical research committed to understanding the social etiology of disease and that, arguably, there is a greater commitment than ever before to understanding how health problems are socially distributed and are liable to arise at key junctures through the social life course.[54] In the field of pain research, moreover, an epistemological revolution is taking place in the understanding of sensory and emotional experience.[55] Put simply, insofar as advancements in the neurobiology of pain bring increasing emphasis to the extent to which feelings are modulated by the meanings people give and acquire for their actions and experiences, issues of "culture" and "association" have acquired a new validity as components of the scientific explanation of how pain works. As the neuroscientist Howard L. Fields explains:

> Although a complete understanding of contextual influences on pain is many years in the future, a general model is emerging. The basic idea is that through the process of association environmental stimuli gain the ability to exert powerful influences on perceived pain intensity. The process of association changes the neural representations (meanings) of the relevant contextual stimuli. Consequently, the contextual stimuli gain the power to change the neural representations elicited by actual or anticipated tissue-damaging stimuli. These changes are exerted via a specific pain-modulatory system with links in limbic forebrain, amygdala and brain stem. The circuit projects to, and selectively controls, pain-transmitting spinothalamic tract neurons.... The study of the stimulus-bound components is advanced and is largely the province of neurobiology. The study of the context-determined components is an inherently inter-disciplinary endeavour and is in its infancy.[56]

Nevertheless, it is also the case that considerable debate remains as to the extent to which this scientific quest for a more "mature" understanding of the sociocultural components of pain experience can recognize any value in the type of data provided by ethnographies of social suffering. If "maturity" of understanding is held to be exhibited in the degree of conceptual refinement and analytical precision with which it is made possible to explain the sociosomatic constitution of human feelings and attitudes, then it may not be possible to achieve the type of interdisciplinary exchange that Fields hopes for. Indeed, when attention is brought to problems of social suffering it is often accompanied by an insistence that for us to recognize how people suffer in experience we must resist the temptation to make this subject to any process of scientific translation that distracts us from its human impact and significance in real-life contexts. To this end, it may well be argued that it is impossible to accomplish an easy accommodation between the quest for social-human understanding that takes place through research and writing on social suffering and the type of knowledge sought by those who would make the sociocultural components of pain a matter for mechanical analysis.[57] Nonetheless, as in other fields of medicine and public health, the provocative focus is on how biosocial processes come together in "local biologies" that mediate social effects on the individual body.[58]

The Social Pathologies of Neoliberalism

Anxiety about the ways in which components of human experience may be strained out of scientific accounts of society also features large in attempts to document the cumulative miseries of everyday life that arise in contexts where "neoliberal" economic policies entail the imposition of extreme austerity on conditions of day-to-day life. Here the focus on social suffering is part of an attempt to draw public attention to forms of "ordinary suffering" that tend to be "explained away" as unfortunate and unavoidable "side effects" of capitalist societies, particularly in connection with the experience of people made unemployed or left surviving on low-paid work and living in poor housing.[59] Bourdieu contends that insofar as metric devices are privileged as the means to document adverse social conditions, all too often these hide too much of the human experience of suffering from view.[60]

For Bourdieu, it is vitally important to understand that social suffering concerns experiences that are "difficult to describe and think about." He calls for a "perspectivism" that involves us in the problem of making sense of "the distress caused by clashing interests, orientations and lifestyles."[61] In terms of his research practice, this leads him to work at documenting the multiple adverse conditions under which people are forced to live and, more important, the languages they use in the struggle to make sense of who they are and what they do. Much of the provocation of the essays collected and published as *The Weight of the World* (1999; *La misère du monde* [1993]) lies in the challenge issued to readers to attend to the ways in which individuals account for their suffering *in their own words*. Adopting a methodological strategy reminiscent of Henry Mayhew's earlier attempts to provide a space in which "ordinary" people can make their voices heard in public debates over conditions of society, large sections of the book document what individuals have to say about their lives without "translating" this into "official" sociological discourse. For example, a passage from an interview with an unemployed woman, "Lydia D.," who is struggling to manage impossible levels of financial debt, is simply recorded as follows.

— You say that you're backed into a corner on all sides, money problems, no car, no work . . .

LYDIA D.: On all sides, that's right, everything gets mixed up together. There's no way out. It's really frustrating that there's no way out. There's no solution. There's no way out, I know . . . there are some solutions, I'd like to learn how to drive, but there'd be the problem of how I'd get to work, I'd like to have a license . . .

— If your husband gets a steady job, wouldn't that take care of things?

LYDIA D.: Yes, but since it's at M.-St-M. and he's got terrible hours, he can't, he starts at four in the morning, there isn't any bus for M.-St-M. at four in the morning, its unbelievable, he has to have the car.

— He does what, at four in the morning?

LYDIA D.: He goes from four in the morning to one in the afternoon, then he has a shift from one in the afternoon to nine at night: shifts like that, that's it, it's just unbelievable.

— He makes a good salary?

LYDIA D.: We don't really know, he's just started, he's only been working for a week, we don't really know.

— He wasn't told how much he was going to make?

LYDIA D.: Ordinarily, it's the minimum wage, that's not much, 5,400 francs, its not clear either how we can pay everything I have to pay and all the back payments, I'll never make it, it's just unbelievable!
I'll have to do without this for I don't know how long, it's unbelievable, really unbelievable!

— You probably don't sleep very well at night?

LYDIA D.: I used to have nightmares before, nightmares, all that to . . .

— Like what?

LYDIA D.: Well, I'd dream about the problems I had, I saw myself, anyway, I saw myself living in the street, because when I saw my mother with all those health problems, I said to myself "that's it, that's it as far as I'm concerned, I'm going to end up in the street, I won't have any house, no one will bother with me at all."[62]

Bourdieu urges us to attend to the ways in which, when asked to explain the misery of their lives, individuals stumble over their words and frequently lapse into silence. He underlines the potential for social suffering to elude formal analysis insofar as it inheres in a welter of daily experience that resists categorization in analytically precise terms. He also aims to bring sociological legitimacy to the everyday languages that are used to register the experience of harm and thereby works to make clear their value as a means to reveal some of the textures of social life that constitute people's distress.

This manner of working has been denounced by some as an impoverished form of social science that is inclined to make overblown claims for its value as a document of social life. For example, Angela McRobbie argues that Bourdieu and his colleagues are "compromised by their own methodologies of intimacy and empathy" on the grounds that these serve to crowd out their text with a "proliferation of voices" to a point where problems of sociological interpretation are treated as a sideline issue.[63] Beyond this, she contends that a great deal of their material is "sociologically banal"or "mere reportage of degrees of misfortune" and that the emotive tone in which it is cast serves more to encourage a response of apathy than one of outrage. McRobbie accuses Bourdieu of both exploiting his respondents for their grief and investing too much hope in the possibility of using his interviews as a means to generate the social resources and political resolve to change people's lives for the better.

It may well be the case that books such as *The Weight of the World* fall short of delivering the kind of "social pedagogy" that Bourdieu hoped for; however, opponents such as McRobbie duck the challenge that is hereby issued to academic sociology, that is, to reflect on the ways in which its privileged methods of knowledge production are ill-suited to reveal how large numbers of people are made to experience their lives. McRobbie seems to be entirely unconcerned to tackle this matter. In her rush to denounce Bourdieu for being caught up in a project of sociological bad faith, she fails to acknowledge that in his concluding essay, "Understanding," Bourdieu himself makes clear that he has deliberately courted such accusations by taking "the risk of writing."[64] He aims to raise the issue of how the "sociological point of view" is made possible and, further, of what kind of social understanding and apprehension of truth is thereby brought within our reach.[65] The possibility that a great deal of sociology operates from a position of bad faith is precisely the issue that Bourdieu would raise for debate. He intended to provoke his readers into questioning how a substantial part of social life, particularly in terms of the ways it is enacted and experienced by individuals trapped in poverty, is blocked from view by the formality of sociological theories and methods.

The Fate of Developing Societies

For many scholars, the extent to which the practice of Western social science contributes to a cultural myopia that seriously distorts how practitioners account for their object of study is most dramatically exposed when considering the fate of populations living in poor societies. The history of Western social science has been overwhelmingly preoccupied with the lives of the 15 percent of the world's population born into the most industrially advanced sectors of the globe. Far more often, it has only ventured to present us with a minority report on conditions of modernity.

This extraordinary bias of privilege and perspective has scarcely entered into the consciousness of social theory, which, for the most part, still prioritizes the cultural perspectives and political concerns of white men reflecting the experience of the Western metropolitan liberal bourgeoisie.[66] It is only in the specialist "subfield" of "development studies" that most students of sociology learn what most anthropologists know: namely, that half the world's population live on less than $2.50 a day and 1.4 billion people live on less than $1.25 a day.[67] The fact that around one billion people are malnourished (including one-third of all children born in developing societies) and that around 22,000 children age five and under die each day from diseases of poverty is unlikely to be included among the key issues profiled by sociological textbooks as a means to unveil the moral character of modern societies.[68] It is a bedrock reality that leads medical anthropologists to bemoan the "immodest claims of cultural causality" in cultural studies.[69] When taking stock of "the way we live now," most Western commentators appear to be largely untroubled by the task of understanding how this may be related to the experience of the 1.5 billion people living in societies afflicted by repeated cycles of extreme political and criminal violence.[70] Here the dominant image of society does not include the 1.6 billion who live without electricity, the 1.1 billion without access to clean drinking water, and the 2.6 billion who do not have adequate sanitation facilities.[71] It is shocking to note the absence of widespread recognition in sociology of the fact that 95 percent of current global population growth takes place in developing societies where more than one billion people live in mass slum districts, in megacities such as Manila, Cairo, São Paolo, Mumbai, Karachi, Jakarta, Caracas, Lagos, and Mexico City.[72] Yet these are the settings in which the majority experience of modernity now takes place.

In this context, research and writing on social suffering not only involves an attempt to radically realign the poles of global understanding, but also a critical questioning of the cultural means by which social experience is represented for public and policy debate. Critical attention is brought to the ways in which official scales of material deprivation and allied metrics of human suffering such as Disability Adjusted Life Years (DALYs), while serving to make social conditions "measurable" and thereby available as an "objective" problem for government, also hide a great deal of social life from view.[73] For example, Maia Green contends that it is not only the case that such technologies of representation, while offering a summary account of global problems, pay no heed to the great varieties of human experience in context, but, more worryingly, they also serve to draw a veil of ignorance over unequal power relations. As far as statistical indicators of global poverty are concerned, she argues that, more often than not, these portray material deprivation as a problem arising "from nowhere" that must simply be "attacked." No invitation is issued to inquire into the social processes of wealth creation and distribution that are implicated in the production and maintenance of gross inequalities.[74]

On this account, the prime value of research and writing on social suffering is its potential to document the cultural categories through which ordinary people struggle to make sense of the world in which they find themselves and, further, to provide them with privileged status in the work of social understanding. More directly, it holds the capacity to expose the ways in which human suffering results at "the conjuncture of specific social and political relations."[75] Urgent public issues are documented and addressed primarily in terms of their "salience for persons."[76] In this context, poverty and ill health are portrayed not so much as attributes of people but rather as the outcome of active social relations, institutional practices, and political economic environments.[77]

For example, in his documentation of the "abject abandonment" of the mentally ill in the poorest sections of Brazilian society, João Biehl details the circumstances and experiences of a single "patient" (Catarina) at an asylum in Porto Alegre. He also aims to expose the dense fabrics of social life that bind people into a system where they are cast as superfluous and beyond the reach of care.[78] Each chapter dwells on the details of significant experiences and events in Catarina's life and also ventures to trace the connections between the harm that is done to her person and the overarching processes of "structural violence" in the Brazilian health care system. Biehl aims to provide us with a strong encounter with a whole person in her immediate circumstances, intimate relationships, life decisions, and personal feelings. In this respect, there is a deliberate courting of our social sympathies; but we are also encouraged to explore how people like Catarina are systematically and routinely produced by societies that are economically and politically organized to treat large segments of the population as if they were human waste.

Similarly, by documenting the expression of emotions such as "rage, sorrow, fright, pining, desire for goods, jealousy and envy" among the poor of Punata, a valley town near the city of Cochabamba in Bolivia, Maria Tapias aims to expose the ways in which social conflicts, material hardship, and "failed sociality" are embodied by mothers, and how this in turn contributes to their ill health as well as that of their children.[79] By tracing the connection between the distress of high emotions and illnesses experienced by breastfeeding infants, she works to explain how economic conditions both infuse women's bodies and cause damage to the mother-infant relationship. Tapias exposes the embodiment of political economic structures that give rise to social suffering both within people and in their most intimate associations with and commitments to others.

Here we are encouraged to move beyond a mere noting of the overall scale and distribution of social problems so as to engage with apprehending how these take place in human experience. We are challenged to involve ourselves in the task of understanding both how social life matters to people and how it is embodied and made a moral reality. Of course, this is also accompanied by the danger that such up close and personal documents of life are left performing no more than an "ornamental function" in the wider reporting of social adversity.[80] It may even be the case that they serve to enact a mere play on feeling more than to inspire concerted actions on behalf of the pursuit of social justice. At the same time, however, there is also the possibility that, as noted above, they work to provoke critical debate over the moral adequacy of the forms and levels of social understanding that are available to us, as well as the space this occupies within the public sphere.[81] For example, with respect to the enormous interest today in health care system reform, this type of critical social inquiry forces us to stop and attend to the way "cost-effectiveness" and "cost benefit" are misused to assess policies and programs without examining what these evaluative strategies leave out by failing to include social suffering either among the programs or the outcomes.

A "Mediatized" Politics of Pity

Research and writing on social suffering tends to bring debate to the roles played by the "politics of pity" in the public realm. In this respect, it is part of a new chapter of inquiry into disputes that began with the first awakenings of "social" consciousness in the eighteenth century. Indeed, at the point where questions are directed to the moral adequacy of the social response to the suffering of distant strangers, commentators return to the original concerns of writers such as Francis Hutcheson, David Hume, and Adam Smith, when they first ventured to understand how human sociability was sustained by moral sentiment. Likewise, when worries are raised over the potential for human suffering to be culturally appropriated in the pursuit of commercial gain or ideological advantage, critics recover moral controversies aroused in response to both the popularization of sentimental literature and the humanitarian campaign culture of the eighteenth and nineteenth centuries

Some of the more recent attempts to understand the moral and political implications of being culturally positioned as a remote witness to distant suffering aim to remind us of this history. Indeed, arguably, in his attempt to delineate the ethical position occupied by spectators of human suffering on television news, Luc Boltanski goes no further than to underline the political frailties of moral sympathy as outlined by Adam Smith as well as the critical suspicions that Hannah Arendt directed to "the passion of compassion."[82] On this account, the seeming impossibility of never being freed from the possibility of questioning the authenticity of the symbolic portrayal of human suffering, coupled with the fact that individuals in their living rooms are never in a position to provide an adequate moral response to the scale of the horror brought to them on their TV screens, most likely serves to create a "crisis of pity." On Boltanski's account, we have now arrived at the point where humanitarian organizations are set to be identified as cynical manipulators of public feeling, while those assailed by images of extreme suffering for their charity are bound to feel an unprecedented sense of political and moral impotence. Indeed, in this context, it is argued that rather than serve to advance an education of compassion, the proliferation of media images of suffering and humanitarian campaign work that seeks to visually shock people into a concern for others serves to create ever more robust cultures of denial.[83]

In a more positive vein, others point to the growth and spread of international nongovernmental humanitarian organizations as evidence for the development of new social arrangements for the institutional channeling of public sentiments of compassion toward a more responsive and productive engagement with human problems on a grand scale.[84] Indeed, it is claimed that we may now be witness to the institutional realization of a "cosmopolitan political community," where for the most of the past two hundred years it has only been possible to refer to this as a utopian ideal.[85] For example, Kate Nash observes that the possibilities afforded by new interactive communication media such as the Internet and mobile phones for a two-way engagement between humanitarian campaign organisations and publics are creating a "cultural politics" in which larger numbers of people than ever before in human history are actively involved in expressing their solidarity with suffering strangers.[86] Accordingly, it is suggested that when it comes to piecing together a clearer understanding of the part played by communication media in the constitution of society, we should recognize that in many instances we are witness to the transformation of cultural forms and social possibilities on an unprecedented scale and at a great pace. In this context, while remaining mindful of many critical and political concerns raised in connection with the moral force and social consequences of media portrayals of human suffering, we are also advised to acknowledge the latent potential for these to be appropriated within the cultural production of political arrangements and social commitments that were scarcely imaginable before the twenty-first century.

When brought to these levels of debate, the symbolic portrayal of social suffering in the public realm is held to comprise cultural forces that are radically transforming the bounds of collective subjectivity.[87] It is argued that we are now witnessing the development of "mediatized" processes of social interaction that are creating unprecedented possibilities for alternative ways of living in and feeling about the world.[88] A critical focus is brought to the immediate ways in which people are set to encounter moments of moral crisis and disturbing states of exception that hold the potential to provoke an enlarged understanding of social possibility and human interconnectedness.[89] Researchers are challenged to engage with the task of understanding the immanent presence and force of new mediatized forms of experience in which individuals are made painfully alert to the human costs and consequences of their social organization as well as to the moral bonds of sociality that bind them to others. Beyond this, moreover, it is in tracing the rise of organizations that make possible the institutional mediation of moral sympathy and outrage toward concerted actions to combat the causes and consequences of human suffering that we may witness the crafting of solidarities to initiate wider practices of social care.

What is also happening is example after example of demonstration projects and occasionally generalized programs that mobilize communities to deal more effectively with some of the major scourges of our era. Nowhere is this more true than in global health, where before and after pictures of patients effectively treated for AIDS, MDR-TB, diabetes, cervical cancer, major depressive disorder, and psychosis show that we cannot focus solely on witnessing and understanding social suffering but must also come to terms with outcomes that demonstrate that informed interventions really matter. Hence the treatment of AIDS has not only turned an acutely lethal disease into a chronic condition but has also, in many places, lessened stigma, saved whole families, and transformed hopelessness into resilience and aspiration. Social interventions are what overcome bottlenecks to implementation of affordable and accessible services, showing that social analysis does not stop with diagnosis and acts of description and interpretation but is central to programs and policies that can make a huge difference in people's lives. The upshot is that such analysis has to query not just access and triage but also the quality of services and the unintended consequences of otherwise effective social interventions. Here through the vantage of social suffering we see disclosed an abiding bias of sociological and anthropological studies, which seem more comfortable identifying problems and witnessing failures of intervention than documenting successes and understanding the sources of such accomplishment. In his long-term ethnographic study of an impoverished, war-affected, and changing area of Sierra Leone, Michael Jackson describes what he calls "life within limits."[90] Within these very narrow and constraining limits, Jackson observes various kinds of achievement and interprets lives that matter even because of those structures. Perhaps what he sees is another kind of limit—the limit of social suffering as a means of interpreting the varieties of moral experience. Perhaps he also identifies a process of constructive interpretation that goes beyond critique to acknowledge and affirm humans enduring in a way that contributes to love and beauty in lives lived at the margin.

CONCLUDING REMARKS

It may be argued that *The Sociological Imagination* has always foundered on its promise and whatever Mills achieved by way of critical posture has been undermined by his failure to devise a viable model of research practice or method of applied sociology. A more charitable view holds that he was alert to this criticism and when writing his text had only just embarked on a new project to redefine the goals of social science. At this point, while convinced that the ability to critically analyze ourselves in social terms should be cultivated as "a common denominator of our general cultural life," he had yet to arrive on a settled point of view on how to carry this out in practice. He died before he was able to complete and see the publication of his major work, *The Cultural Apparatus*, but in this light we might take *The Sociological Imagination* as representing just the first steps along a road whereby he aimed to bring renewed debate to the issue of how "the humanization of man in society" might still be realized and taken up as a matter for action.[91] Commentators observe that it is certainly the case that

Mills was striving to set in place a "politics of culture" that might work to shape reason and "modes of sensibility" so that people would be positioned to relate to their experience of the world with a new set of political coordinates and value orientations.[92] To this end, he was committed to clearing a space for social researchers to question how their roles, personalities, and activities might acquire more progressive value and purpose.[93]

Mills sought to bring critical debate to the morality, politics, practicability, and lived relevance of social inquiry, and on this understanding, he may well have welcomed the methodological frustrations left in the wake of his writing *The Sociological Imagination;* for indeed, more often than not, these are voiced through a yearning to make his sociological "promise" more highly valued and practically relevant to lived experience. In this chapter we have also suggested that there is a considerable affinity between the unfulfilled ambition of his work and that featured in much research and writing on social suffering. Shared anxieties are expressed over the perceived failure of social science to make known the human experience of social life. There is also a shared view that insofar as social research is purely academic and is undertaken as a bystander exercise, it is of questionable value in human terms; rather, it must also be engaged to actions to advance care for people and to make better ways of living in the world.

It must be asked whether it is possible to fashion and sustain such an approach to social investigation from a base within the academy. Certainly, Bourdieu's concern for us to reflect critically upon the moral and political values enacted through our methods of research and writing incorporates not only issues of academic style but also of social environment and institutional affiliation. In questioning how our methods of investigation and terms of cultural representation are suited to make known human-social conditions, we must also be working to understand how our practices of knowledge production are disciplined to the rule of "professional values" and market economies within the modern university. Indeed, when further reviewing Jane Addams's dedication to caregiving as a core component of the quest for social understanding, we shall see that she held that if brought under the direction of the academy, her manner of doing sociology would be excessively compromised and curtailed. For Addams it appeared that the advancement of social research as a humanitarian and progressive concern had little room to flourish once made to comply with the demands of a university career and/or when caught up in a battle for academic recognition (see chapter 6).

Under these circumstances, it may well be the case that, in addition to any movement to criticize social structures and conditions that deliver harm to people, those involved in researching and writing on social suffering must protest against the conditions under which they are made to conduct their work. Of course, here it is also important to pay heed to differences between academic cultures and how these operate. Indeed, a more pronounced culture of critique is often on display in the more sociologically dedicated and theoretical writing on social suffering, and this may be due not only to the critical traditions carried through this field but also to the institutional positioning of academic sociology and the limits placed (either consciously or otherwise) on its role in social understanding. We contend, however, that this must not end at the point of critique, and in this regard, perhaps more than in other formations of social science, there is a risk that sociology is left mired in a pitch of protest. By contrast, we recognise there is more space to advance and develop the approach we advocate within anthropology; and particularly where this has been taken up and fashioned as part of initiatives to set care in action.

There is a fundamental difference between interviews with selected informants in settings in which the social scientist is relatively unfamiliar and the anthropological ethnography of local worlds in which the anthropologist has lived for years, knows the key informants intimately, and has had the everyday experience of observing daily life and participating in mundane practices. Such are the worlds of street people and drug addicts in New York and San Francisco described by Philippe Bourgois, and the drug clinic and drugged families in the old Hispanic community in New Mexico of which Angela Garcia is both ethnographer and family member.[94] The description of a local world broken by the toxic effects of neoliberal policies and programs is more than an anecdote or vignette, but neither is it a statistically "controlled" study of causality. Rather, this kind of study carries ethnographic authority as an illustration of what large-scale social processes do when they come down into local worlds of experience at the collective and individual level as dangers that beat down lives, destroy relationships, animate practices that often intensify injury, and bend subjectivity. The picture that emerges, based in layers of observation and interpretation, illustrates social suffering in narratives, actions, events, interpersonal processes, and subjective feelings. Here the moral, the emotional, and the bodily enactments of experience become visible within a charged field of social entanglements. Connecting their tendrils from bodies through projected feelings to larger unintentional arrangements resocializes personal misfortune and injury. Multiple pictures by different field-workers in the same and other settings provide a kind of scholarly triangulation that supplies authenticity and generalizability to illustration and that is added to by other ways of social knowing, from numbers to biomarkers, to offer if not statistical then epistemological validity. Hence the study of social suffering has contributed to a kind of knowledge generation, which, while more akin to interpretive wisdom about the art of being, is also amenable to use with biosocial and other quantitative forms of inference. The outcome, at its best, offers the potential for a humanly richer and more sophisticated understanding to direct practical policies and programs. And there is accumulating evidence that this can matter for the treatment of disorders in poor communities facing daunting health care challenges of multi-drug-resistant TB, AIDS, and mental illnesses.[95] In this sense, medical anthropological studies of health-related forms of social suffering suggest that this omnibus term is useful not just to think about society but also, at times, to ameliorate its effects on individuals and networks and even, albeit unusually, to change society itself.

Too much that presents itself as "social inquiry" is simply more comfortable with critique than it is with engagement in interventions to enact positive change in our world. The health domain contains numerous examples of where programs succeed, where healing occurs, where life is improved. We contend that the ongoing challenge for sociology and anthropology is to document and interpret when social suffering is ameliorated. This is just as central as witnessing suffering and the failure to alleviate it. By standing aside from men's and women's resilience and their victories, as limited and limiting as they often are, social science itself contributes to social suffering by undermining hope and by reifying bad outcomes. Yet improved health and social circumstance is one of the great stories of our times, as is the building of a middle class in Asia, with greater prosperity, life chances, and satisfaction, and improvements in health and welfare among many in poor societies, in spite of overwhelming negative odds and the fact that many others remain mired in social suffering. The reality of amelioration and prevention also requires social analysis. What impact does good outcome have on society? What possibilities are enlarged by even modest and mixed success? What problems follow on programs that succeed in doing good at individual and collective levels? Large numbers of sociologists and anthropologists may have turned away from these issues. Yet the study of social suffering brings them to the fore as much as it does the inadequacy of measures of cost and benefit and the failure of interventions and the persistence of danger and trauma. We are in a new age of social studies when these issues, unimaginable to an earlier cohort of researchers, are central to what social suffering means for social science. What is more, a new generation of students is demanding that such social studies involve real engagement with the improvement of social life.

4 Learning from Weber

Marianne Weber records that when asked about what his scholarship meant to him, Max Weber replied, "I want to see how much I can stand." She comments that "he regarded it as his task to endure the *antinomies* of existence and, further, to exert to the utmost his freedom from illusions and yet keep his ideals inviolate and preserve his ability to devote himself to them."[1] In working to understand what is at stake here, it is important to recognize that Weber's academic work is informed by his own experience of suffering. The "antinomies of existence" that Marianne Weber refers to should not be thought of as mere intellectual puzzles or scholarly foibles; rather, they relate to problems experienced by Weber at great personal cost. They are rooted in severe physical and mental illness, deep-seated emotional turmoil, protracted career frustrations, thwarted political ambitions, and the calamity of world war. In his personal as well as public life, Weber's experience was one of great "disappointment and failure";[2] and this leaves its marks all over his sociology and social theory.

Weber is particularly alert to the fact that social life is an enactment of substantive human values, and in his sociology he is concerned to emphasize the extent to which, through the constitution of ourselves as social beings, we are set to court many vexed problems of moral meaning. He understands us to be subject to social conditions in which we are set to experience many conflicts and tensions over the values we live by. Weber depicts the cultural experience of modernity as liable to immerse us in a struggle to craft a space that is adequate for the affirmation of our humanity and the practical pursuit of our amelioration. Along with Karl Marx, he shares in the understanding that "men make their own history but . . . they do not make it under circumstances chosen by themselves" and that "the tradition of all the dead generations weighs like a nightmare on the brain of the living."[3] Indeed, insofar as the larger part of his sociological endeavor is committed to explaining the human consequences of modern processes of rationalization, it may be read as amounting to an extended reflection upon Marx's dictum, albeit with a quite different apprehension of the kind of resolve that is required to meet the demands of our day.

In Weber's account of the sociocultural constitution of the problem of suffering we are presented with a series of analytical difficulties that bring considerable volume to these issues. This is an area of his theoretical endeavor where he aims to attend most carefully to how our experience of the antinomies of existence has a propensity to reach a pitch and scale that holds decisive consequences for our social being and development, particularly insofar as these are made subject to ever intensifying processes of rationalization. By working to understand Weber on these matters, students of his work are well placed to grasp his conception of the "calling" (*beruf*) of social science and how this can be taken as a guide to self-understanding and social action.

In this chapter we aim to draw out some lessons from Weber's work for those engaged with the critical praxis of research and writing on social suffering. We believe that Weber's sociological conception of the problem of suffering is of great value for advancing our understanding of how this is constituted as a crisis of moral meaning. We contend that he still has much to teach us about the ways in which the pains and anxieties borne through this experience are set to command people's feelings, thoughts, and actions. In this context, one of Weber's major achievements lies in bringing a measure of sociological understanding to bear on the ways in which people's encounters with problems of suffering are liable to inform the wider dynamics of social and cultural change. More precisely, we understand him to have exposed how a vital part of the impetus behind the development and relentless expansion of modern processes of rationalization resides in the extent to which these are all at once both a cause and a result of social suffering.

We also claim that there is much to learn from Weber when it comes to assessing the ways in which the practice of social research might be crafted as a means to attend to and care for people experiencing suffering. In particular, we contend that his theory is useful for piecing together an understanding of both how and why we are inevitably set to reach limits in the attempt to address such experience within a rational frame of reference or as a problem that is amenable to rational solutions. By highlighting, moreover, the propensity for rationalizing movements to entail consequences that were never intended at their point of initiation, and which might ultimately work in opposition to their original purpose, we suggest that Weber is alert to the fact that the rationalizations of sociology are also subject to this fate. It is not only the case that he understood the problem of suffering to be constituted by social and cultural forces that are set to exceed the bounds of rationalization, but that he also understood the attempt to render it rationally apprehensible—even in terms of sociology—as holding the potential to create new possibilities for suffering. We understand his openly declaring that he pursued his scholarship with an interest to discover how much he could stand as an awareness of how the acquisition of sociological knowledge might amount to a personal undoing, for it often invites not only a painful exposure to the limits of human understanding but also a disconcerting acquaintance with the value contradictions that we enact and inhabit. Moreover, it may well do more to overwhelm us with an appreciation for the intractability of the problems involved in the pursuit of progressive social change than to equip us with the moral wisdom to know how to live and what to do so as to fashion a better, if still not the best, world for ourselves.

In declaring that his commitment to sociology is fueled by a passion to see how much he could stand, Weber very much understood that the practice of social research itself can exact a heavy toll on one's sense of integrity and personhood. It is, moreover, possible to document his acute awareness of this fact in his famous essays on the vocations of science and politics.[4] These are replete with many personal reflections on the existential burdens imposed by his sociological understanding. They also bear testimony to the moral courage and sense of political responsibility that directed his work. Here we are presented with some startling examples of how, while struggling to think without illusions so as to face up to the fate of his times, Weber did not relinquish his concern for human possibility; and we take this as an invaluable guide for those who would marry their passion for humanitarian social reform with critical perspective: a tension we highlighted in the preceding chapter and which is further explored in those that follow from here.

The first section of this chapter is designed to introduce some of the core concerns featured in Weber's conception of the problem of suffering. We also provide a preliminary account of the unresolved and inherently frustrated problems of analysis that are taken up in his attempt to explain possible social responses to this experience. The second section explores how these issues are addressed in Friedrich Tenbruck's celebrated reconstruction of Weber's philosophical anthropology;[5] and in this way, we aim to involve readers in a greater appreciation for the role this plays in Weber's account of the motive force of processes of rationalization. The third section offers a further clarification of the sociological ambition and value of Weber's project by exploring how his theory might be applied to the attempt to explain transformations in the cultural response to outbreaks of epidemic disease. From here, the fourth section outlines the critical debates that are initiated from Weber's depiction of the cultural dynamics of the problem of suffering, particularly in their application to the attempt to understand his declaration on "the fate of our times." In conclusion, we outline the agenda for research that is initiated from this point, and we commend Weber for the resolve with which he sought to make his sociological insights a guide to the practice of social reform. He comes as close to a hero of social theory and practice as we can discern, suggesting that what is at stake for us in this book is more than the analysis of a social theme and the elaboration of a method but rather a way of being in the world to which we can commit ourselves with passion and resolve. Weber teaches us how people endure.

THE PROBLEM OF SUFFERING IN WEBERIAN SOCIOLOGY

In the preceding chapters we offered some insights into the cultural character and genealogy of the modern problem of suffering and, in particular, how this may be encountered in forms of moral experience that open the door to social understanding. We ventured to explain the difficulty of making adequate sense of human suffering as being comprised by a considerable range of cultural conditions, ideological commitments, and social processes. When documenting the origins of social suffering as a cultural term of reference, we attended to some of the ways in which a collective loss of faith in the workings of divine providence contributed to the development of a shared understanding of the experience of suffering as issuing a moral demand for social justice and humanitarian reform (see chapter 1). When it comes to piecing together a historical understanding of how a theological crisis of legitimacy has been transposed into a questioning of the social bounds of moral responsibility, there is still much to question and debate. In addition to any inquiry into the cultural conditions and forms of experience under which providential theologies are made to appear incredible, these matters are greatly complicated by the fact that, from at least the middle of the eighteenth century on, it seems that large numbers of people have been caught up in social processes that have radically transformed their emotional orientation to themselves and others. In this regard, the problem of suffering is not only a matter aggravated by cultural conditions of rational debate; it is also a peculiar form of moral-emotional experience. It is rooted in the social acquisition, cultural shaping, and aesthetic cultivation of moral feelings for which people lack adequate terms of understanding and explanation. Indeed, part of the torment of suffering appears to take place in the frustrations borne under the struggle to fashion symbolic forms of culture that are adequate to convey the moral meanings of the pain met in experience and further, and perhaps especially, when we are beset with the task of making sense of the experience of witnessing and engaging the suffering of others.

Friedrich Nietzsche famously observed that "what really arouses indignation against suffering is not suffering as such but the senselessness of suffering."[6] Perhaps more than any other outstanding figure in modern Western philosophy, he was inclined to treat the moral and existential difficulties experienced under the task of making sense of suffering as a gateway to understanding what makes us ("all too") human. Nietzsche is particularly alert to the ways in which, under conditions of modernity, the apparent senselessness of suffering becomes a pressing matter of moral and popular concern and to the fact that a shared sense of revulsion in the face of the spectacle of excessive suffering is the wellspring for movements of humanitarian social reform.

No doubt a considerable conflict of interpretations will continue to rage over the task of understanding Nietzsche and his philosophy, but it is generally understood that on his terms the radical appearance of suffering as "senseless" holds the potential to draw us toward the abyss of nihilism.[7] He was not inclined to celebrate the rise of modern humanitarianism, for he held that more often than not this is fueled by a ressentiment that is rooted in a "slave morality" that obstructs a proper understanding of the human condition and the limits to which it is set.[8] He also contends that clearing a social space for the exercise of compassion in human affairs ultimately serves to erode our capacity to face up to life with an ethic of self-responsibility and resilience.

Nietzsche understood the experience of modernity as comprised by cultural conditions in which we are made vulnerable to experience a radical loss of selfhood, moral purpose, and social meaning, especially on occasions when we are caught up in the difficulty of making sense of human suffering. He urged us, however, to greet this as holding the potential to enable a better understanding of our human condition as such. Nietzsche advised that there is no morally sufficient meaning for human suffering and that we are always set to fail in the attempt to enact an adequate response to what suffering does to people. On his account, wisdom lies in recognizing that, whatever progress is now made toward the reduction of painful adversity and affliction, we are all destined to perish. Human beings are always bound to suffer; suffering is an inevitable and necessary part of being human. His advocacy of "the will to power" incorporates an urgent call to face up to this as the truth about our existential moral situation. When brought under the guidance of Nietzsche's philosophy we are led to a point where we are asked to practice a "self-mastery and heroic "self-overcoming" that requires that we acknowledge and endure the senselessness of suffering as our lot and even celebrate this as a necessary part of the affirmation of our humanity.[9]

In his comparative studies of religious cultures, Weber sought to cast the apprehension of human suffering articulated in Nietzsche's genealogy of morals in a sociological frame that makes clear its cultural contingencies, psychic consequences, and bearing upon the dynamics of social change.[10] The collected essays published as *The Sociology of Religion* (1966),[11] along with "Religious Rejections of the World and Their Directions"[12] and "The Social Psychology of the World Religions,"[13] are identified as some of the most important works in which Weber addresses the cultural origins and ramifications of the conviction that there is much in suffering that remains "senseless." Aside from piecing together a sociological explanation for modern nihilism, Weber is concerned to expose the cultural circumstances under which this is encountered as a source of cognitive and emotional distress.[14] He aims to attend to the cultural dispositions, moral orientations, and social character of people who, while living out large portions of their lives in wholly secular terms, experience existential dilemmas in which it is made possible for them to apprehend "the death of God." In this regard, the later addition to the Protestant Ethic thesis where he refers to a cultural development that produces "specialists without spirit" and "sensualists without heart" is one of the passages where Weber is understood to echo Nietzsche's fears about "the Last Man,"[15] that is, a type of person who deals with the antinomies of existence by channeling his energies to the pursuit of a comfortable life of dull conformity to routine, mediocrity, and mild distraction.[16] Either through bad faith or moral cowardice, "the Last Man" does not broker with questions of ultimate purpose and the pursuit of human dignity, for he will not risk his comfort for an encounter with unpalatable truths or entrenched moral difficulties.[17]

At the same time, it is important to understand that at no point does Weber declare himself to be intent on devising a sociological elaboration of Nietzsche's philosophy. While sharing in a concern to interrogate the cultural conditions that make possible modern rationality and sympathizing with the view that considerable numbers of academics, politicians, and public officials lack the moral integrity and intellectual courage to face up to many disagreeable truths about modern life, at no point does Weber fully embrace Nietzsche's premises or conclusions. For example, he holds that religious impulses and beliefs are highly complex cultural and psychological phenomena that have an incisive bearing upon practices of day-to-day life and should not be explained away as mere expressions of ressentiment. Moreover, while concerned to document the negative consequences of modern rationality, Weber is also alert to the extent to which this serves to create new opportunities for self-awareness, the apprehension of individual responsibility, and expressions of personal autonomy[18]. There is no doubt that he recognizes Nietzsche's philosophy as holding vital importance for the acquisition of a critical consciousness of cultural conditions of modernity. Indeed, at one point he goes so far as to declare that "the honesty of a contemporary scholar" can be assessed in relation to his judgment on Nietzsche's work.[19] It is rarely the case, however, that Weber allows Nietzsche to have the final word on the important questions he ventures to raise.

Robert Antonio contends that "Weber was no Nietzschean, but he selectively deployed Nietzsche's ideas to challenge modern theorists to recognize the limits of rationality and to rethink their practices accordingly."[20] It is not possible to provide a definitive statement on the purpose of Weber's sociology and its conclusions. Too much is left incomplete and open to interpretation. It is also the case, moreover, that he often appears to be writing more with the aim of opening up questions for debate than for the purpose of articulating a fully resolved point of view. Indeed, we celebrate him for his ability to pioneer channels of inquiry that inspire us to question the conditions of our existence and apply ourselves to the struggle to tell the truth about who we are and what we could be and, further, for the ways in which his scholarship offers serious reflection on moral questions relating to how we should live, what we should do, and what we can hope for.

This spirit of inquiry and critical concern for human possibility is particularly in evidence in his analysis of the problem of suffering. Here Weber holds that there are occasions when the struggle to make sense of experiences of suffering, and to provide moral redress to the harms that are hereby done to people, amounts to a major force of cultural innovation and social change, one that may be decisive for the overall formation of our social character and moral orientations. In this regard, he would have us recognize cultural responses to the problem of suffering as elements comprising the dynamics and directing the course of rationalization. At the same time, however, there is much that remains incomplete and unresolved in his conception and analysis of how this is liable to take place and the consequences it holds.

Weber works under the conviction that the potential for the experience of suffering to be met as something "senseless" grows with the advance and force of modern processes of rationalization. This is grasped by Talcott Parsons when he moves to underline the extent to which Weber believed that with the accomplishment of a more coherent and comprehensive rationalization of reality, the experience of suffering is ever more likely to entail a violent assault on moral meaning and social purpose. Parsons notes, "Weber takes the fundamental position that, *regardless of the particular content of the normative order,* a major element of discrepancy is inevitable. And the more highly rationalized an order, the greater the tension, the greater the exposure of major elements of a population to experiences which are frustrating in the very specific sense, not merely that things happen that contravene their 'interests', but that things happen which are 'meaningless' in the sense that they ought not to happen. Here above all lie the problems of suffering and evil."[21] As modern people, Weber understands us to be made subject to cultural and social conditions in which a great deal of suffering is made to appear senseless and for no purpose. This is the inevitable corollary to our rational mind-set and experience of living in social conditions that are monitored, regulated, and controlled by processes of rationalization. It is not only the case that on occasion we are likely to have painful and distressing experiences that seem "irrational," in that they are unanticipated and unaccounted for at the level of rational expectation and don't add up to anything in rational terms; it is also the case that the more accustomed we are to living in rational systems of association, production, and exchange, the more likely it is that we shall be morally unsettled and emotionally disturbed by events and experiences that painfully expose us to "the irrationality of the world."

On this basis, it might be argued that Weber anticipates the development of social circumstances in which, as we grow accustomed to traveling safely from one place to another in modern trains and airplanes—both being instances of the application of rational techniques and procedures to the orderly control of nature and society—it is more likely that we shall be shocked, distressed, and appalled by occasions when large-scale injury and death occurs as a result of a rail or air "disaster."[22] Here the normative expectations that are acquired, confirmed, and routinized through conditions of everyday life are being made subject to processes of rational efficiency and control but are also the potential source of much suffering. When shattered by the unanticipated failure and breakdown of rational systems, it is in the pain of crushed expectations and the accompanying distress of being made to forge an adequate response to the moral calamity of systemic failure and breakdown that we stand to suffer, perhaps even to the extreme.

There is now, moreover, a considerable amount of sociological, anthropological, and medical literature that documents the human suffering that takes place as an unintended consequence of the ways in which it has become possible to apply modern rationality to the management and regulation of our bodily health. It is widely recognized that at the end of protracted experiences of subjecting ourselves to rational-technical procedures of medical intervention and care, the shock of learning that nothing more can be done to medicate a disease, improve life quality, or prevent death is a major source of emotional distress that can hold devastating consequences for our sense of personhood and capacity to relate to others.[23] Again, in light of such examples, it seems that in his conception of the problem of suffering, Weber apprehends the terrible paradox that many technical and social interventions that are rationally designed to protect and improve the condition of our lives may also give rise to normative expectations that create new possibilities for human suffering and, indeed, for this to take place in unprecedented forms that arouse acute levels of distress.

Weber seems, however, to be far more cautious and uncertain about advancing a firm understanding of how we are set to respond to the occasion of suffering; or at least, when tracing out possible types of cultural reaction and social response to the torment of this experience, he does not provide a definitive statement on their overall consequences or venture to sum up their cumulative effects. He is alert to a range of possibilities, but it is in assessing the sociological importance, psychological consequences, and cultural significance of two predominant forms of response to suffering that he runs into difficulty.

On the one hand, it seems that Weber understands the problem of suffering to often serve as a force that drives us to further rationalize our experience and actions. He would not be surprised to note that when responding to public transportation disasters modern governments now initiate expert inquiries that are designed to gather a more intricate and precise account of "what went wrong" so as to apply such knowledge to the enhancement of rational systems of regulation and control. In this regard, one might speculate that the rapid growth of risk assessment and risk management industries would be precisely what he would expect to take place as part of the modern response to problems of suffering in the world.[24] At one level, Weber's analysis incorporates the understanding that when made subject to modern processes of rationalization we are culturally disposed to respond to human suffering via the pursuit of ever more refined measures of understanding to inform practices designed to "tame" the enduring hazards of uncertainty and chance.[25]

At another level of analysis, he also recognizes that there is a potential for experiences of human suffering to serve as the inspiration for new styles of thinking and action, even to the point where people engage in revolutionary reappraisals of hitherto taken-for-granted understandings of, and practices within, the world.[26] Weber identifies a potential for the response to human suffering to excite "charismatic needs" and for these to incorporate a deep-felt desire for an extraordinary means to overcome situations of adversity and affliction.[27] In their "charismatic praxis" people may well be so emotionally charged that they are driven to radically revise received convention, both at the level of cultural outlook and in their social behavior.[28] Indeed, this may be heavily implicated in the experience and creation of social circumstances that deliver possibilities for momentous social and historical change.[29]

At this point, Weber can be identified as sharing in Theodor Adorno's understanding of the potential for the experience of suffering to inspire critical speculative thinking,[30] but also going further than Adorno to underline the extent to which such thinking is infused by powerful sentiments that defy rational comprehension. In many instances, particularly when noting the potential for charisma to amount to a revolutionary force in human history, Weber depicts this as incorporating an "enthusiasm" that drives people to seek new ways of living in the world.[31] Charisma is experienced as a deeply felt yearning for some kind of magical release from the adversities of present circumstance and, indeed, as an experience that may be attached to associations with heroic individuals who seem possessed by the powers to make this possible.[32] In this regard, his theory cues us to attend to the cultural dynamics, social contexts, and forms of experience that make possible the popular appeal and moral authority of extraordinary individuals such as Mahatma Gandhi, Martin Luther King Jr., or

Nelson Mandela.[33] He provides us with insights into the cultural conditions under which such individuals are empowered to deliver new social possibilities for thought and action. The irony here historically is that Weber did not foresee the charismatic movement in his own country that contributed to the rise of Hitler.[34]

Weber identifies the drive to both shore up and intensify processes of rationalization, as well as actions inspired by charismatic needs, as potential responses to the experience of being made to confront the brute fact of suffering. He does not, however, provide us with a fully elaborated account of when one type of response is more likely to occur than another; neither does he detail how both may take place in creative tension with one another or the possible consequences that such conjunctions hold. On these matters we are dealing with components of Weber's theory that are left tentative and incomplete or are analytical challenges still to be resolved. They are, moreover, aspects of Weber's thought that involve us in scholarly works of reconstruction and creative speculation; and before we venture to explore their implications for our project, it is worth dwelling in more detail on the cultural premises, interpretive understandings, and points of emphasis that set the parameters for analysis and debate.

RECONSTRUCTING WEBER'S CULTURAL ANTHROPOLOGY

Friedrich Tenbruck's seminal article, "The Problem of Thematic Unity in the Works of Max Weber" (1980), revolutionized the interpretation of Weber's sociology and provoked debate over how we should read his work.[35] Here we are mainly concerned with those aspects of Tenbruck's thesis that profile the philosophical and cultural anthropology around which Weber constructed his theory of modernity. This underlines the importance of Weber's analysis of problems of religious theodicy for his understanding of the cultural logics that determine our social character. Indeed, Tenbruck argues that when reading Weber we should privilege those passages in which he contends that the social psychology of entire societies is conditioned by repeated attempts to come to terms with "the experience of the irrationality of the world" as encountered in acute instances of human suffering.[36] Tenbruck holds that, for Weber, this is the "constant and universal anthropological problematic" that conditions the development of every cultural outlook on life and that is heavily implicated in the origins of modern rationality and its potential to inspire processes of "disenchantment."[37]

Tenbruck observes that Weber works with the understanding that in all times and places there are occasions when people encounter extreme forms of suffering that defy moral meaning. The problem of suffering is both intellectual and practical. It leaves people struggling to know how to think and act in their world; and in this sense it is experienced as wholly irrational. Extreme forms of suffering shatter people's purposive-rational categories of understanding and immerse them in a compulsive struggle to overcome, and/or remove themselves from, the experience of pain and affliction.

Such experiences give rise to an intense yearning for some manner of charismatic release, that is, some extraordinary means of overcoming the harsh reality of a world in which there is an unbearable amount of suffering. Herein Weber identifies some of the most vital functions of religions and, in the final analysis, the wellspring of the human search for meaning.[38] At the same time, he emphasizes the extent to which, at some point, religious cultures are always set to fail in the attempt to bestow adequate meaning on, and practical guidance for, the pains and defeats experienced in the context of devastating forms of suffering. Here it is assumed that the irrational force of life always retains a power to confound people's efforts at rational sense making and stands to oppose the work of practical reason.

While on occasion religions may enable people to experience the "emotional life-force" of charisma, the problem of suffering demands much from us aside from the cultural means to vanquish feelings of distress and despair.[39] The charismatic needs aroused by the experience of suffering are also accompanied by intellectual and pragmatic needs; and it is in these connections that religions are forced to engage with questions of theodicy. Following the initial shock of suffering, whatever solace is found through charisma is set to be "routinized" as people resume the practical business of social life and are made to engage with the task of making rational sense of their experience.[40] At one level, the problem of suffering arouses intense charismatic needs, and at another, it enforces a compulsive struggle for routinization. It is comprised both by a passionate yearn-

ing for release and by the struggle to manage its effects within the practices of day-to-day life.

Tenbruck is particularly concerned to dwell upon the extent to which
Weber understood the development of modern rationality to have been
conditioned by people's repeated and inherently frustrated attempts to find
solutions to the problem of suffering. In such instances, the world images
provided by religious ideas, in being made subject to "the spur of charismatic needs," are also placed under intense pressure to satisfy an insatiable
longing for a comprehensive intellectual-rational meaning for suffering, as
well as a means to practically overcome the brute force of affliction.[41]
Tenbruck would have us understand, "What characterises the distinctive-
ness of Weber's approach is that world images, the product of irrational
circumstances, succumb to a double pressure of rationality. First, the image
of the world has to satisfy the structure of theodicy; that is those obscure
aspects of existence that are perceived as unfathomable have, at their own
level, to be explained theoretically and, at a practical level overcome.
Second, in meeting this demand, they have to contribute to a more unified
and comprehensive explanation of the world from the standpoint of a
rational theodicy."[42] This "imperative of consistency," as Weber puts it, is
moderated according to the types of religious ideas that are adopted around
the world as solutions to the problem of theodicy.[43] Theological worldviews
channel the currents of rationalization and its structuring force on thought
and behavior. It is those systems of theology in which an all-powerful and
omniscient God calls upon believers to pursue their salvation through
"active asceticism," which Weber identifies as holding decisive consequences for the course taken by modern Occidental rationality. On this
account, modern processes of rationalization take root and develop as an
unintended consequence of "God-willed" actions taken by believers who
are intent on removing all wickedness from the world. A systematic, uni-
tary, and disciplined approach to thinking about the ultimate meaning of
life bequeaths cultural and institutional formations in which social life is
governed by the "objective" discharge of business and calculable rules.

Here a considerable analytical investment is made in the extent to
which, more than any other Christian denomination, Protestants are set to
encounter the Epicurean paradox[44] as a persistent and insurmountable
source of personal anxiety and distress. The intellectual and moral tensions

borne in the discrepancy between rational ideals and the irrational force of life compel believers to continually work at realizing God's heavenly kingdom on earth. Insofar as Weber holds modern rationality to be inspired and conditioned by religious worldviews, it is in relation to their "dynamic autonomy" as manifested in people's struggles against the apparent contradictions and inconsistencies in their belief systems that he works to expose their potential as social forces and determinants of economic and cultural life.[45]

THE DIFFICULTY OF UNDERSTANDING

Weber makes considerable demands of his readers. His arguments assume an acquaintance with a broad range of philosophical and theological traditions of debate as well as the historical conditions under which belief systems acquire their social appeal and practical relevance. His analysis requires that we are sensitive to the logics set within the religious ideas that comprise contrasting accounts of the causes of human misery and how believers should respond to the brute fact of suffering. He asks us to attend to the ways in which the logical consistency of particular types of theodicy— that is, attempts to defend the character of God (or Gods) and his/her/their actions in light of the occurrence of evil in the world—is made to unfurl with repeated attempts to respond to the calamity of human affliction. It is important to note, however, that here Weber aims to do far more than merely document how people are culturally disposed to interpret the intellectual torments that arise from the experience of adversity. He is also concerned to apprehend their repercussions at the level of social conduct and, further, to understand how such conduct gives rise to new possibilities for thought and practice. Another level of complexity is incorporated in his analysis in his concern to identify the long-term unintended consequences of all this for future conditions of moral belief and social action. Indeed, as far as Protestant traditions of theodicy are concerned, he is particularly attentive to the paradoxical ways in which concerted attempts to uphold and enact religious convictions in the early modern period contributed to the development of sociocultural conditions in which they are made to appear morally undesirable, socially impracticable, and intellectually spurious.

We have already referred to some of the literatures that document the impact of seventeenth-century religious and civil wars on the credibility of divine providence, and "special providence'"in particular.[46] In this context, it appears that the experience of many intractable theological disputes and repeated public failures of prophetic proclamation ultimately made many people more skeptical about claims that the hand of God was at work in the fine details of worldly events.[47] Indeed, from the recorded evidence of seventeenth-century parliamentary speeches, sermons, and theological tracts it is possible to document a considerable revision of popular and elite understandings of how God was liable (if at all) to intervene directly in human affairs[48]. The perceived failures of providential theodicy fed the skepticism of thinkers such as Thomas Hobbes, Pierre Bayle, and Voltaire and, at a more general level of understanding, made people more reluctant to accept that God caused every personal calamity or social disaster to take place as a means to carry out his purposes on earth (see chapter 1). Furthermore, aside from the fact that the credibility of orthodox traditions of Protestant theodicy was strained to the breaking point by the evidence of persistent and unrelieved suffering, it seems that some were driven by the distress of upholding faith in divine providence to work at creating more morally palatable accounts of God's character and his interactions with humanity. Certainly, it appears that this was an important part of the cultural ferment that gave rise to the humanitarian brand of theology promoted by the English Latitudinarian movement.[49] A rejection of providential theodicy on moral and sentimental grounds is also identified as giving encouragement to the development of the modern idea of God as suffering in solidarity with human suffering.[50] Indeed, as Keith Thomas notes, it was not merely the case that adverse events conspired to make providentialism appear incredible; but people grew to be increasingly disaffected by the effort to uphold tenets of belief that identified the experience of suffering as a vital tool of God's admonishment, instruction, and care;[51] they longed for a more humane conception of the divine.

The sophistication of Weber's approach lies in his concern to incorporate in his analysis of the cultural dynamics of theodicy an understanding of how individuals are liable to feel about and to be motivated to act within their world. In this respect, it is more from a concern to divulge the lived experience of the attempt to uphold religious convictions than from an interest in philosophical metaphysics that he conducts his analysis. Weber is working to explain the cultural composition of the trauma of suffering and, further, its consequences for a person's moral dispositions and behaviors. He aims to do far more than merely take note of the results of the historical process whereby faith in divine providence is undone by the struggle to account for the experience of suffering; rather, he seeks to expose the cultural, psychological, and social conditions that coordinate this process and determine its consequences.

It is with a focus on historical transformations in cultural attitudes and social responses to health problems that we are particularly well placed to appreciate Weber's ambition. Historical documents attest to the fact that it is when people are burdened by physical torments and disease that they are inclined to enter into debate with the conditions that govern their fate.[52] Moreover, there is little doubt that while struggling to relieve bodily pains and discomforts individuals are compelled to examine and revise their behaviors and forms of interaction with others. Managing experiences of illness and physical impairment tends to absorb people in the overwhelming practicality of life. In this respect, the social repercussions of theodicy and their wider consequences are often made most explicit.

For example, in his study, *The Impact of Plague in Tudor and Stuart England* (1985), Paul Slack documents the ways in which religious beliefs about the cause and meaning of disease gave rise to social actions that had the unintended consequence of promoting a more "secular" approach to managing outbreaks of plague. He further emphasizes that in order to understand how this took place we need to be sensitive to the ways in which theological disputes were moderated in relation to the practical task of combating the effects of plague. It is by working to understand the character and appeal of knowledge drawn from the experience of dealing with outbreaks of plague that we stand to grasp the dynamics of the process whereby beliefs about God change in response to the problem of suffering.

Slack notes that passages in the Bible such as Exodus 5–12 and the first book of Samuel 4–6 point to the understanding that God was the author of plagues. Such texts promoted the belief that forces of nature as well as social events were used for divine purpose. War, disease, and famine were a means to cast judgment on those who had opposed God's will and, further, served as a warning to those who might yet stray from the path of righteousness.[53] The symbiosis between earthly and spiritual events was generally held to be beyond dispute and a matter of utmost seriousness. Indeed, there is a wealth of evidence to suggest that the urgency with which devout Protestants set about projects of moral and social reform was to a large extent driven by devastating experiences of extreme adversity; the interpretation of these experiences as an injunction and/or reprimand designed to "encourage" them to work harder in their service to God and for the extension of his kingdom in the world[54].

Outbreaks of plague were accompanied by desperate struggles to understand what had gone wrong in the relationship between God and society and what needed to be done in order to appease his wrath.[55] From the record of many plague tracts written at the time, Slack notes that much dispute surrounded the issue of whether it is one's Christian duty to flee from the sinners who are marked out as such by falling prey to plague or, alternatively, whether one should be disposed with compassion to care for the sick and dying.[56] Biblical support could be found for both arguments, and as far as pure matters of principle were concerned, there was no possibility of resolving the issue in favor of one side or the other. Ultimately, however, it was the gathering of empirical evidence in favor of the view that quarantine was the best means to combat the spread of plague that gave rise to the widely shared understanding that God was instructing his chosen people to abandon the victims of plague to their fate.

The administration of quarantine was thus understood to be underwritten by a particular strain of theology (supported by passages such as Mark 9:43–47 and 1 Corinthians 5:9–13). The popular understanding that God favored such measures was also confirmed by the observation that many of those who remained to care for the sick tended to contract the disease. Accordingly, the empirical evidence at hand served to confirm the sacred authority of a particular strand of Christian teaching; it also diminished the credibility and appeal of an alternative tradition of understanding. The more often quarantine was shown to work, the more such convictions and behaviors were adopted as routine common sense.

Slack argues that the waning of theological dispute over how to respond to outbreaks of plague ultimately made possible a more secular approach to combating disease.[57] Once quarantine was established as the customary and demonstrably effective means to halt the spread of plague, people were no longer so inclined and/or compelled to enter into debate over the theological legitimacy of such measures; indeed, it seems that these could be readily recognized as the rational thing to do. Accordingly, here it appears that in the fervor of its belief and practice Protestantism had the unintended consequence of clearing a cultural space for "public health" interventions that by the eighteenth century were administered by authorities who were removed from any compunction to provide a public display of answering to God for their actions.

Slack's study serves as a vivid illustration of a core Weberian insight: namely, that human actions hold consequences that stand "in completely inadequate and often even paradoxical relation to [their] original meaning."[58] This should not, however, be taken as evidence in support of the view that Protestantism was the catalyst for a far-reaching process of secularization that resulted in the wholesale "disenchantment of the world." Rather, it only illustrates how a particular field of health concern, when made to broker with prevailing notions of theodicy, was gradually reconfigured to a point where public authorities were no longer inclined to respond to outbreaks of epidemic disease in open theological dispute over how to act appropriately.

Indeed, Western social historians are increasingly inclined to emphasize that in the seventeenth and eighteenth centuries and most of the nineteenth, there is no evidence to support the view that a major "philosophical turn" promoted the rise of rational medical science and a corresponding denigration of religious convictions in public affairs.[59] In other domains of health care, religious authorities and practitioners of medicine often worked to mutually reinforce their favored beliefs and practices.[60] There was no obvious tension between, on the one hand, the attempt to uphold religious conviction and, on the other, the quest to find the most practicable and rationally appropriate means to heal a person's sickness or ease his physical discomfort.[61] For example, Roy Porter reports that according to the evidence of the eighteenth-century *Gentleman's Magazine*, it was only when public anxieties were raised about premature burials, when it was discovered that people had awoken from comas in their coffins, or when worries were expressed about the ways bodies were used for the purposes of dissection, that people were inclined to question how the practice of medicine might conflict with Christian values.[62]

Porter further emphasizes that it was only on occasions when normative expectations were radically overturned and when moral conventions were breached that people were driven to question established beliefs and practices. He advises that "what most perturbs sufferers is less actual symptoms or quanta of pain, but sickness contrary to expectation."[63] Accordingly, when attempting to understand the dynamics at work in the application of Protestant theodicy to outbreaks of plague, it is particularly important to attend to the ways in which many unanticipated and aggressively indiscriminate outbreaks of epidemic disease precipitated a radical questioning of conventional beliefs about God and his actions. In order for the dynamics of theodicy to unfurl on a grand scale, a sustained period of crisis was required in which large numbers of people were regularly shocked by the mismatch between conviction and experience into revising their beliefs and practices.

When venturing to understand Weber on these matters, we must recognize that in his sociological conception of the problem of suffering he is working to apprehend the dynamics of the interrelationship between a considerable range of cultural experiences and social behaviors, and he aims to document their consequences from the immediate to the long term. In the first place, Weber is attentive to the ways in which the shock of the trauma of suffering serves to greatly aggravate and bring volume to many intellectual tensions, moral dilemmas, and practical difficulties in people's lives. Second, he seeks to understand the particular ways in which, on such occasions, individuals are both culturally and practically compelled to work at alleviating their distress. Third, he aims to trace how protracted struggles to make rational sense of suffering and to combat its deleterious effects on human life have an incisive bearing upon the overall direction of social and cultural change. In this, Weber recognizes that there are occasions when a collective outpouring of charismatic needs and/or a shared drive to rationalize reality may be intensified such that significant modifications are made to cultural beliefs and social practices and, further, that these hold the potential to deliver far-reaching consequences for the institutional formation of a society and its culture. It might be argued that in his analysis of the problem of suffering, Weber is most attentive to the ways in which the "antinomies of existence" enter into a person's moral experience of the world. It is also a context in which we are drawn into speculative debate over the extent to which such contradictory experience, in leaving its marks on people's cultural dispositions and social behaviors, holds lasting consequences for future generations.

ENGAGING WITH WEBER

For the most part, it is only in the context of scholarly debates over how to interpret Weber that his writing on the problem of suffering has been taken up as a serious matter for discussion. His analysis of theodicy tends to preoccupy those concerned to expound upon the moral standpoints and cultural judgments outlined in his celebrated 1948 lectures "Science as a Vocation" and "Politics as a Vocation." Here the focus is brought to his conception of "the fate of our times" and how it constrains the possibilities for thinking and action.

Taking the essay "Religious Rejections of the World and Their Directions" (1948) as their cue, commentators are inclined to highlight the fact that Weber believed that under social conditions of modernity, we are made subject to a cultural experience in which we acquire and create values that are mutually antagonistic and bridled in tension with one another.[64] In this regard, the unfurling dynamics of theodicy are identified as among the significant social and cultural processes that drive the compulsion to rationalize, as well as our conscious awareness of this tendency, to a point where there is intensification of the discord among the values we live by. It is generally held that when documenting "the fate of our times," Weber understood this to entail a great deal of moral and existential anxiety over the conviction that it is no longer possible to harmonize personal beliefs and public standards of value into an ethically unified standpoint for action. On his account we are now made to inhabit social structures and cultural arrangements where the cost of practical efficacy is exacted in ethical compromise. Our moral experience of the world is fragmented, inconsistent, and fraught with tension, at times to a point that is liable to be a cause of great distress.

Gershon Shafir argues that in taking up this thread of Weber's work we are alerted to many unresolved and ambivalent components of his sociological analysis of rationalization and its human consequences and that this is a context where we find Weber operating with a high degree of creative speculation.[65] Similarly, Tenbruck maintains that the task of interpreting Weber's final position on these matters is bound to end in frustration. He contends that we shall always be left struggling to pin down the sociological meaning and substantive claims of the "hieroglyphic sketches" of Weber's later works, particularly when it comes to apprehending his point of view on how we should understand the social possibilities before us.[66]

In taking up this challenge, some are inclined to treat the exacerbated antimonies of Christian theology and the waning public influence and role of the Christian Church in modern times as key matters for debate. For example, at this point Stephen Kalberg responds to Weber's work as an invitation to explore the ways in which tenets of Christian faith are liable to buckle and collapse under the strain of being made to hold public and practical relevance and thereby to leave us wanting for a coherent moral meaning and adequate social purpose.[67] He further argues that we are made particularly alert to this in the context of the attempt to fashion and sustain communities of compassion and mutual care.

On this account, the "communism of loving brethren" is understood to originate among people who are "moved" to value and encourage such practices as part of their Christian duty and calling.[68] Furthermore, doubts are cast on whether it may be possible to nurture or sustain such moral feelings and practices outside these associations; at one point Weber advises, "The religion of brotherliness has always clashed with the orders and values of this world, and the more consistently its demands have been carried through, the sharper the clash has been. The split has usually become wider the more the values of the world have been rationalized and sublimated in terms of their own laws."[69] Kalberg argues that Weber understood the advancement of practical and formal rationality in many areas of our lives to result in "a coldness and harshness to social relations"[70] He suggests that such conditions will always frustrate the attempt to put into practice ideals of human rights and humane society. Here Kalberg contends that Weber understood the relative strength of the "attitude of caritas" to depend on the degree to which it is grounded in the practice of Christian communion; and insofar as this is now theologically uprooted and taken up as a secular matter of "humanitarian concern," it is always liable to be weakened and compromised. Without a religious motivation, he holds, we shall struggle to recover the resolve and sense of purpose to make care for humanity our passion. It is argued that the fading of Christian conviction as the motive force of humanitarianism is a result of the intensification and spread of formal rationality throughout public life and, further, that this is likely to exacerbate many antinomies of moral value and principle among those who would still venture to make sentiments of compassion a guide to action.[71]

It seems clear that Weber greatly feared the potential for bonds of human sympathy to be eroded by the drive to make calculable rules the governing force in social conduct. He was alarmed by the capacity for the increasing "bureaucratization" of society and the tailoring of human exchange to the dictates of commerce to result in institutional arrangements that operate "without regard for persons."[72] On this view, it may well be appropriate to identify his analysis of the problem of theodicy as part of a wider attempt to explain the origins of the drive to rationalize human affairs and to unmask the paradoxical ways in which it serves to create new problems of suffering. Indeed, this very matter is taken up as the central theme of analysis in Michael Herzfeld's exploration of "the social production of indifference" that is set in motion through the ritual practices of modern bureaucrats. Here Herzfeld contends that through carefully crafted attitudes of dispassion and social conduct governed by strict adherence to formal rules, bureaucrats are made distant to human suffering; and insofar as they remain unaffected by the harms done to and/or experienced by others, they risk the possibility that there may be extreme circumstances in which they operate to "tacitly encourage genocide and intracommunal killings."[73] Moreover, Michael Barnett confesses that this is precisely what he identifies as a key part of the explanation for the failure of the UN to respond with concerted actions to halt the mass slaughter of Tutsis by radicalized Hutus in the Rwandan genocide of 1994. He looks back on his socialization into the role of an expert "Adviser for Peacekeeping Operations" for the U.S. Mission to the United Nations as having led him, without at the time giving any particular thought to the wider human consequences of his words and actions, to the point where he was as much interested "in protecting bureaucratic and organizational interests [as] in employing the UN to help those it was supposed to serve."[74] Barnett describes how while learning to be a bureaucrat he was involved in an incremental process of institutionalization that ultimately led him to place greater priority on performing a convincing role as a reliably informed expert and correctly spoken analyst of global affairs than on caring for the ground-level experience of people in adversity.

Albeit with less extreme examples of the brutal and destructive consequences of such social enactments, these concerns also feature large among those now working to understand how Weber's theory can be applied to the attempt to explain the legitimacy of modern medicine, as well as the tendency for the practice of medicine to exacerbate many ethical dilemmas over the value of human life.[75] Indeed, insofar as it is recognized that many processes of "medicalization," which recast social problems as "disease," are motivated by an attempt to render human suffering "manageable" under the auspices of rational administration and technical control, it is now widely understood that these might have the unintended consequence of causing damage to a person's emotional well-being and bonds to others.[76] The sociological critique of medicalization is largely fueled by the concern to expose the unintended human suffering that results from the attempt to promote health and regulate bodies according to purely administrative and technical considerations,[77] while the anthropological critique emphasizes the loss of the human as a moral threat.[78] On these grounds, reading Weber's analysis of the problem of suffering with a focus on its place within his overarching concern to explain the motive force of rationalization is certainly in keeping with a dominant strain in his sociology, particularly where attention is brought to the potential for rationalization—in this instance medical categories that legitimate dangerous, unnecessary, and misrecognized treatment interventions—to be experienced as a human harm.

Under this emphasis, however, we should also be careful to attend to passages where Weber recognizes that there are limits to what is humanely possible to withstand. We recall that in his cultural anthropology Weber holds that at the same time that we may be culturally disposed to respond to suffering via the pursuit of intensifying courses of rationalization we are also likely to be increasingly agitated by the spur of charismatic needs. Insofar as our experience of the problem of suffering is liable to grow in scale and volume along with the accomplishment of a more heavily rationalized society, then where disaster strikes and normative expectations for reality are left shattered, we should expect increasing numbers of people to be charged with the overwhelming desire for some manner of charismatic release from their adversity. Johannes Weiss contends that Weber grew increasingly alert to the potential for processes of rationalization to breed conflicts and tensions that draw people toward the limits of what is intellectually, morally, and socially bearable and that he anticipated the arrival of cultural forces that have the potential to radically unsettle established ideals, conventions, and practices of rationality.[79] Here it may even be possible to suggest that Weber was starting to piece together a conception of revolution as an unintended consequence of rationalization.

Yet, analytically speaking, this remains in pieces. Weber refers to charisma as a "creative revolutionary force in history" and goes so far as to announce that as a form of experience it holds the potential to deliver "a radical alteration of the central system of attitudes and directions of action with a completely new orientation of all attitudes towards the different problems and structures on the world."[80] He does not, however, provide any detailed examples of how charisma actually works to these ends. Furthermore, he does not document and explain the multiple forms in which "charismatic" needs might be manifested, enacted, or expressed or, indeed, the relative degrees to which these may serve to dictate the course of social and cultural change.[81] At the very least, he appears to treat the "revolutionary force" of reason and charisma as equals so as to have us recognize that it is the dynamic interplay between them that matters.[82] But there is no consensus as to how to apply this to social understanding. At one extreme, it is argued that under conditions of disenchantment Weber held that we are only likely to see the revolutionary force of charisma at play in marginal cult settings where people are inspired to follow individuals with "magnetic personalities."[83] At the other extreme, it is suggested that while toward the end of his life he became increasingly preoccupied with the role played by the "irrational force of life" in human experience, Weber was acquiring a greater appreciation for the ways in which cultures and societies were always being adapted in response to an expansive realm of "charismatic needs."[84] At this point, his work is set to attract many conflicts of interpretation, and it is where we must take up the task of social inquiry for ourselves.

CONCLUSION

It has taken almost a century for scholars to recover a proper appreciation for the guiding themes, full range, and complexity of Max Weber's sociology.[85] For most of this period, our understanding of Weber has been curtailed by the appropriation of his work as a critical response to Marxism and, further, by the success of Talcott Parsons's portrayal of him as a theorist of social action and founder of sociology as a value-free "science."[86] Scholars now recognize that distortions and misunderstandings entered into the account of Weber as a consequence of the ways in which his works were originally translated and made available for English speakers.[87] There are many instances in which it appears that we have been laboring not only with a partial grasp of his scholarly concerns but also with conceptual language that is more a product of the interpretive license exercised by his translators than a part of Weber's design.[88]

Taking its cues from the seminal contributions of Friedrich Tenbruck and Wilhelm Hennis, the later reconstructed account of Weber emphasizes the extent to which he was largely concerned to advance a cultural analysis that explains "the consequences of rational life-conduct on the formation of character, especially the rational man of calling (the Berufsmenschentum)."[89] Here Weber is understood to be preoccupied with the task of documenting the conditions under which we acquire our social subjectivity and how, in turn, this shapes our moral, political, and ontological dispositions. A focus is brought to his analysis of how modern people are liable to struggle to "measure up to workaday existence" under cultural conditions "characterized by rationalization and intellectualization and, above all, by the disenchantment of the world."[90] We should approach Weber's sociology on the understanding that it is heavily informed by a philosophical anthropology that is concerned with the ways in which human thought and action change under the compulsion to make "senseless' experiences of death, the suffering of the innocent, and the apparent injustice of the world "somehow *meaningful*."[91] Indeed, on some accounts, the revised approach to reading Weber underlines the extent to which the contents and character of his social theory reflect his own existential dilemmas, political worries, and moral anxieties and that, when writing, he is working to provoke his readers into moral and political debate over their conditions of existence and the fate of their times.[92]

Weber devised his social theory with the basic understanding that in all times and places there will be occasions when people will be existentially burdened by the antinomies of existence. At some point our cultural artifacts and exchanges are destined to fall short of providing us with a morally sufficient meaning for our experience of the world, particularly in contexts of extensive and extreme suffering. In taking up this matter for analysis, he provides us with an intricate account of how the contradictory logics and conflicting value orientations of Protestant theodicy are set to spur the development of modern processes of rationalization. He further attends to how, by providing temporary solutions to the problems that suffering visits upon people's lives, such processes have the unintended consequence of nurturing sociocultural conditions in which the moral senselessness of human affliction is set to intensify in volume and scale. Here the tragedy of modern rationalization lies in the terrible paradox that in being applied to the task of delivering us from suffering, it is fatefully bound to deliver us into new possibilities for suffering.

Insofar as modern societies are made subject to intensifying processes of rationalization, Weber would have us understand that we are also made to inhabit cultural realities that are fraught with intellectual tensions and conflicted moral experience. There can be no escape from this. It is in the texture and grain of every enactment of social life, and he anticipates that there will be many occasions when individuals will struggle to accommodate themselves to their sociocultural constitution as modern people. Among other things, his concern to incorporate an analysis of the problem of suffering in his sociology is driven by the understanding that it is by confronting the brute fact of this experience that we are compelled to negotiate with the cultural conditions that govern our fate.

Here we are set to uncover one of the key motive forces of rationalization: namely, the compulsion to remove ourselves from, or at least render manageable, the negative force of affliction. Weber would have us understand that at the same time that the advancement of rationalization is fueled by the pursuit of cost efficiency and more effective modes of governance it is rooted in, and driven by, the struggle to accommodate our vulnerability to pain and suffering. In this regard, it is in the distress of experiencing the problem of suffering that we are forced to explain our-selves in rational terms and to strive for a more rationally effective means to manage our human frailty and deliver ourselves from harm's way.

Weber cues us to attend to the ways in which the age-old problem of theodicy develops through the cultural experience of modernity. Certainly, on his account, we should anticipate that insofar as problems of human suffering are now addressed via secular forms of "sociodicy,"[93] it is also likely to hold more devastating consequences for our cultural beliefs and practices. He holds that we are now subject to social and cultural condi-tions where it is made particularly difficult for us to endure the contradic-tions of our existence, perhaps more difficult than ever before. His reflec-tions on these matters lend weight to the suggestion that Weber was increasingly inclined to believe there was much within our culture that was unendurable and that we should anticipate the likelihood of revolu-tionary upheaval and a shared urgency to remake our worlds anew.

The value of Weber's social theory lies in its use as a resource for our cultural orientation and social self-understanding. We also commend it for the extent to which it demonstrates his moral resolve to document and explain the cultural conditions under which we might uncover the truth about who we are and how we could be and, indeed, where it may yet be possible for us to clear a space for the development of new and better forms of human society. The conditions under which he delivered his famous lecture "Politics as a Vocation" (1948) are particularly instructive in this regard. The parting advice of this piece serves as a fitting mantle for those who would take up the critical praxis of research and writing on social suffering.

"Politics as a Vocation" is the printed record of a lecture that Weber deliv-ered to students at the University of Munich on January 28, 1919. At this point, German society was reeling under the shocking devastation and defeat of world war. It was also widely feared that the Paris Peace Conference that had begun ten days earlier would impose terms on Germany that guar-anteed a protracted period of economic decline and political instability. Indeed, Germany was already in the throes of revolutionary upheaval, and two weeks earlier two of the leaders of a bloody uprising in Berlin, Rosa Luxembourg and Karl Liebknecht, had been arrested, tortured, and sum-marily executed without trial. Further uprisings and bloodshed seemed inevitable. Marianne Weber records that the mood among the Munich students was very tense and that many of them were caught up in the enthusiasm for Bolshevism. In spite of this, she informs us that Weber "forced his listeners" to attend to the inherently frustrated relationship between politics and ethics,[94] he sought to emphasize the need for a pragmatic urgency that unites passion with perspective.

Weber here provides a stark example of his commitment to think "without illusions" and of the devotion with which he sought to live up to his own sense of calling.[95] Large parts of his address are taken up with an attempt to impress on his audience that they should be careful to temper their enthusiasm for radical regeneration with a sober and proportionate assessment of the practical difficulties involved in making society anew. In this regard, he risks courting their anger and hostility. Weber warns that in the pursuit of "ultimate ends," they must still broker with the "age old problem of theodicy" and that when caught up in the fervor of their ethical idealism they should be wary of the fact that this will inevitably be forced to ground by "the experience of the irrationality of the world."[96] He advises that following this "period of reaction" they must still "[measure] up to the world as it really is in everyday routine."[97] He concludes by declaring:

> Not summer's bloom lies ahead of us, but rather a polar night of icy darkness and hardness, no matter which group may triumph externally now. . . . Politics is a strong and slow boring of hard boards. It takes both passion and perspective. Certainly all historical experience confirms the truth—that man would not have attained the possible unless time and again he had reached out for the impossible. But to do that a man must be a leader, and not only a leader but a hero as well, in a very sober sense of the word. And even those who are neither leaders nor heroes must arm themselves with that steadfastness of heart which can brave even the crumbling of all hopes. This is necessary right now, or else men will not be able to attain even that which is possible today.[98]

5 The Praxis of Social Suffering

The details of Bartolomé de Las Casas's (1474–1566) fifty-year campaign (1516–66) against the abuse of the Amerindians is now studied both for the extent to which, as a cultural event, it marks the birth of modern humanitarian consciousness and for the ways in which it provides insight into the theological concerns and juridical tactics that first established the appeal to "humanity" as part of our moral reasoning and politics.[1] His debates with Juan Gínes de Sepúlveda at Valladolid in 1550–51 are particularly important, for it was here that Las Casas is recorded as founding his case against the enslavement and violent conversion of the Amerindians on the principle that "all the races of the world are men. . . . All have understanding and will and free choice, as all are made in the image and likeness of God. . . . Thus, the entire human race is one."[2] These debates are also significant for the fact that, while working to justify his arguments with support from the Bible and traditions of Christian theology, Las Casas directed his audience to the evidence of his extensive documentation of eyewitness accounts (including his own) of the harms done to the Amerindians by the brutal acts of torture and violent abuse committed by the Spanish conquistadors. Although his efforts only managed to deliver some short-lived reforms of the encomienda system of slavery, Las Casas initiated the craft of using the protest of suffering humanity as the basis for challenging discriminatory cultural beliefs and for exposing the injustices of oppressive political regimes.

His *Short Account of the Destruction of the Indies* (1552) is the first document of human rights abuses in Western history that is explicitly designed with this aim in mind. It was written following a radical conversion of conscience that entailed his public renunciation of his own involvement in slavery. In the prologue Las Casas expressly declares it is dedicated to the cultivation of the Spanish king's moral imagination in the hope that thereby he might be moved to act to halt the massacres taking place in the Spanish colonies. Las Casas writes:

> It is my fervent hope that, once Your Highness perceives the extent of the injustices suffered by these innocent peoples and the way in which they are being destroyed and crushed underfoot, unjustly and for no other reason than to satisfy the greed and ambition of those whose purpose it is to commit such wicked atrocities, Your Highness will see fit to beg and entreat His Majesty to refuse all those who seek royal licence for such evil and detestable ventures, and to put a stop once and for all to their infernal clamour in such a way that nobody will henceforth dare to make such a request nor even to mention ventures of this kind.[3]

What follows is a series of graphic accounts of torture, mass murder, and atrocities as Las Casas builds the vast majority of his case, not on an appeal to matters of Christian conviction and theological principle, but on the evidence of human suffering. He aims to elicit visceral shock in his readers with the moral repugnance of the outrageous experiences that the Amerindians are subjected to. Las Casas works to arouse compassion for the victims of Spanish cruelty. He dwells on the ingenuity of the mechanisms of torture devised by the Spaniards and makes clear the most horrendous details of physical torments and deprivations that are inflicted on Amerindian men, women, and children. The Spanish are decried throughout for their barbarous inhumanity, while he repeatedly moves to bring moral recognition to the humanity of the Amerindians through the most terrible details of their suffering.

Las Casas certainly understood that in his manner of writing he was crafting a text that would scandalize public opinion and, further, that this would have radical social and political repercussions. *A Short Account of the Destruction of the Indies* is a shortened version of a much more detailed record of Spanish brutality that Las Casas compiled under the title *History of the Indies,* which was not published in his lifetime. It is recorded that in 1559 he left written instructions that the longer work should only be published forty years after his death, and only then on the condition that "it is thought to be convenient for the good of the Indians and Spain."[4] It is now recognized, however, that the public outrage and political controversies that followed in the wake of his publication of *A Short Account of the Destruction of the Indies* were so destructive to the national reputation of Spain that thereafter considerable efforts were devoted to suppressing the details of his treatises, and it was not until 1875 that the full *History of the Indies* was finally published.

Right up to the present day it is possible to find writers seeking to defame Las Casas's reputation as a humanitarian and also working to cast doubt on the veracity of his account of the massacre of the Amerindians. In tracing the history of the public reaction to Las Casas's *Short Account,* Benjamin Keen notes that from its first publication through to the twentieth century it has been the subject of heated controversy.[5] This is largely because of the extent to which it is recognized as a key source for those perpetuating the so-called Black Legend of Catholic Spain as a barbaric society.[6] In particular, following the late sixteenth-century publication of the work by the Huguenot de Bry family, which embellished Las Casas's narrative with a series of copper plate engravings of torture scenes, his work was branded as part of an industry of foreign propaganda designed to besmirch the national character of Spain.[7] Moreover, following the eighteenth-century dispute between Voltaire and Corneille de Pauw over the level and form of Las Casas's contribution to the conquest of the Americas, there was regular debate over whether he should be celebrated as a humanitarian or stand condemned as a Spanish imperialist, albeit through his mission to institute a soft-hearted brand of Christian paternalism in the Spanish colonies.[8]

At one level of analysis, the long history of debate over the legacy of Las Casas is important for its illustration of the potential for public documents of human suffering to invite many conflicts of interpretation, particularly with regard to to their reception and standing in the political sphere. In this respect, it also demonstrates how the imagery of suffering might be readily and repeatedly appropriated in ideologically motivated discourses designed to enact power relations in society. The social meaning and historical consequences of Las Casas's humanitarianism have always garnered a great deal of moral and political dispute. At another level of analysis, however, alongside this record of controversy, the history of the critical response to his texts is important for the extent to which it bears testimony to their ongoing power to issue a critical challenge to prevailing codes of social and moral understanding. For centuries they have provoked debate over the moral values enshrined in cultures of social classification. They have also caused many people to question the ties of moral responsibility that are borne by people through their social connections to and social recognition of "others." Indeed, it might be argued that, notwithstanding the history of controversy surrounding his achievement and legacy, in this instance he initiated a critical practice in which experiences of human suffering are framed as issues that channel debate about the moral character of society and about the morality of prevailing forms of social interaction on a grand scale.

It is possible to approach Las Casas's campaign and writings as having had the unintended consequence of drawing the bounds of human sociality and social recognition into debate. The history of the response to *A Short Account* is a startling early example of how the cultural artifacts of a humanitarian campaign also work to provoke a quest for social understanding as well as a critical questioning of the forms in which this takes place. His appropriation of the imagery of the suffering so as to declare our common humanity served not only as an incitement to moral and ontological debate but also to initiate a social awakening.[9] In this process we have gradually acquired a common understanding of ourselves as part of a global human society; or at the very least, we have arrived at a point where this is widely recognized as an issue that raises many new challenges for understanding and action.

We have argued that, among other things, the creation and popularization of social suffering as a category of human understanding marks a conscious realization of the fact that our experience and response to human suffering is bound to the acquisition of social consciousness along with the possibility of recognizing the social realm as an object for care in action. We have also drawn attention to the extent to which, already by the end of the end of the eighteenth century, this was identified as a matter of great controversy (see chapter 1). Insofar as it was taken to involve an active courting and cultivation of moral sentiment, this manner of social understanding was inevitably embroiled in ethical and political dispute. At its origins social suffering raised many troubling questions about the types of actions that should proceed from an identification of human suffering as a social condition and, in particular, in relation to how people should interpret and respond to the moral-social demands that this placed on them to care for the suffering others.

In this chapter we explore the praxis of documenting and writing on problems of social suffering. By taking this up as a matter for analysis, we also aim to clarify how we understand its potential to operate as a provocation to the pursuit of social understanding and as a calling to practical social care. It is important to recognize that very often the praxis of writing on social suffering not only concerns a struggle to create symbolic forms of culture to convey what suffering does to people, but also an anticipation of the possible ways in which readers are disposed to react to this. It is a praxis that aims not only to evoke compassion but also to craft this as a means to *educate* thought and action. It aims to set us on a course whereby we might consciously navigate a path through many troubled and conflicted moral feelings toward a better social understanding of others and to the realization of how we might use this as a guide to responding to them with acts of care.

In order to recognize the critical reflexivity of those writing within this tradition, we are particularly concerned to underline the ways in which the praxis of documenting and writing on social suffering involves a conscious consideration of the critical objections that are likely to arise in response to its work and to proffer these as the kindling for debate so that critical scrutiny is brought to bear on prevailing social values and moral practices. This often concerns the identity and bounds of humanitarianism and humanitarian commitment. Practitioners take a keen interest in the potential for humanitarian impulse to spur the awakening of social consciousness, but alongside this, they also aim to respond to hostile responses to humanitarian values and practices in a manner that makes them productive for further critical thinking and action. A vital component of this praxis is invested in the attempt to corral many disputes and controversies of its own making into a questioning of how we might act to realize humane forms of society.

The following section provides a summary account of key breakthroughs and developments that laid the ground for the conscious realization of the praxis of documenting and writing on social suffering. It refers readers back to some of the details of previous chapters so as to acknowledge the pedigree of the moral and political issues at stake in movements to place problems of social suffering at the center of the attempt to expose our social condition and its constitution. By this we also aim to establish terms of analysis on which to conduct a critical assessment of some dominant strains in critical responses to our standpoint. We then focus on the work of Didier Fassin and his openly hostile and critical dismissal of research and writing on social suffering.[10] We question the value that Fassin places on critique as an end itself and, by contrast, argue for a position of critical pragmatism that aims to establish its worth through the practical results of its work in lived experience. In all this we aim to further clarify the critical and moral commitments that inform our arguments. We explain how these can be taken as a demonstration of the role played by a "humanitarian social imaginary" in the cultivation of social consciousness and of the potential for this to be directed to social care in action.

THE CONSCIOUS REALIZATION OF A NEW PRAXIS

The potential for the spectacle of human misery to awaken social consciousness and provoke moral conscience was more fully realized during the second half of the eighteenth century. Within the critical ferment of the Scottish Enlightenment it was openly recognized that in our capacity to feel for the suffering of others, we are also engaging in "social sympathy." In this context, social experience was identified as being replete with moral feeling and further that our disposition towards sociality was hewn from our capacity to feel for the suffering of others. We have also surveyed some of the critical debates that accompanied this conscious realization of the connection between our feelings for the pains of others and the awakening of social concern. Indeed, it appears that along with the wider recognition that "social sympathy" was an active and powerful force within our culture and politics, there also grew an ever more vociferous culture of critique that sought to decry this development as a danger to principled debate and orderly society.

When the concept of social suffering first acquired currency to denote people's pains and misery as distinctly "social" problems warranting forms of "social" intervention and "social" reform, it was accompanied by a great deal of controversy. At the point at which William Wordsworth first used this term as a means to document experiences of social deprivation, there was already a great deal of critical hostility to the "cult of sensibility," particularly insofar as it was observed that many were inclined to indulge their capacity to feel for the sufferings of others without being moved to care in action. Furthermore, by the turn of the nineteenth century it was widely feared that being fired by "the passion of compassion" made it all too easy for people to endorse acts of bloody vengeance, and for many in the establishment of the time, this served as a compelling reason for them to take steps to erase moral sentiment from public affairs.

From here on, it was almost always the case that those who continued in the effort to encourage the "rebellion of sentiment" as a means to further projects of humanitarian social reform were readily alert to the risks inherent in their literary practices and techniques of social documentation; or if not, they were soon made aware of them by the ferocity of the critical response to their work. Many powerful forces and institutionally privileged groups were allied in their opposition to public displays of fellow feeling, especially those invested in the moral philosophy of classical political economy. As we have seen, in the case of Henry Mayhew we have an example of a pioneering social investigator who though his documentary practices stumbled almost by accident into these controversies (see chapter 2). It is more often the case, however, that where we have historical records of the motives and creative decisions behind the attempt to craft an education of compassion, those fired by humanitarian sentiment recognized the potential for the symbolic portrayal of human suffering to provoke many conflicts of interpretation; they understood also that their texts and imagery could be culturally appropriated in the service of interests that were either far removed from or even openly opposed to their original purposes and design.

For example, mention has already been made of the fact that many of those involved in campaigning against the abolition of slavery were openly concerned with the potential for the imagery of suffering to serve more to "sensationalize" the plight of slaves than to arouse public support for the abolition cause. There are many records of debates between humanitarian campaigners over the extent to which by taking up the "polemics of pain" they were also unwittingly involved in the creation of a morally debased culture in which publics were inclined to gaze upon the spectacle of human misery more as a prurient pleasure than with a concern for humanitarian action and reform.[11] Indeed, there is now a distinct literature devoted to the study of the varied and complex "textual strategies" adopted by anti-slavery campaigners such as Lydia Maria Child as part of their efforts to mitigate the risk that their writing would operate as no more than a form of "erotic exploitation" of people.[12]

Under these circumstances, one might well wonder why it was still worth brokering with such inherently unstable and potentially dangerous senti-ments; and indeed, this question has been a long-standing matter of debate. For example, Gregg Crane records that following the enormous public response to *Uncle Tom's Cabin,* Harriet Beecher Stowe devised *Dred: A Tale of the Great Dismal Swamp* (1856) out of a concern to respond to the many criticisms directed to her sentimental characterization of Uncle Tom and to her strategy of political engagement.[13] Here Stowe offered a standpoint on why and how the impetus for humanitarian reform should be drawn from the conviction of moral feeling rather than from pure principle. Crane con-tends that she believed that all too often the rational culture that presided over systems of law operated in a politically conservative manner and worked to obstruct the possibility of questioning established convention. In this regard, Stowe took "the eruption of moral sympathetic feeling" evoked by the graphic depiction of cruelty to slaves as a "sure signal" that all indi-viduals were entitled to "fundamental human rights."[14] She was also heavily invested in the understanding that it was only by being made to experience such "moral-emotional dissonance" that large numbers of people could be moved to take actions to oppose the apologists for slavery and end its prac-tice. Crane contends that although Stowe recognized the danger that by force of moral sentiment it was possible for people to rush toward the belief that they were morally licensed to seize power at all costs, nevertheless, she remained convinced that such passion was necessary for sustaining the political solidarity and strength of will to realize human rights. Crane argues that even though her characterization of Dred, the revolutionary leader of the slaves living on the swamp, conveys her misgivings about the potential for moral sentiment to breed insurrectionary violence, she held on to the belief that it was by the eruption of moral feeling that alternative social worlds were rendered imaginable and that the struggle to realize more humane forms of society was sustained more by emotion than by point of principle. At the same time that it is possible to argue that Stowe reached an "imaginative impasse" in her literary portrayal of a humanitarian revolution rooted and sustained by social sympathy, she seems to have remained convinced that the struggle to build humane forms of society must first be taken up as a passion so as to be realized in principle and practice. It was as a commitment of praxis that she continued to work at engaging her readers as much through feeling as thought.

THE RECURRENCE OF PASSION AND CRITIQUE

In the more recent gathering of interest around problems of social suffering these moral and critical quandaries have resurfaced and are once again being taken up as key issues for debate. For example, by presenting us with photographs of human suffering and giving privileged space in his work to personal narratives on experiences of material hardship and social deprivation, Paul Farmer acknowledges that he is prepared to traverse many moral and political minefields. He openly worries over the extent to which his publications serve to make his readers "habituated to horror" or encourage them to dismiss "displeasing images" as "gratuitous" or "pornographic."[15] At the same time, however, he remains committed to using visual and viscerally charged representations of human misery as a means to morally unsettle and shock his readers into critical thinking and political action. Farmer holds that the cultivation of moral sentiment is necessary for galvanizing movements to promote the rights of the poor and for forging ties of solidarity with the victims of social injustice.[16] Following Susan Sontag, he operates with the resolve "to locate our privilege on the same map as the suffering of our contemporaries" and to this end contends that "the road from unstable emotions to genuine entitlements—rights—is one we must travel if we are to transform humane values into meaningful and effective programs that will serve precisely those who need our empathy and solidarity most."[17]

In a similar vein, in their photoethnography of "dopefiends" Philippe Bourgois and Jeff Schonberg openly admit to being concerned about the extent to which their images of drug users serve "to fuel a voyeuristic pornography of suffering."[18] They craft their text with the aim of contextualizing visual representations of human suffering with authentic social and cultural meaning; yet they acknowledge the ever present risk that their work leaves too much either distorted or undisclosed. Nevertheless, they hold that it is vitally important to evoke an emotional response from their readers. They aim "to expose the distress of the socially vulnerable" and make the moral disquiet that is thereby experienced by their readers a means to "humanize" the social perception of drug users. Once again, while acknowledging that their methods of social documentation court many contradictory tensions, for the sake of bringing experiences of social suffering to public debate, they hold it necessary to engage with unstable emotions. In this regard, the promotion of practical measures of progressive health care and welfare reform is held to require not only a revision of common cultural categories of social understanding but also a radical reconfiguration of moral feeling.[19]

Farmer, Bourgois, and Schonberg together with an increasing number of younger anthropologists identify many risks inherent in their praxis. Yet they retain a commitment to nourishing moral sentiment as a means to draw public attention to social suffering and to provoke debate over the bounds of the moral and political responsibilities "we" bear toward "others." Like many before them, they operate under the conviction that both the acquisition of social understanding and the desire to take action to create more humane forms of society are allied to a cultural politics of compassion. They acknowledge that they are using unstable cultural practices that often fail to meet their humanitarian ambitions; nevertheless, they recognize these practices as holding the potential to inspire publics to engage in the attempt to build a more caring society. They work to involve us in many of the ethical anxieties and methodological frustrations that they have borne through their research and writing. They do not seek, moreover, to remove themselves from bearing responsibility for the possibility that their texts and photographs might be culturally appropriated to ends opposed to their original design.[20] At the same time, it is by infusing their works with these tensions and by confronting such risks that they aim to make possible forms of social disclosure that would otherwise remain hidden from view. They operate from the understanding that such commitments and practices are necessary for conveying the human experience of the social conditions they document. Indeed, they often credit the most morally difficult, emotionally charged, and semantically unstable passages of their work as being most capable of raising the human social situation up for political recognition and critical debate.[21]

Such strategies of social disclosure are by no means widely endorsed or commonplace. Indeed, more often than not, when the cultural artifacts of humanitarian campaigns are taken up for debate within contemporary social science, it is with the aim of subjecting them to ideological critique. Social commentators and cultural analysts are inclined to devote their attentions to exposing the potential for humanitarian appeals to operate more in the service of the interests of the most institutionally privileged members of society than for those suffering in situations of adversity.[22] In this regard, they are far more concerned to alert us to the ways in which humanitarian culture and its moral sensibilities work more to corrupt than to enhance our capacities for social understanding.[23] They do not recognize, moreover, any valid or desirable role for humanitarianism in the cultures in which they operate.[24] Humanitarianism is placed under suspicion as an ideology that is used to legitimize morally dubious forms of political activity; it is not thought of as holding any value for the advancement of social understanding or for reputable projects of social reform. Nor is it endorsed for responding with social care to grave conditions of human suffering.

A RESPONSE TO FASSIN

Arguably, Didier Fassin has devised the most vociferous objections to the incorporation of "humanitarian reason" in social science.[25] Drawing on traditions of Foucauldian critique, he works to cast humanitarianism as instituting relationships of social domination. Fassin argues that while humanitarianism is widely understood to operate in solidarity with the victims of oppression and to serve as the inspiration for organizations that are militantly opposed to social injustice, it actually works to deny human recognition and operates as a means to uphold radically unequal social relations.[26] On his analysis, "humanitarian government" should be held under suspicion for the extent to which it lends support to the notion that we all share in a common humanity and that all lives hold equal value; for indeed, "by saving lives, it saves something of our idea of ourselves," and "by relieving suffering, it also relieves the burden of this unequal world order."[27] He aims to portray humanitarianism as not only delusional but also as operating to institute the very conditions it decries.

Fassin further identifies research and writing on social suffering as representative of a new cultural trend that, while advancing the claim that "there is more suffering than before and that people are more exposed to the suffering of others," is also inclined to promote an uncritical celebration of the role played by moral sentiments of compassion in the public realm.[28] He contends, moreover, that those involved in such work pay no critical attention to the semantic reconfigurations that they are advancing by their "inflation" of the discourse of suffering and by the move to explicitly identify "the social" as that which "makes people suffer."[29] He maintains that where sociologists and anthropologists venture to document cultural idioms of pain and the lived experience of human suffering, they are unwittingly colluding in the creation of a cultural politics that is inherently repressive. They may understand themselves to be working to promote human rights and as engaging in efforts to care for the misfortune of others, but they are in fact operating as naive purveyors of a discourse that polices moral boundaries between people and imposes categorizations of "victimhood" on the destitute, poor, and misfortunate.[30]

In this regard, Fassin argues that by his involvement in studies of personal experiences of material hardship and social deprivation published in *The Weight of the World* (1999), Bourdieu was involved in an attempt to re-model sociology as a means to police the documentation of human experience but also in the imposition of the common understanding that it is only insofar as we hear, see, and share in feeling for people's suffering that it should be recognized as a pressing social concern (see chapter 3). He argues:

> On the basis of the sociologist's authority, social suffering acquired official status and empathetic listening became a legitimate tool, with the social sciences acting as a model for social work—and all the more because the book's success was partly due to the fact that unlike previous studies of

exclusion, it showed that everyone was or potentially could be affected by suffering. Rather than perpetuating the idea of a social world divided between excluded and included, as the sociologists of the second left asserted, Pierre Bourdieu, who can be seen as representative of the "first left" (neo-Marxist), revealed that everyone suffers, presenting a mirror in which all could recognise themselves.[31]

Fassin then declares that through his work Bourdieu was involved in reinventing human suffering as a matter to be addressed as a "political issue" and that this also involved a recasting of the social as a "vague essentialization of inequality, violence and deviance . . . that makes people suffer."[32] He further contends that "the normalization of social suffering in the public arena and the institution of a national policy of listening do not derive only from new forms of subjectivation resulting in the manifesting of a concern for the misfortune of others; they are also modes of government that strive to make precarious lives livable and elude the social causes of their condition."[33] Accordingly, Bourdieu and his ilk are portrayed as operating not only to diminish our social understanding of the world but also to create a cultural apparatus that serves more to impose a sense of moral order on society than to hold this up for critical investigation.

On Fassin's account, at the same time that medical anthropologists such as Paul Farmer and Philippe Bourgois, and others such as Jim Yong Kim, Veena Das, Rayna Rapp, Mark Nichter, João Biehl, Nancy Scheper-Hughes, Adriana Petryna, Angela Garcia, Sharon Kaufman, and Richard Parker, should be held up for suspicion along with Bourdieu, they may also be criticized for their collusion in a movement to "reduce" people to problems of "biological life."[34] Evoking arguments drawn from the works of Georgio Agamben and informed by Michel Foucault's later concern with issues of "biopower,"[35] Fassin declares that there is an overwhelming disposition within "humanitarian reason" to grant people social recognition only insofar as they can be portrayed as victims of some form of health deprivation, and in this regard, it is people's bodily health conditions that feature as an overwhelming concern for government. He argues that a focus on "biological life" operates to the exclusion of a concern with people's "biographical life" and that humanitarians intent on regulating bodily health conditions operate with no concern to attend to how the subjects of their interventions "give a meaning to their own existence."[36]

Accordingly, research and writing on social suffering within medical anthropology is held to operate as part of a culture that both obfuscates social analysis and diminishes our capacity for human recognition.

Clearly, Fassin aims to advance a wholesale and hostile renunciation of the forms of praxis advocated by writers attending to problems of social suffering; indeed, social suffering itself is denounced as a morally dubious cultural category that operates as part of an insidious discourse of governmental repression and social obfuscation. At the very least, it serves as a further illustration of a point that has already been raised on a number of occasions through this chapter: namely, that those involved in the promotion of a humanitarian social concern are bound to court controversy and criticism. At the same time, to some readers it may appear odd to see such hostility being directed at writers such as Bourdieu, Bourgois, and Farmer from a quarter of academia that aims to present itself as operating at the frontiers of critical thinking and with a strident commitment to the advancement of human social understanding on a radical plane. Given that Fassin professes a concern to critically question society so as to expose unequal power relations, one might think that he would be inclined to identify these fellow scholars more as family relations than as avowed enemies. And it must also be remarkable that Fassin is himself, like Farmer, a physician anthropologist, making one wonder how he squares medicine with humanitarianism.

Fassin appears to be overwhelmingly preoccupied with the development of critique against critique. He aims to persuade us that what we may otherwise identify as operating in the interests of human emancipation is in fact a tool of repression. On his account, the passion of compassion is a moral danger and should not be allowed to color our thinking. His antagonism to the use of moral sentiment in social inquiry is such that he is moved to dismiss all research and writing on social suffering as infected with a pernicious humanitarian ideology. Insofar as we are moved by "social sympathy," Fassin would have us recognize ourselves as caught up in projects of moral coercion. In this regard, he brackets the crudest expressions of sentimentalism along with the subtlest renderings of moral feeling as all amounting to the same thing.

Fassin never acknowledges or concerns himself with the extent to which many of those engaged with problems of social suffering operate from a position of critical pragmatism (see chapter 3). In this regard, the potential for cultures of moral sentiment to be appropriated as a political ideology is openly acknowledged; and further, writers such as Farmer, Bourgois, and Bourdieu expressly understand themselves to be operating with unstable forms of culture. In their writing they are struggling to make possible a sympathetic recognition of human social situations and have this balanced alongside a rational analysis of the structural conditions that govern people's lives. They openly acknowledge that they are engaging with a precarious balancing act that may fall considerably short of achieving their aims. In this chapter we have profiled the extent to which this is due to the indeterminate and inherently wayward disposition of moral feeling, but elsewhere we have also underlined the danger that our capacity for social understanding is emasculated by the drive to have it disciplined within a rationalist frame (see chapter 2). Accordingly, when assessing the critical value of their work, it is important to recognize that although alert to the dangers inherent in cultures of moral sentiment, they are equally concerned to guard against the potential for cultures of rationalization to produce a conceptually sterilized account of social life in which too much of the mess of human experience (i.e., what matters for people) is hidden from view. In this regard, Bourdieu is at pains to point out that it is imminently possible for the language of social science to become a form of "symbolic violence" that contributes to the harms done to people.[37] By our technical manner of writing, we not only risk obscuring more of the world than we bring to light, but we also, and more worryingly, risk a loss of social understanding in human terms. Das has made the issue of how we write of human pain and suffering the most fundamental moral question for and of social science.[38] It is all too easy for social science to operate without human recognition and thereby as a renunciation of care for the human as such. Under this conviction, research and writing on social suffering takes place as an attempt to enact a critical reflexivity that makes social science both consciously and conscientiously committed to exposing the moral experience of people in society.[39] At the same time that an attempt is made to have us critically question the values we live by we are encouraged to take up a critical stance with regard to how the culture of social science operates. Indeed, in almost every instance where researchers are involved with documenting problems of social suffering, they are also inclined to hold up their own practices of knowledge production for critical scrutiny. A critical questioning of the moral values enshrined in their terms of inquiry and an engagement with the attempt to understand the social-human consequences of their work are deemed essential for the advancement of social understanding.

Fassin declares himself to be advocating an approach to critique "that includes us—individually and collectively—and not one that leaves the social scientist alone outside the cave," yet he does not venture to question his own moral standpoint and critical practice.[40] He is overwhelmingly preoccupied with subjecting humanitarian culture to critique. He does not work to expose or debate with the values under which he operates. He does not involve his readers in questioning how his own work might be judged in terms of its practical consequences or human effects. Moreover, he does not offer any alternative mode of reasoning or moral action. Fassin's work seems to be entirely and exclusively geared to upholding critique as an end in itself. But can critique as an end in itself make an adequate contribution? We think not. Nor do we accept its assumption that the critic is above the fray, occupying a higher moral ground. We are all in this together—that is the message of this book.

In this regard, the odd reference Fassin makes to Emmanuel Levinas as offering an approach to ethics that operates "beyond any subjection . . . to humanitarian reason" is telling insofar as it opens up his work to the charge that his critique operates on a plane of metaphysical speculation.[41] Indeed, a common criticism leveled at Levinasian ethics is that it is anti-sociological and is sustained by a critical objection to the fact that humans exist in cultural and social context. It expresses a utopian desire to unmake ourselves as social beings and is enticed by the mythical notion that we might exist in a presocial and extracultural state of being.[42] When diagnosing the problems with our moral dispositions and behaviors, these are located in the inevitable and necessary limitations of our cultural standpoints and socially situated points of view. It would rather locate the source and justification for morality beyond the contingencies of social life and appeals to the trenchantly paradoxical notion that no culture should be permitted to define, and thereby set limits upon, the responsibilities we bear to others. Its critique is sustained by the enticement of metaphysics and the allure of transcendence; it tempts us to engage with an abstract mode of reflection that entertains the possibility that we might exist in, think from, and acquire our meaning beyond the conditions, compromises, and inherent messiness of human social life. While the supposition of "the view from nowhere" may appeal to some quarters of theology, it is untenable from a social perspective. Moreover, it might be argued that Levinas's own ethics requires a human response to the other who suffers; and if it is conceded that this requires an ethical response to human suffering that recognizes the value of caregiving and humanitarian assistance, we contend that this also serves to pull the rug from under Fassin's own cold-blooded above-the-common-key position.

By contrast, it is generally the case that those preoccupied with problems of social suffering operate from a standpoint that holds that human beings are intractably social. This understands our humanity to be immersed and bound in social life and that we have no existence apart from this. Here critical thinking must also be immersed in and proceed from the understanding of ourselves as immanently social beings. Accordingly, the concern for documenting the moral experience of people represents a commitment to understanding how individuals feel, think, and negotiate their actions in the contexts they are made to live, and this must be an encounter with social life in its flow and making, including how people endure, work through, and respond with care to troubling human conditions.

Social life is understood to be constituted by, and to inhere in, our moral experience of the world; and it is further held to be imperative for social scientists to think with and from the moral experience that they are subject to and in the act of creating in their work. It is for these reasons that those engaged in the attempt to document problems of social suffering tend to favor ethnography as their method of social inquiry. Ethnography is valued not only as a means to bear witness to people's lived experience but also for its potential to discomfit and unsettle the researcher.[43] Through their involvement and participation in local moral worlds, researchers such as Philippe Bourgois, Veena Das, Paul Farmer, João Biehl, Nancy Scheper-Hughes, Byron Good, and Mary Jo DelVecchio Good aim to acquire both social understanding and critical self-reflexivity. They hold that it is necessary to expose the values under which they operate as social scientists and, more important, the value conflicts that they are liable to arouse and agitate through their practices of knowledge production. They proceed from the conviction that it is only by raising the volume on the value conflicts and moral tensions that they occupy that it is made possible for them (and their readers) to engage in the struggle for social understanding.[44] And they understand, as we do, and as we have shown the humanitarian founders of the social sciences did, that social understanding is the ground for changing social conditions and for improving social existence, and therefore it is not sufficient in itself unless it leads to human action on the behalf of our fellow human beings.

THE HUMANITARIAN SOCIAL IMAGINARY AND THE CHALLENGE TO CARE

What is social life, and how should it be rendered as an object for study? To what extent should matters of moral feeling be involved in this? How should our moral feelings about human suffering be taken as a guide to social understanding? How should we act on such understanding? For those engaged in research and writing on social suffering, these are all ongoing questions of critical concern for which there are no final or satisfactory answers. Our sensitivity to problems of human suffering, particularly insofar as it involves us in vexed questions of moral meaning and in frustrated debates over the bounds of the moral responsibilities we bear toward others, is taken as a means to awaken human social understanding. Insofar as we are culturally disposed to feel for the suffering of others, it is assumed that we are also primed to think about how social life is met at the level of human experience; or rather, that we are hereby enabled to recognize how social life takes place as an enactment of substantive human values. The study of social life is understood to involve us in experiences, contexts, and connections that greatly matter for people and is thereby an intrinsically moral activity. It binds us in moral commitments to understanding people in terms of what makes their lives hold prime meaning and value in real-life settings of danger and uncertainty. Social inquiry is a high-stakes activity. It is a form of moral epidemiology; not only does it broker with the values by which we are disposed to relate to one another as human beings, but also with those enshrined in our depictions of the social

situations in which humanity takes its shape. It concerns the assignation of
value to humanity; and for the sake of upholding the value of humanity, it
must always be left open to question, revision, and review.

Where priority is given to social suffering as a means to study society,
the provocation of humanitarian conscience is taken both as a sounding of
social alarm and as a call to place conditions of social life radically in question. On this understanding, by charting the history of the portrayal of
human suffering as a humanitarian concern,[45] we are also documenting
the enlivening of social consciousness and social conscience. Humanitarian
impulse inspires the conscious realization of "the social" both as an object
for critical reflection and as a matter for care; and in this regard, a "humanitarian social imaginary"[46] has a vital role to play in the nurturing of our
social understanding.[47]

It is very likely that any movement to ally projects of social investigation
with humanitarian concern will invite criticism over the extent to which
these are left operating as a form of bourgeois class condescension or as
naively duplicitous props for political elites set on regarding people's suffering as no more than an unfortunate side effect of social arrangements that
should otherwise be portrayed as largely benign.[48] There is no doubt that
they will also be left vulnerable to the charge that, by lending succor to
humanitarian concerns, they are subject to the influence of sectional interests and thereby are liable to nurture ideological discourses in which some
people are designated as more or less deserving of our moral recognition,
compassion, and care.[49] Certainly, it is very likely that such work will garner
the disapproval of those who by their status as "academicians" and "scientists" consider themselves duty-bound to operate above the fray of politics
or the moral entanglements of everyday social life and are further moved to
cultivate dispassion as a mark of their professionalism (see chapter 2).

Research and writing on social suffering is bound to court all these criticisms and is vulnerable to all these negative judgments, for it aims to draw
social science in an overtly humanistic and humanitarian direction.[50] In
these quarters the commitment to social understanding is taken up as an
emphatically human concern. We have sought to underline the extent to
which it often incorporates a critical praxis in which a conscious attempt is
made to appropriate the controversies it generates in the promotion of its
causes and concerns. Research and writing on problems of social suffering

are always set to unsettle and provoke. Most obviously, insofar as it invites us to dwell on the harms done to people, conditions of great distress, and the most negative experiences of human pain, then in terms of its featured content it is designed and, perhaps, bound to disturb. For those committed to this endeavor, it is for the possibility of channeling such anguished disruption toward a greater understanding of society in terms of what matters for people that they engage with the risk of writing and for the sake of making this serviceable for the promotion of human care.[51]

At one level, the more recent "rediscovery" of social suffering and its setting within projects of social science might be located as part of a longstanding tradition of humanitarian social inquiry and social concern.[52] At another level, it can be cast as a radically new departure in the development of social understanding and in the practice of social investigation. In almost every instance practitioners are engaged in an attempt to unsettle and overturn conventions of social inquiry as currently established within the academy and within contemporary strictures of rational social science. We strongly disagree with much of Didier Fassin's assessment of this development, yet we stand in agreement with him on one point at least: namely, that by focusing on problems of social suffering, sociology and anthropology are brought to new ground and that here we may be witness to a significant reconfiguration of the bounds of social recognition and human understanding. We would also add, however, that, in contrast to Fassin, we should not be so much preoccupied with the culture of critique as we are with the challenge that is hereby leveled at social science as a practice.

Those involved in this work are committed to the production of knowledge about social life that makes a positive difference in how this takes place in practice. This is not just a venture in social understanding; it is also a calling to care in action. Studies of social suffering operate not only as a plea that we engage in the attempt at social understanding through an attitude of caring concern for the people featured in their texts but also for this to further inspire real practices of caregiving. Indeed, here the practice of caregiving is advanced as a locus for social understanding. The intention is to refashion the practice of social inquiry as a commitment to human care and for the promotion of caregiving as a valued activity in social life. This is what we identify as its most vital provocation.

6   Caregiving

Being cared for and caring for others is a necessary part of human life. We all have basic needs that can only be met through the kindness, help, and support of those who care for us. Particularly through the early and later years of our lives, the realization of our human dignity is dependent upon the quality of care we receive. Through care we are equipped to participate in social life, and in being cared for we are affirmed with recognition and value. In acts of care real things are at stake, including life itself. In relationships of care we are made present to each other and are there for each other. Emotions are invested and worked through and become the grounds of interpersonal solidarity.

In questioning what care involves people doing, the conditions under which care is practiced, who does the care work, and how well particular individuals and groups are cared for, we are set to examine the most elemental conditions of human sociality. A focus on care involves us in attending to relationships of vulnerability in which social values are dramatically exposed in terms of their human consequences and effects. Care settings engage people in social relationships that are saturated with moral meaning as well as material practices and symbolic acts central to lived moral experience. It is often the case that those being cared for are beset by urgent needs and are vitally dependent on the help, kindness, and support of their carers. Furthermore, in many instances the giving of care includes brute materiality: heavy lifting, physical support, and hard work. It exacts a heavy bodily and emotional toll on those doing it. It is a painstaking activity that requires considerable commitments of physical energies and a readiness to involve oneself in troubled and conflicted emotional situations. In this respect, like social suffering, caregiving makes unavoidable the interrelationship between subjectivity and society. Both point to the interpersonal space as the context where human life and life projects succeed and fail, where human beings endure. The practice of care brings considerable volume to the fact that social life takes place as an enactment of substantive human values and thus that it is inextricably moral and political.

Care is a critical issue for understanding how social life is made possible; but all too often a focus on real-life enactments of care reveals people struggling to fulfill their roles and commitments in contexts of social neglect. By attending to present conditions of care work and how this is distributed, we are liable to discover that in many instances social life is organized so as to hide its importance and degrade its value. Care workers are among the lowest paid in our economy, have little political power, and occupy positions of low social status. Full-time carers usually belong to the most socially underprivileged and economically disadvantaged groups in society.[1] Those engaged in the most time-consuming commitments and emotionally difficult and exhausting bodily acts of care tend to be women drawn from lower socioeconomic groups; and it is often the case that they also belong to segments of the population classified as immigrants or people of color.

A focus on who receives the best care and who is doing the actual care work brings a spotlight to contemporary power relations. It sets in bold relief the asymmetry between those who are most valued and those who are hardly valued at all.[2] At the same time that this exposes huge deficiencies in the moral conditions under which social life is governed and set into practice, it highlights the presence of powerful ideological forces that operate to cast debates over the meaning and value of care work to the margins of political concern.

These are among the reasons for Joan Tronto's contention that by venturing to develop a "care perspective" on society we are involving ourselves in "the most important form of contemporary radical political thinking."[3]

In this chapter we follow Tronto in regarding the quality of care given to and received by people as matters to set standards for our critical thinking about the character of our society and the values we live by.[4] We are not, however, so much concerned with the examination of care as an abstract ethical value or matter for utilitarian social policy debate but rather with the experience of how this takes place as a committed human relationship and vital social bond.

We bring a focus to *caregiving*. Our interest lies in *the doing* of care, that is, the visceral, muscular, and sensory work of caring for the health, well-being, and needs of others. In this we are concerned to extol the giving of care not only as a social value but also as a practice that is indispensable to the pursuit of social understanding. In this model, caregiving is treated as a method for getting at what holds social worlds together at the level of moral experience. The effort of building and rebuilding people's lives is taken as a means to acquire knowledge of society. We aim to advance a form of social inquiry engaged to the pedagogy of caregiving, that is, a "social science" that operates with the understanding that it is in the giving of care that we are equipped to piece together a knowledge of how social life is made possible, sustainable, and with a potential for human flourishing. We take caregiving as a *phronesis*[5] that offers the moral and practical wisdom for the art of living socially in networks and community.

In this concern we are advocating a *return* to a form of social investigation pioneered by Jane Addams and others associated with the settlement movement of the Progressive Era.[6] We take Addams's approach to social inquiry as an important illustration of the potential for caregiving to operate as a means to expose the moral texture of social life for understanding. The first part of the chapter reviews the principles that she set into action and explores some of the ways in which her manner of "doing sociology" was configured through her care for the neighborhood of the Near West Side of Chicago around Hull-House over the late nineteenth and early twentieth century.

Addams is of further interest to us here insofar as we understand that her marginalization as a "classical" social theorist and founder of American sociology is in considerable part connected to the extent to which, in its time, her commitment to caregiving was regarded as anathema to the ethos of the academy and the professionalization of social sciences. We hold that analyzing the motives behind the "politics of erasure" that was mobilized in response to Addams's work is important insofar as it serves to alert us to forces and strategies of opposition that still operate to distance and disassociate social science from caregiving. Exposing this history as an issue for critical reflection and debate is a necessary part of the movement to reestablish the pedagogy of caregiving as central to the pursuit of social understanding.

The second part of the chapter reviews recent attempts to rehabilitate projects of social investigation along the lines advocated by Addams through community-based participation research (CBPR). We offer a brief assessment of the progress made in this direction and some of the challenges faced by those working to fashion more "engaged" and "action-oriented" forms of social science. More directly, we explore and question the extent to which these are either alert to or motivated to involve themselves with the pedagogy of caregiving. Here we note that this rarely features as an explicit concern, and insofar as new projects of CBPR look back to the example set by Addams, this appears to be more with an eye cast to her concern with problem solving than to her radical social ethics and political philosophy.

Finally, we note the potential for contexts of social suffering to involve researchers in a heightened critical negotiation with the political meaning and moral consequences of their work but now with a focus on how this might be channeled toward caregiving. In this regard, we highlight the ways in which, perhaps more than any other discipline, medical anthropology is geared to cultivate and, more important, set into practice care work that is at the same time committed to expose social worlds as objects for critical reflection and analysis. Indeed, we argue that as far as contemporary social science is concerned, it may well be in the engagement between medical anthropology and social suffering that we uncover the most productive ground on which to rehabilitate the legacy of Addams.

JANE ADDAMS: CAREGIVING AS "DOING SOCIOLOGY"

Jane Addams's life and her achievements are the subject of many biographies.[7] Born into a relatively prosperous family in Cedarville, Illinois, in 1860, from an early age she was by no means inured to hardship by the trappings of her material privilege. Throughout most of her life, having contracted Potts disease (tuberculosis of the spine) as an infant, Addams suffered from poor health, and it is recorded that, particularly as a young woman, she often felt embarrassed by the "ugliness" of the physical deformity that resulted from this affliction. By the age of twenty-one, moreover, she was already well acquainted with tragedy, bereavement, and loss. Her mother died from internal bleeding after having fallen awkwardly while pregnant when Addams was just two years old. Four of her siblings died in infancy, and at the age of six she was further devastated by the loss of her sixteen-year-old sister, Martha, to typhoid fever and, when she herself was sixteen, by the death of a family servant, Polly, who had cared for Addams throughout her childhood. It was the sudden death of her father in the summer of 1881, however, from acute appendicitis, that left her feeling most shattered and bereft of life purpose; and it was shortly after this shock that Addams was struck down by a deep depression, which at the time was diagnosed as a severe case of neurasthenia. On Addams's own account, it is important to understand her outlook, motives, and character as being shaped from an early age by a profound sense of being left "unsheltered in a wide world of relentless and elemental forces."[8]

Along with most of her biographers, Addams held that such experiences played a significant part in nurturing her sympathy for the plight of the poor; but there was much more than a moral resolve born from grief involved in her decision to collaborate with her friend, Ellen Gates Starr (1859–1940), to found Hull-House on the Near West Side of Chicago in 1889 as a place where they, along with other like-minded individuals, might live as "neighbors" among the poorest members of society in an effort to craft the solidarity required to deliver actions to combat conditions of destitution and disadvantage. It is also widely noted that Addams was driven by a passion to establish a public role outside the domestic sphere for educated women like herself. In this regard, the causes and activities taken up by the residents at Hull-House were shaped by a belief that, due to the gendered division of labor and, in particular, their ascribed roles as carers and guardians of the household, women were particularly well invested with forms of moral experience that could be applied to caring for the conditions of society at large. Beyond this, Addams was influenced by Christian Socialism,[9] and she was inspired by the ways this movement served to institute practices of social care as a means to work at bringing desired forms of society to life. It is widely noted that while recovering from her mental health problems during a visit to England in the summer of 1888, she was particularly impressed by the work of Toynbee Hall,[10] a settlement house based in the slum districts of London's East End. On this point, however, it is important to note that Addams did not seek to affiliate her activities with any Christian organization, and on recognizing that the culture of Toynbee Hall in the late nineteenth century was shaped by an ethos of middle-class paternalism, she sought to distance Hull-House from the Toynbee model of social reform. Under Addams's direction, Hull-House was much more "egalitarian, more female-dominated, and less religious."[11]

Patricia Madoo Lengermann and Gillian Niebrugge observe that since her death in 1935 more often than not Jane Addams has become far more "a name learned in school [rather than] a mind to be reckoned with."[12] She has been celebrated as a "social reformer" and is often portrayed as the embodiment of the political spirit and moral idealism of the Progressive Era.[13] Following her campaign for peace during the First World War, for which, after much political controversy and hostile opposition, she was awarded the Nobel Peace Prize in 1931, she is also remembered as a "peace campaigner." Insofar as her activities have featured as matters of academic interest, more often than not, this has been with a focus on the ways in which these might be portrayed as a pioneering example of "social work."[14] Very little effort tends to be expended in the direction of understanding her methods, ethics, and philosophy and how these developed through her collaborative work at Hull-House. Moreover, it is largely forgotten that she understood herself to be involved in developing a practice of sociology, although it should be emphasized that Addams intended to direct this along an alternative path to that now established in most environments of the academy.

It was only toward the end of the twentieth century that scholars began to reappraise Addams's work as a "sociologist." Those concerned with rehabilitating Addams's status as a founding figure in sociology aim both to underline the role played by women in the creation of sociology and to bring critical scrutiny to bear upon the ideological forces at play in the construction of the history of the so-called classical period of the discipline, particularly insofar as this privileges the achievements of white male academics to the exclusion of those of women, African Americans, and immigrants working outside universities.[15]While reminding us that Addams was a founding member of the American Sociological Association and a frequent contributor to the *American Journal of Sociology* and that she wrote nine books of social theory and analysis, this work of recovery and revision also highlights the possibility of understanding the purpose, value, and practice of "sociology" under terms radically different from those advanced by most modern-day university courses and introductory textbooks.[16]

Working and writing at a time before the compartmentalization of social inquiry into separate fields of sociology, anthropology, social policy, and social work, Addams advocated an approach to studying social life that involved active participation in the lived experience of people's lives. She also maintained that this should be normatively geared to alleviate hardship, conflict, and suffering and that it should be intent on devising and setting into practice better ways of living together in society. On the model advocated by Addams, the conduct of sociology should not only be shaped by a commitment to social reform, but also by collaborative movements to bring humane forms of society into existence. She rejected the view that sociology should be developed as a professionally accredited "objective science." Moreover, insofar as social researchers working within universities were institutionally positioned to operate at an academic distance from the immediate realities of the subjects of their inquiries, she held that a proper knowledge of social life remained beyond their reach. Heavily informed by pragmatist teachings and philosophy, Addams's work can be approached as a practical and political realization of the philosophy of knowledge advocated by William James and John Dewey.[17] Addams held that social understanding could only be gathered through immersion in the *experience* of real-life conditions.[18] It required social researchers to operate in sympathy with individuals dealing with the practicalities of lived perplexities and everyday problems. Indeed, she stressed that working to empathize with people's subjective points of view was not only an indispensable component of social research but also a moral obligation without which it was impossible to grasp the reality of their social situation.

With these interests set to the fore, Addams's methods of social investigation involved a heavy investment in strategies designed to expose and unsettle her own class and cultural prejudices and those whose backgrounds were similar to hers.[19] In her writings she frequently refers to events that served to awaken her to the fact that she was a particular "social type" (i.e., an institutionally privileged, relatively affluent, well-educated, white woman) and that this not only shaped her way of seeing the world but also how she was set to be seen by others.[20] She aimed to equip and empower individuals living in the community around Hull-House to communicate their experience of the world. In *Twenty Years at Hull-House* (1910) she records that, on realizing that the Hull-House Settlement was regarded in some quarters as Addams's "sociological laboratory experiment" in living among the lowly, she always involved members of the neighborhood in public lectures on her work. Addams writes, "I never addressed a Chicago audience on the subject of the Settlement and its vicinity without inviting a neighbor to go with me, that I might curb any hasty generalization by the consciousness that I had an auditor who knew the conditions more intimately than I could hope to."[21] Moreover, in essays such as "The Subjective Necessity for Social Settlements" (1892) she contends that, on her model, the settlement aimed to "socialize democracy" and that this required a movement to create social environments in which people from different class and ethnic backgrounds could share together in the attempt to understand the problems of their community and the possible actions by which they might be best solved.[22] Such initiatives were based on the conviction that "much of the insensibility and hardness of the world is due to the lack of imagination which prevents a realization of the experiences of other people."[23] Addams argued that experiences "determine our understanding of life" and "the scope of our ethics."[24] She held that all too often, by the refinements of their education and the comfort of their material circumstances, many from privileged social and cultural backgrounds are made too removed from the experience of their poorer neighbors and are thereby unable to extend the empathy required to make possible social understanding. At the same time, she aimed to create social settings that made it possible for those deprived of the status and learning of the middle and upper classes to participate in attempts at problem solving, so that all would benefit from the experience of collaboration with others. As Charlene Haddock Seigfried notes, under Addams's direction the settlement aimed to set into practice transactions that "criticized top down approaches to problem solving in favor of working with others in a way calculated to change the attitudes and habits of both the settlement workers, mostly middle- and upper-class women, and members of the impoverished working-class neighborhood with whom they worked."[25]

In *Twenty Years at Hull-House* Addams explains how this culture of cooperation was founded on and sustained by caregiving. Hull-House was ostensibly set up to provide educational and social opportunities for the local community, but Addams and her associates quickly found that residing in one of the poorest areas of the city where most people of working age were employed in some form of sweatshop labor brought many desperate human needs to their door. She writes of the first days at Hull-House, "In addition to the neighbors who responded to the receptions and classes we found those who were too battered and oppressed to care for them. To these, however, was left that susceptibility to the bare offices of humanity which raises such offices into a bond of fellowship. From the first it seemed understood that we were ready to perform the humblest neighborhood services. We were asked to wash the new-born babies, and to prepare the dead for burial, to nurse the sick, and to 'mind the children.'"[26] Addams records that at first it was by creating space in Hull-House for the provision of child care in the form of a kindergarten that it subsequently won the affection and trust of the local community as a place for local gatherings to address more deeply entrenched problems of work and family life. Through actively caring for the most vulnerable members of the community, the residents at Hull-House were involved in attending to wider social needs; for, indeed, it was often the case that families were unable to provide adequate care for the young, sick, and elderly due to the harsh conditions under which adults were made to work and the squalor of their local tenement housing. While the creation of a public bathhouse, public kitchen, and coffeehouse further established Hull-House as a place of care for the body and the community, its activities were soon extended to include more far-reaching initiatives of collaborative social reform.

The Hull-House Women's Club, which was formed as a branch of the kindergarten, devoted itself to a campaign to clean the streets of garbage, filth, and dead animals, and eventually succeeded in persuading the city council to regularly organize the collection of refuse and to repair the streets. This success encouraged them to apply themselves to the task of improving the plumbing of tenement buildings so as to combat the insanitary conditions that contributed to epidemics of typhoid and dysentery as well as the overcrowding that helped tuberculosis to spread. Moreover, this ended in the successful criminal prosecution of landlords who failed to provide adequate housing for their tenants.[27] It is, however, in connection with their attempts to reform the culture and organization of the workplace that Jane Addams and her collaborators at Hull-House initiated some of the boldest and most controversial movements of care for those in their neighborhood.

Addams records that her involvement in actions to care for people in work and in campaigning for better conditions of employment began with the founding of the "Jane Club" in 1891. This provided young girls working at a local shoe factory with safe and cheap local apartments where they could board. At first these were rented out by Hull-House, but thereafter they were paid for by members of the club for themselves. Addams mentions that the initial impetus for the founding of the club came from the desire to support those striking for better pay and working conditions. The provision of an affordable place to live enabled the girls to participate in the strike without fear of being pressured to return to work by the threat of being turned out of their homes through periods of strike action when they had no money for rent.[28]

As Addams and her associates became more alert to the dangers and depravity of sweatshop work, especially in terms of its impact on the lives of women and children (some as young as four years old) working in the factories, they became more organized in their attempt to apply social science to the task of documenting people's living and working conditions so as to gather information for campaigns for social reform. Major studies of work and living conditions in the local area, such as *Hull-House Maps and Papers* (1895),[29] were among the arsenal of information that was used to campaign for legislation to protect the health and safety of factory workers and to help unions agitate for improved wages and shorter workdays. Indeed, insofar as Hull-House became associated with helping to organize trade unions, Addams notes that it was often portrayed in arenas of public life as a hotbed of "radicalism" and as a movement conspiring to undermine capitalist industry. Particularly in the aftermath of the Pullman strike of 1894,[30] which finally collapsed after federal troops were used to stop strikers obstructing the movement of trains (resulting in the deaths of

thirty strikers and the serious injury of many more), insofar as it was publicly identified as operating in "fellowship with trades-unions," Addams
records that "Hull-House lost many friends."[31] At the same time, in *Twenty
Years at Hull-House,* she contends that being brought into conflict with
"public opinion" and powerful interest groups was an inevitable and necessary part of caring for the suffering of those working in the local factories
and industry, especially insofar as it involved taking actions to protect the
most vulnerable members of the community from institutionalized cruelty,
socioeconomic hardship, and physical harm.[32]

In an effort to highlight the radicalism of Addams's approach to caregiving, Maurice Hamington notes that, while it was founded on embodied openness to the experience of others and material acts of care, it also
demonstrates how the practice of care may be channeled to promote policies and institutions that are attentive to human social conditions and
responsive to people's social needs.[33] Her caregiving operated not only for
the good of particular individuals but also for "the betterment of society."[34]
Addams and her associates involved themselves physically and emotionally in caring for people's health, well-being, and potential for flourishing.
It was exhausting, and on many occasions, difficult and upsetting work;
but it also made possible much comradeship and mutual social understanding. Here caregiving involved committed work of "active listening"
to others.[35] It also served to cultivate moral solidarities, practices of civic
participation, and friendships through which "caring knowledge" could be
applied in actions for the good of society as a shared corporeal concern.

It is also important to understand that Addams's caregiving courted
much public controversy, professional hostility, and political opposition.
Indeed, it might well be identified as the essential ingredient in her sociology that made it most unpalatable to many of those working to promote
social science within the academy. Mary Jo Deegan provides a detailed
breakdown of how Jane Addams and her associates at Hull-House were
increasingly brought into conflict with the University of Chicago and the
interests of key actors in its Department of Sociology.[36] She also highlights
the extent to which these hostilities were aggravated in large part by
Addams's social morality and her attempt to install this as a vital part of her
sociological practice. In her public and practical support for the trade union
movement, Addams was identified as a politically dangerous radical operat-

ing in opposition to leaders of the Chicago business community. This led the University of Chicago Board of Trustees to work at disassociating the university from any public support for her work, particularly insofar as a public endorsement of Addams and Hull-House was believed to place the funding of the academy at risk.[37] Deegan also contends that Ernest W. Burgess and (especially) Robert E. Park worked hard to set up an approach to sociology that was opposed to the values and methods advocated by Addams. On her account, Park was possessed by "a virulent ideology against social reform and 'do-gooders,'"[38] but beyond this, along with Burgess, Park was heavily invested in a movement to promote sociology as a "scientific" enterprise that operated above the fray of politics. Deegan holds that in writing their *Introduction to the Science of Sociology* (1921), a book that was widely adopted in American universities as the standard textbook introduction to the discipline, Park and Burgess were also engaged in a campaign to demote the intellectual standing of Addams's work (along with that of other women sociologists of the time, as well as men associated with the work of Hull-House) and to erase it from the corporate memory of the founding of sociology within the academy.[39]

It may be argued that with the creation of "social work" as a discipline of applied sociology and as a field of activity more heavily associated with women, Addams's sociological legacy was still afforded a place within the academy. More often than not, however, it is now generally conceded that social work was founded and developed on a set of principles quite different from those advocated by Addams. In its emphasis on "case work," "service provision," and "professional" assistance to individuals in need, modern social work operates more in the tradition of the Charity Organization Society than that of the settlement movement.[40] Addams herself declared that in their use of "moral means testing" and their concern to relieve poverty with charitable assistance and "friendly visitor" advice on how individuals living in dire circumstances should work at rehabilitating themselves, in their methods, ethical standards, and political beliefs "charity visitors" clashed "absolutely" with the values and practices of Hull-House.[41] In addition, insofar as Addams was not only committed to living as a "neighbor" among the poor and working alongside people to solve their problems but also helping to organize movements for large-scale social reform that brought her into open conflict with employers, landlords, politicians, university trustees, and cultures of hierarchy within the academy, her activities are regarded as too radical for modern social work.[42]

Our argument here is that, so as to grasp both the form and the enduring presence of the controversies generated by Addams's work at Hull-House, it is important to understand how these were coupled to her advocacy of a radical approach to caregiving. Through her manner of caregiving, Addams was cast as a politically subversive radical; even to a point where, in the Red Scare of the 1920s she was not only named at the top of a list of the "sixty-two most dangerous and destructive people in the country" that was presented to a Senate subcommittee investigating individuals who posed a threat to national security, but she was also featured along with other women sociologists from Hull-House in a Daughters of the American Revolution "spider web chart" denoting "dangerous citizens" operating as part of "un-American organizations."[43] It is also her commitment to caregiving both as a means to acquire social understanding and as a means to involve herself in collaborative acts of social reform that served to mark out her approach to doing sociology as radically opposed to the ethos and culture of that practiced within the academy. Indeed, while her advocacy of a sociology committed to caregiving was rejected by those working to advance sociology as an accredited "science," it also led Addams to distance herself and her activities from those of the academy. As Deegan explains, her decision to decline Albion Small's invitation to have Hull-House affiliated with the University of Chicago and to take up a half-time faculty position was due to Addams's reluctance to have her sociology disciplined to the rule of the University of Chicago's philosophy of education.[44] In addition to this, she feared that an association with the university would damage the moral meaning and practice of her work through its academic portrayal as a "sociological laboratory" experiment.[45] Quite simply, it was not only that she had no need for the status of an academician but also that she understood a great deal of the culture and practice of academic sociology to operate along lines that were antithetical to the practices of democratic citizenship, collaborative learning, humanitarianism, and social fellowship that she sought to promote through her work.

A NEW BEGINNING?

In recent years a considerable number of books and articles have been dedicated to announcing the renaissance of "community engagement" and "participatory research" in academic programs across the United States and Europe.[46] On many accounts, a renewed movement to promote community-based participatory research has taken root and is gathering force. This is particularly noticeable in the field of public health. Articles have been published on the value of CBPR as a method for assessing the social determinants of health and as a strategy for encouraging greater communal participation in health promotion initiatives.[47] It has also been taken up as a key concern for educationalists committed to fostering good community links between universities and their localities, especially where these come under political pressures to demonstrate their value to society as sites of privilege located in areas of social deprivation. There are many reports on "outreach initiatives" from universities that involve students and faculty in various "service learning" activities in their local communities.[48]

Jane Addams is frequently referred to as providing a model for this work.[49] She is often credited with being the first to put participatory research into action, and in noting her practices of democratic citizenship, practitioners openly declare themselves to be operating with the aim of revitalizing her politics and philosophy.[50] When introducing CBPR, authors tend to celebrate its value as a method that gathers together people from different social backgrounds with a common interest in solving a particular problem and/or improving a shared area of life.[51] A CBPR approach is lauded as a means to initiate and enact processes of civic participation. It is further argued that, when properly established and maintained, it holds the potential to expand the critical consciousness of participants, even to the point where they may be inspired to work together to transform fundamental social structures and relationships.[52] In all these respects, the pioneering work of figures such as Addams is referenced not only as a point of academic validation but also for its value as a guide for practice.[53]

Questions may be raised, however, about the extent to which new projects of CBPR are prepared to adopt Addams's critical standpoint and social morality. Indeed, in most instances, contemporary research does not venture to trouble itself with her pedagogy of caregiving. It is only on very rare occasions that the experience of caring for people and of practitioner involvement in actions to care for their needs is profiled as an explicit aim for the new generation of scholars engaged in participatory/action research. For the most part, technical considerations take precedence over any concern to establish and sustain social relationships of care. Rather than take their experience of conducting CBPR as a cue for critical reflections on the qualities and conditions of human relationships, more often than not practitioners are inclined to treat it as a model strategy for disciplining health-related behaviors or as a means to improve student test scores.

Mary Brydon-Miller and Patricia Maguire claim that as CBPR has become more widely established as a component of health promotion initiatives and as part of nonformal adult and teen education, it has often been disconnected from more critical traditions of social inquiry.[54] They argue that the new generation of practitioners tends to be possessed by a technocratic ethos that essentially commits CBPR to problem solving and is thereby not much concerned to provoke critical debate over unjust and inequitable social conditions.[55] More directly, Brydon-Miller and Maguire contend that rather than approach their research as "a political engagement" that warrants that practitioners question their own involvement in maintaining networks of power and privilege, the majority are inclined to treat it as a "formulaic strategy" for implementing more effective measures of social control.

Evidence to support this view may be found in articles that reflect on the difficulties of incorporating CBPR with strategies of health promotion and, in particular, where practitioners write with the aim of clarifying lessons learned through the experience of failing to achieve desired levels of communal participation and/or qualities of partnership. For example, when reviewing the possibility of developing CBPR as a "mainstream" strategy for "engaging multiple stakeholders" in health promotion initiatives designed to prevent and control cardiovascular diseases, Carol Horowitz and colleagues portray many of the conflicts and disputes encountered in the attempt to forge partnerships between academics and "at risk" communities as largely matters to be solved via further expert training in appropriate research methods and communication skills.[56] Similarly, when summarizing the successes and failures of a suite of public health initiatives in poor districts of Seattle that incorporated a CBPR approach, James Krieger and associates contend that where they sometimes found it difficult to recruit adequate numbers of people to participate effectively in their projects, this should be attributed to technical difficulties in their manner of conveying information to community partners and inefficiencies in the management and design of procedures for involving participants in decision making.[57]

In this setting, the example set by Nina Wallerstein and Bonnie Duran, which shows the ways in which CBPR initiatives are liable to be compromised by researchers' attachments to the culture of academy, is not so common.[58] Wallerstein and Duran argue that insofar as academics are endowed with "higher" social status and are apt to display educated conduct and manners of speaking, this can make "lower" status and less educated lay participants feel socially awkward and averse to collaboration. Beyond this, they contend that one of the main reasons for a breakdown in relationships of trust between researchers and their "partners" in the community lies in the extent to which scholars are identified as operating not so much in the interests of the community but more for the advancement of their university careers. Arguing in a vein similar to that of Diane Calleson and colleagues, they claim that where academics are institutionally and professionally committed to placing a priority on cultivating research partnerships that provide opportunities for advancing scholarship and furthering research funding applications, CBPR initiatives tend to be hamstrung by practitioners' mixed motives and conflicting value orientations.[59] On this view, while most scholars would think it culturally acceptable and even recognize themselves to be under a professional obligation to confront the shortcomings of their work by airing problems of method, by contrast, it is more of a taboo to take the frustration of failing to establish productive relationships with their community partners as a cue to critically question the cultural values and material interests that govern their profession.

Yet a preparedness to critically question, actively disrupt, and even break with academic convention and criteria of value may be required to establish an ethos and practice of care. Indeed, this is precisely what Helen Meyer and colleagues report as part of the "unexpected learning" that took place through their involvement in various "action research" projects that handed resources and initiative to students from socially deprived backgrounds so that they might define research problems and set terms of discussion in an exploration of their educational experience.[60] Meyer and colleagues report that among the more surprising discoveries made through establishing a more collaborative ethos in the classroom was that they found themselves to be nurturing social bonds of care. In this instance they arrived at the point of valuing their work not for the steps toward solving problems but rather for the "journey" into care for their students, as well as the mutual respect, empathy, and social understanding that this made possible. They emphasize, however, that on many occasions this required them to work at making themselves vulnerable to one another and to their students by openly confronting problems encountered in their own educational experience and also by confessing to ongoing tensions connected to their working values and motivations. In short, by disrupting their "front stage" performance as professional educators, students were made alert to their teachers' "backstage" nerves, self-doubts, and moral conflicts.

In light of the fact that care work and acts of caregiving, though vital and indispensable for social life, are frequently devalued or hidden as matters for serious academic and policy debate, Virginia Olesen argues that we should be particularly concerned to examine the contexts that determine our "socialization to ethical thinking."[61] She contends that we need to work at sensitizing ourselves to how we are being conditioned to think, feel, and act either with or without care for others. Certainly, it appears that when conducted with the aim of nurturing a critical self-reflexive orientation to one's social field and concerns, CBPR appears particularly well suited to serve this purpose. While Meyer and colleagues appear to have stumbled upon this discovery, this is precisely the recognition that guided Jane Addams in her work. As Erik Schneiderhan emphasizes,[62] while taking steps to distance the work of Hull-House from the economistic logic and paternalism of a "charity organization" approach to poor relief, Addams made a special effort to involve herself in relationships, physical activities, and social situations that brought a critical challenge to her cultural prejudices, traditional beliefs, and moral values. She took the view that she needed to take actions to disrupt and unsettle her own social condition so as to be open to understanding the social condition of others. Indeed, on his account, we should never allow her achievements in implementing measures of social reform to obscure the fact that this was driven by a passion to acquire greater human understanding and *social intelligence*. She was actively working to convert herself and her neighbors to a heightened level of social consciousness and, further, for this to be applied to the goals of communal solidarity and mutual care.

Schneiderhan would have us understand such conviction and sensibility as rooted and sustained in a conjunction between, on the one hand, her maternalist ethics and, on the other, her philosophical commitment to pragmatism. While acknowledging that her standpoint was heavily informed by her struggle to find a valued role in public life, he tends to explain Addams's modus operandi as largely a product of political conviction and moral outlook. On this point, Schneiderhan stands with a number of other commentators who when accounting for her project and method tend to dwell on her "purposeful idealism," as Louise Knight puts it, and its fashioning through a carefully considered process of ethical deliberation.[63]

On another tack, Christopher Lasch contends that while Addams was possessed by a moral sensibility cultivated through careful reading and reflection on the cultural malaise and social divisions of her times, we should not let this obscure the fact that, by her own testimony, she was shocked into action by a dramatic encounter with human suffering.[64] In a chapter titled "The Snare of Preparation" in *Twenty Years at Hull-House*, she takes steps to emphasize that it was the experience of participating in "slumming" in the East End of London,[65] that is, being taken as a "tourist" to gaze down from the top of an omnibus on the Saturday night sale of rotting vegetables to the poor, that left an indelible impression on her. Having witnessed the swaying crowd of desperate people with empty hands "clutching forward for food which was already unfit to eat" and one starving man tear into and devour a raw and decaying cabbage, she writes, "Perhaps nothing is so fraught with significance as the human hand, this oldest tool with which man has dug his way from savagery, and with which he is constantly groping forward. I have never since been able to see a number of hands held upward, even when they are moving rhythmically in a calisthenic exercise, or when they belong to a class of chubby children who wave them in eager response to a teacher's query, without a certain revival of this memory, a clutching at the heart reminiscent of the despair and resentment which seized me then."[66] In elaborating on the experience, she adds that she was further agitated and disgusted by the fact that, in the struggle to master her feelings, she was immediately prompted to indulge in literary reflections. Addams records that she was suddenly made painfully aware of the fact that she was caught up in a "hateful and vicious circle" in which she was guilty of using cultural reminiscences as a means "to cloud the really vital situation spread before our eyes." Paraphrasing Matthew Arnold, she goes on to confess that at this point she was deeply and irrevocably admonished by the understanding that "conduct and not culture is three fourths of human life."[67]

SOCIAL SUFFERING AS INCITEMENT TO CAREGIVING

In their review of CBPR as a radical "epistemological orientation" to research, Maxine Jacobson and Chris Rangeley's writing is distinguished by an emphasis on the extent to which the coupling of CBPR to critical social justice agendas takes place in contexts where practitioners have a shared experience of suffering.[68] They work to make clear that while radical traditions of CBPR are well established in countries in southern and eastern Africa and South America but remain a more peripheral concern in countries such as the United States and the United Kingdom, this is related to the different degrees to which researchers are apt to identify themselves as all in the same boat as victims of gross abuses of power, economic disparities, and social injustice. They argue that there must be a "foundational level" of corporate concern and interest. People need to be "joined with" one another in experiences of disappointment, distress, and abandonment. It is by sharing in the burden of social suffering that they are brought under the compulsion to question their social state and are driven to develop practices of mutual aid and communal care.

In the final analysis, our interest in problems of social suffering lies in the extent to which it might be rendered productive for this end. We take people's experiences of the brute fact of human suffering to be a necessary part of the dialectical process through which they may not only be critically awakened to their social condition, but also moved to care for others. Of course, as should be clear by now, we also understand that there are many other possible responses and reactions to human suffering and, indeed, that many of these are geared to operate as a means to obstruct the cultivation of social conscience, to distance "us" from ties of moral responsibility to "others," and to devalue and/or disable practices of care. People's sensitivities, interpretations, and moral responses to the problem of human suffering are heavily conditioned by cultural context and social circumstance. Throughout this book we have worked to frame a broad range of cultural and social possibilities with historical, sociological, and anthropological understanding. It is the case, however, that insofar as our efforts might serve as a spur to critical thinking and moral debate, our overriding aim is to promote the social value and practice of caregiving.

We hold that the "cash-value," as William James put it,[69] of research and writing on social suffering should be sought in the extent to which it serves to advance caregiving both as a response to human suffering and as an indispensable component of the pursuit of human social understanding. At the same time, we recognize that much of the work that takes place in this domain falls short of meeting these goals. A great deal of current research and writing on problems of social suffering seems to be more caught up in a protest against the conditions that do harm to people than in the task of devising more effective means to actively engage in caregiving.

Insofar as they remain mired in this pitch of protest, some have been moved to make clear the moral disquiet they experience through their conditions of research and manner of writing, particularly as these leave them in the role of "voyeurs" of human misery operating to collect and publish documents of human pain and distress. For example, at one point in her study of suffering endured by Latvians in their struggle to make sense of the damage done to their cultural history and identities under Soviet rule, Vieda Skultans confesses to be being burdened by the conviction that in accounting for people's experience within the cultural grammar of social science her actions were akin to "the well-fed anthropologist carrying out a participant observation study of famine."[70] Similarly, Pierre Bourdieu admits that in according a dominant role to the voice of people in his studies of social suffering published in *The Weight of the World* (1999), he was working to combat the "symbolic violence" that is done to their experience when it is appropriated as part of an "objectifying" script of social science.[71] Here Bourdieu explains that he intends his work to be a protest against established conventions of sociological understanding and the role of the contemporary sociologist as a morally detached "expert" and "scholar." Not only does he aim to provoke critical debate over the moral responsibilities that social researchers bear toward their subjects in the field; he also seeks to expose their role as agents of cultural reproduction that have a moral and political stake in shaping *"the way we look at* other people in ordinary circumstances of life."[72] Indeed, he declares that his ultimate aim is to fashion an approach to social research and social understanding by which it is made possible for the problems of "respondents" to become our own.[73] Bourdieu hankers after the remaking of sociology as a civic engagement and as a cultural movement untrammeled by "intellectualism" so that it is made to operate with care for people in their life context.[74]

These are among the reasons for the value that we place on medical anthropology, and particularly its more critical and politically engaged variants; for we hold that when compared to other disciplines and domains of social science, it is better equipped than most to advance the praxis of caregiving.[75] More directly, it is the fact that medical anthropology is configured around a meeting between, on the one hand, an applied engagement with health care and, on the other, a commitment to ethnographic method that is most important here. While possessing valuable knowledge, training, and skill to potentially make a practical and positive contribution to people's bodily experience and health conditions, practitioners are also engaged in processes of data collection and knowledge production in which they aim to share in people's lived experience and to participate in their way of life. At the same time that they are working to grasp and absorb "the insiders view of the world," they are involved in significant practices of care.[76]

An earlier form of anthropology as "care" can be found in Benjamin Paul's effort to integrate anthropology into public health. The case studies in his *Health, Care, and Community* (1955) show ethnographers seeking to integrate local knowledge and practices into public health intervention programs to make them more culturally congruent and thereby more effective in improving local health conditions. These applied anthropological efforts did not extend to an idea of social care.[77] Over the past two decades, a small but rising cohort of medical anthropologists has included social and cultural anthropologists who are also physicians and public health experts. This cohort straddles medicine and social science. Its members notably include the current president of the World Bank (Jim Yong Kim), as well as arguably the leading figure in global health (Paul

Farmer), and researchers who have situated their work at the intersection of clinical interventions and social inquiry.[78] Humanitarian assistance and human rights activities are led by such scholar-practitioners, as are some of the most notable activities in global public health, including, for example, programs focused on providing care for poor patients with multi-drug-resistant tuberculosis, AIDS, and chronic noncommunicable diseases like diabetes and cancer, as well as mental illness.[79]

Obviously, the dual training in medicine and social science legitimates and empowers these researchers to build professional caregiving activities into social programs that include such things as the accompaniment by community workers of patients taking complex and dangerous treatments (Rwanda, Peru), postearthquake relief and reconstruction among those most deeply traumatized (Haiti), and caregiving activities with special populations, such as prisoners with tuberculosis in Siberian prisons and vulnerable people in postconflict settings (Rwanda). These projects are simultaneously social and medical. They build out of ethnographic knowledge projects that are explicitly meant to help the most vulnerable people who are beset by the cascading of deep poverty and deadly infectious diseases. The projects are also meant to generate knowledge that can assist communities and the individuals in them to better understand the social problems they face and to partner resources and practices that can make a difference in people's lives. Not all medical anthropologists work in this way; and yet the MD-PhD cohort offers a particular kind of model in which implementation of interventions is as important as generating social knowledge; and non-MD anthropologists now work in this way as well.[80] Indeed, global health in this mode is reset as a resocializing biosocial field. Local knowledge and global social theory complement each other with the explicit goal of delivering services that in many areas of the world are backlogged and balked.[81]

One of us (AK) developed such a pilot project in China, immediately on the heels of the greatly destructive Cultural Revolution.[82] In 1980, at the then Hunan Medical College, formerly (and again now) the Yale-in-China Medical School, we investigated the traumatic consequences of mass violence on the lives of intellectuals, cadres, and workers who had developed symptoms of neurasthenia. The one hundred individuals studied suffered from dizziness, deep fatigue, and pain, among other complaints. Almost all were disabled. Few had recovered or received any lasting professional medical benefit. They were accompanied by family members and friends— many of whom were worn out and frustrated by the years of failed quest for therapy of any kind. The upshot of the study, which extended over several years, was to show that although patients could be rediagnosed as suffering from clinical depression and related psychiatric conditions, their somatic complaints did not improve with conventional treatment until they had resolved work, family, and political problems that had become inseparable from their debilitating symptoms in long, drawn-out social courses that were as much life history as disease syndromes. The cardinal complaints themselves were a threnody performed as a cultural bereavement for a lost time.

The social knowledge became part of the interviews and life stories. "You listened to me. No one else did. You heard what I said. You helped me say it. You showed you cared for me. I felt better just talking to you. I always wanted to thank you for that," several wrote years later. Not all; and yet a surprising number got better in the course of the research, which increasingly became a mutual exploration of the great danger and personal and collective injury they suffered. Some of the lessons learned were carried over to the treatment of other patients with neurasthenia in the Medical School's Second Affiliated Hospital.

The Chinese psychiatrists who participated in the study were surprised and concerned by the research: both because of its social process and because of the type of knowledge it was utilizing, which struck them as only partly medical. They realized that they were part of the story. Some of them shared the symptoms, and almost all had been injured by the mass violence. The stories of suffering were ones they could and did share, deepening the witnessing and bringing a compassion that was rare at that time in clinical work or societal interactions. The purpose of the research was as much caregiving, it is now clear, as it was a quest for social wisdom about how ordinary people get through a terribly destructive era. Symptoms, both bodily and emotional, offered medical legitimation for treatment that included social care, otherwise unavailable and disguised as medical intervention.

We acknowledge that it may be possible to shape ethnographic research techniques to the practice of caregiving without the researcher being actively involved in medicine or possessing professional training in some formal discipline of health care, like nursing, occupational therapy, and clinical social work, where such efforts are taking place. Indeed, we recognize that some of the most impressive ethnographies in medical anthropology have been written by social and cultural anthropologists who are not trained clinicians but have committed themselves to ethnography as a caregiving form of knowledge generation and use.[83] These works make many valuable contributions to a search for wisdom in the art of living, through caring for their subjects and using what they learned through research to dignify and uplift their fellow beings. There is still, however, something of great importance to underline in the more formal engagements between anthropology, medicine, and clinical study: namely, the particular urgency that is brought to the ethics of social practice.

In their review of the history and development of medical anthropology, Hans Baer and colleagues note that this is particularly distinguished by a concern to debate and clarify moral codes and behaviors.[84] This is due to the fact that in their work, practitioners are not only repeatedly being confronted with real experiences of human affliction, misery and distress, but also by the moral imperative and practical opportunities to apply their skills and training to take actions to secure processes of healing, recovery, and regeneration. In their praxis they are directly involved in many morally challenging situations in which it is made all too clear to them that by their actions they hold the potential to either do good or harm. While other disciplines might readily find the space in their work to entertain dichotomies of theory and practice and to separate thought from action, by contrast, in medical anthropology this is either severely curtailed or totally denied. More often than most, its practitioners are immersed in contexts of social suffering where their actions hold great consequence for what really matters for people, and even life itself. Implementing effective services so that they can be generalized to poor populations at risk can bring needed technology via community accompaniment in a human way to bear on some of the great threats to health of our era, and to do so with care complementing prevention and with social good as an outcome.

It is here that we identify developments taking place that come close to rehabilitating the approach to social understanding first pioneered by Addams, an approach in which knowledge is sought through "the doing" of care and where there is a ready understanding that this is only gained through an intimate involvement in the deep perplexities, hardships, and miseries of people's lives. Here it is also important to take note of the fact that in their manner of work, medical anthropologists are also more motivated, and more *legitimated,* than most other academics to move beyond the environs of the academy. In this regard, they are presented with rare opportunities for molding a social research practice beyond the disciplinary reach of the academy and also a more obvious and greater demand for this to be informed by the pedagogy of caregiving. We don't present this example as an exception; it is for us an illustration of how the rest of social science can encompass the implementation of social care as an intended outcome.

CONCLUSION

A passion for society requires that we do more than expose the social conditions that bring harm to people. It also calls us to actively involve ourselves in movements to deliver the care that makes possible their recovery and healing. At the same time that we embark on a quest to understand the embodied interpersonal experience of local social worlds, we must be engaged in practices to make people's living conditions more socially beneficent and humane. Moreover, not only does this involve us in a moral commitment to do good to others; it also involves us in efforts to acquire the social wisdom that is only made possible through caregiving.

It is important to understand here that we hold this to be more than a matter of political calling or expression of humanitarian resolve; we also contend that this is the route toward proper social understanding. In this respect, we hold a considerable portion of the knowledge of society produced within the academy to be morally deficient and lacking in human substance. Quite simply, it cannot serve as an adequate means to make known how people socially experience, morally inhabit, and embody their world. It also fails to trouble researchers and students over the moral and political values they are enacting through their institutional conduct, modes of disciplinary study, and manner of academic writing and further how these might often be implicated in the perpetration of considerable social harm.

In their introduction to participatory research Randy Stoecker and Edna Bonacich work to make clear that to engage in efforts to democratize the production of social knowledge and to apply this to the task of empowering disadvantaged and oppressed peoples with the means to positively change their lives, we must not flinch from making clear the social values we either choose or, rather, are *made* to live by. Moreover, as far as the institutional cultures of contemporary Western universities and the configuration of the social sciences within them are concerned, it may well require us to begin from a position where we acknowledge that in the pursuit of social justice, much that takes place here is more a part of the problem than any solution. Indeed, they contend that disciplines such as sociology are often to be found operating as "one more element in the structures of control that maintain oppression and exploitation, sustaining a class of professional experts who are linked to those with power and who proclaim what is legitimate knowledge, thereby drowning out the knowledge of those who lack power."[85] We would also add here that it certainly is the case that this tends to be divorced from any concern with practices of caregiving and the creation of effective relations of care in society.

Care does not feature as a privileged matter for debate within either "classical" or "contemporary" traditions of anthropological and sociological inquiry; and as far as the latter is concerned, it is almost entirely absent as a recognized component of social life. While it might be argued, moreover, that later developments of the "sociology of the body" and the "sociology of gender" as distinct fields of study signal a new disciplinary openness to issues of care, it is still the case that it is never addressed as a core topic for analysis within contemporary social theory.[86] At best, care remains a peripheral and specialist area of medical sociological and medical anthropological interest. While care in practice may be studied by those seeking to apply social science to issues of health and medicine (especially with a focus on the conduct of nursing) and while the organization and funding of care provision is debated as an issue of social policy, care is not identified as a vital matter of interest within studies of society and social experience at a broad level of concern. In this regard, the "revolutionary" impact of the so-called feminist ethics of care has not been felt much beyond a fringe community of moral philosophers and associated scholars invested in the task of reforming practices of social work or with criticizing the quality of professional care provided for marginalized groups of vulnerable people.[87]

In this environment it remains the case that Addams's approach to "doing sociology" is only of interest to those with a dissident view of contemporary social science. Her legacy is most likely to feature as part of an arsenal of protest against the institutionalized conventions, presiding values, and professionalized practices of social research and its favored methods of knowledge production. Very few are disposed, are permitted, or have the courage to take this as an imminently realizable model for their practice. Indeed, as we have already sought to emphasize, there is evidence to suggest that it is only in contexts where social suffering is plainly abundant and where there are meager opportunities for social researchers to keep themselves cocooned in positions of institutional and material privilege that Addams's example is embraced as a guide to social understanding.

We are left with the fragile hope that current initiatives in medical anthropology will be further nurtured as part of institutional arrangements configured for a renewed caregiving approach to understanding human social life. By itself, however, this is unable to deliver either the scale or the full substance of the reforms we are looking for. In order for these to be more widely recognized as matters of urgency, it is very likely that it will take much more than the inspiration to be drawn from outlying examples of caregiving social science in practice. Ultimately, it may only come where it is made painfully clear that the current setting of social science education and social research within the modern university is both inadequate and unsustainable. Indeed, one of the more worrying lessons to gather from the history of social science to date is that, more often than not, its human value and practical worth for living well with others are only grasped at the point where social conditions have fallen to a desperate state.

Conclusion

In our era, we tend to see all human problems as those of individuals. We ask why did he or she pull the trigger, run away, become infected with HIV, commit suicide, join a radical Islamist group. The moral space of the individual—as a source of problems, as the root of resistance, as responsible for resilience or defeat—has increased greatly. Reporters interview victims of natural disasters or political violence and ask, how did that make *you* feel? Stories of war, genocide, religious conflict, and street violence that we seem most comfortable listening to are about what a person or a few family members saw or did. Even policy experts when responding to a "crisis" like the Ebola epidemic or the failure of the war on drugs are more comfortable telling stories about particular victims to explain group statistics on vulnerability than addressing the "crisis" in social structure, social relations, social institutions, and society as a whole that contribute to those problems. They can make us understand what is at stake for a particular person or several family members; yet what is at stake for society cannot be articulated in the same way to mobilize our moral indignation and readiness to act. We have lost sight of "the social question"; we don't feel the weight of placing "the social" in question. It has become a fuzzy concept, an abstraction that seems far removed from real persons who possess real needs and do real things. It has been morally neutralized.

In other periods of modern society, however, "the social" and its "question" were matters of passionate concern. In nineteenth-century Western Europe and the United States, "the social question" held currency as a term to evoke the misery of the poor and was taken as an open invitation to debate what should be done to ameliorate their condition and alleviate their plight.[1] The same held for twentieth-century China and India. In this context the social was recognized as being infused with moral meaning; it was taken as issuing a call for actions to combat human suffering and for there to be an urgency of care for humanity. As Hannah Arendt sought to emphasize in her famous essay on the revolutionary character of this matter, "the social question" aroused "the passion of compassion";[2] it served to aggravate dispute over the social meaning of human misery and involved people in questioning how they should negotiate with the upwelling of moral feelings aroused before the spectacle of collective affliction. In questioning the social and by setting priority on it as a "problem" for public concern, individuals engaged humanitarian sentiment and how this should serve as a guide to understanding and action. Here "the social question" signaled a radical transformation in how many people were disposed to think and feel about the hardships and pains of others. Traditions of religious theodicy were being superseded by debates over the social causes of human misery.[3] Human suffering was no longer being addressed as a problem for religious instruction or spiritual healing; rather, it was being taken as a moral outrage in demand of social investigation and concerted efforts at social reform. In Britain, France, and Germany, "the social question" was the preoccupation of new "social movements" intent on combating the immiseration of populations caught up in the maelstrom of capitalist industrialization.[4] In America, the urgency with which people engaged with this matter was intensified by the struggle to rebuild society out of the rubble of vicious civil war. The May 4th Movement in China (1918), similarly, called for a renewal of the nation in terms of science and democracy; and in India the anticolonial movement also turned on understanding colonialism as the issue. In both cases, people engaged what they took to be the social question. In these contexts it was generally understood that social life takes place in enactments of substantive human values and that in these enactments lies the possibility of rebuilding society for the good of humanity. "The social question" brought volume to our moral responsibility to care for the suffering of others; and it further emphasized the need for the implementation of caring actions to deliver humanitarian social reform: in Europe, for immiserated urban poor; in the United States, for freed slaves and the families of 750,000 dead soldiers; in China, for "the Sick Man of Asia" who was perceived as being dismembered by colonial powers; and in India, for the unfree whom the Raj had allowed to suffer famine and the privations of wars that were not theirs.

A range of factors are identified as having made the social far less questionable and at the same time transformed its meaning and set it within a distinctly new frame of reference and under new rules of cultural exchange. Some of these are related to subsequent advancements made toward alleviating the worst effects of poverty, extending state welfare provision, and widening the bounds of citizenship and people's civil and social rights. There is no doubting the fact that, at least as far as the more developed industrial nations are concerned, a great deal of the original urgency of "the social question" was removed as improvements were made to the quality of people's housing conditions, workplace environments, and basic health. As a matter of Western public debate, "the social question" was relegated farther down the list of priorities, the more it appeared that industrial societies were no longer courting revolutionary social upheaval through the brutal treatment of workers, the threat of mass starvation, or the health catastrophe of insanitary living conditions. There is also, however, a distinctly ideological component to this story that is related to the conditions of knowledge production that prevailed within the development of "social science" as an accredited profession and the terms under which it was established within the academy as a set of disciplinary concerns.

It is now widely acknowledged that the early development of the disciplines of sociology, social policy, and anthropology was wedded to a "scientizing" mission that, more often than not, sought to divest itself of humanitarian sentiment.[5] Here it was generally accepted that the disciplined study of society should be divorced from moral feeling and, in order to be taken seriously as "science," should locate itself above the provinces of do-gooderism and its dispensation of "indiscriminate charity." Practitioners of social science were to engage with their object of study with studied disinterest and to refrain from moral judgment, for their credibility and authority would rest on the extent to which they succeeded in presenting themselves as immune to the distortions of sensationalism and the corruptions of interpersonal sympathy.

In this setting "the social question" was reconfigured through the discipline of "science." While on the one hand the development of social survey techniques, social statistics, and refined social taxonomies served to bestow credibility and authority on "social science" as equipped to provide an "objective" view of society that stood above mere opinion; on the other, it served to establish "official talk" about social life as though it did not matter directly for people: it was designed to be void of moral sentiment and to operate with no sympathetic attachment to persons. The pursuit of social understanding within the disciplinary regimes of "social science" entailed a revolutionary transformation in terms of social representation. As a condition of their licensing as "science," such disciplines would have no part in the social question as originally conceived, and it was in their interest to portray it as a matter for disparagement.[6]

At its origins some moved to protest against this development and worried over the depreciation of humanity that was being demanded as the cost for academic recognition. In America figures such as Jane Addams and Albion Small, while at first celebrating the potential for sociology to operate in conjunction with projects of humanitarian social reform, increasingly found themselves at odds with its culture and values. As Addams came to recognize the new scientific sociology as having little or no interest in making the world a better place in which to live, and as moving to celebrate its existence in terms of the pursuit of knowledge as an end in itself, she took steps to disassociate her manner of doing sociology from the newly founded Chicago school.[7] For his part, the more Small found his original vision for the discipline corrupted by academic careerism and an ethos of detachment, the more he was inclined to regard his involvement in the founding of American sociology as making him party to the creation of a "Frankenstein's monster."[8] The early Boasian cultural anthropologists Paul Radin and Edward Sapir similarly resisted the scientific movement in sociology and its influence on anthropology, which they feared would lose its concern for existential human experiences.

For most of its history, and especially since its inception within the academy, Western social science has been largely unconcerned with associating itself with projects of humanitarian social reform. Largely, and especially when engaged in abstract debate on a grand scale, social theorists have seen no cause to treat the meanings and qualities of human care as a principal concern and have expressed no interest in how caregiving is either carried out in real-life settings or made possible in practice. Moreover, through the course of their training, most students would not be presented with the contention that it is by the cultivation of social sympathy that they stand to acquire social understanding or that they should be particularly concerned to have their learning about society shaped by active participation in caring for the suffering and needs of others. More often than not, the virtues of sound methodology are portrayed in terms of the extent to which they locate the practice of social research above the conflicts of daily moral experience and beyond the fray of public quarrel.

Over the past century, it is only on rare occasions that sociologists and anthropologists have been moved to identify their motivations and interests in terms of a deliberate attempt to alleviate human suffering and to promote humane conditions of society. In this regard, at the same time that figures such as Margaret Mead and C. Wright Mills are celebrated for their championing of the potential for anthropology and sociology to be made attentive to the harms done to people in lived experience and to be fashioned for the pursuit of human healing and progressive social change, they are distinguished by their exceptionality and by the extent to which they operated against the tide of their times. They disrupted academic convention and embraced the social question in a manner closer to its original form. They were intent on reinitiating social inquiry as a passion for humanity and as a humanitarian endeavor committed to improving people's life conditions and terms of association.

We understand ourselves to be living through a period when forces shaping the conduct of academic social science are perhaps more disposed than ever before to making it morally sterile, practically worthless, and void of human passion. The market imperatives governing neoliberal universities and the purely utilitarian standards that dictate the terms of value on academic achievement tend to afford little space for the nurturing of social understanding as a commitment to human care and the promotion of humane society.[9] So much of academic life is now regulated by the drumbeat of careerism, the relentless marketization of education, and the pursuit of utilitarian efficiency and sheer bureaucratic indifference. Yet at the same time there is potential for the ever intensifying moral and political conflicts aggravated under the struggle to endure these conditions to provoke people into acts of resistance.

Important disruptions and countermovements are taking place that hold out the possibility of restoring vitality to the social question as a pressing human concern and on a renewed scale. Many of these have been fired into life by the provocations encountered in meeting "the problem of suffering" in our times, the knowledge of which is more abundant than ever before in human history. There is a renewed urgency to make social science responsive to global conditions of human tragedy and to the harms met in lived experience. Debates over the character, value, and purpose of social science are far from being settled; and it is often readily understood that the social science we have is not the one we need.

In this book we have reviewed some of the ways in which a focus on social suffering holds the potential to inspire a new approach to social theory and practices of social research. It is our hope that it also contains material that is useful for the cultivation of the moral resolve to inspire the pursuit of social understanding through real acts of care for others. While each chapter might be read as a discrete report on a pressing issue or analytical theme, the book has been organized in a sequence that invites reflection on how the points of analysis developed in earlier parts inform the logics, terms of emphasis, and critical concerns featured in later parts. There are some lines of argument running throughout the book that have served to shape our interests and to guide our writing. These may be summarized as follows.

First, we contend that in attempting to understand the peculiar character and lived experience of the problem of suffering, we are addressing a concern that determines our personal and social being. We are set to work at understanding how social life matters for people in the extreme; and under such desperate and trying circumstances the values enshrined in human conduct are made raw. In bringing a focus to the ways people in different times and places struggle to endow suffering with positive meaning and in documenting the actions taken to counter its harmful consequences and effects, we are gathering insights into how human social life is forged as an intensively moral experience. We are also presented with opportunities to grasp how the problem of suffering, as met in experience, operates to alert us to our social circumstance and cultural condition. In this respect, the particular ways in which individuals manifest and address their experience of suffering, as well as the quality of efforts taken by others to respond to their plight, are recognized as holding the potential to expose our social character and cultural state. In research and writing on social suffering it is generally held that by concentrating on the ways individuals struggle to make suffering productive for thought and action, we are particularly well positioned to gather insights into the moral character of social life, especially in terms of its human consequences. We understand the originators of social inquiry and the progenitors of social science to have envisaged understanding that would respond to serious social problems by improving society and human conditions. The professionalization of social science has marginalized these founding values such that social science has itself become marginal to the great issues of social life: practical, moral, political.

Second, we maintain that the origins of social suffering, as a distinct form of cultural representation and as a category of human understanding, are intimately linked to the modern discovery of "the social" as such. Here many painful interpersonal problems, existential anxieties, and embodied traumas that would otherwise preoccupy individuals with issues of providential meaning and the parameters of divine action are instead channeled toward debates over how to characterize conditions of *social* life, the morality of *social* conduct, and the human consequences of our *social* organization. In this context, we are challenged to identify and explain the peculiar conjunction of circumstances that made it possible for people to take suffering not so much as a cue for theology but rather as a provocation to engage with questions of social cause and societal response. Max Weber provides us with valuable insights into the existential dimensions of the cultural changes involved in the creation of the secular space for thinking and acting in social terms, particularly where he focuses on the propensity for the intellectual logics set within Western traditions of Christian theodicy to play themselves out in this secular social direction. Weber's account also invites further investigation of the ways in which the lived experience of material conditions, technological advancement, political events, and, not least, the brute fact of suffering itself served to make people more pragmatically geared to attempts at social reform. In our account, moreover, an emphasis is brought to the pivotal role played by the dynamics of cultural emotions and social sentiment. The development of social consciousness and of a shared desire for the acquisition of social understanding is inspired by shifts in intellectual and practical orientation. Yet it is also vitally important to recognize the extent to which this is sustained by forces of moral feeling, and in particular those of humanitarian conviction. Here there is no doubting the fact that modern religious cultures have contributed a great deal to the relative ways in which moral sentiment has been cultivated and expressed through modern history, but many other social and cultural forces, particularly in connection with the advance of "civilizing processes" and media technologies that render the lived experience of suffering more widely visible, are heavily implicated in the development of prevailing cultures of humanitarian feeling. Indeed, on this view, we are particularly concerned to attend to the distinct ways in which shared understandings of social life and experience are made possible through our cultural propensity to feel for the suffering of others.

Third, we argue that humanitarian culture has made a vital contribution to the cultivation of modern social consciousness and that in this respect it is intimately involved in the development of social understanding. Research and writing on social suffering operates within a peculiarly modern tradition of inquiry where human experiences of pain and distress are identified not only as serving to expose the reality of social conditions in terms of the harms they do to people but also as issues that, when brought to public attention, hold the potential to mobilize social bonds. Notwithstanding the fact that social sentiments born from the witness of suffering may be appropriated in the service of ideological agendas and in the enactment of exploitative relationships, such sensibilities are also held to be an integral part of the cultural process whereby it is made possible for us to relate to others with social conscience and fellow feeling. In this regard, a critical praxis, in which social researchers are made to broker with many unstable emotions and value conflicts through their attempts at documenting events and experiences of human suffering, is taken up as a necessary part of the attempt to make known the antihuman social conditions under which many people are made to live. This invites further sociological and anthropological study of the role played by modern expressions of humanitarianism in the cultivation of social consciousness. It also challenges us to identify how humanitarian motives, sensibilities, and actions can be applied to the methods by which we venture to acquire valid knowledge of human social life. In no way should this blind us to the misadventures of humanitarian programs, the repeated failures of programs that are poorly grounded in local worlds or that misconstrue what is locally at stake for participants, and the inadequacy of good intentions to address structured violence that is unexamined via critical reflection and evaluation. Nor do we discount Weber's appreciation of the human failure of bureaucracy. On the contrary, we believe that social suffering and caregiving make these failures more visible and approachable.

Fourth, we are commending an approach to social inquiry that stands opposed to the view that researchers should work at presenting themselves as dispassionate experts operating above the fray of morality and politics. All social life takes place as an enactment of substantive human values, and the practice of social research, as much as any other social practice, involves us in unavoidable commitments of value. The proper development of our social understanding requires us to acknowledge ourselves as passionate beings and to be motivated by a passionate concern for understanding the social lives of others. More directly, this should make us particularly attentive to the moral experience borne through our interactions with other people, particularly where this makes us troubled by conflicts of value, ruptures of attitude, and matters of practical perplexity; for here there are opportunities for us to be made particularly alert to the human interests at stake in social life. In this regard, following C. Wright Mills, we are interested in the potential for social research to be redeveloped as a venture in critical pragmatism. Perhaps more than Mills, however, we take seriously Williams James's injunction that the "cash-value" of ideas should be sought in the experiences they make possible and in how they are mobilized in practice. We are wary of the potential for the work of critique to operate as an end in itself and for this to hold no value beyond some rarefied domain of intellectual abstraction. Our interest lies in what we should do and how we should live so as to bring desired forms of society into existence. Moreover, it is due to the fact that more interactive methods of social inquiry, and ethnography in particular, involve researchers in examining how their conduct is involved in the creation of the experiences they aim to document that we consider them to hold particular value for the type of social understanding we are seeking to develop. This should not be taken as a standpoint opposed to the application of quantitative methods to the documentation of aggregate social conditions; but it certainly aims to accentuate the value of social research that profiles how social life is encountered, negotiated, and made in human experience.

Fifth and finally, we are arguing for the practice of caregiving to be regarded not only as a matter to expose social values for critical debate but also as a valued means to acquire knowledge of social life. The practice of care is particularly important to us insofar as it often involves an attempt to alleviate some form of suffering and is thereby frequently addressed to the social and cultural conditions that cause people damage, pain, and distress and that are obstacles to the implementation of intervention programs. Through the effort to care for others we are immersed in problems of social suffering in contexts of health care and settings of critical social need. It is frequently the case that care in practice, and perhaps even more in conditions of social suffering, involves carers in many moral dilemmas concerning the human consequences of their actions. Social life as a human matter is rendered intensively distinct as a critical and practical concern. Moreover, given that, more often than not, care work is poorly paid, is treated as a low-status activity, and is carried out by lower-class women, often of color, with few employment options, in dramatic terms it serves to expose presiding hierarchies of value and structures of power relations. In our critical thinking about society we aim to profile the people who do care work, the conditions under which they carry this out in practice, and how they are valued; and further, we aim to enshrine the place of caregiving in society as a key matter for political and moral debate. By setting this as a prime concern, we also intend to involve ourselves, as practitioners of social science, in critically questioning our roles, values, and activities in terms of their contribution to the task of realizing social conditions in which all people are adequately cared for. Here we take the pioneering example of Jane Addams as a demonstration of how methods of social inquiry, and the criteria of value placed on the human knowledge this makes possible, might be rooted in a concern to understand and alleviate problems of social suffering. Social care must be as important for policy analysis and program planning as are issues of cost benefit;

and a commitment to cost benefit is inadequate and distorting when social suffering and social care are excluded from practical consideration.

In sum, then, this book has traced a line of criticism of how social science has absconded from conditions of social suffering and practices of social care that were central at its origin via the discontent of Max Weber, Jane Addams, C. Wright Mills, and others who were passionately struggling to create a more human form of social knowledge that was more responsive to people's actual lived experiences. This line of social critique calls into question the development of social science.

THE CHALLENGE AHEAD

We aim to promote and institute a new project of social science. We recognize, however, that on many fronts this is likely to encounter opposition and resistance. Some are bound to take issue with our arguments on intellectual grounds. No doubt others will dismiss our critical standpoint and practical concerns as politically unacceptable. It is also the case that within current configurations of academic social science, those researchers, writers, and teachers who may be disposed to welcome this book as an encouragement to their work are most likely to be preoccupied by issues that are marginal to mainstream interests.

At various points we have underlined a commitment to include the institutional settings and practical conventions of social science in any venture to render prevailing conditions of society and culture as objects for critique. In this respect, it is vitally important to make the political and moral economy of university life a part of the attempt to understand the economic conditions, political attitudes, and criteria of moral value governing society at large. The advancement of a more explicitly humanitarian and care-oriented practice of social inquiry requires that we attend carefully to how this is currently set to be left frustrated, distorted, and compromised by the disciplinary force of the career values and institutional practices that govern the professional conduct of social science.

Such concerns lead us to welcome recent debates surrounding the value of more "public" and "engaged" forms of sociology and anthropology as a positive development. At the very least, these serve as a provocation for practitioners of social science to question what is achieved by their work beyond the goal of accumulating peer-reviewed units of publication or winning out in the competition for research funding.[10] These interventions are also useful for their attempts at delineating the domain interests that govern contrasting approaches to the conduct of social inquiry and for their efforts to link these to divergent views on what should be valued as knowledge of social life; especially where a space is cleared for questioning how more policy oriented and professionally committed brands of social research are configured so as to dispose practitioners to set aside issues of critical value and public relevance.

In these contexts, there is a tendency to identify social suffering as a problem tailored for the promotion of anthropology and sociology as a public concern or as a matter to be raised as an encouragement to activism on behalf of the poor and vulnerable.[11] We certainly concur with these identifications, but we also hold some reservations with regard to the extent to which they leave our ambitions overly compromised and muted; for on our account, research and writing on social suffering involves far more than an attempt to relegitimize more critical and/or activist traditions of social inquiry. Engagements with problems of social suffering should have far more than a bit part to play in any critical agitation against the disciplining of social science as a purely academic exercise.

In one of the most famous statements on "the promise and challenge of public sociology," Michael Burawoy places considerable emphasis on the extent to which he regards his efforts at championing such initiatives as a reflection of the beleaguered state of social science in contexts where neoliberal market values hold sway over the organization and ethos of the academy. In this regard, he urges us to "provincialize" his terms of analysis and points of argument, as these are very much fashioned with his experience of American universities in mind. Burawoy makes clear that his argument that "public sociology" has the potential to serve as an important complement to more stridently "professional" or "policy" geared brands of social science is a pragmatic position that he has arrived at through an assessment of the compromised position in which he works. Quite rightly, he points out that that in many countries of the Global South, and especially in South Africa and Latin America, more publicly engaged, openly political, and critically motivated forms of social inquiry are taken to comprise the very essence of sociology (and anthropology). In these contexts little space is afforded for projects of social investigation to be taken up as a purely academic enterprise; rather, their purpose is cast as a commitment to the making of social movements for humanitarian social change.[12] It is the privilege of Western academics cocooned by positions of material affluence, and whose working days are largely taken up with the packaging of social science for delivery in marketable degree courses, to approach such activities more as objects for study than as something in which they should be involved for the sake of acquiring valid knowledge of social life.

For many of us working within Western neoliberal universities it may well be the case that, for now at least, there are few options but to approach problems of social suffering as a subaltern cause. However, courses may still be developed and taught that review how problems of social suffering feature as part of a distinct approach to social inquiry with its own dedicated methods of data collection and analysis. It may also be possible for colleagues to forge cross-disciplinary alliances and collaborations with activist groups so that problems of social suffering are more widely established on the agenda for research and scholarship. Indeed, in some institutions funding may even be found for the establishment of research centers where the task of understanding and alleviating conditions of social suffering is championed as a core concern. At the same time, readers should understand that on no account could we hold such positive initiatives as adequate to deliver the level of reform we are seeking. All such efforts may be a necessary part of the critical pragmatism required to advance social suffering as a key concern and to this end may well inspire a great deal of positive change in academic conduct and university life; but when set against the demands of our day, we fear that this is too ad hoc and piecemeal.

In contrast to Burawoy and others involved in calls for sociologists and anthropologists to recognize the value and make room for more public and engaged forms of social inquiry, we are not so much concerned to have our interests tailored to what can be made to fit within the university as we find it; and further we have no interest in the validation of our work in terms of the conventions set by Western academic tradition. Indeed, in this book we have worked to make clear that we are concerned with an approach to social understanding that for the most part has operated without academic recognition, or has often been left emasculated when disciplined to the conventions and ethos of the Western academy. We are seeking to develop an alternative history of social understanding and to promote new departures in current methods of social investigation and theoretical terms of understanding. As far as the present is concerned, this may well require that, where possible, we take steps to unshackle the work of research and writing on social suffering from the deadweight of university bureaucracy. Most certainly, moreover, if our efforts are welcomed only in terms of how they might feature in some "public" outreach initiative or for their potential to be molded in the direction of "engagements" for demonstrating the positive "impact" of university research on civic life, then we would regard them as more a failure than a success.

Now more than ever before, in a world where conditions of modernity are being taken to new and unprecedented extremes, we need to critically review and revise established conventions of social science. The very fact that most traditions of social inquiry have been championed and shaped under the direction of individuals born into the most institutionally privileged and materially affluent sectors of Western societies should be a grave cause for concern, particularly insofar as, more often than not, these only involve themselves with championing minority reports on conditions of social life and, even then, with many more esoteric concerns set to the fore.

The Chinese, for example, have a long tradition of indigenous commentary on human nature, society, interpersonal relationships, and subjectivity. Out of this tradition of knowledge creation has come not only powerful critiques but also practices of social care. While the industrialization of philanthropy and humanitarian assistance only emerged in China in the 1980s as a result of increasing wealth and globalization, local forms of charity, compassion, and practical assistance have long been associated with Buddhism, Confucianism, and Taoism as well as Christianity and Islam in China. Also, communities and the Chinese state have for millennia responded to human catastrophes. This points to the comparative reality that in the West much of social action for humanitarian aid has also come from the religious tradition that has supported social care with theological ideas and values. And here too in the West, the state and communities long preceded social science in organizing what we would now call humanitarian assistance and social care. Hence the story we are telling about social science and care must be understood against this broad religious tradition of responding to human suffering with social support, practical assistance, and moral solidarity, along with more narrowly salvific efforts.

In the Chinese tradition, as the great Chinese sociologist and anthropologist Fei Xiaotong emphasized, efforts to respond to collective suffering centered on the networks of social connection (*guanxi*) that circled around each individual and included the family and close friends who were under moral and emotional obligation (*renqing*) to acknowledge and assist those in distress.[13] The Taiwanese psychologist Yang Kuo-shu and sociologist Hwang Kwang-kuo, in their effort to sinicize social science, regarded the theory of social networks as a powerful Chinese contribution to universal social theory that involved both a different and more interdependent understanding of research and a commitment to social care as a goal of social science.[14] Criticism of the way social science in America functions by the distinguished Indian anthropologist Veena Das suggests that Indian culture too may harbor approaches to social inquiry in which acknowledgment of the existential rights of the other and the need to join inquiry to care are important. Thus, the cross-cultural research record would seem to support the position we have advanced in these pages.

If sociology and anthropology are to be credited with the possibility of making us more consciously alert to the peculiarity of our social makeup and condition, then there is still much to be done by way of awakening our intellect and sensibilities to the world state of our humanity. The Swedish social scientist Göran Therborn argues that the novelty of our times is distinguished by the technological possibility of acquiring a "mass awareness of a common humanity" and that we should understand this to "have opened up a new horizon of social understanding and action."[15] However, in this light it is also very likely that most of the works privileged by current sociology and anthropology and the possible roles they might play in advancing the self-consciousness of modernity are set to appear excessively parochial and as fit for the benefit of the few. It is very doubtful that we possess terms of social understanding and analysis that are suitably geared to convey what matters for people in global-social terms, particularly insofar as social researchers, with a few exceptions, guided by the priorities set for funding in affluent Western societies, are unlikely to treat the majority experience of a global modernity as anything more than a marginal concern.

The economic and industrial developments of Southeast Asia and South America over the past thirty years have removed huge swaths of population from conditions of absolute poverty.[16] On many counts these developments have also initiated processes of modernization that have allowed historically unprecedented numbers of people to experience major life-changing advancements in their health and material comfort. China, for example, has had unprecedented success in raising hundreds of millions out of poverty in just a few decades. By any standards, this is a wonderful achievement. At the same time, however, this still leaves approximately one billion people living on less than $1.25 a day, more than 3 billion living on less than $2.50 a day, and around 5.6 billion people (close to 80 percent of the world's population) living on less than $10 a day.[17] The scale and extremes of social division and economic inequality in our global society are without precedent, particularly if one ventures to compare the majority experience of modernity to that of the richest 1 percent of the world's population that own and control around half the world's wealth.[18] Indeed, in a recent report on global trends in economic inequality, which among other things highlights the fact that the richest eighty-five people in the world now possess more wealth than over half the world's population (the poorest 3.5 billion people), the U.K. charity Oxfam contends that in many countries the gap between the super rich and the mass ranks of the poor has reached a point where sustained periods of political and social unrest seem almost inevitable.[19]

The UN anticipates that by 2050 there will be around 9 billion people living on our planet, compared to 3 billion at the end of the Second World War and 7 billion today. The vast majority will be located in areas of the globe plagued by food insecurity. Huge numbers will also be left struggling to piece together a living in areas that are afflicted by the more extreme effects of climate change and that are blighted by ever more persistent problems of water scarcity and environmental pollution.[20] As they are left reeling under the pressures of tumultuous social change, and often change for the worse, it looks like many countries are facing a high risk of societal breakdown, particularly in contexts where the majority of poorer households are occupied by politically disaffected young adults.[21] Some fear that the emergence of such conditions is already tempting ruling elites in the direction of authoritarianism as a means to uphold the status quo and maintain business as usual.[22] Indeed, when it comes to the analysis of current policies being implemented to "manage" problems relating to the movement of migrant populations seeking to escape conditions of poverty, violence, and environmental disaster, it is already widely noted that the governments of wealthier nations are increasingly inclined to adopt authoritarian measures to impose stricter border controls and speed up processes of deportation.[23]

Our worry is for the current state of the world. We fear for the possibility that as a global community we shall fail to extend the bounds of social justice and squander whatever opportunities now lie before us for fashioning society around relationships of mutual respect and care. While our global risk society contains many developments and processes that hold the potential to further improve people's health and social well-being, the simultaneous countervailing tendencies that point to a possible future of extreme conditions of social suffering are all too palpable and real. Our struggle is for a social science fitted with the critical insight, practical motivation, and moral courage to meet the demands of our day. In this book we have tried to clear a space not only for new works of sociological and anthropological imagination but also for making the pursuit of social understanding inextricably linked to care for the human, and for its value to be judged in terms of the production of humanitarian social care in action. Our hope is for research and writing on social suffering to serve as a means to provoke critical public debate over the forms of action required to realize humane social conditions on a global scale. We seek to cultivate sociologies and anthropologies motivated by global humanitarian social concern and, more important, for these to result in real and effective practices of care for all people. This is our passion for society.

Notes

INTRODUCTION

1. This is an extract from an interview featured in the documentary film *Mardi Gras: Made in China*, directed by David Redmon. It is also featured in the book that explains the film in terms of its methodology and analyzes its material through the lens of social theory. See D. Redmon, *Beads, Bodies and Trash: Public Sex, Global Labor and the Disposability of Mardi Gras* (New York: Routledge, 2015), pp. 29–30.

2. See Redmon, *Beads, Bodies and Trash*, pp. 112–15.

3. Z. Bauman, *Wasted Lives: Modernity and Its Outcasts* (Cambridge: Polity Press, 2003).

4. T. Miller, *China's Urban Billion: The Story Behind the Biggest Migration in Human History* (London: Zed Books, 2012).

5. D. F. K. Wong, Y. L. Chang, and X. S. He, "Rural Migrant Workers in Urban China: Living a Marginalised Life," *International Journal of Social Welfare* 16.1 (2007): 32–40.

6. K. A. Mason, "Mobile Migrants, Mobile Germs: Migration, Contagion and Boundary building in Shenzhen, China after SARS," *Medical Anthropology* 31.2 (2012): 113–31.

7. M. D. Loyakla, *Eating Bitterness: Stories from the Front Lines of China's Great Urban Migration* (Berkeley: University of California Press, 2013).

8. J. Mou, J. Cheng, S. M. Griffiths, S. Y. S. Wong, S. Hillier, and D. Zhang, "Internal Migration and Depressive Symptoms among Migrant Factory Workers in Shenzhen, China," *Journal of Community Psychology* 39.2 (2011): 212–30; J. Mou, S. M. Griffiths, H. Fong, and M. G. Dawes, "Health of China's Rural-Urban Migrants and Their Families: A Review of Literature from 2000 to 2012," *British Medical Bulletin* 106.1 (2013): 19–43.

9. D. Morgan, "Pain: The Unrelieved Condition of Modernity," *European Journal of Social Theory* 5.3 (2002): 307–22.

10. A. Kleinman, *What Really Matters: Living a Moral Life amidst Uncertainty and Danger* (New York: Oxford University Press, 2006).

11. See M. Davis, *Planet of Slums* (London: Verso, 2007); P. Farmer, *Pathologies of Power: Health, Human Rights, and the New War on the Poor* (Berkeley: University of California Press, 2003).

12. See J. Glover, *Humanity: A Moral History of the Twentieth Century* (London: Pimlico, 2001).

13. A phrase used in J. P. Sniadecki, *Digital Jianghu: Independent Documentary in a Beijing Art Village* (2013), available at http://dash.harvard.edu/handle/1/11064403.

14. E. Levinas, "Useless Suffering," in *The Provocation of Levinas: Rethinking the Other*, ed. R. Bernasconi and D. Wood (London: Routledge, 1988), p. 156.

15. An argument pursued by Arthur Frank in his "Can We Research Suffering?," *Qualitative Health Research* 11.3 (2001): 353–62.

16. G. Steiner, *Language and Silence* (London: Faber & Faber, 1967).

17. This argument is developed by Gillian Rose in her *Mourning Becomes the Law: Philosophy and Representation* (Cambridge: Cambridge University Press, 1996), p. 43.

18. See S. Cohen, *States of Denial: Knowing about Atrocities and Suffering* (Cambridge: Polity Press, 2001).

19. H. Arendt, *Men in Dark Times* (Harmondsworth: Pelican, 1968), pp. 7–8.

20. A. Schopenhauer, "On the Suffering of the World," in *Essays and Aphorisms* (Harmondsworth: Penguin, 1970), pp. 43–47.

21. J. Hick, *Evil and the God of Love* (London: Macmillan, 1966), pp. 354–55.

22. P. Levi, *The Drowned and the Saved* (London: Abacus, 1987), pp. 142–50.

23. E. J. Cassell, *The Nature of Suffering and the Goals of Medicine* (Oxford: Oxford University Press, 2004), pp. 38–42.

24. See I. Wilkinson, *Suffering: A Sociological Introduction* (Cambridge: Polity Press, 2005), esp. chap. 3.

25. E. Hobsbawm, *An Age of Extremes: The Short History of the Twentieth Century, 1914–1991* (London: Penguin Books, 1994).

26. R. J. Rummel, *Death by Government* (New Brunswick, NJ: Transaction Publishers, 1994).

27. H. Arendt, *Eichmann in Jerusalem: A Report on the Banality of Evil* (Harmondsworth: Penguin, 1963).

28. See H. Arendt, *The Origins of Totalitarianism* (Cleveland: Meridian, 1958); Z. Bauman, *Modernity and the Holocaust* (Cambridge: Polity Press, 1989); U. Beck and E. Beck-Gernsheim, *Individualization: Institutionalized Individualism and Its Social and Political Consequences* (London: Sage, 2002); M. Herzfeld, *The Social Production of Indifference: Exploring the Symbolic Roots of Western Bureaucracy* (Chicago: University of Chicago Press, 1992).

29. R. K. Merton, "The Unanticipated Consequences of Purposive Action," *American Sociological Review* 1.6 (1936): 894–904.

30. P. Kirby, *Vulnerability and Violence: The Impact of Globalization* (London: Pluto Press, 2006).

31. M. Herzfeld, *The Body Impolitic: Artisans and Artifice in the Global Hierarchy of Value* (Chicago: University of Chicago Press, 2004).

32. E. Durkheim, "Individualism and the Intellectuals" (1898), in *Emile Durkheim on Morality and Society,* ed. R. Bellah (Chicago: University of Chicago Press, 1973).

33. See J. A. Amato, *Victims and Values: A History and a Theory of Suffering* (New York: Greenwood Press, 1990); B. H. Rosenwein, "Worrying about Emotions in History," *American Historical Review* 107.3 (2002): 821–45.

34. See G. J. Barker-Benfield, *The Culture of Sensibility: Sex and Society in Eighteenth-Century Britain* (Chicago: University of Chicago Press, 1992); D. Denby, *Sentimental Narrative and the Social Order in France, 1760–1820* (Cambridge: Cambridge University Press, 1994); M. Ellis, *The Politics of Sensibility: Race, Gender and Commerce in the Sentimental Novel* (Cambridge: Cambridge University Press, 1996); S. Pinker, *The Better Angels of Our Nature: A History of Violence and Humanity* (London: Penguin, 2011); and A. Vincent-Buffault, *The History of Tears: Sensibility and Sentimentality in France* (Basingstoke: Macmillan, 1986).

35. L. Hunt, *Inventing Human Rights: A History* (New York: Norton, 2007).

36. See Ellis, *The Politics of Sensibility,* pp. 190–221.

37. See H. Arendt, "The Social Question," in *On Revolution* (Harmondsworth: Penguin, 1963); W. M. Reddy, *The Navigation of Feeling: A Framework for the History of Emotions* (Cambridge: Cambridge University Press, 2001); M. J. Sandel, *Justice: What's the Right Thing to Do?* (New York: Farrar, Straus and Giroux, 2009); M. J. Sandel, *What Money Can't Buy: The Moral Limits of Markets* (New York: Farrar, Straus and Giroux, 2012); A. Sen, *The Idea of Justice* (Cambridge, MA: Belknap Press, 2009).

38. See H. Gardner, ed., *Responsibility at Work: How Leading Professionals Act (or Don't Act) Responsibly* (New York: John Wiley & Sons, 2010); S. R. Krause, *Civil Passions: Moral Sentiment and Democratic Deliberation* (Princeton, NJ: Princeton University Press, 2008); A. Lazare, *On Apology* (New York: Oxford

University Press, 2004); N. Sznaider, *The Compassionate Temperament: Care and Cruelty in Modern Society* (Lanham, MD: Rowman & Littlefield, 2001); D. Wickberg, "What Is the History of Sensibilities? On Cultural Histories, Old and New," *American Historical Review* 112.3 (2007): 661–84.

39. J. B. Thompson, *The Media and Modernity: A Social Theory of the Media* (Cambridge: Polity Press, 1995).

40. M. Ignatieff, *The Warrior's Honour: Ethnic War and the Modern Conscience* (London: Vintage, 1999). See also A. Kleinman and J. Kleinman, "The Appeal of Experience, the Dismay of Images: Cultural Appropriations of Suffering in Our Times," *Daedalus* 125.1 (1996): 1–23; S. Sontag, *Regarding the Pain of Others* (London: Hamish Hamilton, 2003).

41. L. Boltanski, *Distant Suffering: Morality, Media and Politics* (Cambridge: Cambridge University Press, 1999).

42. J. Biehl, B. Good, and A. Kleinman, "Introduction: Rethinking Subjectivity," in *Subjectivity: Ethnographic Investigations*, ed. J. Biehl, B. Good, and A. Kleinman (Berkeley: University of California Press, 2007).

43. See J. W. Bowker, *Problems of Suffering in Religions of the World* (Cambridge: Cambridge University Press, 1975).

44. Kleinman, *What Really Matters.*

45. This is the title of the English translation of Pierre Bourdieu and colleagues' classic study of social suffering. See P. Bourdieu et al., eds., *The Weight of the World: Social Suffering in Contemporary Society* (Cambridge: Polity Press, 1999).

46. This is a major concern in Paul Farmer's accounts of social suffering. See P. Farmer, *Infections and Inequalities: The Modern Plagues* (Berkeley: University of California Press, 1999); P. Farmer, *Pathologies of Power: Health, Human Rights and the New War on the Poor* (Berkeley: University of California Press, 2003); P. Farmer, "Conversation in the Time of Cholera: A Reflection on Structural Violence and Social Change," in *In the Company of the Poor: Conversations with Dr. Paul Farmer and Fr. Gustavo Gutierrez*, ed. M. Griffin and J. W. Block (New York: Orbis Books, 2013).

47. For examples of studies that take this approach, see P. Hillyard, C. Pantazis, S. Tombs, and D. Gordon, *Beyond Criminology: Taking Harm Seriously* (London: Macmillan, 2004); B. Moore Jr., *Reflections on the Causes of Human Misery and upon Certain Proposals to Eliminate Them* (Boston: Beacon Press, 1972).

48. M. Jay, *Songs of Experience: Modern American and European Variations on a Universal Theme* (Berkeley: University of California Press, 2006).

49. For examples of other studies that take this approach, see K. Plummer, *Documents of Life 2: An Invitation to Critical Humanism* (London: Sage, 2001); B. S. Turner, *Vulnerability and Human Rights* (University Park: Pennsylvania State University Press, 2006); J. C. Tronto, *Moral Boundaries: A Political Argument for an Ethic of Care* (New York: Routledge, 1993); J. C. Tronto, *Caring*

Democracy: Markets, Equality, and Social Justice (New York: New York University Press, 2013).

50. There is already an example of this taking place in global medical ethics. See J.-B. Nie, *Medical Ethics in China: A Transcultural Interpretation* (London: Routledge, 2013).

51. A phrase used by Joan Tronto to describe the ambition of her approach to social inquiry. See Tronto, *Moral Boundaries*.

52. In this regard our approach bears some similarities to that developed by George Marcus and Michael Fischer. G. E. Marcus and M. M. Fischer, *Anthropology as Cultural Critique: An Experimental Moment in the Human Sciences* (Chicago: University of Chicago Press, 1999).

53. On this point we offer a critical assessment of Didier Fassin's work. See D. Fassin, *Humanitarian Reason: A Moral History of the Present* (Berkeley: University of California Press, 2012).

54. This text is taken from the concluding section of Max Weber's famous lecture/essay, "Politics as a Vocation" (featured in chap. 4 below). See M. Weber, "Politics as a Vocation," in *From Max Weber*, ed. H. H. Gerth and C. W. Mills (London: Routledge, 1948).

CHAPTER 1. THE ORIGINS OF SOCIAL SUFFERING

1. R. Williams, *The Country and the City* (London: Chatto & Windus, 1973), p. 96.

2. See J. Harrington, "Wordsworth's Descriptive Sketches and the Prelude, Book VI," *Publications of the Modern Languages Association (PMLA)* 44.4 (1929): 1144–58; G. H. Hartman, "Wordsworth's Descriptive Sketches and the Growth of a Poet's Mind," *Publications of the Modern Language Association (PMLA)* 76.5 (1961): 519–27; J. Williams, *Wordsworth: Romantic Poetry and Revolution Politics* (Manchester: Manchester University Press, 1989), pp. 36–68.

3. E. Durkheim, "Individualism and the Intellectuals" (1898), in *Emile Durkheim on Morality and Society*, ed. R. Bellah (Chicago: University of Chicago Press, 1973), p. 49.

4. See A. Thompson, *The Art of Suffering and the Impact of Seventeenth-Century Anti-Providential Thought* (Aldershot: Ashgate, 2003), p. 1.

5. See, e.g., W. J. Brandt, *The Shape of Medieval History: Studies in Modes of Perception* (New Haven, CT: Yale University Press, 1966); K. Thomas, *Religion and the Decline of Magic: Studies in Popular Beliefs in Sixteenth- and Seventeenth-Century England* (London: Penguin, 1971), pp. 90–132; A. Walsham, *Providence in Early Modern England* (Oxford: Oxford University Press, 1999); B. Ward, *Miracles and the Medieval Mind: Theory, Record, and Event, 1000–1215* (Philadelphia: University of Pennsylvania Press, 1982).

6. From the New Testament and St. Paul's Letter to the Romans 9:22.

7. See, e.g., the Gospel of Matthew 5:10–12 and St. Paul's Letter to the Romans 5:3–4.

8. M. Bloch, *Feudal Society* (London: Routledge, 1989), p. 73.

9. Ibid.

10. Walsham, *Providence in Early Modern England*, p. 17.

11. A. Kibbey, "Mutations of the Supernatural: Witchcraft, Remarkable Providences and the Power of Puritan Men," *American Quarterly* 34.2 (1982): 125–48.

12. Thomas, *Religion and the Decline of Magic*, p. 95.

13. Ibid.

14. D. F. Tinsley, *The Scourge of the Cross: Ascetic Mentalities of the Later Middle Ages* (Walpole: Peeters, 2010).

15. A. Cunningham and O. P. Grell, *The Four Horsemen of the Apocalypse: Religion, War, Famine and Death in Reformation Europe* (Cambridge: Cambridge University Press, 2000).

16. Thomas, *Religion and the Decline of Magic*, pp. 129–30.

17. For a selection of texts that explore this matter, see D. D. Hall, *Worlds of Wonder, Days of Judgement: Popular Religious Belief in Early New England* (New York: Alfred A. Knopf, 1989); Kibbey, "Mutations of the Supernatural"; Walsham, *Providence in Early Modern England;* M. Winship, *Seers of God: Puritan Providentialism in the Restoration and Early Modern Enlightenment* (Baltimore, MD: Johns Hopkins University Press, 1996).

18. Walsham, *Providence in Early Modern England*, p. 9.

19. For a more elaborated analysis of this matter as set within the frameworks of contrasting world religions, see J. Bowker, *Problems of Suffering in Religions of the World* (Cambridge: Cambridge University Press, 1975).

20. W. E. Burns, *An Age of Wonders: Prodigies, Politics and Providence in England, 1657–1727* (Manchester: Manchester University Press, 2002); C. Hill, *The Word Turned Upside Down* (Harmondsworth: Penguin, 1975).

21. B. Worden, "Providence and Politics in Cromwellian England," *Past and Present* 109.1 (1985): 55–99.

22. C. Hill, *The English Bible and the Seventeenth-Century Revolution* (London: Penguin, 1993); J. Morrill and P. Baker, "Oliver Cromwell, the Regicide and the Sons of Zeruiah," in *Cromwell and the Interregnum: Essential Readings*, ed. D. L. Smith (Oxford: Wiley Blackwell, 2003).

23. Worden, "Providence and Politics in Cromwellian England," p. 57.

24. Walsham, *Providence in Early Modern England*, p. 333.

25. See Hill, *The English Bible*, p. 414. For more detailed reflections on this point, see B. S. Gregory, *The Unintended Reformation: How Religious Revolution Secularized Society* (Cambridge, MA: Harvard University Press, 2012).

26. Worden, "Providence and Politics in Cromwellian England," p. 86.

27. Hill, *The English Bible*, pp. 432–34.

28. For a detailed account of this process, see Burns, *An Age of Wonders.*

29. M. Winship, "Prodigies, Puritanism and the Perils of Natural Theology: The Example of Cotton Mather," *William and Mary Quarterly* 51.1 (1994): 92–105; Winship, *Seers of God.*

30. For a more detailed analysis of this matter that also includes a focus on the cultural and political impacts of climate change through this period, see G. Parker, *Global Crisis: War, Climate Change, and Catastrophe in the Seventeenth Century* (New Haven, CT: Yale University Press, 2013), esp. chaps. 11, 12.

31. See Hill, *The English Bible*, pp. 413–35; Walsham, *Providence in Early Modern England*, pp. 333–34.

32. See Burns, *An Age of Wonders.*

33. Thomas, *Religion and the Decline of Magic*, p. 132.

34. See S. J. Barnett, *The Enlightenment and Religion: Myths of Modernity* (Manchester: Manchester University Press, 2004).

35. This matter is featured in L. O. Saum, *The Popular Mood of America, 1860–1890* (Lincoln: University of Nebraska Press, 1990).

36. Thompson, *The Art of Suffering*, p. 169.

37. Hill, *The English Bible*, pp. 415–35.

38. J. A. Herdt, "The Rise of Sympathy and the Question of Divine Suffering," *Journal of Religious Ethics* 29.3 (2001): 367–99.

39. Herdt, "The Rise of Sympathy," pp. 389–95.

40. Voltaire "The Lisbon Earthquake" (1756), in *The Portable Voltaire*, ed. B. R. Redman (Harmondsworth: Penguin, 1949), pp. 560–61.

41. Voltaire, *Candide or Optimism* (Harmondsworth: Penguin, [1759] 1947).

42. Ibid., pp. 143–44.

43. P. Gay, *The Enlightenment, an Interpretation*, vol. 1, *The Rise of Modern Paganism* (New York: Norton, 1966), p. 200.

44. See R. C. Bartlett, "On the Politics of Faith and Reason: The Project of Enlightenment in Pierre Bayle and Montesquieu," *Journal of Politics* 63.1 (2001): 1–28; P. Bayle, *Historical and Critical Dictionary* (Indianapolis: Bobbs-Merrill, [1695–97] 1965); Z. Porat, "Who, Me? Evil and the Rhetoric of Interminable Interrogation in Pierre Bayle's Critical and Historical Dictionary," *Literature & Theology* 9.1 (1995): 46–65.

45. F. H. Wines, "Sociology and Philanthropy," *Annals of the American Academy of Political and Social Science* 12 (1898): 49–57.

46. "Social suffering" features as a shared point of reference and problem for debate in the following nineteenth-century texts: E. B. Andrews, "The Bimetallist Committee of Boston and New England," *Quarterly Journal of Economics* 8.3 (1894): 319–27; W. G. Blaickie, *Heads and Hands in the World of Labour* (London: Alexander Strathern, 1865), p. 30; C. Brooks, *A Statement of Facts from Each Religious Denomination in New England Respecting Ministers Salaries*

(Boston: Crocker & Brewster, Gould & Lincoln, C. Stimpson and J. Munroe & Co, 1854), p. 24; A. J. Davis, *The History and Philosophy of Evil with Suggestions for More Ennobling Institutions and Philosophical Systems of Education* (Boston: William White & Co., 1869), p. 107; D. R. De Morier, *What Has Religion to Do with Politics? The Question Considered in Letters to His Son by DR De Morier* (London: John W. Parker, 1848), p. 45; R. Mayo-Smith, "Levasseur's 'La Population Française,'" *Political Science Quarterly* 8.1 (1893): 124–36, p. 125; J. Noble, *Fiscal Legislation, 1842-1865* (London: Longmans, Green, Reader & Dyer, 1867), pp. 34, 113, 142; C. E. Norton, *Considerations on Some Recent Social Theories* (Boston: Little, Brown, 1853), p. 59; H. Spencer, "The New Toryism," *Contemporary Review* 45 (1884): 153–67; C. H. Toy, "On the Asaph-Psalms," *Journal of the Society of Biblical Literature and Exegesis* 6.1 (1886): 73–85; W. G. Ward, *On Nature and Grace* (London: G. Barkley, 1859), p. 35.

47. K. Thomas, *Man and the Natural World: Changing Attitudes in England, 1500-1800* (London: Penguin, 1983), pp. 173–80; L. Hunt, *Inventing Human Rights: A History* (New York: Norton, 2007), pp. 70–112; S. Pinker, *The Better Angels of Our Nature: A History of Violence and Humanity* (London: Penguin, 2011), pp. 155–227.

48. K. Halttunen, "Humanitarianism and the Pornography of Pain in Anglo-American Culture," *American Historical Review* 100.2 (1995): 303–34.

49. A. Kleinman and B. Good, eds., *Culture and Depression: Studies in the Anthropology and Cross-Cultural Psychiatry of Affect and Disorder* (Berkeley: University of California Press, 1985); R. Williams, *Marxism and Literature* (Oxford: Oxford University Press, 1985), pp. 128–35.

50. E. Cohen, "The Animated Pain of the Body," *American Historical Review* 105.1 (2000): 36–68.

51. See Cohen, "The Animated Pain of the Body," pp. 54–58.

52. This matter is explored in A. R. Hochschild, *The Managed Heart: Commercialization of Human Feeling* (Berkeley: University of California Press, 1983).

53. W. M. Reddy, *The Navigation of Feeling: A Framework for the History of Emotions* (Cambridge: Cambridge University Press, 2001).

54. This quotation is featured in R. S. Crane, "Suggestions towards a Genealogy of the 'Man of Feeling,'" *English Literary History* 1.3 (1934): 205–30, on pp. 208–9.

55. Crane, "Suggestions towards a Genealogy of the 'Man of Feeling,'" 208–9.

56. For more detail on this intellectual and moral-emotional development, see C. Chapin, "Shaftsbury and the Man of Feeling," *Modern Philology* 81.1 (1983): 47–50; N. S. Fiering, "Irresistible Compassion: An Aspect of Eighteenth-Century Sympathy and Humanitarianism," *Journal of the History of Ideas* 37.2 (1976): 195–218; S. Gaston, "The Impossibility of Sympathy," *Eighteenth Century* 51.1-2 (2010): 129–52; L. E. Klein, *Shaftsbury and the Culture of Politeness: Moral*

Discourse and Cultural Politics in Early Eighteenth-Century England (Cambridge: Cambridge University Press, 1994); L. Turco, "Sympathy and Moral Sense: 1725–1740," *British Journal for the History of Philosophy* 7.1 (1999): 79–101.

57. T. Paine, *Rights of Man, Common Sense and Other Political Writings*, Oxford: Oxford University Press,[1776] 1995), p. 29.

58. Fiering, "Irresistible Compassion," p. 195.

59. See E. B. Clark, "The Sacred Rights of the Weak: Pain, Sympathy and the Culture of Individual Rights in Antebellum America," *Journal of American History* 82.2 (1995): 463–93; M. Ellis, *The Politics of Sensibility: Race, Gender and Commerce in the Sentimental Novel* (Cambridge: Cambridge University Press, 1996).

60. Thomas, *Man and the Natural World*, pp. 173–75.

61. Hill, *The English Bible*, p. 426.

62. Hunt, *Inventing Human Rights*, pp. 70–76.

63. R. McGowan, "A Powerful Sympathy: Terror, the Prison, and Humanitarian Reform in Early Nineteenth-Century Britain," *Journal of British Studies* 25.3 (1986): 312–34.

64. N. Elias, *The Civilizing Process* (Oxford: Blackwell, 1994).

65. For an analysis for this development from an Eliasian perspective, see P. Spierenburg, *Violence & Punishment: Civilizing the Body through Time* (Cambridge: Polity Press, 2013). Also see J. S. Cockburn, "Punishment and Brutalization in the English Enlightenment," *Law and History Review* 12.1 (1994): 155–79; McGowan, "A Powerful Sympathy."

66. N. Sznaider, *The Compassionate Temperament: Care and Cruelty in Modern Society* (Lanham, MD: Rowman & Littlefield, 2001), p. 9.

67. T. L. Haskell, "Capitalism and the Origins of the Humanitarian Sensibility, Part 1," American Historical Review 90.2 (1985): 339–61; and "Capitalism and the Origins of the Humanitarian Sensibility, Part 2," American Historical Review 90.3 (1985): 547–66.

68. G. J. Barker-Benfield, *The Culture of Sensibility: Sex and Society in Eighteenth-Century Britain* (Chicago: University of Chicago Press, 1992).

69. C. Campbell, *The Romantic Ethic and the Spirit of Modern Consumerism* (Oxford: Blackwell, 1987).

70. See J. Plamper, "The History of Emotions: An Interview with William Reddy, Barbara Rosenwein, and Peter Stearns," *History and Theory* 49.2 (2010): 237–65; B. H. Rosenwein, "Worrying about Emotions in History," *American Historical Review* 107.3 (2002): 821–45; R. C. Solomon, *The Passions: Emotions and the Meaning of Life* (Indianapolis: Hackett, 1993).

71. Reddy, *The Navigation of Feeling*.

72. Gaston, "The Impossibility of Sympathy," p. 146.

73. This is explored in more detail in M. L. Frazer, *The Enlightenment of Sympathy: Justice and the Moral Sentiments in the Eighteenth Century and Today* (Oxford: Oxford University Press, 2010).

74. F. Hutcheson, *A Short Introduction to Moral Philosophy in Three Books Containing Elements of Ethicks and the Law of Nature* (Glasgow: Glasgow University Press, 1747), pp. 49–50.

75. P. Harth, "The Satiric Purpose of 'The Fable of the Bees,'" *Eighteenth-Century Studies* 2.4 (1969): 321–40.

76. D. Carey, "Hutcheson's Moral Sense and the Problem of Innateness," *Journal of the History of Philosophy* 38.1 (2000): 103–10.

77. E. Sprague, "Francis Hutcheson and the Moral Sense," *Journal of Philosophy* 51.24 (1954): 794–800.

78. See J. Mullan, *Sentiment and Sociability: The Language of Feeling in the Eighteenth Century* (London: Clarendon Press, 1988), pp. 18–56.

79. D. Hume, *A Treatise of Human Nature* (London: Penguin, [1739–40] 1969), p. 630.

80. Ibid., p. 540.

81. R. Vitz, "Sympathy and Benevolence in Hume's Moral Psychology," *Journal of the History of Philosophy* 42.3 (2004): 261–75.

82. See G. R. Morrow, "The Significance of the Doctrine of Sympathy in Hume and Adam Smith,"*Philosophical Review* 32.1 (1923): 60–78; and Mullan, *Sentiment and Sociability*, pp. 36–43.

83. See, e.g., L. Boltanski, *Distant Suffering: Morality, Media and Politics* (Cambridge: Cambridge University Press, 1999); F. Forman-Barzilai, "Sympathy in Space(s): Adam Smith on Proximity," *Political Theory* 33.2 (2005): 189–217.

84. D. Marshall, "Adam Smith and the Theatricality of Moral Sentiments," *Critical Inquiry* 10 (1984): 592–613.

85. A. Smith, *The Theory of Moral Sentiments* (Mineola: Dover Publications, [1759] 2006), p. 113.

86. Ibid., p. 227.

87. Mullan, *Sentiment and Sociability*, p. 56.

88. R. Williams, *Keywords: A Vocabulary of Culture and Society* (Glasgow: Fontana, 1976), p. 237.

89. Ellis, *The Politics of Sensibility*, pp. 190–221.

90. H. Mackenzie, "Henry Mackenzie, *The Lounger*, No. 20 (Saturday, 18 June 1785)," in *The Man of Feeling* (Oxford: Oxford University Press, [1785] 2001), p. 101.

91. Cited in Ellis, *The Politics of Sensibility*, p. 207.

92. Barker-Benfield, *The Culture of Sensibility*, pp. 351–95; M. Wollstonecraft, *A Vindication of the Rights of Woman and A Vindication of the Rights of Man* (Oxford: Oxford University Press, [1792] 1994).

93. C. Jones, "Radical Sensibility in the 1790s," in *Reflections of Revolution: Images of Revolution*, ed. A. Yarrington and K. Everest (London: Routledge, 1993); W. M. Reddy, "Sentimentalism and Its Erasure: The Role of Emotions in the Era of the French Revolution," *Journal of Modern History* 72.1 (2000): 109–52.

94. D. Denby, *Sentimental Narrative and the Social Order in France, 1760–1820* (Cambridge: Cambridge University Press, 1994); A. Vincent-Buffault, *The History of Tears: Sensibility and Sentimentality in France* (Basingstoke: Macmillan, 1986).

95. Arendt, "The Social Question."

96. Ellis, *The Politics of Sensibility*, pp. 190–221.

97. W. Wordsworth, "Preface to *Lyrical Ballads*," in *Wordsworth and Coleridge Lyrical Ballads and Other Poems* (Ware: Wordsworth Editions, [1802] 2003), p. 10.

98. K. G. Blank, "The Degrading Thirst after Outrageous Stimulation: Wordsworth as Cultural Critic," *Journal of Popular Culture* 39.1 (2006): 365–82.

2. IN DIVISION AND DENIAL

1. E. Wilson, *Patriotic Gore: Studies in the Literature of the American Civil War* (New York: Oxford University Press, 1966), p. 3.

2. K. Carabine, Introduction to H. Beecher Stowe, *Uncle Tom's Cabin or Negro Life in the Slave States of America* (Ware: Wordsworth Classics, 2002), p. v.

3. Cited in F. J. Klingberg, "Harriet Beecher Stowe and Social Reform in England," *American Historical Review* 43.3 (1938): 545.

4. R. S. Levine, "*Uncle Tom's Cabin* in Frederick Douglass' Paper: An Analysis of Reception," *American Literature*, 64.1 (1992): 71–93.

5. Wilson, *Patriotic Gore*, p. 3.

6. Klingberg, "Harriet Beecher Stowe and Social Reform." Also see E. V. Spelman, *Fruits of Sorrow: Framing Our Attention to Suffering* Boston: Beacon Press, 1997), pp. 113–32.

7. J. Tomkins, *Sensational Designs: The Cultural Work of American Fiction, 1790–1860* (New York: Oxford University Press, 1985), p. 125.

8. L. Berlant, *The Female Complaint: The Unfinished Business of Sentimentality in American Culture* (Durham, NC: Duke University Press, 2008); J. Noble, "The Ecstasies of Sentimental Wounding in *Uncle Tom's Cabin*," *Yale Journal of Criticism* 10.2 (1997): 295–320.

9. Wilson, *Patriotic Gore*, p. 3.

10. Ibid., p. 5.

11. For a detailed exploration and extended reflection on the traumatic impact of the American Civil War on the collective consciousness of American society at this time, see D. G. Faust, *This Republic of Suffering: Death and the American Civil War* (New York: Vintage, 2008).

12. See, e.g., A. Douglas, "The Art of Controversy: Introduction to *Uncle Tom's Cabin*," in H. Beecher Stowe, *Uncle Tom's Cabin: Or, Life among the Lowly* (Harmondsworth: Penguin, 1983).

13. T. Hovet Jr. "Harriet Martineau's Exceptional American Narratives: Harriet Beecher Stowe, John Brown and the Redemption of Your National Soul," *American Studies* 48.1 (2007): 63–76.

14. J. Baldwin, "Everybody's Protest Novel," *Partisan Review* 16 (1949): 578–79.

15. See, e.g., E. B. Clark, "The Sacred Rights of the Weak: Pain, Sympathy and the Culture of Individual Rights in Antebellum America," *Journal of American History* 82.2 (1995): 463–93; G. D. Crane, "Dangerous Sentiments: Sympathy, Rights, and Revolution in Stowe's Antislavery Novels," *Nineteenth-Century Literature* 51.2 (1996): 176–204; N. Greyser, "Affective Geographies: Sojourner Truth's Narrative: Feminism and the Ethical Bind of Sentimentalism," *American Literature* 79.2 (2007): 275–305; K. Halttunen, "Humanitarianism and the Pornography of Pain in Anglo-American Culture," *American Historical Review* 100.2 (1995): 303–34; N. Roberts, "Character in the Mind: Citizenship, Education and Psychology in Britain, 1880–1914," *History of Education: Journal of the History of Education Society* 33.2 (2004): 177–97; C. Sorisio, "The Spectacle of the Body: Torture in the Antislavery Writing of Lydia Maria Child and Frances E.W. Harper," *Modern Language Studies* 30.1 (2000): 45–66.

16. Spelman, *Fruits of Sorrow*, pp. 1–17.

17. C. J. Barker-Benfield, *The Culture of Sensibility: Sex and Society in Eighteenth Century Britain* (Chicago: University of Chicago Press, 1992); D. Denby, *Sentimental Narrative and the Social Order in France, 1760–1820*, (Cambridge: Cambridge University Press, 1994); M. L. Frazer, *The Enlightenment of Sympathy: Justice and the Moral Sentiments in the Eighteenth Century and Today* (Oxford: Oxford University Press, 2010); S. Maza, *Private Lives and Public Affairs: The Causes Célèbres of Prerevolutionary France* (Berkeley: University of California Press, 1993); R. Porter, *The Enlightenment* (Basingstoke: Palgrave, 2001); A. Vincent-Buffault, *The History of Tears: Sensibility and Sentimentality in France* (Basingstoke: Macmillan, 1986).

18. For a book that takes this up as a central concern, see J. Riskin, *Science in the Age of Sensibility: The Sentimental Empiricists of the French Enlightenment* (Chicago: University of Chicago Press, 2002).

19. R. E. Norton, "The Myth of the Counter-Enlightenment," *Journal of the History of Ideas* 68.4 (2007): 638–58.

20. For an excellent account of this development, see M. Poovey, *A History of the Modern Fact: Problems of Knowledge in the Sciences of Wealth and Society* (Chicago: University of Chicago University, 1998).

21. This is now featured as a matter for investigation in a range of studies. See, e.g., L. Daston, "Objectivity and the Escape from Perspective," *Social Studies of Science* 22.4 (1992): 597–618; C. Fox, R. S. Porter, and R. Wolker, eds., *Inventing Human Science: Eighteenth-Century Domains* (Berkeley: University of California Press, 1995); J. Morrell and A. Thackray, *Gentlemen of Science: Early Years of*

the British Association for the Advancement of Science (Oxford: Clarendon Press, 1981); R. Porter, "The Scientific Revolution: A Spoke in the Wheel?," in *Revolution in History*, ed. R. Porter and M. Teich (Cambridge: Cambridge University Press, 1986); R. Porter and M. Teich, *The Scientific Revolution in National Context* (Cambridge: Cambridge University Press, 1992).

22. H. Arendt, "The Social Question," in *On Revolution* (Harmondsworth: Penguin, 1963).

23. W. M. Reddy, "Sentimentalism and Its Erasure: The Role of Emotions in the Era of the French Revolution," *Journal of Modern History* 72.1 (2000): 109–52.

24. M. Berg, *The Machinery Question and the Making of Political Economy, 1815–1848* (Cambridge: Cambridge University Press, 1980); E. Hobsbawm, *The Age of Revolution, 1789–1848* (London: Wiedenfeld and Nicolson, 1962); M. Poovey, *Making a Social Body: British Cultural Formation, 1830–1864* (Chicago: University of Chicago Press, 1995); F. D. Roberts, *The Social Conscience of the Early Victorians* (Stanford, CA: Stanford University Press, 2002), pp. 75–112.

25. Roberts, *The Social Conscience*, pp. 104, 134–82.

26. Hobsbawm, *The Age of Revolution*, pp. 288–91. Some of the most devastating consequences of this ideology were visited upon Ireland between 1845 to 1852 as mass starvation and disease wrought havoc through the country. Cecil Woodeham-Smith contends that the political and moral convictions held by the liberal prime minister, Lord John Russell, were largely responsible for decisions that resulted in the deaths of approximately one million people. It was a blind commitment to neoliberal market-driven policies and Malthusian population theory that served to deny proper relief to a population that during the famine was reduced in size by around 50 percent (through death and emigration). See C. Woodham-Smith, *The Great Hunger: Ireland, 1845–9* (London: Penguin, 1962).

27. Roberts, *The Social Conscience*, pp. 150–51.

28. M. Brown, "Medicine, Reform and the 'End' of Charity in Early Nineteenth-Century England," *English Historical Review* 124.511 (2009): 1353–88.

29. M. Poovey, "Figures of Arithmetic, Figures of Speech: The Discourse of Statistics in the Late 1830s," *Critical Inquiry* 19.2 (1993): 256–76; Poovey, *Making a Social Body*; Poovey, *A History of the Modern Fact*.

30. For key works by Michel Foucault that inspire this project, see *Discipline and Punish: The Birth of the Prison*, New York: Vintage, 1977); *The History of Sexuality, Vol. 3: The Care of the Self*, New York: Vintage, 1988); *The History of Sexuality, Vol. 1: An Introduction* (New York: Vintage, 1990); *The History of Sexuality, Vol. 2: The Use of Pleasure* (New York: Vintage, 1990).

31. Poovey, *Making a Social Body*, pp.7–13, 98–131.

32. Poovey, *A History of the Modern Fact*, pp. 278–306.

33. Ibid., p. 317.

34. Poovey, "Figures of Arithmetic, Figures of Speech."

35. L. Goldman, "The Origins of British 'Social Science': Political Economy, Natural Science and Statistics, 1830–35," *Historical Journal* 26.3 (1983): 587–616; L. Goldman, "Statistics and the Science of Society in Early Victorian Britain: An Intellectual Context for the General Register Office," *Social History of Medicine* 4.3 (1991): 415–34.

36. E. Yeo, *The Contest for Social Science: Relations and Representations of Gender and Class* (London: Rivers Oram Press, 1996), pp. 95–98.

37. Goldman, "Statistics and the Science of Society," p. 422.

38. R. Porter, *The Greatest Benefit to Mankind: A Medical History of Humanity from Antiquity to the Present* (London: HarperCollins, 1997), pp. 409–11.

39. C. Hamlin, "Could You Starve to Death in England in 1839? The Chadwick-Farr Controversy and the Loss of the 'Social' in Public Health," *American Journal of Public Health* 85.6 (1995): 862.

40. It was only following Joseph Lister's pioneering work in the 1870s applying the germ theory of disease to sanitation in medical settings and aseptic surgical techniques—partly through the use of carbolic acid (phenol) as an antiseptic—that it started to widely supplant miasmic theory as the preferred scientific explanation for disease. See R. P. Gaynes, *Germ Theory: Medical Pioneers in Infectious Diseases* (Washington, DC: American Society for Microbiology, 2011); and M. Worboys, *Spreading Germs: Disease Theories and Medical Practice in Britain, 1865–1900* (Cambridge: Cambridge University Press, 2006).

41. C. Hamlin, "Predisposing Causes and Public Health in Early Nineteenth-Century Medical Thought," *Social History of Medicine* 5.1 (1992): 43–70.

42. Hamlin, "Could You Starve to Death in England in 1839?," p. 862.

43. Ibid.

44. See Poovey, *Making a Social Body*, pp. 117–31.

45. See Roberts, *The Social Conscience*, p. 290; E. P. Thompson, "Mayhew and the *Morning Chronicle*," in *The Unknown Mayhew: Selections from the "Morning Chronicle*," ed. E. P. Thompson and E. Yeo (London: Merlin Press, 1971), pp. 34–41.

46. R. H. Crocker, "The Victorian Poor Law in Crisis and Change: Southampton,1870–1895," *Albion* 19.1 (1987)): 30.

47. Roberts, *The Social Conscience*, p. 258.

48. Ibid., pp. 258–95.

49. F. Kaplan, *Sacred Tears: Sentimentality in Victorian Literature* (New York: Open Road Media, 2013); S. Ledger, "From Queen Caroline to Lady Dedlock: Dickens and the Popular Radical Imagination," *Victorian Literature and Culture* 32.2 (2004): 575–600; S. Ledger, *Dickens and the Popular Radical Imagination* (Cambridge: Cambridge University Press, 2007); E. Mason, "Feeling Dickensian Feeling," *19: Interdisciplinary Studies in the Long Nineteenth Century* 4 (2007), www.19.bbk.ac.uk; Poovey, *Making a Social Body*, pp. 155–81; R. Williams, *The Country and the City* (London: Chatto & Windus, 1973), pp. 218–19.

50. C. Dickens, *Hard Times*, London: Penguin, [1854] 2003); C. Dickens, *The Mudfog Papers* (Richmond: Alma Classics, [1843] 2014). As far as this matter is concerned, readers may also be interested to note the early influence of Thomas Wakley on Charles Dickens. Thomas Wakley was a surgeon, a British Member of Parliament, a social reformer, and the founding editor the *Lancet*. Through his work as a coroner he came to be celebrated as humanitarian campaigner on behalf of the interests of underprivileged members of society. In his reports on deaths caused by flogging, police violence, the adulteration of foodstuffs, and accidents in the workplace, he sought to bring a critical challenge to official discourses designed to operate without regard for the social conditions of the poor. Through the *Lancet* he also campaigned for a system of compensation for employees injured in the workplace. It is recorded that in his own work Dickens was inspired by Wakley's passion for social justice and his humanitarian example. See E. Cawthon, "Thomas Wakley and the Medical Coronership: Occupational Death and the Judicial Process," *Medical History* 30.2 (1986): 191–202; D. Sharp, "Thomas Wakley (1795–1862): A Biographical Sketch," *Lancet* 379.9829 (2012): 1914–1921; C. Tomalin, *Charles Dickens: A Life* (London: Penguin, 2011).

51. Poovey, "Figures of Arithmetic, Figures of Speech," p. 269.

52. Mason, "Feeling Dickensian Feeling."

53. A. Jaffe, "Spectacular Sympathy: Visuality and Ideology in Dickens's *A Christmas Carol*," *Publication of the Modern Languages Association (PMLA)* 109.2 (1994): 254–65; A. Jaffe, *Scenes of Sympathy: Identity and Representation in Victorian Literature* (Ithaca, NY: Cornell University Press, 2000).

54. H. James, "Our Mutual Friend," *The Nation* 1 (1865): 786–87.

55. Roberts, *The Social Conscience*, pp. 267–73.

56. S. Solicari, "Selling Sentiment: The Commodification of Emotion in Victorian Visual Culture," *19: Interdisciplinary Studies in the Long Nineteenth Century* 4 (2007), www.19.bbk.ac.uk.

57. W. James, "Pragmatism's Conception of Truth," *Journal of Philosophy, Psychology and Scientific Methods* 4.6 (1907): 153.

58. R. Douglas-Fairhurst, Introduction to H. Mayhew, *London Labour and the London Poor* (Oxford: Oxford University Press, [1861–62] 2010), p. xxv.

59. Cited in Douglas-Fairhurst, Introduction, p. xxvii.

60. G. Himmelfarb, "Mayhew's Poor: A Problem of Identity," *Victorian Studies* 14.3 (1971): 307–20.

61. Mayhew, *London Labour and the London Poor*, pp. 274–78.

62. E. P. Thompson and E. Yeo, eds., *The Unknown Mayhew: Selections from the "Morning Chronicle"* (London: Merlin Press, 1971).

63. Cited in E. P. Thompson, "Mayhew and the *Morning Chronicle*," in Thompson and Yeo, *The Unknown Mayhew*, pp. 46–47; original emphasis.

64. A. Humphreys, *Travels into the Poor Man's Country: The Work of Henry Mayhew* (Athens: University of Georgia Press, 1977), p. 19.

65. In this regard Mayhew is also celebrated as a pioneering figure in the development of photojournalism and its use as a form of political activism. See M. Bogre, *Photography as Activism: Images for Social Change* (Oxford: Focal Press, 2012).

66. Cited in Humphreys, *Travels into the Poor Man's Country*, p. 62.

67. P. Quennell, *Mayhew's London: Being Selections from "London Labour and the London Poor"* (London: Pilot Press, 1949); Thompson, "Mayhew and the *Morning Chronicle*"; G. Woodcock, "Henry Mayhew and the Undiscovered Country of the Poor," *Sewanee Review* 92.4 (1984): 556–73; Yeo, *The Contest for Social Science.*

68. Williams, *The Country and the City*, pp. 215–32.

69. Cited in Thompson, "Mayhew and the *Morning Chronicle*," p. 39.

70. Humphreys, *Travels into the Poor Man's Country*, pp. 21–30.

71. M.D. Freeman, "Social Investigation in Rural England, 1870–1914" (PhD diss., University of Glasgow, 1999); B. Harrison, *Peaceable Kingdom: Stability and Change in Modern Britain* (Oxford: Clarendon Press, 1982); Yeo, *The Contest for Social Science.*

72. S. Koven, *Slumming: Sexual and Social Politics in Victorian England* (Princeton, NJ: Princeton University Press, 2006).

73. Harrison, *Peaceable Kingdom*, p. 306.

74. Ibid., p. 276.

75. R.C. Bannister, *Sociology and Scientism: The American Quest for Objectivity, 1880–1940* (Chapel Hill: University of North Carolina Press, 1991); T.L. Haskell, *The Emergence of Professional Social Science: The American Social Science Association and the Crisis of Authority* (Baltimore: Johns Hopkins University Press, 2000); Yeo, *The Contest for Social Science.*

76. D. Englander, "Comparisons and Contrasts: Henry Mayhew and Charles Booth as Social Investigators," in *Retrieved Riches: Social Investigation in Britain, 1840–1914*, ed. D. Englander and R. O'Day (Aldershot: Scolar Press, 1955), pp. 132–33.

77. For a more elaborated account of this development, see G. Himmelfarb, *Poverty and Compassion: The Moral Imagination of the Late Victorians* (New York: Alfred A. Knopf, 1992).

78. R.H. Bremner, "'Scientific Philanthropy' 1873–93," *Social Science Review* 30.1 (1956): 168–73; M.J.D. Roberts, "Charity Disestablished? The Origins of the Charity Organisation Society Revisited, 1868–1871," *Journal of Ecclesiastical History* 54.1 (203): 40–61.

79. G. Bowpitt, "Evangelical Christianity, Secular Humanism and the Genesis of British Social Work," *British Journal of Social Work* 28 (1998): 675–93; C.L. Mowat, *The Charity Organisation Society, 1869–1913: Its Ideas and Work* (London: Methuen, 1961); M.J. Smith, *Professional Education for Social Work in Britain: An Historical Account* (London: Allen & Unwin, 1965).

80. Yeo, *The Contest for Social Science.*

81. Hovet, "Harriet Martineau's Exceptional American Narratives."

82. L. F. Ward, "Mind as a Social Factor," *Mind* 9.36 (1884): 571.

83. C. Calhoun, ed. *Sociology in America: A History* (Chicago: University of Chicago Press, 2007); P. M. Lengermann and J. Niebrugge-Brantley, "Back to the Future: Settlement Sociology, 1885–1930," *American Sociologist* (Fall 2002): 5–20; J. E. Williams and V. M. MacLean, "Studying Ourselves: Sociology Discipline-Building in the United States," *American Sociologist* 36.1 (2005): 111–33; F. H. Wines, "Sociology and Philanthropy," *Annals of the American Academy of Political and Social Science* 12 (July 1898): 49–57.

84. A. J. Todd, "Sentimentality and Social Reform," *American Journal of Sociology* 22.2 (1916): 159–76.

85. J. Addams, *Democracy and Social Ethics* (Urbana: University of Illinois, [1902] 2002); M. Fischer, "Addams's Internationalist Pacifism and the Rhetoric Maternalism," *National Women's Studies Association (NWSA) Journal* 18.3 (2006): 1–19; M. R. Leffers, "Pragmatists Jane Addams and John Dewey Inform the Ethics of Care," *Hypatia* 8.2 (1993): 64–77. Also see chapter 6.

86. R. A. Beauregard, "City of Superlatives," *City & Community* 2.3 (2003): 183–99; P. Lannoy, "When Robert. E. Park was (Re)Writing 'The City': Biography, the Social Survey and the Science of Sociology," *American Sociologist* (Spring 2004): 34–62; S. P. Turner and J. H. Turner, *The Impossible Science: An Institutional Analysis of American Sociology* (New York: Sage, 1990).

87. M. J. Deegan, "Early Women Sociologists and the American Sociological Society: The Patterns of Exclusion and Participation," *American Sociologist* 16 (February 1981): 14–24; M. J. Deegan, *Jane Addams and the Men of the Chicago School, 1892–1918* (New Brunswick, NJ: Transaction Books, 1988); M. J. Deegan, "W. E. B. Du Bois and the Women of Hull-House, 1865–1899," *American Sociologist* 23 (Winter 1988): 301–11.

88. L. Berlant, *The Female Complaint: The Unfinished Business of Sentimentality in American Culture* (Durham, NC: Duke University Press, 2008).

89. See, e.g., A. Rai, *Rule of Sympathy: Sentiment, Race, and Power, 1750–1850* (New York: Palgrave, 2002).

CHAPTER 3. A BROKEN RECOVERY

1. C. W. Mills, *The Sociological Imagination* (Oxford: Oxford University Press, 1959), p. 6.

2. Ibid., p. 23.

3. J. D. Brewer, "Imagining *The Sociological Imagination*: The Biographical Context of a Sociological Classic," *British Journal of Sociology* 55.3 (2004): 317–33.

4. J. R. Abbott, "Critical Sociologies and Ressentiment: The Examples of C. Wright Mills and Howard Becker," *American Sociologist* 37.3 (2006): 15–30.

5. C. J. Calhoun and J. VanAntwerpen, "Orthodoxy. Heterodoxy and Hierarchy: Mainstream Sociology and Its Challengers," in *Sociology in America: A History*, ed. C. J. Calhoun (Chicago: University of Chicago Press, 2007), pp. 382–84.

6. Z. Bauman and T. May, *Thinking Sociologically*, 2nd ed. (Oxford: Wiley-Blackwell, 2001).

7. G. Delanty and P. Strydom, eds., *Philosophies of Social Science: The Classical and Contemporary Readings* (Milton Keynes: Open University Press, 2003), p. 284.

8. I. L. Horowitz, "The Intellectual Genesis of C. Wright Mills," in C. W. Mills, *Sociology and Pragmatism: The Higher Learning in America*, ed. I. V. Horowitz (New York: Oxford University Press, 1964).

9. For a further elaboration on Mills's position, see C. W. Mills, *Sociology and Pragmatism: The Higher Learning in America* (New York: Oxford University Press, 1964); J. L. Simich and R. Tilman, "Radicalism vs. Liberalism: C. Wright Mills' Critique of John Dewey's Ideas," *American Journal of Economics and Sociology* 37.4 (1978): 413–30.

10. C. West, *The American Evasion of Philosophy: A Genealogy of Pragmatism* (Basingstoke: Macmillan, 1989), pp. 124–38.

11. N. K. Denzin, "Presidential Address on *The Sociological Imagination* Revisited," *Sociological Quarterly* 31.1 (1990): p. 9.

12. H. Arendt, *Men in Dark Times* (Harmondsworth: Pelican, 1968, p. 8.

13. J. J. Kaag, "Pragmatism and the Lessons of Experience," *Daedalus* 138.2 (2009): 63–72; J. T. Kloppenberg, "Pragmatism: An Old Name for Some New Ways of Thinking?," *Journal of American History* 83.1 (1996): 100–38; E. A. MacGilvray, "Experience as Experiment: Some Consequences of Pragmatism for Democratic Theory," *American Journal of Political Science* 43.2 (1999): 542–65; J. J. Stuhr, *Genealogical Pragmatism: Philosophy, Experience and Community* (Albany: State University of New York Press, 1997).

14. J. Dewey, *On Experience, Nature and Freedom* (New York: Liberal Arts Press, 1960).

15. W. James, "A World of Pure Experience II," *Journal of Philosophy, Psychology and Scientific Methods* 1.21 (1904): 561–70; W. James, "Pragmatism's Conception of Truth," *Journal of Philosophy, Psychology and Scientific Methods* 4.6 (1907): 141–55.

16. See, e.g., R. Bernstein, *The Pragmatic Turn* (Cambridge: Polity Press, 2010), pp. 125–52; R. Rorty, *The Linguistic Turn: Recent Essays in Philosophical Method* (Chicago: University of Chicago Press, 1967); R. Rorty, "Is Truth a Goal of Enquiry? Davidson vs. Wright," *Philosophical Quarterly* 45.180 (1995): 281–300.

17. H. Putnam, *Pragmatism: An Open Question* (Cambridge: Blackwell, 1995); P. M. Shields, "Classical Pragmatism: Engaging Practitioner Experience," *Administration & Society* 36.3 (2004): 351–61.

18. S. Cameron, "Representing Grief: Emerson's Experience," *Representations* 15 (Summer 1986): 15–41; R. W. Emerson, "Experience," in *Essays and Lectures* (New York: Library of America, [1842] 1983).

19. M. Jay, *Songs of Experience: Modern American and European Variations on a Universal Theme* (Berkeley: University of California Press, 2006), pp. 257–77. Also see R. D. Richardson, *William James in the Maelstrom of American Modernism* (Boston: Mariner Books, 2006).

20. For an account of the suffering experienced through this time, see D. G. Faust, *The Republic of Suffering: Death and the American Civil War* (New York: Vintage, 2008).

21. L. Menand, *The Metaphysical Club: A Story of Ideas in America* (New York: Farrar, Straus and Giroux, 2001), p. x.

22. J. Dewey, "The Need for a Recovery of Philosophy," in *On Experience, Nature and Freedom*, ed. R. Bernstein (New York: Liberal Arts Press, [1917] 1960), pp. 23–67.

23. J. Conway, "Women Reformers and American Culture, 1870–1930," *Journal of Social History* 5.2 (1971): 164–77 (see p. 173); C. H. Seigfried, "Socializing Democracy: Jane Addams and John Dewey," *Philosophy of the Social Sciences* 29.2 (1999): 207–30; C. H. Seigfried, "Introduction to the Illinois Edition," in J. Addams, *Democracy and Social Ethics* (Urbana: University of Illinois Press, 2002).

24. P. Bourdieu and L. Wacquant, *An Invitation to Reflexive Sociology* (Chicago: University of Chicago Press, 1992), p. 122; A. Kleinman, *The Illness Narratives: Suffering, Healing and the Human Condition* (New York: Basic Books, 1988); A. Kleinman, "Everything That Really Matters: Social Suffering, Subjectivity, and the Remaking of Human Experience in a Disordering World," *Harvard Theological Review* 90.3 (1997): 315–36; A. Kleinman, "Experience and Its Moral Modes: Culture, Human Conditions and Disorder," in *The Tanner Lectures on Human Values*, vol. 20, ed. G. B. Peterson (Salt Lake City: University of Utah Press, 1999), p. 360.

25. A. Kleinman, V. Das, and M. Lock, eds., *Social Suffering* (Berkeley: University of California Press, 1997).

26. Bourdieu and Wacquant, *An Invitation to Reflexive Sociology*, p. 200.

27. For some key works and commentaries, see P. Bourdieu et al. *The Weight of the World: Social Suffering in Contemporary Society* (Cambridge: Polity Press, 1999); C. Dejours, *Souffrances en France: La banalization de l'injustice sociale* (Paris: Seuil, 1998); Kleinman, Das, and Lock, *Social Suffering;* E. Renault, *Souffrances sociales* (Paris: La Découverte, 2008); I. Wilkinson, *Suffering: A Sociological Introduction* (Cambridge: Polity Press, 2005).

28. P. Farmer, *Pathologies of Power: Health, Human Rights, and the New War on the Poor* (Berkeley: University of California Press, 2003); P. Farmer, "Conversation in the Time of Cholera: A Reflection on Structural Violence and Social Change," in *In the Company of the Poor: Conversations with Dr. Paul Farmer and Fr. Gustavo Gutierrez*, ed. M. Griffin and J. W. Block (New York: Orbis Books, 2013).

29. M. Herzfeld, *The Social Production of Indifference: Exploring the Symbolic Roots of Western Bureaucracy* (Chicago: University of Chicago Press, 1992); R. K. Merton, "The Unanticipated Consequences of Purposive Action," *American Sociological Review* 1.6 (1936): 894–904.

30. V. Das, *Life and Worlds: Violence and the Descent into the Ordinary* (Berkeley: University of California Press, 2006).

31. Kleinman, Das, and Lock, *Social Suffering*, p. ix.

32. This is a featured matter of concern in Das, *Life and Worlds;* M. J. Good, P. Brodwin, B. Good, and A. Kleinman, eds., *Pain as Human Experience: An Anthropological Perspective*, Comparative Studies of Health Systems and Medical Care (Berkeley: University of California Press, 1994); P. Farmer, *AIDS and Accusation: Haiti and the Geography of Blame* (Berkeley: University of California Press, 1992); S. Kaufman, *And a Time to Die: How American Hospitals Shape the End of Life* (Chicago: University of Chicago Press, 2006); M. Jackson, *Life within Limits: Well-Being in a World of Want* (Durham, NC: Duke University Press, 2011); E. C. James, *Democratic Insecurities: Violence, Trauma, and Intervention in Haiti* (Berkeley: University of California Press, 2010).

33. This issue is raised by J. Biehl, *Vita: Life in a Zone of Social Abandonment* (Berkeley: University of California Press, 2005); R. Desjarlais, *Shelter Blues: Sanity and Selfhood among the Homeless* (Philadelphia: University of Pennsylvania Press, 1997); A. Garcia, *The Pastoral Clinic: Addiction and Dispossession along the Rio Grande* (Berkeley: University of California Press, 2010); C. Han, *Life in Debt: Times of Care and Violence in Neoliberal Chile* (Berkeley: University of California Press, 2012); James, *Democratic Insecurities;* A. Petryna, *Life Exposed: Biological Citizens after Chernobyl* (Princeton, NJ: Princeton University Press, 2002).

34. P. Bourdieu, "Understanding," in Bourdieu et al., *The Weight of the World*, p. 608.

35. See, e.g., the accounts featured in V. Das, "Sufferings, Theodicies, Disciplinary Practices, Appropriations," *International Journal of Social Science* 49 (1997): 563–57; V. Das, 'The Act of Witnessing: Violence, Poisonous Knowledge, and Subjectivity," in *Violence and Subjectivity*, ed. V. Das, A. Kleinman, M. Ramphele, and P. Reynolds (Berkeley: University of California Press, 2000).

36. Das, *Life and Worlds*.

37. This is a repeated theme in the case studies featured in A. Kleinman, *What Really Matters: Living a Moral Life amidst Uncertainty and Danger* (New York: Oxford University Press, 2006).

38. A. Becker, *Body, Self, and Society: The View from Fiji* (Philadelphia: University of Pennsylvania Press, 1995); L. Cohen, "No Aging in India: The Uses of Gerontology," *Culture, Medicine and Psychiatry* 16.2 (1991): 123–61; Farmer, *AIDS and Accusation.*

39. In this regard, while not always sharing in their terms of analysis, politics, or conclusions, we pay careful heed to critiques such as H. Arendt, "The Social Question," in *On Revolution* (Harmondsworth: Penguin, 1963); D. Fassin, "Compassion and Repression: The Moral Economy of Immigration Policies in France," *Cultural Anthropology* 20.3 (2005): 362–87; D. Fassin, *When Bodies Remember: Experiences and Politics of AIDS in South Africa* (Berkeley: University of California Press, 2007); D. Fassin, "Beyond Good and Evil? Questioning the Anthropological Discomfort with Morals," *Anthropological Theory* 8.4 (2008): 333–44; D. Fassin, "Another Politics of Life Is Possible," *Theory, Culture & Society* 26.5 (2009): 44–60; D. Fassin, "Heart of Humaneness: The Moral Economy of Humanitarian Intervention," in *Contemporary States of Emergency: The Politics of Military and Humanitarian Interventions,* ed. D. Fassin and M. Pandolfini (New York: Zone Books, 2010); D. Fassin, *Humanitarian Reason: A Moral History of the Present* (Berkeley: University of California Press, 2012); M. Givoni, "Beyond the Humanitarian/Political Divide: Witnessing and the Making of Humanitarian Ethics," *Journal of Human Rights* 10.1 (2011): 55–75.

40. Farmer, *AIDS and Accusation;* P. Farmer, *Infections and Inequalities: The Modern Plagues* (Berkeley: University of California Press, 1999); Farmer, *Pathologies of Power;* J. Galtung, "Violence, Peace, and Peace Research," *Journal of Peace Research* 6.3 (1969): 167–91; J. Roberts, "Structural Violence and Emotional Health: A Message from Easington, a Former Mining Community in Northern England," *Anthropology & Medicine* 16.1 (2009): 37–48.

41. H. A. Baer, M. Singer, and I. Susser, *Medical Anthropology and the World System* (Westport, CT: Praeger, 2013).

42. R. Desjarlais, L. Eisenberg, B. Good, and A. Kleinman, *World Mental Health: Problems and Priorities in Low-Income Countries* (New York: Oxford University Press, 1995).

43. See P. Farmer, J. Y. Kim, A. Kleinman, and M. Basilico, eds., *Reimagining Global Health: An Introduction* (Berkeley: University of California Press, 2013); M. Lock and V. K. Nguyen, *An Anthropology of Biomedicine* (Oxford: Wiley-Blackwell, 2010); M. Singer and S. Clair, "Syndemics and Public Health: Reconceptualizing Disease in Bio-Social Context," *Medical Anthropology Quarterly* 17.4 (2003): 423–41.

44. See R. Brown and R. Lewis-Fernandez, "Culture and Conversion Disorder: Implications for DSM-5," *Psychiatry* 74.3 (2011): 187–206; P. I. Bourgois, *In Search of Respect: Selling Crack in El Barrio* (Cambridge: Cambridge University Press, 2002); P. I. Bourgois and J. Schonberg, *Righteous Dopefiend* (Berkeley: University of California Press, 2009); D. Fullwiley, *The Encultured Gene:*

Sickle Cell Health Politics and Biological Difference in West Africa (Princeton, NJ: Princeton University Press, 2011); Garcia, *The Pastoral Clinic;* Han, *Life in Debt;* M. Lock and N. Scheper-Hughes, "A Critical-Interpretive Approach in Medical Anthropology: Rituals and Routines of Discipline and Dissent," in *Medical Anthropology: A Handbook of Theory and Method,* ed. T.M. Johnson and C.F. Sargent (New York: Greenwood Press, 1990).

45. M.D. Good, S.S. Willen, S.D. Hannah, K. Vickory, and L.T. Park, eds., *Shattering Culture: American Medicine Responds to Cultural Diversity* (New York: Russell Sage Foundation, 2011); A.L. Hinton, ed., *Annihilating Difference: The Anthropology of Genocide* (Berkeley: University of California Press, 2002); S. Keshavjee, *Blind Spot: How Neoliberalism Infiltrated Global Health* (Berkeley: University of California Press, 2014).

46. L. Duffy, "Suffering, Shame, and Silence: The Stigma of HIV/AIDS," *Journal of the Association of Nurses in AIDS Care* 16.1 (2005): 13–20; A. Kleinman, W.Z. Wang, S.C. Li, X.M. Cheng, X.Y. Dai, K.T. Li, and J. Kleinman, "The Social Course of Epilepsy: Chronic Illness as Social Experience in Interior China," *Social Science & Medicine* 40.10 (1995): 1319–30; T. Rhodes, M. Singer, P. Bourgois, S.R. Friedman, and S.A. Strathdee, "The Social Structural Production of HIV Risk among Injecting Drug Users," *Social Science & Medicine* 61.5 (2005): 1026–44; M. Rock, "Sweet Blood and Social Suffering: Rethinking Cause-Effect Relationships in Diabetes, Distress, and Duress," *Medical Anthropology* 22.2 (2003): 131–74.

47. Bourgois and Schonberg, *Righteous Dopefiend;* M. Todeschini, "The Bomb's Womb? Women and the Atom Bomb," in *Remaking a World: Violence, Social Suffering and Recovery,* ed. V. Das et al. (Berkeley: University of California Press, 2001); L.H. Yang, A. Kleinman, B.G. Link, J.C. Phelan, S. Lee, and B. Good, "Culture and Stigma: Adding Moral Experience to Stigma Theory," *Social Science & Medicine* 64.7 (2007): 1524–35.

48. Farmer, *AIDS and Accusation.*

49. N. Scheper-Hughes, *Death without Weeping: The Violence of Everyday Life in Brazil* (Berkeley: University of California Press, 1992).

50. For an alternative view of how this moral-emotional process actually works, see M. Nations and L. Rebhun, "Angels with Wet Wings Won't Fly: Maternal Sentiment in Brazil and the Image of Neglect," *Culture, Medicine, and Psychiatry* 12.2 (June 1988): 141–200.

51. Biehl, *Vita;* Bourgeois and Schonberg, *Righteous Dopefiend;* Farmer, *Infections and Inequalities;* Farmer, *Pathologies of Power;* Han, *Life in Debt;* N. Scheper-Hughes, "Three Propositions for a Critically Applied Medical Anthropology." *Social Science & Medicine* 30.2 (1990): 189–97.

52. Fullwiley, *The Enculturated Gene;* M.C. Inhorn, "Global Infertility and the Globalization of New Reproductive Technologies: Illustrations from Egypt," *Social Science & Medicine* 56.9 (2003): 1837–51; T.M. Luhrmann, *Of*

Two Minds: The Growing Disorder in American Psychiatry (New York: Alfred A. Knopf, 2000).

53. A. Kleinman, *Patients and Healers in the Context of Culture: An Exploration of the Borderland between Anthropology, Medicine, and Psychiatry* (Berkeley: University of California Press, 1980); A. Kleinman, "How Is Culture Important for DSM-IV?," in *Culture and Psychiatric Diagnosis: A DSM-IV Perspective*, ed. J. E. Mezzich, D. L. Parron, and A. Kleinman (Arlington, VA: American Psychiatric Press, 1996); Lock and Nguyen, *An Anthropology of Biomedicine*; Luhrmann, *Of Two Minds*; Scheper-Hughes, "Three Propositions for a Critically Applied Medical Anthropology."

54. J. Y. Kim, J. V. Millen, A. Irwin, and J. Gershman, eds., *Dying for Growth: Global Inequality and the Health of the Poor* (Monroe, ME: Common Courage Press, 2002); K. Krieger, *Epidemiology and the People's Health: Theory and Context* (New York: Oxford University Press, 2011); M. Marmot and R. Wilkinson, eds., *Social Determinants of Health* (Oxford: Oxford University Press, 2009); Farmer et al., *Reimagining Global Health*.

55. For some useful reviews of this literature see E. J. Cassell, *The Nature of Suffering and the Goals of Medicine* (Oxford: Oxford University Press, 2004); S. Coakley and K. K. Shelemay, eds., *Pain and Its Transformations: The Interface of Biology and Culture* (Cambridge, MA: Harvard University Press, 2007).

56. H. L. Fields, "Setting the Stage for Pain: Allegorical Tales from Neuroscience," in Coakley and Shelemay, *Pain and Its Transformations*, p. 59.

57. See A. Kleinman, "Response: The Incommensurable Richness of 'Experience,'" in Coakley and Shelemay, *Pain and Its Transformations*, pp. 122–25.

58. See Lock and Nguyen, *An Anthropology of Biomedicine*.

59. Bourdieu et al., *The Weight of the World*; S. J. Charlesworth, "Understanding Social Suffering: A Phenomenological Investigation of the Experience of Inequality," *Journal of Community & Applied Social Psychology* 15.4 (2005): 296–312; Dejours, *Souffrances en France*; Kim et al., *Dying for Growth*; J. Peck, "Zombie Neoliberalism and the Ambidextrous State," *Theoretical Criminology* 14.1 (2010): 104–10; Renault, *Souffrances sociales*; L. Wacquant, *Punishing the Poor: The Neoliberal Government of Social Insecurity* (Durham, NC: Duke University Press, 2009).

60. Bourdieu, "Understanding."

61. P. Bourdieu, "The Space of Points of View," in Bourdieu et al., *The Weight of the World*, pp. 3–4.

62. P. Bourdieu, "Hanging by a Thread," in Bourdieu et al., *The Weight of the World*, pp. 375–76.

63. A. McRobbie, "A Mixed Bag of Misfortunes? Bourdieu's *Weight of the World*," *Theory, Culture & Society* 19.3 (2002): 131–33.

64. Bourdieu, "Understanding," pp. 621–26.

65. Bourdieu and Wacquant, *An Invitation to Reflexive Sociology*.

66. See R. Connell, *Southern Theory: Social Science and the Global Dynamics of Knowledge* (Cambridge: Polity Press, 2007).

67. S. Chen and M. Ravallion, *The Developing World Is Poorer than We Thought, but No Less Successful in the Fight against Poverty*, World Bank Policy Research Working Paper 4703 (Washington, DC: World Bank, 2008).

68. See H. K. Atrash, "Childhood Mortality: Still a Global Priority," *Journal of Human Growth and Development* 23.3 (2013): 257–60; FAO, *The State of Food Insecurity in the World: Addressing Food Insecurity in Protracted Crises* (Rome: FAO, 2010); B. Thompson, M. J. Cohen, and J. Meerman, "World Food Insecurity and Malnutrition: Scope, Trends, Causes and Consequences," in *The Impact of Climate Change and Bioenergy on Nutrition*, ed. B. Thompson and M. J. Cohen (Dordrecht: Springer, 2012); UNICEF, *Levels and Trends in Child Mortality: Report 2010* (New York: UNICEF, 2010).

69. Farmer, *Pathologies of Power*.

70. World Bank, *World Development Report 2011: Conflict, Security, and Development* (Washington, DC: World Bank, 2011).

71. UNDP, *Human Development Report 2006. Beyond Scarcity: Power, Poverty and the Global Water Crisis* (New York: UNDP, 2006).

72. M. Davis, *Planet of Slums* (London: Verso, 2007); M. Dogan, "Four Hundred Giant Cities Atop the World," *International Social Science Journal* 56.181 (2004): 347–60; P. D. Smith, *City: A Guidebook for the Urban Age* (London: Bloomsbury Press, 2012).

73. A. Kleinman and J. Kleinman, "The Appeal of Experience, the Dismay of Images: Cultural Appropriations of Suffering in Our Times," *Daedalus* 125.1 (1996): 1–23.

74. M. Green, "Representing Poverty and Attacking Representations: Perspectives on Poverty from Social Anthropology," *Journal of Development Studies* 42.7 (2006): 1108–29.

75. Ibid., p. 1116.

76. Ibid.

77. See, e.g., J. James, *Technology, Globalization and Poverty* (Cheltenham: Edward Elgar, 2002); J. Quesada, "Suffering Child: An Embodiment of War and Its Aftermath in Post-Sandinista Nicaragua," *Medical Anthropology Quarterly* 12.1 (1998): 51–73; A. Sayad, *The Suffering of the Immigrant* (Cambridge: Polity Press, 2004); C. Zarowsky, "Writing Trauma: Emotion, Ethnography, and the Politics of Suffering among Somali Returnees in Ethiopia," *Culture, Medicine and Psychiatry* 28.2 (2004): 189–209.

78. Biehl, *Vita*.

79. M. Tapias, "Emotions and the Intergenerational Embodiment of Social Suffering in Rural Bolivia," *Medical Anthropology Quarterly* 20.3 (2006): 399–415.

80. Such concerns are expressed by Veena Das. See V. Das, *Critical Events: An Anthropological Perspective on Contemporary India* (Delhi: Oxford University Press, 1995).

81. L. Butt, "The Suffering Stranger: Medical Anthropology and International Morality," *Medical Anthropology* 21.1 (2002): 1–24.

82. L. Boltanski, *Distant Suffering: Morality, Media and Politics* (Cambridge: Cambridge University Press, 1999).

83. S. Cohen, *States of Denial: Knowing about Atrocities and Suffering* (Cambridge: Polity Press, 2001).

84. B. Höijer, "The Discourse of Global Compassion: The Audience and Media Reporting of Human Suffering," *Media, Culture & Society* 26.4 (2004): 513–31; K. Tester, *Compassion, Morality, and the Media* (Buckingham: Open University Press, 2001); Wilkinson, *Suffering*.

85. U. Beck, *The Cosmopolitan Vision* (Cambridge: Polity Press, 2006); U. Beck and J. Willms, *Conversations with Ulrich Beck* (Cambridge: Polity Press, 2004).

86. K. Nash, "Global Citizenship as Show Business: The Cultural Politics of Make Poverty History," *Media, Culture and Society* 30.2 (2008): 167–81.

87. J. Biehl, B. Good, and A. Kleinman, "Introduction: Rethinking Subjectivity," in *Subjectivity: Ethnographic Investigations*, ed. J. Biehl, B. Good, and A. Kleinman (Berkeley: University of California Press, 2007).

88. J. Rifkin, *The Empathic Civilization: The Race to Global Consciousness in a World in Crisis* (Cambridge: Polity Press, 2009).

89. For examples of how this is taking place in contemporary China, see A. Kleinman, Y. Yan, J. Jun, S. Lee, E. Zhang, P. Tianshu, W. Fei, and G. Jinhua, *Deep China: The Moral Life of the Person* (Berkeley: University of California Press, 2011).

90. Jackson, *Life within Limits*.

91. C. W. Mills, "The Cultural Apparatus," in *Power, Politics and People: The Collected Essays of C. Wright Mills*, ed. I. L. Horowitz (New York: Oxford University Press, 1963), pp. 405–22.

92. K. Sawchuk, "The Cultural Apparatus: C. Wright Mills' Unfinished Work," *American Sociologist* 32.1 (2001): 27–49.

93. In his biography of Mills, Daniel Geary draws a spotlight to the ways this agenda shaped his intellectual career, relations within the academy, and political standpoint. See D. Geary, *Radical Ambition: C. Wright Mills, the Left, and American Social Thought* (Berkeley: University of California Press, 2009).

94. See Bourgois, *In Search of Respect;* Bourgois and Schonberg, *Righteous Dopefiend;* Garcia, *The Pastoral Clinic.*

95. A. Cohen, A. Kleinman, and B. Saraceno, eds., *World Mental Health Casebook: Social and Mental Programs in Low-Income Countries* (New York:

Springer, 2002); Farmer, *Pathologies of Power;* Farmer et al., *Reimagining Global Health;* Good et al., *Shattering Culture;* L.J. Kirmayer, "Multicultural Medicine and the Politics of Recognition," *Journal of Medicine and Philosophy* 36.4 (2014): 410–23; L.J. Kirmayer, G.M. Brass, T. Holton, K. Paul, C. Simpson, and C. Tait, *Suicide among Aboriginal People in Canada* (Ottawa: Aboriginal Healing Foundation, 2007).

CHAPTER 4. LEARNING FROM WEBER

1. Marianne Weber, *Max Weber: A Biography* (New York: John Wiley & Sons, 1975), p. 678; original emphasis.

2. L.A. Scaff, *Max Weber in America* (Princeton, NJ: Princeton University Press, 2011), p. 1.

3. K. Marx, "The Eighteenth Brumaire of Louis Bonaparte," in *Karl Marx: Selected Writings,* ed. D. Mclellan (Oxford: Oxford University Press, [1851] 1977), p. 300.

4. M. Weber, "Science as a Vocation," in *From Max Weber,* ed. H.H. Gerth and C.W. Mills (London: Routledge, 1948); M. Weber, "Politics as a Vocation," in Gerth and Mills, *From Max Weber.*

5. F. Tenbruck, 'The Problem of the Thematic Unity in the Works of Max Weber," *British Journal of Sociology* 31.3 (1980): 316–51.

6. F. Nietzsche, "On the Genealogy of Morals," in *Basic Writings of Nietzsche,* ed. W. Kaufmann (New York: Modern Library, [1887] 2000), p. 504.

7. P.J. Kain, "Nietzsche, Eternal Recurrence, and the Horror of Existence," *Journal of Nietzsche Studies* 33 (2007): 49–63; P.J. Kain, "Nietzsche, Virtue, and the Horror of Existence," *British Journal for the History of Philosophy* 17.1 (2009): 153–67.

8. R.J. Antonio, "Nietzsche's Antisociology: Subjectified Culture and the End of History," *American Journal of Sociology* 101.1 (1995): 1–43, esp. pp.7–12.

9. M. Warren, "The Politics of Nietzsche's Philosophy: Nihilism, Culture and Power," *Political Studies* 33.3 (1985): 418–38.

10. R. Schroeder, "Nietzsche and Weber: Two 'Prophets' of the Modern World," in *Max Weber, Rationality and Modernity,* ed. S. Whimster and S. Lash (London: Routledge, 1987); T.B. Strong, "What Have We to Do with Morals? Nietzsche and Weber on History and Ethics," *History of the Human Sciences* 5.3 (1992): 9–18.

11. M. Weber, *The Sociology of Religion* (London: Methuen, 1966).

12. M. Weber, "Religious Rejections of the World and Their Directions," in Gerth and Mills, *From Max Weber.*

13. M. Weber, "The Social Psychology of the World Religions," in Gerth and Mills, *From Max Weber.*

14. See N. Gane, *Max Weber and Postmodern Theory: Rationalization versus Re-enchantment* (Basingstoke: Macmillan, 2004), pp. 19–23.

15. M. Weber, *The Protestant Ethic and the Spirit of Capitalism* (New York: Charles Scribner's & Sons, 1958), p. 182. For some commentary on this matter, see P. Baehr, "The 'Iron Cage' and the 'Shell as Hard as Steel': Parsons, Weber, and the Stahlhartes Gehäuse Metaphor in the *Protestant Ethic and the Spirit of Capitalism*," *History and Theory* 40.2 (2001): 153–69.

16. S. A. Kent, "Weber, Goethe, and the Nietzschean Allusion: Capturing the Source of the 'Iron Cage' Metaphor," *Sociology of Religion* 44.4 (1983): 297–319.

17. F. Nietzsche, *Thus Spoke Zarathustra: A Book for Everyone and No One* (Harmondsworth: Penguin Books, [1883] 1961), pp. 45–47.

18. S. Seidman, "Modernity, Meaning, and Cultural Pessimism in Max Weber," *Sociology of Religion* 44.4 (1983): 267–78; S. Seidman, "The Main Aims and Thematic Structures of Max Weber's Sociology," *Canadian Journal of Sociology* 9.4 (1984): 381–404; Weber, "Science as a Vocation."

19. W. Schluchter, *Rationalism, Religion, and Domination: A Weberian Perspective* (Berkeley: University of California Press, 1989), p. 316.

20. Antonio, "Nietzsche's Antisociology," p. 23.

21. T. Parsons, Introduction to Weber, *The Sociology of Religion*, p. xlvi; original emphasis.

22. For a discussion of how this might apply to modern practices of risk management, see I. Wilkinson, *Risk Vulnerability and Everyday Life*, London: Routledge, 2010), pp. 27–35.

23. N. A. Christakis, *Death Foretold: Prophecy and Prognosis in Medical Care* (Chicago: University of Chicago Press, 2001); J. E. Dunphy, "Annual Discourse: On Caring for the Patient with Cancer," *New England Journal of Medicine* 295.6 (1976): 313–19; M. Lock, "On Dying Twice: Culture, Technology and the Determination of Death," in *Living and Working with the New Medical Technologies: Intersections of Inquiry,* ed. M. Lock, A. Young, and A. Cambrosio (New York: Cambridge University Press, 2000); A. Girgis and R. W. Sanson-Fisher, "Breaking Bad News: Consensus Guidelines for Medical Practitioners," *Journal of Clinical Oncology* 13.9 (1995): 2449–56.

24. Wilkinson, *Risk Vulnerability and Everyday Life.*

25. I. Hacking, *The Taming of Chance* (Cambridge: Cambridge University Press, 1990).

26. M. Weber, "The Nature of Charismatic Authority and Its Routinization," in *Max Weber on Charisma and Institution Building,* ed. S. N. Eisenstadt (Chicago: University of Chicago Press, 1968), pp. 53–54.

27. F. Tenbruck, "The Problem of the Thematic Unity in the Works of Max Weber (with Prefatory Remarks)," in *Reading Weber,* ed. K. Tribe (London: Routledge, 1989), p. 70.

28. P. L. Wasielewski, "The Emotional Basis of Charisma," *Symbolic Interaction* 8.2 (1985): 207–22.

29. E. A. Tiryakian, "Collective Effervescence, Social Change and Charisma: Durkheim, Weber and 1989," *International Sociology* 10.3 (1995): 269–81.

30. T. W. Adorno, *Negative Dialectics* (New York: Continuum, 1973), pp. 202–3.

31. Weber, "The Nature of Charismatic Authority," p. 53.

32. M. Riesebrodt, "Charisma in Max Weber's Sociology of Religion," *Religion* 29.1 (1999): 1–14.

33. W. Spinrad, "Charisma: A Blighted Concept and an Alternative Formula," *Political Science Quarterly* 106.2 (1991): 295–311.

34. I. Kershaw, *The "Hitler Myth": Image and Reality in the Third Reich* (Oxford: Oxford University Press, 1987).

35. P. Lassman, ed., *Max Weber* (Aldershot: Ashgate, 2006), pp. viii–xv; B. S. Turner, "Introduction: Marx and Nietzsche," in *For Weber: Essays on the Sociology of Fate* (London: Sage, 1996), p. xix; B. S. Turner, *Classical Sociology* (London: Sage, 1999), p. 14.

36. Also see J. W. Bowker, *Problems of Suffering in Religions of the World* (Cambridge: Cambridge University Press, 1975), pp. 361–63; Weber, "Politics as a Vocation," pp. 122–23.

37. Tenbruck, "The Problem of the Thematic Unity in the Works of Max Weber" (1980), p. 338.

38. Weber, "Politics as a Vocation," pp. 122–23.

39. T. E. Dow Jr., "An Analysis of Weber's Work on Charisma," *British Journal of Sociology* 29.1 (1978): 83–93, esp. 85.

40. M. Weber, "The Routinization of Charisma," in *Max Weber: The Theory of Social and Economic Organization,* ed. T. Parsons (New York: Free Press, 1947), p. 370.

41. Tenbruck, 'The Problem of the Thematic Unity in the Works of Max Weber" (1989), p. 70.

42. Ibid., p. 67.

43. Weber, "Religious Rejections of the World," p. 324.

44. For those who believe in a just, all-knowing, all-loving, and all-powerful God, the problem of evil was formulated by Epicurus (341–270 BCE) and is quoted by Lactanius (ca. 260–340 CE) as "God either wishes to take away evils, and is unable; or He is able, and is unwilling; or He is neither willing nor able, or He is both willing and able. If He is willing and is unable, He is feeble, which is not in accordance with the character of God; if He is able and unwilling, He is envious, which is equally at variance with God; if He is neither willing nor able, He is both envious and feeble, and therefore not God; if He is both willing and able, which alone is suitable to God, from what source then are evils? Or why does He not remove them?" (cited in J. Hick, *Evil and the God of Love* [London: Macmillan, 1966], p. 5).

45. S. Kalberg, "The Past and Present Influence of World Views: Max Weber on a Neglected Sociological Concept," *Journal of Classical Sociology* 4.2 (2004): 139–63.

46. See, e.g., D. Randall, "Providence, Fortune, and the Experience of Combat: English Printed Battlefield Reports, circa 1570–1637," *Sixteenth Century Journal* 35.4 (2004): 1053–77; A. Walsham, *Providence in Early Modern England* (Oxford: Oxford University Press, 1999).

47. W. E. Burns, *An Age of Wonders: Prodigies, Politics and Providence in England, 1657–1727* (Manchester: Manchester University Press, 2002); C. Hill, *The English Bible and the Seventeenth-Century Revolution* (London: Penguin, 1993), pp. 413–35.

48. A. Thompson, *The Art of Suffering and the Impact of Seventeenth-Century Anti-Providential Thought* (Aldershot: Ashgate, 2003).

49. J. A. Herdt, "The Rise of Sympathy and the Question of Divine Suffering," *Journal of Religious Ethics* 29.3 (2001): 367–99.

50. A. Foyle, "Human and Divine Suffering," *Ars Disputandi* 5 (2005), http://dx.doi.org/10.1080/15665399.2005.10819894.

51. K. Thomas, *Religion and the Decline of Magic: Studies in Popular Beliefs in Sixteenth- and Seventeenth-Century England* (London: Penguin, 1971), pp. 90–132.

52. Bowker, *Problems of Suffering in Religions of the World;* E. B. Gilman, *Plague Writing in Early Modern England* (Chicago: University of Chicago Press, 2009); R. B. Hays, *All in the Family: Faith Issues for Families Dealing with Addiction* (Nashville, TN: West Bow Press, 2010); B. S. Turner, "The History of the Changing Concepts of Health and Illness: Outline of a General Model of Illness Categories," in *The Handbook of Social Studies in Health and Medicine,* ed. G. L. Albrecht, R. Fitzpatrick, and S. C. Scrimshaw (London: Sage, 2000).

53. See, e.g., T. Beard, *The Theatre of God's Judgements* (Memphis, TN: Rare Books Club, [1597] 2012).

54. J. Crawford, *Marvelous Protestantism: Monstrous Births in Post-Reformation England* (Baltimore: Johns Hopkins University Press, 2005); A. Cunningham and O. P. Grell, *The Four Horsemen of the Apocalypse: Religion, War, Famine and Death in Reformation Europe* (Cambridge: Cambridge University Press, 2000).

55. Gilman, *Plague Writing.*

56. P. Slack, *The Impact of Plague in Tudor and Stuart England* (London: Routledge & Kegan Paul, 1985), pp. 227–54.

57. Ibid., p. 48.

58. Weber, "Politics as a Vocation," p. 117.

59. H. J. Cook, "The History of Medicine and the Scientific Revolution," *Isis* 102.1 (2011): 102–8; S. Sturdy and R. Cooter, "Science, Scientific Management

and the Transformation of Medicine in Britain, c. 1870–1950," *History of Science* 36 (1998): 421–66.

60. P. Harrison, "'Science' and 'Religion': Constructing the Boundaries," *Journal of Religion* 86.1 (2006): 81–106; A. Wear, ed., *Medicine in Society: Historical Essays* (Cambridge: Cambridge University Press, 1992).

61. D. Porter and R. Porter, *Patient's Progress: Doctors and Doctoring in Eighteenth-Century England* (Redwood City, CA: Stanford University Press, 1989).

62. R. Porter, "The Patient's View: Doing Medical History from Below," *Theory and Society* 14.2 (1985): 175–98; R. Porter, *Patients and Practitioners: Lay Perceptions of Medicine in Pre-Industrial Society* (Cambridge: Cambridge University Press, 1985).

63. Porter, "The Patient's View," p. 184.

64. Scaff, *Max Weber in America*, p. 250; Seidman, "The Main Aims and Thematic Structures of Max Weber's Sociology.".

65. G. Shafir, "The Incongruity between Destiny and Merit: Max Weber on Meaningful Existence and Modernity," *British Journal of Sociology* 36.4 (1985): 516–30.

66. Tenbruck, 'The Problem of the Thematic Unity in the Works of Max Weber" (1989), pp. 76–79.

67. S. Kalberg, "The Rationalization of Action in Max Weber's Sociology of Religion," *Sociological Theory* 8.1 (1990): 58–84; S. Kalberg, "Should the 'Dynamic Autonomy' of Ideas Matter to Sociologists?," *Journal of Classical Sociology* 1.3 (2001): 291–327; Kalberg, "The Past and Present Influence of World Views."

68. Weber, "Religious Rejections on the World," p. 330.

69. Ibid.

70. Kalberg, "The Past and Present Influence of World Views," p. 156.

71. Kalberg, "Should the 'Dynamic Autonomy' of Ideas Matter?"

72. Weber, "Bureaucracy," in Gerth and Mills, *From Max Weber*, p. 215.

73. M. Herzfeld, *The Body Impolitic: Artisans and Artifice in the Global Hierarchy of Value* (Chicago: University of Chicago Press, 2004), p. 33.

74. M. N. Barnett, "The UN Security Council, Indifference, and Genocide in Rwanda," *Cultural Anthropology* 12.4 (1997): 551–78, esp. 575–76.

75. S. Hewa, "Medical Technology: A Pandora's Box?," *Journal of Medical Humanities* 15.3 (1994): 171–81.

76. K. Charmaz, "Loss of Self: A Fundamental Form of Suffering in the Chronically Ill," *Sociology of Health & Illness* 5.2 (1983): 168–95; P. Conrad, *The Medicalization of Society: On the Transformation of Human Conditions into Treatable Disorders* (Baltimore: Johns Hopkins University Press, 2008); S. J. Williams, *Medicine and the Body* (London: Sage, 2003).

77. J. E. Davis, "Medicalization, Social Control, and the Relief of Suffering," in *The New Blackwell Companion to Medical Sociology*, ed. W. C. Cockerham

(Malden, MA: Blackwell, 2009); R. Fox, *Essays in Medical Sociology: Journeys into the Field* (New Brunswick, NJ: Transaction Publishers, 1988).

78. A. Kleinman, V.. Das, and M. Lock, eds., *Social Suffering* (Berkeley: University of California Press, 1997).

79. J. Weiss, "On the Irreversibility of Western Rationalization and Max Weber's Alleged Fatalism," in *Max Weber, Rationality and Modernity*, ed. S. Whimster and S. Lash (London: Allen & Unwin, 1987).

80. Weber, "The Nature of Charismatic Authority," pp. 53–54.

81. W. H. Swatos, "The Disenchantment of Charisma: A Weberian Assessment of Revolution in a Rationalized World," *Sociological Analysis* 42.2 (1981): 119–36.

82. Weber, "The Nature of Charismatic Authority," pp. 53–54.

83. S. Turner, "Charisma Reconsidered," *Journal of Classical Sociology* 3.1 (2003): 5–26, esp. 20.

84. C. Adair-Toteff, "Max Weber's Charisma," *Journal of Classical Sociology* 5.2 (2005): 189–204.

85. For useful summaries, see D. Chalcraft, M. F. Howell, M. L. Menendez, and M. H. Vera, eds., *Max Weber Matters: Interweaving Past and Present* (Farnham: Ashgate, 2008); S. Whimster, *Understanding Weber* (London: Routledge, 2007).

86. Tribe, *Reading Weber;* ; B. S. Turner, *Max Weber: From History to Modernity* (London: Routledge, 1992).

87. G. J. Hinkle, "The Americanization of Max Weber," *Current Perspectives in Social Theory* 7 (1986): 87–104; Scaff, *Max Weber in America*, pp. 197–252.

88. This is especially the case as far as Weber's association with the "iron cage" metaphor is concerned. See Baehr, "The 'Iron Cage' and the 'Shell as Hard as Steel'"; D. Chalcraft, "Bringing the Text Back In: On Ways of Reading the Iron Cage Metaphor in the Two Editions of *The Protestant Ethic*," in *Organizing Modernity: New Weberian Perspectives on Work, Organization and Society*, ed. L. Ray and M. Reed (London: Routledge, 1994).

89. W. Hennis, *Max Weber: Essays in Reconstruction* (London: Allen & Unwin, 1988); Tenbruck, 'The Problem of the Thematic Unity in the Works of Max Weber" (1980, 1989); Turner, *Max Weber*, p. 228.

90. Weber. "Science as a Vocation," pp. 149, 155.

91. Weber, "Politics as a Vocation," p. 353; original emphasis.

92. S. S. Wolin, "Max Weber: Legitimation, Method, and the Politics of Theory," *Political Theory* 9.3 (1981): 401–24.

93. A term coined by Raymond Aron: see J. Elster, "Functional Explanation in Social Science," in *Readings in the Philosophy of Social Science*, ed. M. Martin and L. C. McIntyre (Cambridge, MA: MIT Press, 1994), p. 403. It is also used by Arthur Vidich and Stanford Lyman: see A. J. Vidich. and S. J. Lyman, *American Sociology: Worldly Rejections of Religions and Their Directions* (New Haven, CT: Yale University Press, 1985).

94. Weber, *Max Weber: A Biography*, p. 682.
95. Ibid., pp. 678–84.
96. Weber, "Politics as a Vocation," pp. 122–23.
97. Ibid., p. 128.
98. Ibid.

CHAPTER 5. THE PRAXIS OF SOCIAL SUFFERING

1. H. R. Alker Jr., "The Humanistic Moment in International Studies: Reflections on Machiavelli and Las Casas: 1992 Presidential Address," *International Studies Quarterly* 36.4 (1992): 347–71; D. R. Brunstetter, "Sepúlveda, Las Casas, and the Other: Exploring the Tension between Moral Universalism and Alterity," *Review of Politics* 72.3 (2010): 409–35; S. McFarland, "The Slow Creation of Humanity," *Political Psychology* 32.1 (2011): 1–20; K. Pennington, "Bartolomé de las Casas and the Tradition of Medieval Law," *Church History* 39.2 (1970): 149–61; P. Wright-Carozza, "From Conquest to Constitutions: Retrieving a Latin American Tradition of the Idea of Human Rights," *Human Rights Quarterly* 25.2 (2003): 281–313.

2. R. Marrero-Fente, "Human Rights and Academic Discourse: Teaching the Las Casas–Sepúlveda Debate at the Time of the Iraq War," Human Rights and Latin American Cultural Studies, *Hispanic Issues On Line* 4.1 (2009): 252; available at http://hispanicissues.umn.edu/assets/doc/Marrero_Fente.pdf.

3. B. de Las Casas, *A Short Account of the Destruction of the Indies* (London: Penguin, [1552] 1992), p. 7.

4. A. Pagden, Introduction to Las Casas, *A Short Account of the Destruction of the Indies*, p. xviii.

5. B. Keen, "The Black Legend Revisited: Assumptions and Realities," *Hispanic American Historical Review* 49.4 (1969): 703–19.

6. J. Juderías, *La Leyenda negra y la verdad histórica* (Madrid: Revista de, 1914).

7. T. Conley, "De Bry's Las Casas," in *Amerindian Images and the Legacy of Columbus,* ed. R. Jara and N. Spadaccini (Minneapolis: University of Minnesota Press, 1992); L. Hanke, *Bartolomé de las Casas, Historian: An Essay in Spanish Historiography* (Gainesville: University Press of Florida, 1952).

8. S. Arias and E. M. Merediz, eds., *Approaches to Teaching the Writings of Bartolomé de Las Casas* (New York: Modern Languages Association, 2008); D. R. Brunstetter, *Tensions of Modernity: Las Casas and His Legacy in the French Enlightenment* (New York: Routledge, 2012); D. Castro, *Another Face of Empire: Bartolomé de Las Casas, Indigenous Rights, and Ecclesiastical Imperialism* (Durham, NC: Duke University Press, 2007).

9. Following the seminal contribution of Tzvetan Todorov's *The Conquest of America: The Question of the Other* (1984), it has become increasingly fashionable

to look back to the European colonization of the New World in the sixteenth century as the period that initiated a series of cultural debates over the extent to which people possess a common humanity. Here political historians are also especially attentive to the ways in which, from the moment of its inception, humanitarian discourse has featured as a key element in ideological disputes that not only involve debates over the moral responsibilities we bear toward others but also the attempt to justify people's enslavement and the violent exploitation of foreign lands. In this context, it is recognized that in charting the cultural development of humanitarian forms of political protest, we are also exposing the fissures of power relations and that very often these concern extreme circumstances in which many people's lives are at stake. See R. Blackburn, *The Making of New World Slavery: From the Baroque to the Modern, 1492–1800* (London: Verso, 1997), pp. 127–81.

10. Didier Fassin is one of the most theoretically sophisticated critics of modern humanitarianism. In many of his studies he exposes humanitarian thought and practice as operating to promote unequal power relations. More often than not, Fassin appears to be intent on denouncing humanitarianism as a force of social oppression and as a pernicious assault on human dignity. See, e.g., D. Fassin, "Compassion and Repression: The Moral Economy of Immigration Policies in France," *Cultural Anthropology* 20.3 (2005): 362–87; D. Fassin, *When Bodies Remember: Experiences and Politics of AIDS in South Africa* (Berkeley: University of California Press, 2007); D. Fassin, "Another Politics of Life Is Possible," *Theory, Culture & Society* 26.5 (2009): 44–60; D. Fassin, "Heart of Humaneness: The Moral Economy of Humanitarian Intervention," in *Contemporary States of Emergency: The Politics of Military and Humanitarian Interventions*, ed. D. Fassin and M. Pandolfini (New York: Zone Books, 2010). Here our attention is largely focused on his recent book *Humanitarian Reason: A Moral History of the Present* (2012), in which he makes direct reference to research and writing on social suffering as one of the developments within contemporary social science to which he is most strongly opposed. We identify him as among the sternest of our critics.

11. K. Halttunen, "Humanitarianism and the Pornography of Pain in Anglo-American Culture," *American Historical Review* 100.2 (1995): 303–34.

12. See, e.g., C. Sorisio, "The Spectacle of the Body: Torture in the Antislavery Writing of Lydia Maria Child and Frances E. W. Harper," *Modern Language Studies* 30.1 (2000): 45–66; E. V. Spelman, *Fruits of Sorrow: Framing Our Attention to Suffering* (Boston: Beacon Press, 1997).

13. G. D. Crane, "Dangerous Sentiments: Sympathy, Rights, and Revolution in Stowe's Antislavery Novels," *Nineteenth-Century Literature* 51.2 (1996): 176–204.

14. Ibid., pp. 177–86.

15. P. Farmer, "Never Again? Reflections on Human Values and Human Rights," in *Tanner Lectures on Human Values*, vol. 26, ed. G. B. Peterson (Salt Lake City: University of Utah Press, 2006), pp. 153, 164.

16. Farmer also famously contrasts before and after treatment images of AIDS and TB patients in Haiti and Rwanda to make the visual case that accompanies the quantitative outcome data, so that we all can see why treatment matters, how it can be provided in the poorest of places, and why we must overcome implementation bottlenecks and barriers in order to intervene. As a medical anthropologist-physician Farmer demonstrates that social scientists can in fact lead intervention programs in global health. Richard Parker, a medical anthropologist who leads an NGO for AIDS treatment in Brazil, and Jim Yong Kim, who organized the WHO's AIDS treatment program in Africa and is now president of the World Bank, are notable examples of this growing trend of social scientists going beyond advocacy and policy development to actually develop and lead intervention programs. Dual training in a social science discipline and medicine may distinguish certain ones of this new brand of practitioners, but increasing numbers of social scientists in practical roles in public health, medicine, poverty reduction, human rights, and humanitarian assistance activities speak to practices far beyond those thought of in the past as part of what social scientists do (see chapter 6).

17. Farmer, "Never Again?," pp. 152–56; S. Sontag, *Regarding the Pain of Others* (London: Hamish Hamilton, 2003).

18. P. I. Bourgois and J. Schonberg, *Righteous Dopefiend* (Berkeley: University of California Press, 2009), p. 9; Michael Taussig's *Shamanism, Colonialism, and the Wild Man: A Study in Terror and Healing* (1987) begins with ninety pages of graphic descriptions of terror, atrocity, and brutal violence carried out by Spaniards in the conquest of Latin America against Amerindians. The sheer repetition and detailed portrayals of gratuitous, sadistic, and unrelieved violence has been criticized as pornography, and it is hard to argue that this unleashing of violent images is anything less than a perverse fetishization of violence intended to titillate readers.

19. Viram Patel and like-minded colleagues insist that seeing the actual faces of the mentally ill who are experiencing the abjection of social death, marginalization, and social rejection is crucial—no matter the ethical issue of protecting privacy to the contrary—forcing viewers to engage the overwhelming human rights abuse of those with serious mental illness, in order to provoke a moral movement for global mental health along the lines of that developed for HIV/AIDS sufferers. See V. Patel, A. Kleinman, and B. Saraceno, "Protecting the Human Rights of People with Mental Illnesses: A Call to Action for Global Mental Health," in *Mental Health and Human Rights: Vision, Praxis and Courage*, ed. M. Dudley, D. Silove, and F. Gale (New York: Oxford University Press, 2012), pp. 362–75.

20. They are also not unaware of the potential serious misuses of images of suffering to mislead audiences about the actual causes of the particular forms of human misery they are studying. See A. Kleinman and J. Kleinman, "The Appeal of Experience; the Dismay of Images: Cultural Appropriations of Suffering in

Our Times," *Daedalus* 125.1 (1996): 1–23. Indeed, this problem is frequently cited by Farmer in his critique of "immodest claims of causality."

21. Veena Das has been concerned with this issue throughout her career. See V. Das, *Life and Worlds: Violence and the Descent into the Ordinary* (Berkeley: University of California Press, 2006). Nancy Scheper-Hughes uses the provocation "benign material neglect" to encourage a passionate commitment to improving the lives of mothers in Brazil's favelas and to demonizing the perpetrators to stop abuses in the global organ trade. See N. Scheper-Hughes, *Death without Weeping: The Violence of Everyday Life in Brazil* (Berkeley: University of California Press, 1992).

22. See, e.g., C. Calhoun, "A World of Emergencies: Fear, Intervention, and the Limits of Cosmopolitan Order," *Canadian Review of Sociology* 41.4 (2004): 373–95; C. Calhoun, "The Imperative to Reduce Suffering: Charity, Progress, and Emergencies in the Field of Humanitarian Action," in *Humanitarianism in Question*, ed. M. Barnett and T.G. Weiss (Ithaca, NY: Cornell University Press, 2008).

23. See, e.g., L. Boltanski, *Distant Suffering: Morality, Media and Politics* (Cambridge: Cambridge University Press, 1999); L. Chouliaraki, *The Ironic Spectator: Solidarity in the Age of Post-Humanitarianism* (Cambridge: Polity Press, 2013).

24. See, e.g., M. Pandolfi, "Humanitarianism and Its Discontents," in *Forces of Compassion: Humanitarianism between Ethics and Politics*, ed. E. Bornstein and P. Redfield (Santa Fe, NM: School for Advanced Research Press, 2010).

25. In this regard, insofar as it draws attention to moral and political hazards relating to the attempt to mobilize humanitarian concerns in practice, we acknowledge that Fassin's work holds value as an aid to critical thinking and praxis in the field of medical humanitarianism. We also acknowledge the value of the contributions made by scholars such as Vinh-Kim Nguyen. See V.K. Nguyen, *The Republic of Therapy: Triage and Sovereignty in West Africa's Time of AIDS* (Durham, NC: Duke University Press, 2010).

26. Fassin, "Compassion and Repression"; Fassin, *When Bodies Remember*; D. Fassin, "Beyond Good and Evil? Questioning the Anthropological Discomfort with Morals," *Anthropological Theory* 8.4 (2008): 333–44; Fassin, "Another Politics of Life Is Possible"; Fassin "Heart of Humaneness"; D. Fassin, *Humanitarian Reason: A Moral History of the Present* (Berkeley: University of California Press, 2012).

27. Fassin, *Humanitarian Reason*, p. 252.

28. Ibid., pp. 25–29.

29. Ibid.

30. Ibid., pp. 252–57.

31. Ibid., p. 32.

32. Ibid., p. 41.

33. Ibid., p. 42.

34. J. Y. Kim, J. V. Millen, A. Irwin, and J. Gershman, eds., *Dying for Growth: Global Inequality and the Health of the Poor* (Monroe, ME: Common Courage Press, 2002); V. Das, *Critical Events: An Anthropological Perspective on Contemporary India* (Delhi: Oxford University Press, 1995); R. Rapp, *Testing Women, Testing the Fetus: The Social Impact of Amniocentesis in America* (New York: Psychology Press, 1999); M. Nichter, *Global Health: Why Cultural Perceptions, Social Representations, and Biopolitics Matter* (Tucson: University of Arizona Press, 2008); J. Biehl, *Vita: Life in a Zone of Social Abandonment* (Berkeley: University of California Press, 2005); Scheper-Hughes, *Death without Weeping*; A. Petryna, *Life Exposed: Biological Citizens after Chernobyl* (Princeton, NJ: Princeton University Press, 2002); A. Garcia, *The Pastoral Clinic: Addiction and Dispossession along the Rio Grande* (Berkeley: University of California Press, 2010); S. Kaufman, *And a Time to Die: How American Hospitals Shape the End of Life* (Chicago: University of Chicago Press, 2006); G. Parker, *Global Crisis: War, Climate Change, and Catastrophe in the Seventeenth Century* (New Haven, CT: Yale University Press, 2013).

35. In particular, see G. Agamben, *Homo Sacer: Sovereign Power and Bare Life* (Stanford, CA: Stanford University Press, 1998). M. Foucault, *The History of Sexuality, Volume 1: An Introduction* (New York: Pantheon Books, 1978)

36. Fassin, *Humanitarian Reason*, p. 254.

37. P. Bourdieu, "Understanding," in *The Weight of the World: Social Suffering in Contemporary Society*, ed. P. Bourdieu et al. (Cambridge: Polity Press, 1999), pp. 607-26.

38. Das, *Life and Worlds*.

39. A. Kleinman, "Experience and Its Moral Modes: Culture, Human Conditions and Disorder," in Peterson, *The Tanner Lectures on Human Values*.

40. Fassin, *Humanitarian Reason*, p. 246.

41. Ibid., pp. 254-55.

42. See, e.g., F. C. Alford, "Bauman and Levinas: Levinas Cannot Be Used," *Journal for Cultural Research* 18.3 (2014): 249-62; R. Kilminster, "Critique and Overcritique in Sociology," *Human Figurations* 2.2 (2013), available at http://hdl.handle.net/2027/spo.11217607.0002.205; O. Makridis, "Is a Levinasian Theory of Justice Possible? A Response to Murray," *New Jersey Journal of Communication* 11.1 (2003): 24-44.

43. Kleinman, "Experience and Its Moral Modes," pp. 414-45.

44. Readers may be also be interested to explore how this ethical understanding and moral practice is applied in relation to the work of Médecins Sans Frontières. See Peter Redfield's study, *Life in Crisis: The Ethical Journey of Doctors Without Borders* (Berkeley: University of California Press, 2013).

45. A considerable amount of scholarship is now devoted to tracing the cultural origins and social history of modern humanitarianism. In the twenty-first

century, the problem of explaining modern humanitarianism as a form of moral culture, a mode of social sensibility, and an approach to politics has been taken up as key concerns across the humanities and social sciences. By no means has the dust settled on the dispute over how to set this within a framework of historical or historiographical analysis. It might be argued that over recent years the level of controversy surrounding this matter has risen to an unprecedented scale. There is now an enhanced awareness of the historical peculiarity of modern humanitarianism and its influence over our moral dispositions and political outlooks and the difficulty of making this amenable to social understanding. See, e.g., M. Abruzzo, *Polemical Pain: Slavery, Cruelty, and the Rise of Humanitarianism* (Baltimore: Johns Hopkins University Press, 2010); M. Barnett, *Empire of Humanity: A History of Humanitarianism* (Ithaca, NY: Cornell University Press, 2011); Barnett and Weiss, *Humanitarianism in Question;* J.M. Headley, *The Europeanization of the World: On the Origins of Human Rights and Democracy* (Princeton, NJ: Princeton University Press, 2008); L. Hunt, *Inventing Human Rights: A History* (New York: Norton, 2007); M.R. Ishay, *The History of Human Rights: From Ancient Times to the Globalization Era* (Berkeley: University of California Press, 2008); S. Moyn, *The Last Utopia: Human Rights in History* (Cambridge, MA: Harvard University Press, 2010); P. Stamatov, *The Origins of Global Humanitarianism: Religion, Empires and Advocacy* (Cambridge: Cambridge University Press, 2013).

46. This notion draws on Charles Taylor's suggestion that in any period it is possible to identify distinct ways in which "people imagine their social existence, how they fit together with others, how things go on between them and their fellows, the expectations that are normally met, and the deeper normative notions and images that underlie these expectations" (C. Taylor, *Modern Social Imaginaries* [Durham, NC: Duke University Press, 2004], p. 23). We contend that the form of the "social imaginary" that tends to be in evidence in the context of research and writing on social suffering is distinctly "humanitarian," for it designates the welfare of humanity as its overriding concern; in addition to this, it aims to excite moral debate over how we should respond to, and care for, the suffering of others (see chapter 6). In this context, the active courting of moral sentiment that takes place through the documentation of cultural idioms of pain and distress is designed to engage us in the attempt to understand people in social terms. At the same time as humanitarian culture may be taken up as a matter for critical analysis, a keen interest is taken in the potential for humanitarian impulse to serve as a spur for the awakening of social consciousness. It offers an approach to social understanding that is overtly motivated by humanitarian concern and aims to shape humanitarian sentiment as a means to extend the bounds of social understanding. We fully recognize, and go so far as to celebrate, the fact that the "humanitarian social imaginary" is bound to attract criticism. Given the human values at stake, we hold that it will inevitably court

dispute and that there will be many instances where it will, and moreover should, be taken up for ideological critique. For a recent example of this, see Chouliaraki, *The Ironic Spectator*, pp. 26–53.

47. For further developments of these ideas, see M. Abramovitz, "Social Work and Social Reform: An Arena of Struggle," *Social Work* 43.6 (1998): 512–26; J. H. Grayman, "Humanitarian Encounters in Post-Conflict Aceh, Indonesia" (PhD diss, Harvard University), available at http://dash.harvard.edu/handle/1 /10433473.

48. This is a common standpoint in critical theory. See, e.g., M. Horkheimer and T. W. Adorno, *Dialectic of Enlightenment* (London: Allen Lane, 1973), p. 121; C. Calhoun, "A World of Emergencies"; S. Žižek, *Violence* (London: Picador, 2008), pp. 1–39.

49. Fassin, *Humanitarian Reason*.

50. For some of the fullest expressions of this standpoint, see P. Farmer, *AIDS and Accusation: Haiti and the Geography of Blame* (Berkeley: University of California Press, 1992); P. Farmer, *Infections and Inequalities: The Modern Plagues* (Berkeley: University of California Press, 1999); P. Farmer, *Pathologies of Power: Health, Human Rights and the New War on the Poor* (Berkeley: University of California Press, 2003); Farmer, "Never Again?"; P. Farmer, "Conversation in the Time of Cholera: A Reflection on Structural Violence and Social Change," in *In the Company of the Poor: Conversations with Dr. Paul Farmer and Fr. Gustavo Gutierrez*, ed. M. Griffin and J. W. Block (New York: Orbis Books, 2013); N. Scheper-Hughes, "Undoing: Social Suffering and the Politics of Remorse in the New South Africa," *Social Justice* 24.4 (1998): 114–42.

51. See Das, *Life and Worlds*.

52. We have already noted that there is a long-standing tradition of debate within social science over the extent to which it should operate in sympathy with projects of humanitarian social reform (see chapter 2 for a brief survey of some of its founding terms and interest). Many have argued that the value of knowledge about society, and of us as social beings, should be sought not so much in the forms of enlightenment it delivers, but, more important, in the practical difference it makes to the care of human life. On this view, social science should have the project of building a more humane society as its aim and its practitioners should be committed to producing knowledge that can be usefully applied to this end Under this emphasis, the fact that social life takes place as an enactment of substantive human values is readily acknowledged and the practice of social inquiry is openly addressed as a form of moral conduct that is loaded with practical and political significance. It is generally held that its value lies in the extent to which it promotes sympathy for all that is human and in its contribution to the founding and maintenance of institutional arrangements in which care for the human is a prime concern. For a further selection of studies that feature this matter as a core concern, see E. Becker, *The Structure of Evil: An Essay on the*

Unification of the Science of Man (New York: Free Press, 1968); E. Becker, *The Lost Science of Man* (New York: George Braziller, 1971); M. Burawoy, "For Public Sociology," *American Sociological Review* 70.1 (2005): 4–28; W. D. Du Bois and R. D. Wright, *Applying Sociology: Making a Better World* (Boston: Allyn and Bacon, 2001); W. D. Du Bois and R. D. Wright, *Politics in the Human Interest: Applying Sociology in the Real World* (Lanham, MD: Rowman & Littlefield, 2008); A. M. Lee, *Toward Humanist Sociology* (Englewood Cliffs, NJ: Prentice-Hall, 1973); A. M. Lee, *Sociology for Whom?* (New York: Oxford University Press, 1978); R. S. Lynd, *Knowledge for What? The Place of Social Science in American Culture* (Princeton, NJ: Princeton University Press, 1939).

6. CAREGIVING

1. See, e.g., M. Duffy, *Making Care Count: A Century of Gender, Race, and Paid Care Work* (Piscataway, NJ: Rutgers University Press, 2011); P. England, M. Budig, and N. Folbre, "Wages of Virtue: The Relative Pay of Care Work," *Social Problems* 49.4 (2002): 455–73; N. Folbre, *For Love and Money: Care Provision in the United States* (New York: Russell Sage Foundation, 2012).

2. P. England, "Emerging Theories of Care Work," *Annual Review of Sociology* 31 (2005): 381–99.

3. J. C. Tronto, "Care as a Basis for Radical Political Judgments," *Hypatia* 10.2 (1995): 141.

4. J. C. Tronto, *Moral Boundaries: A Political Argument for an Ethic of Care* (New York: Routledge, 1993); J. C. Tronto, *Caring Democracy: Markets, Equality and Social Justice* (New York: New York University Press, 2013).

5. In book 6 of the *Nicomachean Ethics*, Aristotle distinguishes between two intellectual virtues, *sophia* and *phronesis*. While *sophia* refers to wisdom acquired through rational thinking, *phronesis* refers to the wisdom that applies this to actions to deliver desirable outcomes. *Phronesis* is "practical wisdom." It involves a person in moral and political decisions in the attempt to realize conditions for human flourishing.

6. For some useful histories of the settlement movement and this period, see M. Carson, *Settlement Folk: Social Thought and the American Settlement Movement, 1885–1930* (Chicago: University of Chicago Press, 1990); A. F. Davis, *Spearheads of Reform: The Social Settlements and the Progressive Movement, 1890–1914* (New York: Oxford University Press, 1967); J. L. Recchiuti, *Civic Engagement: Social Science and Progressive Era Reform in New York City* (Philadelphia: University of Pennsylvania Press, 2007).

7. R. K. Berson, *Jane Addams: A Biography* (Westport, CT: Greenwood Press, 2004); A. F. Davis, *American Heroine: The Life and Legend of Jane Addams* (New York: Oxford University Press, 1973); J. W. Linn, *Jane Addams: A Biography*

(Chicago: University of Illinois Press, 1935); S. Opdycke, *Jane Addams and Her Vision of America* (Upper Saddle River, NJ: Pearson, 2011); L.W. Knight. *Jane Addams: Spirit in Action* (New York: Norton, 2010).

8. J. Addams, *Twenty Years at Hull-House* (New York: Penguin, [1910] 1998), p. 18.

9. For some useful surveys of this movement, see P.D.A. Jones, *The Christian Socialist Revival, 1877–1914: Religion, Class, and Social Conscience in Late-Victorian England* (Princeton, NJ: Princeton University Press, 1968); C.H. Hopkins, *The Rise of the Social Gospel in American Protestantism* (New Haven, CT: Yale University Press, 1940).

10. For more information on the founding and early history of Toynbee Hall, see S. Meacham, *Toynbee Hall and Social Reform, 1880–1914: The Search for Community* (New Haven, CT: Yale University Press, 1987).

11. M.J. Deegan, *Jane Addams and the Men of the Chicago School, 1892–1918* (New Brunswick, NJ: Transaction Publishers, 1988), p. 5.

12. P.M. Lengermann and J. Niebrugge-Brantley, *The Women Founders* (Boston: McGraw-Hill, 1998), p. 72.

13. See, e.g., J.B. Elshtain, *Jane Addams and the Dream of American Democracy: A Life* (New York: Basic Books, 2002); Knight, *Jane Addams: Spirit in Action*.

14. See, e.g., D.L. Franklin, "Mary Richmond and Jane Addams: From Moral Certainty to Rational Inquiry in Social Work Practice," *Social Service Review* 60.4 (1986): 504–25; K.S. Lundblad, "Jane Addams and Social Reform: A Role Model for the 1990s," *Social Work* 40.5 (1995): 661–69.

15. M.J. Deegan, "W.E.B. Du Bois and the Women of Hull-House, 1865–1899," *American Sociologist* 23 (Winter 1988): 301–11; Lengermann and Niebrugge-Brantley, *The Women Founders*.

16. For a useful summary of her sociological contribution, see E. Schneiderhan, "Pragmatism and Empirical Sociology: The case of Jane Addams and Hull-House, 1889–1895," *Theory and Society* 40.6 (2011): 589–617. In light of the issues covered in chapter 4, readers may be interested to note that in her own time, Jane Addams's standing as a leading figure in the development of American sociology was recognized by Marianne and Max Weber. Lawrence Scaff records that in their 1904 visit to the United States, the Webers sought out the company of Jane Addams in a visit to Hull House and took an interest in her work in support of the Chicago trade union movement (L.A. Scaff, *Max Weber in America* [Princeton, NJ: Princeton University Press, 2011], pp. 40–48).

17. Charlene Haddock Seigfried records that John Dewey "credited Addams with the paradigm shift from thinking of democracy only as a political system to thinking of it as a way of life" (C.H. Seigfried, "Introduction to the Illinois Edition," in J. Addams, *Democracy and Social Ethics* [Urbana: University of Illinois Press, 2002]). Also see Deegan, *Jane Adams and the Men of the Chicago*

School, pp. 247–308; C. H. Seigfried, "Socializing Democracy: Jane Addams and John Dewey," *Philosophy of the Social Sciences* 29.2 (1999): 207–30.

18. On this point readers may care to review the section on the pragmatist understanding of "experience" in chapter 3.

19. Seigfried, "Socializing Democracy," p. 224.

20. Lengermann and Niebrugge-Brantley, *The Women Founders,* p. 86.

21. Addams, *Twenty Years at Hull-House,* p. 67.

22. J. Addams, "The Subjective Necessity for the Social Settlements," in *The Social Thought of Jane Addams,* ed. C. Lasch (Indianapolis: Bobbs-Merrill, [1892] 1965), p. 35.

23. Addams, *Democracy and Social Ethics,* p. 8.

24. Ibid.

25. Seigfried, "Socializing Democracy," pp. 212–13. Debate surrounds the extent to which Addams applied this ethic to her interactions with African Americans. See M. Hamington, "Public Pragmatism: Jane Addams and Ida B. Wells on Lynching," *Journal of Speculative Philosophy* 19.2 (2005): 167–74; K. G. Muhammad, *The Condemnation of Blackness* (Cambridge, MA: Harvard University Press, 2010), esp. pp. 88–145; R. S. Lissak, *Pluralism and Progressives: Hull House and the New Immigrants, 1890–1919* (Chicago: University of Chicago Press, 1989); T. L. Philpott, *The Slum and the Ghetto: Immigrants, Blacks, and Reformers in Chicago, 1880–1930* (Belmont, CA: Wadsworth, 1991).

26. Addams, *Twenty Years at Hull-House,* p. 75.

27. Ibid., pp. 185–201.

28. Ibid., pp. 93–95.

29. Residents of Hull-House, *Hull-House Maps and Papers* (Urbana: University of Illinois Press, [1895] 2007). This study was largely devised under the direction of Florence Kelley.

30. For further information on the Pullman strike of 1894, see A. Lindsey, *The Pullman Strike: The Story of a Unique Experiment and of a Great Labor Upheaval* (Chicago: University of Chicago Press, 1943); D. R. Papke, *The Pullman Case: The Clash of Labor and Capital in Industrial America* (Lawrence: University Press of Kansas, 1999).

31. Addams, *Twenty Years at Hull-House,* p. 150.

32. Ibid., pp. 131–52.

33. M. Hamington, *Embodied Care: Jane Addams, Maurice Merleau-Ponty, and Feminist Ethics* (Urbana: University of Illinois Press, 2004); M. Hamington, "An Inverted Home: Socializing Care at Hull-House," in *Socializing Care: Feminist Ethics and Public Issues,* ed. M. Hamington and D. C. Miller (Lanham, MD: Rowman & Littlefield, 2006).

34. Hamington, *Embodied Care,* p. 92.

35. Ibid., p. 112.

36. Deegan, *Jane Addams and the Men of the Chicago School.*

37. Ibid., pp. 167–90.

38. Ibid., p. 23.

39. Ibid., pp. 143–66. Also see H. S. Becker, "The Chicago School, So-Called," *Qualitative Sociology* 22.1 (1999): 3–12; M. Bulmer, *The Chicago School of Sociology: Institutionalization, Diversity, and the Rise of Sociological Research* (Chicago: University of Chicago Press, 1986).

40. D. Brieland, "The Hull-House Tradition and the Contemporary Social Worker: Was Jane Addams Really a Social Worker?," *Social Work* 35.2 (1990): 134–38.

41. Addams, *Democracy and Social Ethics,*. pp. 11–34.

42. See, e.g., M. Abramovitz, "Social Work and Social Reform: An Arena of Struggle," *Social Work* 43.6 (1988): 512–26; J. Ehrenreich, *The Altruistic Imagination: A History of Social Work and Social Policy in the United States* (Ithaca, NY: Cornell University Press, 1985); H. Specht and M. E. Courtney, *Unfaithful Angels: How Social Work Has Abandoned Its Mission* (New York: Free Press, 1995).

43. Davis, *American Heroine*, p. 265; Deegan, *Jane Addams and the Men of the Chicago School*, p. 320.

44. Deegan, *Jane Addams and the Men of the Chicago School*, pp. 80–83.

45. Ibid., p. 50.

46. E. L. Boyer, *Scholarship Reconsidered: Priorities of the Professoriate* (Princeton, NJ: Carnegie Foundation for the Advancement of Teaching, 1990); D. E. Giles Jr., "Understanding an Emerging Field of Scholarship: Toward a Research Agenda for Engaged Public Scholarship," *Journal of Higher Education Outreach and Engagement* 12.2 (2008): 97–106; K. Hacker, *Community-Based Participatory Research* (New York: Sage, 2013); B. L. Hall, "From Margins to Center? The Development and Purpose of Participatory Research," *American Sociologist* 23.4 (1992): 15–28; K. O'Meara and A. J. Jaeger, "Preparing Future Faculty for Community Engagement: Barriers, Facilitators, Models, and Recommendations," *Journal of Higher Education Outreach and Engagement* 11.4 (2007): 3–26; K. J. Strand, N. Cutforth, R. Stoecker, S. Marullo, and P. Donohue, *Community-Based Research and Higher Education: Principles and Practices* (New York: John Wiley & Sons, 2003); M. Minkler and N. Wallerstein, eds., *Community-Based Participatory Research for Health: From Process to Outcomes* (New York: John Wiley & Sons, 2010).

47. F. Gong, S. Baron, L. Ayala, L. Stock, S. McDevitt, and C. Heaney, "The Role for Community-Based Participatory Research in Formulating Policy Initiatives: Promoting Safety and Health for In-Home Care Workers and Their Consumers," *American Journal of Public Health* 99.3 (2009): 531–39; J. Krieger, C. Allen, A. Cheadle, S. Ciske, J. K. Schier, K. Senturia, and M. Sullivan, "Using Community-Based Participatory Research to Address Social Determinants of Health: Lessons Learned from Seattle Partners for Healthy Communities,"

Health Education & Behavior 29.3 (2002): 361–82; M.W. Leung, I.H. Yen, and M. Minkler, "Community-Based Participatory Research: A Promising Approach for Increasing Epidemiology's Relevance in the 21st Century," *International Journal of Epidemiology* 33.3 (2004): 499–506; T.C. Lewis, T.G. Robins, J.T. Dvonch, G.J. Keeler, F.Y. Yip, G.B. Mentz, X. Xihong Lin, E.A. Parker, B.A. Israel, L. Gonzalez, and Y. Hill, "Air Pollution–Associated Changes in Lung Function among Asthmatic Children in Detroit," *Environmental Health Perspectives* 113.8 (2005): 1068–75; M. Minkler, V.B. Vasquez, and P. Shepard, "Promoting Environmental Health Policy through Community-Based Participatory Research: A Case Study from Harlem, New York," *Journal of Urban Health* 83.1 (2006): 101–10; S.D. Rhodes, E. Eng, K.C. Hergenrather, I.M. Remnitz, R. Arceo, J. Montao, and J. Alegra-Ortega, "Exploring Latino Men's HIV Risk Using Community-Based Participatory Research," *American Journal of Health Behavior* 31.2 (2007): 146–58; J.J. Schensul, J. Robison, C. Reyes, K. Radda, S. Gaztambide, and W. Disch, "Building Interdisciplinary/Intersectoral Research Partnerships for Community-Based Mental Health Research with Older Minority Adults," *American Journal of Community Psychology* 38.1–2 (2006): 79–93.

48. J.H. Backman, "Law Schools, Law Students, Civic Engagement, and Community-Based Research as Resources for Improving Access to Justice in Utah," *Utah Law Review* 4 (2006): 953–1209; J.F. Ibáñez-Carrasco and E.R. Meiners, eds., *Public Acts: Disruptive Readings on Making Curriculum Public* (New York: Routledge, 2004); M. Kenny, ed., *Learning to Serve: Promoting Civil Society through Service Learning* (New York: Springer, 2002).

49. There are many other notable sources mentioned in accounts of the origins of community-based participatory research. The research and work of Kurt Lewin (1946), the Highlander Folk School (see Lewis 2001), and Paulo Friere (1970, 1993) are particularly noteworthy. Budd Hall (1992) provides a useful overview of early participatory research projects in Tanzania and South America, as well as their routes to influence North American initiatives.

50. See, e.g., J.R. Feagin, "Social Justice and Sociology: Agendas for the Twenty-First Century," in *Critical Strategies for Social Research*, ed. W.K. Carroll (Toronto: Canadian Scholars Press, 2004); Giles, "Understanding an Emerging Field of Scholarship"; B. Holland, "New Views of Research for the 21st Century: The Role of Engaged Scholarship," *Scholarship in Action: Applied Research and Community Change* (November 2005): 1–9, 10; M. Jacobson and C. Rugeley, "Community-Based Participatory Research: Group Work for Social Justice and Community Change," *Social Work with Groups* 30.4 (2007): 21–39; H.A. Lawson, "An Appreciation and a Selective Enhancement of the Developing Model for University-Assisted Community Schools," *Universities and Community Schools* 8.1–2 (2010): 5–20; K.J. Strand, N. Cutforth, R. Stoecker, S. Marullo, and P. Donohue, *Community-Based Research and Higher Education: Principles and Practices* (New York: John Wiley & Sons, 2003), pp. 4–5.

51. Hacker, *Community-Based Participatory Research.*

52. N. Wallerstein and B. Duran, "Community-Based Participatory Research Contributions to Intervention Research: The Intersection of Science and Practice to Improve Health Equity," *American Journal of Public Health* 100.1 (2010): 40–46.

53. I. Harkavy and J. L. Puckett, "Lessons from Hull House for the Contemporary Urban University," *Social Service Review* 68.3 (1994): 299–321.

54. M. Brydon-Miller and P. Maguire, "Participatory Action Research: Contributions to the Development of Practitioner Inquiry in Education," *Educational Action Research* 17.1 (2009): 79–93.

55. Brydon-Miller and Maguire are not alone in taking this view. See also G. L. Anderson, "The Politics of Participatory Reforms in Education," *Theory into Practice* 38.4 (1999): 191–95; G. L. Anderson and K. Herr, "The New Paradigm Wars: Is There Room for Rigorous Practitioner Knowledge in Schools and Universities?," *Educational Researcher* 28.5 (1999): 12–40; L. Valli, ed., *Reflective Teacher Education: Cases and Critiques* (Albany: State University of New York Press, 1992).

56. C. R. Horowitz, B. L. Brenner, S. Lachapelle, D. A. Amara, and G. Arniella, "Effective recruitment of Minority Populations through Community-Led Strategies," *American Journal of Preventive Medicine* 37.6 (2009): 195–200.

57. Krieger et al., "Using Community-Based Participatory Research."

58. Wallerstein and Duran, "Community-Based Participatory Research Contributions."

59. D. C. Calleson, C. Jordan, and S. D. Seifer, "Community-Engaged Scholarship: Is Faculty Work in Communities a True Academic Enterprise?," *Academic Medicine* 80.4 (2005): 317–21.

60. H. Meyer, B. Hamilton, S. Kroeger, S. Stewart, and M. Brydon-Miller, "The Unexpected Journey: Renewing our Commitment to Students through Educational Action Research," *Educational Action Research* 12.4 (2004): 557–74.

61. V. L. Olesen, "Caregiving, Ethical and Informal: Emerging Challenges in the Sociology of Health and Illness," *Journal of Health and Social Behavior* 30.1 (1989): 1–10.

62. Schneiderhan, "Pragmatism and Empirical Sociology."

63. Elshtain, *Jane Addams and the Dream of American Democracy*; Knight, *Jane Addams: Spirit in Action*, p. 68.

64. Lasch, *The Social Thought of Jane Addams*, pp. 1–43.

65. For a useful history of "slumming" in 1880s London, see S. Koven, *Slumming: Sexual and Social Politics in Victorian England* (Princeton, NJ: Princeton University Press, 2006.

66. Addams, *Twenty Years at Hull-House*, pp. 50–51.

67. Ibid.

68. Jacobson and Rugeley, "Community-Based Participatory Research."

69. W. James, "Pragmatism's Conception of Truth," *Journal of Philosophy, Psychology and Scientific Methods* 4.6 (1907): 141–55.

70. V. Skultans, *The Testimony of Lives: Narrative and Memory in Post-Soviet Latvia* (London: Routledge, 1998), p. 21.

71. P. Bourdieu, "Understanding," in *The Weight of the World: Social Suffering in Contemporary Society,* ed. P. Bourdieu et al. (Cambridge: Polity Press, 1999), p. 609. Also see chapter 3.

72. Bourdieu, "Understanding," p. 614; original emphasis.

73. Ibid.

74. P. Bourdieu and L. Wacquant, *An Invitation to Reflexive Sociology* (Chicago: University of Chicago Press, 1992), pp. 122, 200–202.

75. For an introduction to critical medical anthropology see H.A. Baer, M. Singer, and I. Susser, *Medical Anthropology and the World System* (Westport, CT: Praeger, 2013).

76. For more elaborated reflections on this matter, see A. Kleinman, "Experience and Its Moral Modes: Culture, Human Conditions and Disorder," in *The Tanner Lectures on Human Values,* vol. 20, ed. G.B. Peterson (Salt Lake City: University of Utah Press, 1999).

77. For more recent examples, see R.A. Hahn and M.C. Inhorn, *Anthropology and Public Health: Bridging Differences in Culture and Society* (New York: Oxford University Press, 2008).

78. See, e.g., A. Becker, *Body, Self, and Society: The View from Fiji* (Philadelphia: University of Pennsylvania Press, 1995); S. Keshavjee, *Blind Spot: How Neoliberalism Infiltrated Global Health* (Berkeley: University of California Press, 2014).

79. See Baer, Singer, and Susser, *Medical Anthropology and the World System,* for an extended review of this work

80. J.H. Grayman, "Humanitarian Encounters in Post-Conflict Aceh, Indonesia" (PhD diss., Harvard University, 2013), available at http://dash.harvard .edu/handle/1/10433473; J.H. Grayman, M.J.D. Good, and B.J. Good, "Conflict Nightmares and Trauma in Aceh," *Culture, Medicine, and Psychiatry* 33.2 (2009): 290–312.

81. P. Farmer, J.Y. Kim, A. Kleinman, and M. Basilico, eds., *Reimagining Global Health: An Introduction* (Berkeley: University of California Press, 2013).

82. A. Kleinman, *Patients and Healers in the Context of Culture: An Exploration of the Borderland between Anthropology, Medicine, and Psychiatry* (Berkeley: University of California Press, 1980); A. Kleinman, J.M. Anderson, K. Finkler, R.J. Frankenberg, and A. Young, "Social Origins of Distress and Disease: Depression, Neurasthenia, and Pain in Modern China," *Current Anthropology* 24.5 (1986): 499–509.

83. See, e.g., S.C. Abramowitz, *Searching for Normal in the Wake of the Liberian War* (Philadelphia: University of Pennsylvania Press, 2014); P. Benson, *Tobacco Capitalism: Growers, Migrant Workers, and the Changing Face of a Global Industry* (Princeton, NJ: Princeton University Press, 2012); J. Biehl, *Vita: Life in a Zone of Social Abandonment* (Berkeley: University of California Press, 2005); P.I. Bourgois and J. Schonberg, *Righteous Dopefiend* (Berkeley: University of California Press, 2009); P. Brodwin, *Everyday Ethics: Voices from the Front Line of Community Psychiatry* (Berkeley: University of California Press, 2012); A. Garcia, *The Pastoral Clinic: Addiction and Dispossession along the Rio Grande* (Berkeley: University of California Press, 2010); C. Han, *Life in Debt: Times of Care and Violence in Neoliberal Chile* (Berkeley: University of California Press, 2012); K.L. Moore, *The Joy of Noh: Embodied Learning and Discipline in Urban Japan* (New York: State University of New York Press, 2014); A. Petryna, *Life Exposed: Biological Citizens after Chernobyl* (Princeton, NJ: Princeton University Press, 2002); N. Scheper-Hughes, *Death without Weeping: The Violence of Everyday Life in Brazil* (Berkeley: University of California Press, 1992).

84. See Baer, Singer, and Susser, *Medical Anthropology and the World System*.

85. R. Stoecker and E. Bonacich, "Why Participatory Research? Guest Editors' Introduction," *American Sociologist* 23.4 (1992): 6.

86. M. Fine, "Individualization, Risk and the Body: Sociology and Care," *Journal of Sociology* 41.3 (2005): 247–66.

87. See, e.g., L. Lloyd, "A Caring Profession? The Ethics of Care and Social Work with Older People," *British Journal of Social Work* 36.7 (2006): 1171–85; G. Meagher, "Modernising Social Work and the Ethics of Care," *Social Work & Society* 2.1 (2004): 10–27; J. Morris, "Impairment and Disability: Constructing an Ethics of Care that Promotes Human Rights," *Hypatia* 16.4 (2001): 1–16; N. Parton, "Rethinking Professional Practice: The Contributions of Social Constructionism and the Feminist 'Ethics of Care,'" *British Journal of Social Work* 33.1 (2003): 1–16.

CONCLUSION

1. For some of the most elaborated historical accounts of this matter, see G. Himmelfarb, *The Idea of Poverty: England in the Early Industrial Age* (London: Faber & Faber, 1984); and G. Himmelfarb, *Poverty and Compassion: The Moral Imagination of the Late Victorians* (New York: Alfred A. Knopf, 1992).

2. H. Arendt, "The Social Question," in *On Revolution* (Harmondsworth: Penguin, 1963).

3. For some theological reactions to this development at the time, see K. Bocock, "The Social Question and the Christian Answer," *Sewanee Review* 10.4

(1902): 450–57; F. G. Peabody, *Jesus Christ and the Social Question* (New York: Grosset and Dunlap, 1900); W. Rauschenbusch, *Christianity and the Social Crisis* (London: Macmillan, 1908). For a more recent survey of the debates that took shape during this period, see M. Ossewaarde, "Settling the Social Question: Three Variants of Modern Christian Social Thought," *Journal of Markets and Morality* 14.2 (2011): 301–17. See chapter 1 of this book for a more detailed discussion of how this relates to the issue of theodicy.

4. See C. Calhoun, "New Social Movements of the Early Nineteenth Century," *Social Science and History* 17.3 (1993): 385–427; C. Calhoun, *The Roots of Radicalism: Tradition, the Public Sphere, and Early Nineteenth-Century Social Movements* (Chicago: University of Chicago Press, 2012); P. Owens, "From Bismarck to Patraeus: The Question of the Social and the Social Question in Counterinsurgency," *European Journal of International Relations* 19.1 (2013): 135–57; G. Steinmetz, "Reflections on the Role of Social Narratives in Working-Class Formation: Narrative Theory in the Social Sciences," *Social Science History* 16.3 (1992): 489–516.

5. See R. C. Bannister, *Sociology and Scientism: The American Quest for Objectivity, 1880–1940* (Chapel Hill: University of North Carolina Press, 1991); T. L. Haskell, *The Emergence of Professional Social Science: The American Social Science Association and the Crisis of Authority* (Baltimore: Johns Hopkins University Press, 2000); B. Mazlish, *A New Science: The Breakdown of Connections and the Birth of Sociology* (Oxford: Oxford University Press, 1989).

6. The development of philanthropic institutions, often religiously based, and the separation of social work as an "applied" helping profession doubtless made it easier for the social sciences to sustain this otherwise unsustainable position.

7. See M. J. Deegan, *Jane Addams and the Men of the Chicago School, 1892–1918* (New Brunswick, NJ: Transaction Publishers, 1988).

8. See E. Becker, *The Lost Science of Man* (New York: George Braziller, 1971).

9. Such critical concerns were also raised by Thorstein Veblen in *The Higher Learning in America* (1908) and by Alvin Gouldner in *The Future of Intellectuals and the Rise of the New Class* (1979).

10. M. Burawoy, "For Public Sociology," *American Sociological Review* 70.1 (2005): 4–28; S. M. Low and S. E. Merry, "Engaged Anthropology: Diversity and Dilemmas," *Current Anthropology* 51.2 (2010): 203–26.

11. M. Burawoy, "Introduction: Sociology as a Combat Sport," *Current Sociology* 62.1 (2014): 1–16; R. A. Hahn and M. C. Inhorn, *Anthropology and Public Health: Bridging Differences in Culture and Society* (New York: Oxford University Press, 2008); B. Rylko-Bauer, M. Singer, and J. V. Willigen, "Reclaiming Applied Anthropology: Its Past, Present, and Future," *American Anthropologist* 108.1 (2006):178–90; N. Scheper-Hughes, "Making Anthropology Public," *Anthropology Today* 25.4 (2009): 1–3.

12. Burawoy, "For Public Sociology," pp. 21–22.

13. X. Fei, *From the Soil: The Foundations of Chinese Society* (Berkeley: University of California Press, 1992).

14. K. K. Hwang, "Face and Favor: The Chinese Power Game," *American Journal of Sociology* 92.4 (1987): 944–74; K. S. Yang, "Chinese Social Orientation: An Integrative Analysis," in *Chinese Societies and Mental Health*, ed. T. Y. Lin, W. S. Tseng, and Y. Ye (Oxford: Oxford University Press, 1995), pp. 19–39; U. Kim, K. S. Yang, and K. K. Hwang, *Indigenous and Cultural Psychology: Understanding People in Context* (New York: Springer, 2006).

15. G. Therborn, *The World: A Beginner's Guide* (Cambridge: Polity Press, 2011).

16. A. Sumner, "Global Poverty and the New Bottom Billion: What If Three Quarters of the World's Poor Live in Middle-Income Countries?," *IDS Working Papers* 349 (2010): 1–43; A. Sumner and M. Tiwari, "Global Poverty Reduction to 2015 and Beyond: What Has Been the Impact of the MDGs and What Are the Options for a Post-2015 Global Framework?," *IDS Working Papers* 348 (2010): 1–31.

17. P. J. Albert, P. Werhane, and T. Rolph, *Global Poverty Alleviation: A Case Book* (New York: Springer, 2014); L. Chandy and G. Gertz, *Poverty in Numbers: The Changing State of Global Poverty from 2005 to 2015* (Washington, DC: Brookings Institution, 2011); R. Kanbur and A. Sumner, "Poor Countries or Poor People? Development Assistance and the New Geography of Global Poverty," *Journal of International Development*, 26.6 (2012): 686–95.

18. J. B. Davies, S. Sandström, A. Shorrocks, and E. N. Wolff, *The World Distribution of Household Wealth* (No. 2008/03), WIDER Discussion Papers (Helsinki: World Institute for Development Economics, 2008).

19. R. Fuentes-Nieva and N. Galasso, *Working for the Few: Political Capture and Economic Inequality* (Oxford: Oxfam, 2014), available at www.oxfam.org/en/policy/working-for-the-few-economic-inequality.

20. FAO, *The State of Food Insecurity in the World: Addressing Food Insecurity in Protracted Crises* (Rome: FAO, 2010); FAO, *Coping with Water Scarcity: An Action Framework for Agriculture and Food Security* (Rome: FAO), available at www.fao.org/docrep/016/i3015e/i3015e.pdf.

21. I. Ortiz and M. Cummins, *When the Global Crisis and Youth Bulge Collide: Double the Jobs Trouble for Youth* (New York: UNICEF, 2010), available at www.unicef.org/socialpolicy/files/Global_Crisis_and_Youth_Bulge_FINAL.pdf.

22. I. Bremmer, "The End of the Free Market: Who Wins the War between States and Corporations?," *European View* 9.2 (2010): 249–52.

23. P. Andreas and T. Snyder, *The Wall around the West: State Borders and Immigration Controls in North America and Europe* (Lanham, MD: Rowman & Littlefield, 2000); J. Hampshire, *The Politics of Immigration: Contradictions of the Liberal State* (Cambridge: Polity Press, 2013); T. J. Hatton, *Seeking Asylum:*

Trends and Policies in the OECD (London: Centre for Economic Policy Research, 2011); A. Kundnani, *The End of Tolerance: Racism in 21st Century Britain* (London: Pluto Press, 2007); M. Maguire, C. Frois, and N. Zurawksi, eds., *The Anthropology of Security: Perspectives from the Frontline of Policing, Counter-Terrorism and Border Control* (London: Pluto Press, 2014); S. Scuzzarello and C. Kinnvall, "Rebordering France and Denmark Narratives and Practices of Border-Construction in Two European Countries," *Mobilities* 8.1 (2013): 90–106.

Bibliography

Abbott, J. R. "Critical Sociologies and Ressentiment: The Examples of C. Wright Mills and Howard Becker." *American Sociologist* 37.3 (2006): 15–30.

Abramovitz, M. "Social Work and Social Reform: An Arena of Struggle." *Social Work* 43.6 (1998): 512–26.

Abramowitz, S. C. *Searching for Normal in the Wake of the Liberian War.* Philadelphia: University of Pennsylvania Press, 2014.

Abruzzo, M. *Polemical Pain: Slavery, Cruelty, and the Rise of Humanitarianism.* Baltimore: Johns Hopkins University Press, 2010.

Adaair-Toteff, C. "Max Weber's Charisma." *Journal of Classical Sociology* 5.2 (2005): 189–204.

Addams, J. *Democracy and Social Ethics.* Urbana: University of Illinois Press, [1902] 2002.

———. "The Subjective Necessity for the Social Settlements." In *The Social Thought of Jane Addams*, ed. C. Lasch. Indianapolis: Bobbs-Merrill, [1892] 1965.

———. *Twenty Years at Hull-House.* New York: Penguin, [1910] 1998.

Adorno, T. W. *Negative Dialectics.* New York: Continuum, 1973.

Agamben, G. *Homo Sacer: Sovereign Power and Bare Life.* Stanford, CA: Stanford University Press, 1998.

Albert, P. J., P. Werhane, and T. Rolph. *Global Poverty Alleviation: A Case Book.* New York: Springer, 2014.

Alker, H. R., Jr. "The Humanistic Moment in International Studies: Reflections on Machiavelli and Las Casas. 1992 Presidential Address." *International Studies Quarterly* 36.4 (1992): 347–71.

Alford, F. C. "Bauman and Levinas: Levinas Cannot Be Used." *Journal for Cultural Research* 18.3 (2014): 249–62.

Amato, J. A. *Victims and Values: A History and a Theory of Suffering.* New York: Greenwood Press, 1990.

Anderson, G. L. "The Politics of Participatory Reforms in Education." *Theory into Practice* 38.4 (1999): 191–95.

Anderson, G. L., and K. Herr. "The New Paradigm Wars: Is There Room for Rigorous Practitioner Knowledge in Schools and Universities?" *Educational Researcher* 28.5 (1999): 12–40.

Andreas, P., and T. Snyder, eds. *The Wall around the West: State Borders and Immigration Controls in North America and Europe.* Lanham, MD: Rowman & Littlefield, 2000.

Andrews, E. B. "The Bimetallist Committee of Boston and New England." *Quarterly Journal of Economics* 8.3 (1894): 319–27.

Antonio, R. J. 1995. "Nietzsche's Antisociology: Subjectified Culture and the End of History." *American Journal of Sociology* 101.1 (1995): 1–43.

Arendt, H. 1963. *Eichmann in Jerusalem: A Report on the Banality of Evil.* Harmondsworth: Penguin.

———. *Men in Dark Times.* Harmondsworth: Pelican, 1968.

———. *The Origins of Totalitarianism.* Cleveland, OH: Meridian, 1958.

———. "The Social Question." In *On Revolution.* Harmondsworth: Penguin, 1963.

Arias, S., and E. M. Merediz, eds. *Approaches to Teaching the Writings of Bartolomé de Las Casas.* New York: Modern Languages Association, 2008.

Atrash, H. K. "Childhood Mortality: Still a Global Priority." *Journal of Human Growth and Development* 23.3 (2013): 257–60.

Averill, J. H. *Wordsworth and the Poetry of Human Suffering.* Ithaca, NY: Cornell University Press, 1980.

Backman, J. H. "Law Schools, Law Students, Civic Engagement, and Community-Based Research as Resources for Improving Access to Justice in Utah." *Utah Law Review* 4 (2006): 953–1209.

Baehr, P. "The 'Iron Cage' and the 'Shell as Hard as Steel': Parsons, Weber, and the Stahlhartes Gehäuse Metaphor in the Protestant Ethic and the Spirit of Capitalism." *History and Theory* 40.2 (2001): 153–69.

Baer, H. A., M. Singer, and I. Susser. *Medical Anthropology and the World System.* Westport, CT: Praeger, 2013.

Baldwin, J. "Everybody's Protest Novel." *Partisan Review* 16 (1949): 578–85.

Bannister, R. C. *Sociology and Scientism: The American Quest for Objectivity, 1880–1940.* Chapel Hill: University of North Carolina Press, 1991.

Barker-Benfield, G. J. *The Culture of Sensibility: Sex and Society in Eighteenth-Century Britain.* Chicago: University of Chicago Press, 1992.

Barnett, M. N. *Empire of Humanity: A History of Humanitarianism.* Ithaca, NY: Cornell University Press, 2011.

———. "The UN Security Council, Indifference, and Genocide in Rwanda." *Cultural Anthropology* 12.4 (1997): 551–78.

Barnett, M., and T. G. Weiss, eds. *Humanitarianism in Question: Politics, Power, Ethics.* Ithaca, NY: Cornell University Press, 2008.

Barnett, S. J. *The Enlightenment and Religion: Myths of Modernity.* Manchester: Manchester University Press, 2004.

Bartlett, R. C. "On the Politics of Faith and Reason: The Project of Enlightenment in Pierre Bayle and Montesquieu." *Journal of Politics* 63.1 (2001): 1–28.

Bauman, Z. *Modernity and the Holocaust.* Cambridge: Polity Press, 1989.

———. *Wasted Lives: Modernity and Its Outcasts.* Cambridge: Polity Press, 2003.

Bauman, Z., and T. May. *Thinking Sociologically.* 2nd ed. Oxford: Wiley-Blackwell, 2001.

Bayle, P. *Historical and Critical Dictionary.* Indianapolis: Bobbs-Merrill, [1695–97] 1965.

Beard, T. *The Theatre of God's Judgements.* Memphis, TN: Rare Books Club, [1597] 2012.

Beauregard, R. A. "City of Superlatives." *City & Community* 2.3 (2003): 183–99.

Beck, U. *The Cosmopolitan Vision.* Cambridge: Polity Press, 2006.

Beck, U., and E. Beck-Gernsheim. *Individualization: Institutionalized Individualism and Its Social and Political Consequences.* London: Sage, 2002.

Beck, U., and J. Willms. *Conversations with Ulrich Beck.* Cambridge: Polity Press, 2004.

Becker, A. *Body, Self, and Society: The View from Fiji.* Philadelphia: University of Pennsylvania Press, 1995.

Becker, E. *The Lost Science of Man.* New York: George Braziller, 1971.

———. *The Structure of Evil: An Essay on the Unification of the Science of Man.* New York: Free Press, 1968.

Becker, H. S. 1999. "The Chicago School, So-Called." *Qualitative Sociology* 22.1 (1999): 3–12.

Benson, P. *Tobacco Capitalism: Growers, Migrant Workers, and the Changing Face of a Global Industry.* Princeton, NJ: Princeton University Press, 2012.

Berg, M. *The Machinery Question and the Making of Political Economy, 1815–1848.* Cambridge: Cambridge University Press, 1980.

Berger, P. L., B. Berger, and H. Kellner. *The Homeless Mind: Modernization and Consciousness.* Oxford: Penguin, 1973.

Berlant, L. *The Female Complaint: The Unfinished Business of Sentimentality in American Culture*. Durham, NC: Duke University Press, 2008.

Bernstein, R. *The Pragmatic Turn*. Cambridge: Polity Press, 2010.

Berson, R. K. *Jane Addams: A Biography*. Westport, CT: Greenwood Press, 2004.

Besterman, T. "Voltaire and the Lisbon Earthquake or, The Death of Optimism." In *Voltaire: Essays*, ed. T. Besterman. Oxford: Oxford University Press, 1962.

Biehl, J. *Vita: Life in a Zone of Social Abandonment*. Berkeley: University of California Press, 2005.

Biehl, J., B. Good, and A. Kleinman. "Introduction: Rethinking Subjectivity." In *Subjectivity: Ethnographic Investigations*, ed. J. Biehl, B. Good, and A. Kleinman. Berkeley: University of California Press, 2007.

Blackburn, R. *The Making of New World Slavery: From the Baroque to the Modern, 1492–1800*. London: Verso, 1997.

Blaickie, W. G. *Heads and Hands in the World of Labour*. London: Alexander Strathern, 1865.

Blank, K. G. "The Degrading Thirst after Outrageous Stimulation: Wordsworth as Cultural Critic." *Journal of Popular Culture* 39.1 (2006): 365–82.

Bloch, M. *Feudal Society*. London: Routledge, 1989.

Bocock, K. "The Social Question and the Christian Answer." *Sewanee Review* 10.4 (1902): 450–57.

Bogre, M. *Photography as Activism: Images for Social Change*. Oxford: Focal Press, 2012.

Boltanski, L. *Distant Suffering: Morality, Media, and Politics*. Cambridge: Cambridge University Press, 1999.

Bourdieu, P. "Hanging by a Thread." In *The Weight of the World: Social Suffering in Contemporary Society*, ed. P. Bourdieu et al. Cambridge: Polity Press, 1999.

———. *Homo Academicus*. Stanford, CA: Stanford University Press, 1988.

———. *Pascalian Meditations*. Stanford, CA: Stanford University Press, 2000.

———. "The Space of Points of View." In *The Weight of the World: Social Suffering in Contemporary Society*, ed. P. Bourdieu et al. Cambridge: Cambridge University Press, 1999.

———. "Understanding." In *The Weight of the World: Social Suffering in Contemporary Society*, ed. P. Bourdieu et al. Cambridge: Polity Press, 1999.

Bourdieu, P., et al., eds. *The Weight of the World: Social Suffering in Contemporary Society*. Cambridge: Polity Press, 1999.

Bourdieu, P., and L. Wacquant. *An Invitation to Reflexive Sociology*. Chicago: University of Chicago Press, 1992.

Bourgois, P. I. *In Search of Respect: Selling Crack in El Barrio*. Cambridge: Cambridge University Press, 2002.

Bourgois, P. I., and J. Schonberg. *Righteous Dopefiend.* Berkeley: University of California Press, 2009.

Bowker, J. W. *Problems of Suffering in Religions of the World.* Cambridge: Cambridge University Press, 1975.

Bowpitt, G. "Evangelical Christianity, Secular Humanism and the Genesis of British Social Work." *British Journal of Social Work* 28 (1998): 675–93.

Boyer, E. L. *Scholarship Reconsidered: Priorities of the Professoriate.* Princeton, NJ: Carnegie Foundation for the Advancement of Teaching, 1990.

Brandt, W. J. *The Shape of Medieval History: Studies in Modes of Perception.* New Haven, CT: Yale University Press, 1966.

Bremmer, I. "The End of the Free Market: Who Wins the War between States and Corporations?" *European View* 9.2 (2010): 249–52.

Bremner, R. H. "'Scientific Philanthropy,' 1873–93." *Social Science Review* 30.1 (1956): 168–73.

Brewer, J. D. "Imagining the Sociological Imagination: The Biographical Context of a Sociological Classic." *British Journal of Sociology* 55.3 (2004): 317–33.

Brieland, D. "The Hull House Tradition and the Contemporary Social Worker: Was Jane Addams Really a Social Worker?" *Social Work* 35.2 (1990): 134–38.

Brodwin, P. *Everyday Ethics: Voices from the Front Line of Community Psychiatry.* Berkeley: University of California Press, 2012.

Brooks, C. *A Statement of Facts from Each Religious Denomination in New England Respecting Ministers Salaries.* Boston: Crocker & Brewster, Gould & Lincoln, C. Stimpson & J. Munroe & Co., 1854.

Brown, M. "Medicine, Reform and the 'End' of Charity in Early Nineteenth-Century England." *English Historical Review* 124.511 (2009): 1353–88.

Brown, R., and R. Lewis-Fernandez. "Culture and Conversion Disorder: Implications for DSM-5." *Psychiatry* 74.3 (2011): 187–206.

Brunstetter, D. R. "Sepúlveda, Las Casas, and the Other: Exploring the Tension between Moral Universalism and Alterity." *Review of Politics* 72.3 (2010): 409–35.

———.*Tensions of Modernity: Las Casas and His Legacy in the French Enlightenment.* New York: Routledge, 2012.

Brydon-Miller, M., and P. Maguire. "Participatory Action Research: Contributions to the Development of Practitioner Inquiry in Education." *Educational Action Research* 17.1 (2009): 79–93.

Bulmer, M. *The Chicago School of Sociology: Institutionalization, Diversity, and the Rise of Sociological Research.* Chicago: University of Chicago Press, 1986.

Burawoy, M. "For Public Sociology." *American Sociological Review* 70.1 (2005): 4–28.

———. "Introduction: Sociology as a Combat Sport." *Current Sociology* 62.1 (2014): 1–16.

Burns, W. E. *An Age of Wonders: Prodigies, Politics and Providence in England, 1657–1727.* Manchester: Manchester University Press, 2002.

Butt, L. "The Suffering Stranger: Medical Anthropology and International Morality." *Medical Anthropology* 21.1 (2002): 1–24.

Calhoun, C. "The Imperative to Reduce Suffering: Charity, Progress and Emergencies in the Field of Humanitarian Action." In *Humanitarianism in Question: Politics, Power, Ethics,* ed. M. Barnett and T. G. Weiss. Ithaca, NY: Cornell University Press, 2008.

———. "A World of Emergencies: Fear, Intervention, and the Limits of Cosmopolitan Order." *Canadian Review of Sociology* 41.4 (2004): 373–95.

———, ed. 2007. *Sociology in America: A History.* Chicago: University of Chicago Press.

Calhoun, C. J., and J. VanAntwerpen. "Orthodoxy, Heterodoxy, and Hierarchy: Mainstream Sociology and Its Challengers." In *Sociology in America: A History,* ed. C. J. Calhoun. Chicago: University of Chicago Press, 2007.

Calleson, D. C., C. Jordan, and S. D. Seifer. "Community-Engaged Scholarship: Is Faculty Work in Communities a True Academic Enterprise?" *Academic Medicine* 80.4 (2005): 317–21.

Cameron, S. "Representing Grief: Emerson's Experience." *Representations* 15 (1986): 15–41.

Campbell, C. *The Romantic Ethic and the Spirit of Modern Consumerism.* Oxford: Blackwell, 1987.

Carabine, K. Introduction to H. Beecher Stowe, *Uncle Tom's Cabin or Negro Life in the Slave States of America.* Ware: Wordsworth Classics, 2002.

Carey, D. "Hutcheson's Moral Sense and the Problem of Innateness." *Journal of the History of Philosophy* 38.1 (2000): 103–10.

Carson, M. *Settlement Folk: Social Thought and the American Settlement Movement, 1885–1930.* Chicago: University of Chicago Press, 1990.

Cassell, E. J. *The Nature of Suffering and the Goals of Medicine.* Oxford: Oxford University Press, 2004.

Castro, D. *Another Face of Empire: Bartolomé de Las Casas, Indigenous Rights, and Ecclesiastical Imperialism.* Durham, NC: Duke University Press, 2007.

Cawthon, E. "Thomas Wakley and the Medical Coronership: Occupational Death and the Judicial Process." *Medical History* 30.2 (1986): 191–202.

Chapin, C. "Shaftsbury and the Man of Feeling." *Modern Philology* 81.1 (1983): 47–50.

Chalcraft, D. "Bringing the Text Back In: On Ways of Reading the Iron Cage Metaphor in the Two Editions of *The Protestant Ethic.*" In *Organizing Modernity: New Weberian Perspectives on Work, Organization and Society,* ed. L. Ray and M. Reed. London: Routledge, 1994.

Chalcraft, D., M. F. Howell, M. L. Menendez, and M. H. Vera, eds. *Max Weber Matters: Interweaving Past and Present.* Farnham: Ashgate, 2008.

Chandy, L., and G. Gertz. *Poverty in Numbers: The Changing State of Global Poverty from 2005 to 2015.* Washington, DC: Brookings Institution, 2011.

Charlesworth, S.J. "Understanding Social Suffering: A Phenomenological Investigation of the Experience of Inequality." *Journal of Community & Applied Social Psychology* 15.4 (2005): 296–312.

Charmaz, K. "Loss of Self: A Fundamental Form of Suffering in the Chronically Ill." *Sociology of Health & Illness* 5.2 (1983): 168–95.

Chen, S., and M. Ravallion. *The Developing World Is Poorer than We Thought, but No Less Successful in the Fight against Poverty.* World Bank Policy Research Working Paper 4703. Washington, DC: World Bank, 2008.

Chouliaraki, L. *The Ironic Spectator: Solidarity in the Age of Post-Humanitarianism.* Cambridge: Polity Press, 2013.

Christakis, N.A. *Death Foretold: Prophecy and Prognosis in Medical Care.* Chicago: University of Chicago Press, 2001.

Clark, E.B. "The Sacred Rights of the Weak: Pain, Sympathy and the Culture of Individual Rights in Antebellum America." *Journal of American History* 82.2 (1995): 463–93.

Coakley, S., and K.K. Shelemay, eds. *Pain and Its Transformations: The Interface of Biology and Culture.* Cambridge, MA: Harvard University Press, 2007.

Cockburn, J.S. "Punishment and Brutalization in the English Enlightenment." *Law and History Review* 12.1 (1994): 155–79.

Cohen, A., A. Kleinman, and B. Saraceno, eds. *World Mental Health Casebook: Social and Mental Programs in Low-Income Countries.* New York: Springer, 2002.

Cohen, E. "The Animated Pain of the Body." *American Historical Review* 105.1 (2000): 36–68.

Cohen, L. "No Aging in India: The Uses of Gerontology." *Culture, Medicine and Psychiatry* 16.2 (1992): 123–61.

Cohen, S. *States of Denial: Knowing about Atrocities and Suffering.* Cambridge: Polity Press, 2001.

Conley, T. "De Bry's Las Casas." In *Amerindian Images and the Legacy of Columbus,* ed. R. Jara and N. Spadaccini. Minneapolis: University of Minnesota Press, 1992.

Connell, R. *Southern Theory: Social Science and the Global Dynamics of Knowledge.* Cambridge: Polity Press, 2007.

Conrad, P. *The Medicalization of Society: On the Transformation of Human Conditions into Treatable Disorders.* Baltimore: Johns Hopkins University Press, 2008.

Conway, J. "Women Reformers and American Culture, 1870–1930." *Journal of Social History* 5.2 (1971): 164–77.

Cook, H.J. "The History of Medicine and the Scientific Revolution." *Isis* 102.1 (2011): 102–8.

Crane, G. D. "Dangerous Sentiments: Sympathy, Rights, and Revolution in Stowe's Antislavery Novels." *Nineteenth-Century Literature* 51.2 (1996): 176–204.

Crane, R. S. "Suggestions towards a Genealogy of the 'Man of Feeling.'" *English Literary History* 1.3 (1934): 205–30.

Crawford, J. *Marvelous Protestantism: Monstrous Births in Post-Reformation England.* Baltimore: Johns Hopkins University Press, 2005.

Crocker, R. H. "The Victorian Poor Law in Crisis and Change: Southampton, 1870–1895." *Albion* 19.1 (1987): 19–44.

Csengei, I. *Sympathy, Sensibility and the Literature of Feeling in the Eighteenth Century.* Basingstoke: Palgrave, 2012.

Cunningham, A., and O. P. Grell. *The Four Horsemen of the Apocalypse: Religion, War, Famine and Death in Reformation Europe.* Cambridge: Cambridge University, 2000.

Das, V. "The Act of Witnessing: Violence, Poisonous Knowledge, and Subjectivity." In *Violence and Subjectivity,* ed. V. Das, A. Kleinman, M. Ramphele, and P. Reynolds. Berkeley: University of California Press, 2000.

———. *Critical Events: An Anthropological Perspective on Contemporary India.* Delhi: Oxford University Press, 1995.

———. *Life and Worlds: Violence and the Descent into the Ordinary.* Berkeley: University of California Press, 2006.

———. "Sufferings, Theodicies, Disciplinary Practices, Appropriations." *International Journal of Social Science* 49 (1997): 563–57.

Daston, L. "Objectivity and the Escape from Perspective." *Social Studies of Science* 22.4 (1992): 597–618.

Davies, J. B., S. Sandström, A. Shorrocks, and E. N. Wolff. *The World Distribution of Household Wealth.* WIDER Discussion Papers, No. 2008/03. Helsinki: World Institute for Development Economics, 2008.

Davis, A. F. *American Heroine: The Life and Legend of Jane Addams.* New York: Oxford University Press, 1973.

———. *Spearheads of Reform: The Social Settlements and the Progressive Movement, 1890–1914.* New York: Oxford University Press, 1967.

Davis, A. J. *The History and Philosophy of Evil with Suggestions for More Ennobling Institutions and Philosophical Systems of Education.* Boston: William White & Co, 1869.

Davis, J. E. "Medicalization, Social Control, and the Relief of Suffering." In *The New Blackwell Companion to Medical Sociology,* ed. W. C. Cockerham. Malden, MA: Blackwell, 2009.

Davis, M. *Planet of Slums.* London: Verso, 2007.

Deegan, M. J. "Early Women Sociologists and the American Sociological Society: The Patterns of Exclusion and Participation." *American Sociologist* 16 (February 1981): 14–24.

———. *Jane Addams and the Men of the Chicago School, 1892–1918.* New Brunswick, NJ: Transaction Books, 1988.

———. "W. E. B. Du Bois and the Women of Hull-House, 1865–1899." *American Sociologist* 23 (Winter 1988): 301–11.

Dejours, C. *Souffrances en France: La banalization de l'injustice sociale.* Paris: Seuil, 1998.

Delanty, G., and P. Strydom. eds. *Philosophies of Social Science: The Classical and Contemporary Readings.* Milton Keynes: Open University Press, 2003.

De Morier, D. R. *What Has Religion to Do with Politics? The Question Considered in Letters to His Son.* London: John W. Parker, 1848.

Denby, D. *Sentimental Narrative and the Social Order in France, 1760–1820,* Cambridge: Cambridge University Press, 1994.

Denzin, N. K. "Presidential Address on the Sociological Imagination Revisited." *Sociological Quarterly* 31.1 (1990): 1–22.

Desjarlais, R. *Shelter Blues: Sanity and Selfhood among the Homeless.* Philadelphia: University of Pennsylvania Press, 1997.

Desjarlais, R., L. Eisenberg, B. Good, and A. Kleinman. *World Mental Health: Problems and Priorities in Low-Income Countries.* Oxford: Oxford University Press, 1995.

Dewey, J. "The Need for a Recovery of Philosophy." In *On Experience, Nature and Freedom,* ed. R. Bernstein. New York: Liberal Arts Press, [1917] 1960.

———. *On Experience, Nature and Freedom.* New York: Liberal Arts Press, [1917] 1960.

Dickens, C. *Hard Times.* London: Penguin, [1854] 2003.

———. *The Mudfog Papers.* Richmond, VA: Alma Classics, [1843] 2014.

Dogan, M. "Four Hundred Giant Cities Atop the World." *International Social Science Journal* 56.181 (2004): 347–60.

Douglas, A. "The Art of Controversy: Introduction to *Uncle Tom's Cabin.*" In *Uncle Tom's Cabin: Or, Life among the Lowly,* by H. Beecher Stowe. Harmondsworth: Penguin, 1983.

Douglas-Fairhurst, R. Introduction to *London Labour and the London Poor,* by H. Mayhew. Oxford: Oxford University Press, 2010.

Dow, T. E., Jr. "An Analysis of Weber's Work on Charisma." *British Journal of Sociology* 29.1 (1978): 83–93.

Du Bois, W. D., and R. D. Wright. *Applying Sociology: Making a Better World.* Boston: Allyn and Bacon, 2001.

———. *Politics in the Human Interest: Applying Sociology in the Real World.* Lanham, MD: Rowman and Littlefield, 2008.

Duffy, L. "Suffering, Shame, and Silence: The Stigma of HIV/AIDS." *Journal of the Association of Nurses in AIDS Care* 16.1 (2005): 13–20.

Duffy, M. *Making Care Count: A Century of Gender, Race, and Paid Care Work.* Piscataway, NJ: Rutgers University Press, 2011.

Dunphy, J. E. "Annual Discourse: On Caring for the Patient with Cancer." *New England Journal of Medicine* 295.6 (1976): 313–19.

Durkheim, E. "Individualism and the Intellectuals." in *Emile Durkheim on Morality and Society*, ed. R. Bellah. Chicago: University of Chicago Press, [1898] 1973.

Ehrenreich, J. *The Altruistic Imagination: A History of Social Work and Social Policy in the United States*. Ithaca, NY: Cornell University Press, 1985.

Elias, N. *The Civilizing Process*. Oxford: Blackwell, 1994.

Ellis, M. *The Politics of Sensibility: Race, Gender and Commerce in the Sentimental Novel*. Cambridge: Cambridge University Press, 1996.

Elshtain, J. B. *Jane Addams and the Dream of American Democracy: A Life*. New York: Basic Books, 2002.

Elster, J. "Functional Explanation in Social Science." in *Readings in the Philosophy of Social Science*, ed. M. Martin and L. C. McIntyre. Cambridge, MA: MIT Press, 1994.

Emerson, R. W. "Experience." In *Essays and Lectures*. New York: Library of America, [1842] 1983.

England, P. "Emerging Theories of Care Work." *Annual Review of Sociology* 31 (2005): 381–99.

England, P., M. Budig, and N. Folbre. "'Wages of Virtue': The Relative Pay of Care Work." *Social Problems* 49.4 (2002): 455–73.

Englander, D. "Comparisons and Contrasts: Henry Mayhew and Charles Booth as Social Investigators." in *Retrieved Riches: Social Investigation in Britain, 1840–1914*, ed. D. Englander and R. O'Day. Aldershot: Scholar Press, 1995.

Farmer, P. *Aids and Accusation: Haiti and the Geography of Blame*. Berkeley: University of California Press, 1992.

———. "Conversation in the Time of Cholera: A Reflection on Structural Violence and Social Change." In *In the Company of the Poor: Conversations with Dr. Paul Farmer and Fr. Gustavo Gutierrez*, ed. M. Griffin and J. W. Block. New York: Orbis Books, 2013.

———. *Infections and Inequalities: The Modern Plagues*. Berkeley: University of California Press, 1999.

———. "Never Again? Reflections on Human Values and Human Rights." In *Tanner Lectures on Human Values*,,vol. 26, ed. G. B. Peterson. Salt Lake City: University of Utah Press, 2006.

———. *Pathologies of Power: Health, Human Rights, and the New War on the Poor*. Berkeley: University of California Press, 2003.

Farmer, P., J. Y. Kim, A. Kleinman, and M. Basilico, eds. *Reimagining Global Health: An Introduction*. Berkeley: University of California Press, 2013.

Fassin, D. "Another Politics of Life Is Possible." *Theory, Culture & Society* 26.5 (2009): 44–60.

———. "Beyond Good and Evil? Questioning the Anthropological Discomfort with Morals." *Anthropological Theory* 8.4 (2008): 333–44.

———. "Compassion and Repression: The Moral Economy of Immigration Policies in France." *Cultural Anthropology* 20.3 (2005): 362–87.

———. "Heart of Humaneness: The Moral Economy of Humanitarian Intervention." In *Contemporary States of Emergency: The Politics of Military and Humanitarian Interventions*, ed. D. Fassin and M. Pandolfini. New York: Zone Books, 2010.

———. *Humanitarian Reason: A Moral History of the Present*. Berkeley: University of California Press, 2012.

———. *When Bodies Remember: Experiences and Politics of AIDS in South Africa*. Berkeley: University of California Press, 2007.

Faust, D. G. *The Republic of Suffering: Death and the American Civil War*. New York: Vintage Books, 2008.

Feagin, J. R. "Social Justice and Sociology: Agendas for the Twenty-First Century." In *Critical Strategies for Social Research*, ed. W. K. Carroll. Toronto: Canadian Scholars Press, 2004.

Fei, X. *From the Soil: The Foundations of Chinese Society*. Berkeley: University of California Press, 1992.

Fields, H. L. "Setting the Stage for Pain: Allegorical Tales from Neuroscience." In *Pain and Its Transformations: The Interface of Biology and Culture*, ed. S. Coakley and K. K. Shelemay. Cambridge, MA: Harvard University Press, 2007.

Fiering, N. S. "Irresistible Compassion: An Aspect of Eighteenth-Century Sympathy and Humanitarianism." *Journal of the History of Ideas* 37.2 (1976): 195–218.

Fine, M. "Individualization, Risk and the Body: Sociology and Care." *Journal of Sociology* 41.3 (2005): 247–66.

Fischer, M. "Addams's Internationalist Pacifism and the Rhetoric of Maternalism." *National Women's Studies Association (NWSA) Journal* 18.3 (2006): 1–19.

Folbre, N. *For Love and Money: Care Provision in the United States*, New York: Russell Sage Foundation, 2012.

Food and Agricultural Organization of the United Nations (FAO). *Coping with Water Scarcity: An Action Framework for Agriculture and Food Security*. Rome: FAO, 2012. Available at www.fao.org/docrep/016/i3015e/i3015e.pdf.

———. *The State of Food Insecurity in the World: Addressing Food Insecurity in Protracted Crises*. Rome: FAO, 2010.

Forman-Barzilai, F. "Sympathy in Space(s): Adam Smith on Proximity." *Political Theory* 33.2 (2005): 189–217.

Foucault, M. *Discipline and Punish: The Birth of the Prison*. New York: Vintage, 1977.

———. *The History of Sexuality, Vol. 1: An Introduction.* New York: Pantheon, 1978.

———. *The History of Sexuality, Vol. 2: The Use of Pleasure.* New York: Vintage, 1985.

———. *The History of Sexuality, Vol. 3: The Care of the Self.* New York: Vintage, 1988.

Foyle, A. "Human and Divine Suffering." *Ars Disputandi* 5 (2001). Available at www.arsdisputandi.org/.

Fox, C., R. S. Porter, and R. Wolker, eds. *Inventing Human Science: Eighteenth-Century Domains.* Berkeley: University of California Press, 1995.

Fox, R. *Essays in Medical Sociology: Journeys into the Field.* New Brunswick, NJ: Transaction Publishers, 1988.

Frank, A. W. "Can We Research Suffering?" *Qualitative Health Research* 11.3 (2001): 353–62.

Franklin, D. L. "Mary Richmond and Jane Addams: From Moral Certainty to Rational Inquiry in Social Work Practice."*Social Service Review* 60.4 (1986): 504–25.

Frazer, M. L. *The Enlightenment of Sympathy: Justice and the Moral Sentiments in the Eighteenth Century and Today.* Oxford: Oxford University Press, 2010.

Freeman, M. D. "Social Investigation in Rural England, 1870–1914." PhD diss., University of Glasgow, 1999.

Freire, P. 1993. *Pedagogy of Hope.* New York: Continuum, 2004.

———. *Pedagogy of the Oppressed.* New York: Continuum, 1993.

Frothingham, N. L., et al. *Society for the Relief of Aged and Destitute Clergymen: Extracts from Records Relating to Its History and Objects.* Boston: John Wilson & Son, 1862.

Fuentes-Nieva, R., and N. Galasso. *Working for the Few: Political Capture and Economic Inequality.* Oxford: Oxfam, 2014. Available at www.oxfam.org/en /policy/working-for-the-few-economic-inequality.

Fullwiley, D. *The Encultured Gene: Sickle Cell Health Politics and Biological Difference in West Africa.* Princeton, NJ: Princeton University Press, 2011.

Galtung, J. "Violence, Peace, and Peace Research." *Journal of Peace Research* 6.3 (1969): 167–91.

Gane, N. *Max Weber and Postmodern Theory: Rationalization versus Re-enchantment.* Basingstoke: Macmillan, 2004.

Gardner, H., ed. *Responsibility at Work: How Leading Professionals Act (or Don't Act) Responsibly.* New York: John Wiley & Sons, 2010.

Garcia, A. *The Pastoral Clinic: Addiction and Dispossession along the Rio Grande.* Berkeley: University of California Press, 2010.

Gaston, S. "The Impossibility of Sympathy." *Eighteenth Century* 51.1–2 (2010): 129–52.

Gay, P. *The Enlightenment, an Interpretation*, vol. 1: *The Rise of Modern Paganism*. New York: Norton, 1966.

Gaynes, R. P. *Germ Theory: Medical Pioneers in Infectious Diseases*. Washington, DC: American Society for Microbiology, 2011.

Geary, D. *Radical Ambition: C. Wright Mills, the Left, and American Social Thought*. Berkeley: University of California Press, 2009.

Giddens, A. *Modernity and Self-Identity: Self and Identity in the Late Modern Age*. Cambridge: Polity Press, 1991.

Giles, D. E., Jr. "Understanding an Emerging Field of Scholarship: Toward a Research Agenda for Engaged Public Scholarship." *Journal of Higher Education Outreach and Engagement* 12.2 (2008): 97–106.

Gilman, E. B. *Plague Writing in Early Modern England*. Chicago: University of Chicago Press, 2009.

Girgis, A., and R. W. Sanson-Fisher. "Breaking Bad News: Consensus Guidelines for Medical Practitioners." *Journal of Clinical Oncology* 13.9 (1995): 2449–56.

Givoni, M. "Beyond the Humanitarian/Political Divide: Witnessing and the Making of Humanitarian Ethics." *Journal of Human Rights* 10.1 (2011): 55–75.

Glover, J. *Humanity: A Moral History of the Twentieth Century*. London: Pimlico, 2001.

Goldman, L. "The Origins of British 'Social Science': Political Economy, Natural Science and Statistics, 1830–35." *Historical Journal* 26.3 (1983): 587–616.

———. "Statistics and the Science of Society in Early Victorian Britain: An Intellectual Context for the General Register Office." *Social History of Medicine* 4.3 (1991): 415–34.

Gong, F., S. Baron, L. Ayala, L. Stock, S. McDevitt, and C. Heaney. "The Role for Community-Based Participatory Research in Formulating Policy Initiatives: Promoting Safety and Health for In-Home Care Workers and Their Consumers." *American Journal of Public Health* 99.3 (2009): 531–39.

Good, M. D., S. S. Willen, S. D. Hannah, K. Vickory, and L. T. Park, eds. *Shattering Culture: American Medicine Responds to Cultural Diversity*. New York: Russell Sage Foundation, 2011.

Good, M. J., P. Brodwin, B. Good, and A. Kleinman, eds. *Pain as Human Experience: An Anthropological Perspective*. Comparative Studies of Health Systems and Medical Care. Berkeley: University of California Press, 1994.

Grayman, J. H. "Humanitarian Encounters in Post-Conflict Aceh, Indonesia." PhD diss., Harvard University, 2013. Available at http://dash.harvard.edu/handle/1/10433473.

Grayman, J. H., M. J. D. Good, and B. J. Good. "Conflict Nightmares and Trauma in Aceh." *Culture, Medicine, and Psychiatry* 33.2 (2009): 290–312.

Green, M. "Representing Poverty and Attacking Representations: Perspectives on Poverty from Social Anthropology." *Journal of Development Studies* 42.7 (2006): 1108–29.

Gregory, B. S. *The Unintended Reformation: How Religious Revolution Secularized Society.* Cambridge, MA: Harvard University Press, 2012.

Greyser, N. "Affective Geographies: Sojourner Truth's Narrative: Feminism and the Ethical Bind of Sentimentalism." *American Literature* 79.2 (2007): 275–305.

Hacker, K. *Community-Based Participatory Research.* New York: Sage, 2013.

Hacking, I. *The Taming of Chance.* Cambridge: Cambridge University Press, 1990.

Hahn, R. A., and M. C. Inhorn. *Anthropology and Public Health: Bridging Differences in Culture and Society.* New York: Oxford University Press, 2008.

Hall, B. L. "From Margins to Center? The Development and Purpose of Participatory Research." *American Sociologist* 23.4 (1992): 15–28.

Hall, D. D. *Worlds of Wonder, Days of Judgement: Popular Religious Belief in Early New England.* New York: Alfred A. Knopf, 1989.

Halttunen, K. "Humanitarianism and the Pornography of Pain in Anglo- American Culture." *American Historical Review* 100.2 (1995): 303–34.

Hamington, M. *Embodied Care: Jane Addams, Maurice Merleau-Ponty, and Feminist Ethics.* Urbana: University of Illinois Press, 2004.

———. "An Inverted Home: Socializing Care at Hull-House." In *Socializing Care: Feminist Ethics and Public Issues,* ed. M. Hamington and D.C. Miller. Lanham, MD: Rowman and Littlefield, 2006.

———. "Public Pragmatism: Jane Addams and Ida B. Wells on Lynching." *Journal of Speculative Philosophy* 19.2 (2005): 167–74.

Hamlin, C. "Could You Starve to Death in England in 1839? The Chadwick-Farr Controversy and the Loss of the 'Social' in Public Health." *American Journal of Public Health* 85.6 (1995): 856–66.

———. "Predisposing Causes and Public Health in Early Nineteenth-Century Medical Thought." *Social History of Medicine* 5.1 (1992): 43–70.

Hampshire, J. *The Politics of Immigration: Contradictions of the Liberal State.* Cambridge: Polity Press, 2013.

Han, C. *Life in Debt: Times of Care and Violence in Neoliberal Chile.* Berkeley: University of California Press, 2012.

Hanke, L. *Bartolomé de Las Casas, Historian: An Essay in Spanish Historiography.* Gainesville: University Press of Florida, 1952.

Harkavy, I., and J. L. Puckett. "Lessons from Hull House for the Contemporary Urban University." *Social Service Review* 68.3 (1994): 299–321.

Harrington J. "Wordsworth's Descriptive Sketches and the Prelude, Book VI." *Publications of the Modern Languages Association (PMLA)* 44.4 (1929): 1144–58.

Harrison, B. *Peaceable Kingdom: Stability and Change in Modern Britain*. Oxford: Clarendon Press, 1982.

Harrison, P. "'Science' and 'Religion': Constructing the Boundaries." *Journal of Religion* 86.1 (2006): 81–106.

Harth, P. "The Satiric Purpose of the Fable of the Bees." *Eighteenth-Century Studies* 2.4 (1969): 321–40.

Hartman, G. H. "Wordsworth's Descriptive Sketches and the Growth of a Poet's Mind." *Publications of the Modern Language Association (PMLA)* 76.5 (1961): 519–27.

Haskell, T. L. "Capitalism and the Origins of the Humanitarian Sensibility, Part 1." American Historical Review 90.2 (1985): 339–61.

———. "Capitalism and the Origins of the Humanitarian Sensibility, Part 2." American Historical Review 90.3 (1985): 547–66.

———. *The Emergence of Professional Social Science: The American Social Science Association and the Crisis of Authority*. Baltimore: Johns Hopkins University Press, 2000.

Hatton, T. J. *Seeking Asylum: Trends and Policies in the OECD*. London: Centre for Economic Policy Research, 2011.

Hays, R. B. *All in the Family: Faith Issues for Families Dealing with Addiction*. Nashville, TN: WestBow Press, 2010.

Headley, J. M. *The Europeanization of the World: On the Origins of Human Rights and Democracy*. Princeton, NJ: Princeton University Press, 2008.

Hennis, W. *Max Weber: Essays in Reconstruction*. London: Allen & Unwin, 1988.

Herdt, J. A. "The Rise of Sympathy and the Question of Divine Suffering." *Journal of Religious Ethics* 29.3 (2001): 367–99.

Herzfeld, M. *The Body Impolitic: Artisans and Artifice in the Global Hierarchy of Value*. Chicago: University of Chicago Press, 2004.

———. *The Social Production of Indifference: Exploring the Symbolic Roots of Western Bureaucracy*. Chicago: University of Chicago Press, 1992.

Hewa, S. "Medical Technology: A Pandora's Box?" *Journal of Medical Humanities* 15.3 (1994): 171–81.

Hick, J. *Evil and the God of Love*. London: Macmillan, 1966.

Hill, C. *The English Bible and the Seventeenth Century Revolution*. London: Penguin, 1993.

———. *The Word Turned Upside Down*. Harmondsworth: Penguin, 1975.

Hillyard, P., C. Pantazis, S. Tombs, and D. Gordon. *Beyond Criminology: Taking Harm Seriously*. London: Macmillan, 2004.

Himmelfarb, G. *The Idea of Poverty: England in the Early Industrial Age*. London: Faber & Faber, 1984.

———. "Mayhew's Poor: A Problem of Identity." *Victorian Studies* 14.3 (1971): 307–20.

———. *Poverty and Compassion: The Moral Imagination of the Late Victorians.* New York: Alfred A. Knopf, 1992.

Hinkle, G. J. "The Americanization of Max Weber." *Current Perspectives in Social Theory* 7 (1986): 87–104.

Hinton, A. L., ed. *Annihilating Difference: The Anthropology of Genocide.* Berkeley: University of California Press, 2002.

Hobsbawm, E. *An Age of Extremes: The Short History of the Twentieth Century, 1914–1991.* London: Penguin Books, 1994.

———. *The Age of Revolution, 1789–1848.* London: Wiedenfeld and Nicolson, 1962.

Hochschild, A. R. *The Managed Heart: Commercialization of Human Feeling.* Berkeley: University of California Press, 1983.

Höijer, B. "The Discourse of Global Compassion: The Audience and Media Reporting of Human Suffering." *Media, Culture & Society* 26.4 (2004): 513–31.

Holland, B. "New Views of Research for the 21st Century: The Role of Engaged Scholarship." *Scholarship in Action: Applied Research and Community Change* (November 2005): 1–9.

Hopkins, C. H. *The Rise of the Social Gospel in American Protestantism.* New Haven, CT: Yale University Press, 1940.

Horkheimer, M., and T. W. Adorno. *Dialectic of Enlightenment.* London: Allen Lane, 1973.

Horowitz, C. R., B. L. Brenner, S. Lachapelle, D. A. Amara, and G. Arniella. "Effective Recruitment of Minority Populations through Community-Led Strategies." *American Journal of Preventive Medicine* 37.6 (2009): 195–200.

Horowitz, I. L. "The Intellectual Genesis of C. Wright Mills." In C. W. Mills, *Sociology and Pragmatism: The Higher Learning in America,* ed. and introd. I. L. Horowitz. New York: Oxford University Press, 1964.

Hovet, T., Jr. "Harriet Martineau's Exceptional American Narratives: Harriet Beecher Stowe, John Brown and the Redemption of Your National Soul." *American Studies* 48.1 (2007): 63–76.

Hume, D. *An Enquiry Concerning the Principles of Morals.* Indianapolis, IN: Hackett, [1751] 1987.

———. *A Treatise of Human Nature.* London: Penguin, [1739–40] 1969.

Humphreys, A. *Travels into the Poor Man's Country: The Work of Henry Mayhew.* Athens: University of Georgia Press, 1977.

Hunt, L. *Inventing Human Rights: A History.* New York: Norton, 2007.

Hutcheson, F. *A Short Introduction to Moral Philosophy in Three Books Containing Elements of Ethicks and the Law of Nature.* Glasgow: Glasgow University Press, 1747.

Hwang, K. K. "Face and Favor: The Chinese Power Game." *American Journal of Sociology* 92.4 (1987): 944–74.

Ibáñez-Carrasco, J. F., and E. R. Meiners, eds. *Public Acts: Disruptive Readings on Making Curriculum Public*. New York: Routledge, 2004.

Ignatieff, M. *The Warrior's Honour: Ethnic War and the Modern Conscience*. London: Vintage, 1999.

Inhorn, M. C. "Global Infertility and the Globalization of New Reproductive Technologies: Illustrations from Egypt." *Social Science & Medicine* 56.9 (2003): 1837–51.

Ishay, M. R. *The History of Human Rights: From Ancient Times to the Globalization Era*. Berkeley: University of California Press, 2008.

Jackson, M. *Life within Limits: Well-Being in a World of Want*. Durham, NC: Duke University Press, 2011.

Jacobson, M., and C. Rugeley. "Community-Based Participatory Research: Group Work for Social Justice and Community Change." *Social Work with Groups* 30.4 (2007): 21–39.

Jaffe, A. *Scenes of Sympathy: Identity and Representation in Victorian Literature*. Ithaca, NY: Cornell University Press, 2000.

———. "Spectacular Sympathy: Visuality and Ideology in Dickens's *A Christmas Carol*." *Publication of the Modern Languages Association (PMLA)* 109.2 (1994): 254–65.

James, E. C. *Democratic Insecurities: Violence, Trauma, and Intervention in Haiti*. Berkeley: University of California Press, 2010.

James, H. "Our Mutual Friend." *The Nation* 1 (1865): 786–87.

James, J. *Technology, Globalization and Poverty*. Cheltenham: Edward Elgar, 2002.

James, W. "Pragmatism's Conception of Truth." *Journal of Philosophy, Psychology and Scientific Methods* 4.6 (1907): 141–55.

———. "A World of Pure Experience II." *Journal of Philosophy, Psychology and Scientific Methods* 1.21 (1904): 561–70.

Jay, M. *Songs of Experience: Modern American and European Variations on a Universal Theme*. Berkeley: University of California Press, 2006.

Jones, C. "Radical Sensibility in the 1790s." In *Reflections of Revolution: Images of Revolution*, ed. A. Yarrington and K. Everest. London: Routledge, 1993.

Jones, P. D. A. *The Christian Socialist Revival, 1877–1914: Religion, Class, and Social Conscience in Late-Victorian England*. Princeton, NJ: Princeton University Press, 1968.

Juderías, J. *La Leyenda negra y la verdad histórica*. Madrid: Revista de, 1914.

Kaag, J. J. "Pragmatism and the Lessons of Experience." *Daedalus* 138.2 (2009): 63–72.

Kain P. J. "Nietzsche, Eternal Recurrence, and the Horror of Existence." *Journal of Nietzsche Studies* 33 (2007): 49–63.

———. "Nietzsche, Virtue and the Horror of Existence." *British Journal for the History of Philosophy* 17.1 (2009): 153–67.

Kalberg, S. "The Past and Present Influence of World Views: Max Weber on a Neglected Sociological Concept." *Journal of Classical Sociology* 4.2 (2004): 139–63.

———. "The Rationalization of Action in Max Weber's Sociology of Religion." *Sociological Theory* 8.1 (1990): 58–84.

———. "Should the 'Dynamic Autonomy' of Ideas Matter to Sociologists?" *Journal of Classical Sociology* 1.3 (2001): 291–327.

Kanbur, R., and A. Sumner. "Poor Countries or Poor People? Development Assistance and the New Geography of Global Poverty." *Journal of International Development* 26.6 (2012): 686–95.

Kaplan, F. *Sacred Tears: Sentimentality in Victorian Literature*. New York: Open Road Media, 2013.

Kaufman, S. *And a Time to Die: How American Hospitals Shape the End of Life*. Chicago: University of Chicago Press, 2006.

Keen, B. "The Black Legend Revisited: Assumptions and Realities." *Hispanic American Historical Review* 49.4 (1969): 703–19.

Kenny, M., ed. *Learning to Serve: Promoting Civil Society through Service Learning*. New York: Springer, 2002.

Kent, S. A. "Weber, Goethe, and the Nietzschean Allusion: Capturing the Source of the 'Iron Cage' Metaphor." *Sociology of Religion* 44.4 (1983): 297–319.

Keshavjee, S. *Blind Spot: How Neoliberalism Infiltrated Global Health*. Berkeley: University of California Press, 2014.

Kershaw, I. *The "Hitler Myth": Image and Reality in the Third Reich*. Oxford: Oxford University Press, 1987.

Kibbey, A. "Mutations of the Supernatural: Witchcraft, Remarkable Providences and the Power of Puritan Men." *American Quarterly* 34.2 (1982): 125–48.

Kilminster, R. "Critique and Overcritique in Sociology." *Human Figurations* 2.2 (2013). Available at http://hdl.handle.net/2027/spo.11217607.0002.205.

Kim, J. Y., J. V. Millen, A. Irwin, and J. Gershman, eds. *Dying for Growth: Global Inequality and the Health of the Poor*. Monroe, ME: Common Courage Press, 2002.

Kim, U., K. S. Yang, and K. K. Hwang. *Indigenous and Cultural Psychology: Understanding People in Context*. New York: Springer, 2006.

Kirby, P. *Vulnerability and Violence: The Impact of Globalization*. London: Pluto Press, 2006.

Kirmayer, L. J. "Multicultural Medicine and the Politics of Recognition." *Journal of Medicine and Philosophy* 36.4 (2014): 410–23.

Kirmayer, L. J., G. M. Brass, T. Holton, K. Paul, C. Simpson, and C. Tait. *Suicide among Aboriginal People in Canada*. Ottawa: Aboriginal Healing Foundation, 2007.

Klein, L. E. *Shaftsbury and the Culture of Politeness: Moral Discourse and Cultural Politics in Early Eighteenth-Century England*. Cambridge: Cambridge University Press, 1994.

Kleinman, A. "Caregiving as Moral Experience." *Lancet* 380.9853 (2012): 1550–51.

———. "Everything That Really Matters: Social Suffering, Subjectivity, and the Remaking of Human Experience in a Disordering World." *Harvard Theological Review* 90.3 (1997): 315–36.

———. "Experience and Its Moral Modes: Culture, Human Conditions, and Disorder." In *The Tanner Lectures on Human Values*, vol. 20, ed. G. B. Peterson. Salt Lake City: University of Utah Press, 1999.

———. "From Illness as Culture to Caregiving as Moral Experience." *New England Journal of Medicine* 368.15 (2013): 1376–77.

———. "How Is Culture Important for DSM-IV?" In *Culture and Psychiatric Diagnosis: A DSM-IV Perspective*, ed. J. E. Mezzich, D. L. Parron, and A. Kleinman. Arlington, VA: American Psychiatric Press, 1996.

———. *The Illness Narratives: Suffering, Healing, and the Human Condition*. New York: Basic Books, 1988.

———. "Neurasthenia and Depression: A Study of Somatization and Culture in China." *Culture, Medicine and Psychiatry* 6.2 (1982): 117–90.

———. *Patients and Healers in the Context of Culture: An Exploration of the Borderland Between Anthropology, Medicine, and Psychiatry*. Berkeley: University of California Press, 1980.

———. "Response: The Incommensurable Richness of 'Experience.'" In *Pain and Its Transformations: The Interface of Biology and Culture*, ed. S. Coakley and K. K. Shelemay. Cambridge, MA: Harvard University Press, 2007.

———. *What Really Matters: Living a Moral Life amidst Uncertainty and Danger*. New York: Oxford University Press, 2006.

Kleinman, A., J. M. Anderson, K. Finkler, R. J. Frankenberg, and A. Young. "Social Origins of Distress and Disease: Depression, Neurasthenia, and Pain in Modern China." *Current Anthropology* 24.5 (1986): 499–509.

Kleinman, A., and B. Good, eds. *Culture and Depression: Studies in the Anthropology and Cross-Cultural Psychiatry of Affect and Disorder*. Berkeley: University of California Press, 1985.

Kleinman, A., V. Das, and M. Lock, eds. *Social Suffering*. Berkeley: University of California Press, 1997.

Kleinman, A., and J. Kleinman. "The Appeal of Experience, the Dismay of Images: Cultural Appropriations of Suffering in Our Times." *Daedalus* 125.1 (1996): 1–23.

Kleinman, A., W. Z. Wang, S. C. Li, X. M. Cheng, X. Y. Dai, K. T. Li, and J. Kleinman. "The Social Course of Epilepsy: Chronic Illness as Social Experience in Interior China." *Social Science & Medicine* 40.10 (1995): 1319–30.

Kleinman, A., Y. Yan, J. Jun, S. Lee, E. Zhang, P. Tianshu, W. Fei, and G. Jinhua. *Deep China: The Moral Life of the Person*. Berkeley: University of California Press, 2011.

Klingberg, F.J. "Harriet Beecher Stowe and Social Reform in England." *American Historical Review* 43.3 (1938): 542–52.

Kloppenberg, J.T. "Pragmatism: An Old Name for Some New Ways of Thinking?" *Journal of American History* 83.1 (1996): 100–138.

Knight, L.W. *Jane Addams: Spirit in Action*. New York: Norton, 2010.

Koven, S. *Slumming: Sexual and Social Politics in Victorian England*. Princeton, NJ: Princeton University Press, 2006.

Krause, S.R. *Civil Passions: Moral Sentiment and Democratic Deliberation*. Princeton, NJ: Princeton University Press, 2008.

Krieger, J., C. Allen, A. Cheadle, S. Ciske, J.K. Schier, K. Senturia, and M. Sullivan. "Using Community-Based Participatory Research to Address Social Determinants of Health: Lessons Learned from Seattle Partners for Healthy Communities." *Health Education & Behavior* 29.3 (2002): 361–82.

Krieger, N. *Epidemiology and the People's Health: Theory and Context*. New York: Oxford University Press, 2011.

Kundnani, A. *The End of Tolerance: Racism in 21st Century Britain*. London: Pluto Press, 2007.

Lannoy, P. "When Robert E. Park was (Re)Writing 'The City': Biography, the Social Survey and the Science of Sociology." *American Sociologist* 35.1 (Spring 2004): 34–62.

Las Casas, B. de. *A Short Account of the Destruction of the Indies*. London: Penguin, [1552] 1992.

Lasch, C., ed. *The Social Thought of Jane Addams*. Indianapolis, IN: Bobbs-Merrill, 1965.

Lassman, P., ed. *Max Weber*. Aldershot: Ashgate, 2006.

Lawson, H.A. "An Appreciation and a Selective Enhancement of the Developing Model for University-Assisted Community Schools." *Universities and Community Schools* 8.1–2 (2010): 5–20.

Lazare, A. *On Apology*. New York: Oxford University Press, 2004.

Ledger, S. *Dickens and the Popular Radical Imagination*. Cambridge: Cambridge University Press, 2007.

———. "From Queen Caroline to Lady Dedlock: Dickens and the Popular Radical Imagination." *Victorian Literature and Culture* 32.2 (2004): 575–600.

Lee, A.M. *Sociology for Whom?* New York: Oxford University Press, 1978.

———. *Toward Humanist Sociology*. Englewood Cliffs, NJ: Prentice-Hall, 1973.

Leffers, M.R. "Pragmatists Jane Addams and John Dewey Inform the Ethics of Care." *Hypatia* 8.2 (1993): 64–77.

Lengermann, P.M., and J. Niebrugge-Brantley. "Back to the Future: Settlement Sociology, 1885–1930." *American Sociologist* (Fall 2002): 5–20.

———. *The Women Founders.* Boston: McGraw-Hill, 1998.

Leung, M.W., I.H. Yen, and M. Minkler. "Community-Based Participatory Research: A Promising Approach for Increasing Epidemiology's Relevance in the 21st Century." *International Journal of Epidemiology* 33.3 (2004): 499–506.

Levi, P. *The Drowned and the Saved.* London: Abacus, 1987.

Levinas, E. "Useless Suffering." In *The Provocation of Levinas: Rethinking the Other,* ed. R. Bernasconi and D. Wood. London: Routledge, 1988.

Levine, R.S. "*Uncle Tom's Cabin* in Frederick Douglass' Paper: An Analysis of Reception." *American Literature* 64.1 (1992): 71–93.

Lewin, K. "Action Research and Minority Problems." *Journal of Social Issues* 2.4 (1946): 34–46.

Lewis, H.M. *Participatory Research and Education for Social Change: Highlander Research and Education Center.* Thousand Oaks, CA: Sage, 2001.

Lewis, T.C., T.G. Robins, J.T. Dvonch, G.J. Keeler, F.Y. Yip, G.B. Mentz, X. Xihong Lin, E.A. Parker, B.A. Israel, L. Gonzalez, and Y. Hill. "Air Pollution–Associated Changes in Lung Function among Asthmatic Children in Detroit." *Environmental Health Perspectives* 113.8 (2005): 1068–75.

Lindsey, A. *The Pullman Strike: The Story of a Unique Experiment and of a Great Labor Upheaval.* Chicago: University of Chicago Press, 1943.

Linn, J.W. *Jane Addams: A Biography.* Chicago: University of Illinois Press, 1935.

Lissak, R.S. *Pluralism and Progressives: Hull House and the New Immigrants, 1890–1919.* Chicago: University of Chicago Press, 1989.

Lloyd, L. "A Caring Profession? The Ethics of Care and Social Work with Older People." *British Journal of Social Work* 36.7 (2006): 1171–85.

Lock, M. "On Dying Twice: Culture, Technology and the Determination of Death." In *Living and Working with the New Medical Technologies: Intersections of Inquiry,* ed. M. Lock, A. Young, and A. Cambrosio. New York: Cambridge University Press, 2000.

Lock, M., and V.K. Nguyen. *An Anthropology of Biomedicine.* Oxford: Wiley-Blackwell, 2010.

Lock, M., and N. Scheper-Hughes. "A Critical-Interpretive Approach in Medical Anthropology: Rituals and Routines of Discipline and Dissent." In *Medical Anthropology: A Handbook of Theory and Method,* ed. T.M. Johnson and C.F. Sargent. New York: Greenwood Press, 1990.

Low, S.M., and S.E. Merry. "Engaged Anthropology: Diversity and Dilemmas." *Current Anthropology* 51.2 (2010): 203–26.

Loyakla, M.D. *Eating Bitterness: Stories from the Front Lines of China's Great Urban Migration.* Berkeley: University of California Press, 2013.

Luhrmann, T. M. *Of Two Minds: The Growing Disorder in American Psychiatry.* New York: Alfred A. Knopf, 2000.

Lundblad, K. S. "Jane Addams and Social Reform: A Role Model for the 1990s." *Social Work* 40.5 (1995): 661–69.

Lynd, R. S. *Knowledge for What? The Place of Social Science in American Culture.* Princeton, NJ: Princeton University Press, 1939.

MacGilvray, E. A. "Experience as Experiment: Some Consequences of Pragmatism for Democratic Theory." *American Journal of Political Science* 43.2 (1999): 542–65.

Mackenzie, H. "Henry Mackenzie, *The Lounger*, No. 20 (Saturday, 18 June 1785)." In *The Man of Feeling.* Oxford: Oxford University Press, [1785] 2001.

Maguire, M., C. Frois, and N. Zurawksi, eds. *The Anthropology of Security: Perspectives from the Frontline of Policing, Counter-Terrorism and Border Control.* London: Pluto Press, 2014.

Makridis, O. "Is a Levinasian Theory of Justice Possible? A Response to Murray." *New Jersey Journal of Communication* 11.1 (2003): 24–44.

Mandeville, B. *The Fable of the Bees.* Harmondsworth: Penguin, [1723] 1970.

Marcus, G. E., and M. M. Fischer. *Anthropology as Cultural Critique: An Experimental Moment in the Human Sciences.* Chicago: University of Chicago Press, 1999.

Marmot, M., and R. Wilkinson, eds. *Social Determinants of Health.* Oxford: Oxford University Press, 2009.

Marrero-Fente, R. "Human Rights and Academic Discourse: Teaching the Las Casas-Sepúlveda Debate at the Time of the Iraq War." Human Rights and Latin American Cultural Studies. *Hispanic Issues On Line* 4.1 (2009). http://hispanicissues.umn.edu/assets/doc/Marrero_Fente.pdf.

Marshall, D. "Adam Smith and the Theatricality of Moral Sentiments." *Critical Inquiry* 10 (1984): 592–613.

Marx, K. "The Eighteenth Brumaire of Louis Bonaparte." In *Karl Marx: Selected Writings*, ed. D. Mclellan. Oxford: Oxford University Press, [1851] 1977.

Mason, E. "Feeling Dickensian Feeling." *Interdisciplinary Studies in the Long Nineteenth Century* 19.4 (2007). Available at www.19.bbk.ac.uk.

Mason, K. A. "Mobile Migrants, Mobile Germs: Migration, Contagion and Boundary building in Shenzhen, China after SARS." *Medical Anthropology* 31.2 (2012): 113–31.

Mayo-Smith R. "Levasseur's *La Population Française.*" *Political Science Quarterly* 8.1 (1893): 124–36.

Mayhew, H. *London Labour and the London Poor.* Oxford: Oxford University Press, [1861–62] 2010.

Maza, S. *Private Lives and Public Affairs: The Causes Célèbres of Prerevolutionary France.* Berkeley: University of California Press, 1993.

McFarland, S. "The Slow Creation of Humanity." *Political Psychology* 32.1 (2011): 1–20.

McGowan, R. "A Powerful Sympathy: Terror, the Prison, and Humanitarian Reform in Early Nineteenth-Century Britain." *Journal of British Studies* 25.3 (1986): 312–34.

McRobbie, A. "A Mixed Bag of Misfortunes? Bourdieu's *Weight of the World*." *Theory, Culture & Society* 19.3 (2002): 129–38.

Meacham, S. *Toynbee Hall and Social Reform, 1880–1914: The Search for Community*. New Haven, CT: Yale University Press, 1987.

Meagher, G. "Modernising Social Work and the Ethics of Care." *Social Work & Society* 2.1 (2004): 10–27.

Menand, L. *The Metaphysical Club: A Story of Ideas in America*. New York: Farrar, Straus and Giroux, 2001.

Merton, R. K. "The Unanticipated Consequences of Purposive Action." *American Sociological Review* 1.6 (1936): 894–904.

Meyer, H., B. Hamilton, S. Kroeger, S. Stewart, and M. Brydon-Miller. "The Unexpected Journey: Renewing our Commitment to Students through Educational Action Research." *Educational Action Research* 12.4 (2004): 557–74.

Miller, T. *China's Urban Billion: The Story Behind the Biggest Migration in Human History*. London: Zed Books, 2012.

Mills, C. W. "The Cultural Apparatus." In *Power, Politics and People: The Collected Essays of C. Wright Mills*, ed. I. L. Horowitz. New York: Oxford University Press, 1963.

———. *The Sociological Imagination*. Oxford: Oxford University Press, 1959.

———. *Sociology and Pragmatism: The Higher Learning in America*. New York: Oxford University Press, 1964.

Minkler, M., V. B. Vasquez, and P. Shepard. "Promoting Environmental Health Policy through Community-Based Participatory Research: A Case Study from Harlem, New York." *Journal of Urban Health* 83.1 (2006): 101–10.

Minkler, M., and N. Wallerstein, eds. *Community-Based Participatory Research for Health: From Process to Outcomes*. New York: John Wiley & Sons, 2010.

Moore, B., Jr. *Reflections on the Causes of Human Misery and upon Certain Proposals to Eliminate Them*. Boston: Beacon Press, 1972.

Moore, K. L. *The Joy of Noh: Embodied Learning and Discipline in Urban Japan*. New York: State University of New York Press, 2014.

Morgan, D. "Pain: The Unrelieved Condition of Modernity." *European Journal of Social Theory* 5.3 (2002): 307–22.

Morrell, J., and A. Thackray. *Gentlemen of Science: Early Years of the British Association for the Advancement of Science*. Oxford: Clarendon Press, 1981.

Morrill, J., and P. Baker. 'Oliver Cromwell, the Regicide and the Sons of Zeruiah." In *Cromwell and the Interregnum: Essential Readings*, ed. D. L. Smith. Oxford: Wiley-Blackwell, 2003.

Morris, J. "Impairment and Disability: Constructing an Ethics of Care that Promotes Human Rights." *Hypatia* 16.4 (2001): 1–16.

Morrow, G. R. "The Significance of the Doctrine of Sympathy in Hume and Adam Smith." *Philosophical Review* 32.1 (1923): 60–78.

Mou, J., J. Cheng, S. M. Griffiths, S. Y. S. Wong, S. Hillier, and D. Zhang. "Internal Migration and Depressive Symptoms among Migrant Factory Workers in Shenzhen, China." *Journal of Community Psychology* 39.2 (2011): 212–30.

Mou, J., S. M. Griffiths, H. Fong, and M. G. Dawes. "Health of China's Rural-Urban Migrants and Their Families: A Review of Literature from 2000 to 2012." *British Medical Bulletin* 106.1 (2013): 19–43.

Mowat, C. L. *The Charity Organisation Society, 1869–1913: Its Ideas and Work.* London: Methuen, 1961.

Moyn, S. *The Last Utopia: Human Rights in History.* Cambridge, MA: Harvard University Press, 2010.

Mullan, J. *Sentiment and Sociability: The Language of Feeling in the Eighteenth Century.* London: Clarendon Press, 1988.

Nash, K. "Global Citizenship as Show Business: The Cultural Politics of Make Poverty History." *Media, Culture and Society* 30.2 (2008): 167–81.

Nations, M., and L. Rebhun. "Angels with Wet Wings Won't Fly: Maternal Sentiment in Brazil and the Image of Neglect." *Culture, Medicine and Psychiatry* 12.2 (1988): 141–200.

Nguyen, V. K. *The Republic of Therapy: Triage and Sovereignty in West Africa's Time of AIDS.* Durham, NC: Duke University Press, 2010.

Nichter, M. *Global Health: Why Cultural Perceptions, Social Representations, and Biopolitics Matter.* Tucson: University of Arizona Press, 2008.

Nie, J.-B. *Medical Ethics in China: A Transcultural Interpretation.* London: Routledge, 2013.

Nietzsche, F. "On the Genealogy of Morals." In *Basic Writings of Nietzsche*, ed. W. Kaufmann. New York: Modern Library, [1887] 2000.

———. *Thus Spoke Zarathustra: A Book for Everyone and No One.* Harmondsworth: Penguin Books, [1883] 1961.

Noble, J. *Fiscal Legislation, 1842–1865.* London: Longmans, Green, Reader & Dyer, 1867.

Noble, M. "The Ecstasies of Sentimental Wounding in *Uncle Tom's Cabin*." *Yale Journal of Criticism* 10.2 (1997): 295–320.

Norton, C. E. *Considerations on Some Recent Social Theories.* Boston: Little, Brown, 1853.

Norton, R. E. "The Myth of the Counter-Enlightenment." *Journal of the History of Ideas* 68.4 (2007): 638–58.

Olesen, V. L. "Caregiving, Ethical and Informal: Emerging Challenges in the Sociology of Health and Illness." *Journal of Health and Social Behavior* 30.1 (1989): 1–10.

O'Meara, K., and A. J. Jaeger. "Preparing Future Faculty for Community Engagement: Barriers, Facilitators, Models, and Recommendations." *Journal of Higher Education Outreach and Engagement* 11.4 (2007): 3–26.

Opdycke, S. *Jane Addams and Her Vision of America*. Upper Saddle River, NJ: Pearson, 2011.

Ortiz, I., and M. Cummins. "When the Global Crisis and Youth Bulge Collide: Double the Jobs Trouble for Youth." UNICEF, New York, 2012. Available at www.unicef.org/socialpolicy/files/Global_Crisis_and_Youth_Bulge_FINAL. pdf.

Ossewaarde, M. "Settling the Social Question: Three Variants of Modern Christian Social Thought." *Journal of Markets and Morality* 14.2 (2011): 301–17.

Pagden, A. 1992. Introduction to B. de Las Casas, *A Short Account of the Destruction of the Indies*. London: Penguin, [1552] 1992.

Paine, T. *Rights of Man, Common Sense and Other Political Writings*. Oxford: Oxford University Press, [1776] 1995.

Pandolfi, M. "Humanitarianism and Its Discontents." In *Forces of Compassion: Humanitarianism between Ethics and Politics*, ed. E. Bornstein and P. Redfield. Santa Fe, NM: School for Advanced Research Press, 2010.

Papke, D. R. *The Pullman Case: The Clash of Labor and Capital in Industrial America*. Lawrence: University Press of Kansas, 1999.

Parker, G. *Global Crisis: War, Climate Change and Catastrophe in the Seventeenth Century*. New Haven, CT: Yale University Press, 2013.

Parker, R. *Beneath the Equator: Cultures of Desire, Male Homosexuality, and Emerging Gay Communities in Brazil*. London: Routledge, 1998.

Parsons, T. Introduction to M. Weber, *The Sociology of Religion*. London: Methuen, 1966.

Parton, N. "Rethinking Professional Practice: The Contributions of Social Constructionism and the Feminist 'Ethics of Care.'" *British Journal of Social Work* 33.1 (2003): 1–16.

Patel, V., A. Kleinman, and B. Saraceno. "Protecting the Human Rights of People with Mental Illnesses: A Call to Action for Global Mental Health." In *Mental Health and Human Rights: Vision, Praxis and Courage*, ed. M. Dudley, D. Silove, and F. Gale. New York: Oxford University Press, 2012.

Paul, B. D., ed. *Health, Culture, and Community*. New York: Russell Sage Foundation, 1955.

Peabody, F. G. *Jesus Christ and the Social Question*. New York: Grosset and Dunlap, 1900.

Peck, J. "Zombie Neoliberalism and the Ambidextrous State." *Theoretical Criminology* 14.1 (2010): 104–10.

Pennington, K. "Bartolomé de las Casas and the Tradition of Medieval Law." *Church History* 39.2 (1970): 149–61.

Petryna, A. *Life Exposed: Biological Citizens after Chernobyl*. Princeton, NJ: Princeton University Press, 2002.

Philpott, T. L. *The Slum and the Ghetto: Immigrants, Blacks, and Reformers in Chicago, 1880–1930*. Belmont, CA: Wadsworth, 1991.

Pinker, S. *The Better Angels of Our Nature: A History of Violence and Humanity*. London: Penguin, 2011.

Plamper, J. "The History of Emotions: An Interview with William Reddy, Barbara Rosenwein and Peter Stearns." *History and Theory* 49.2 (2010): 237–65.

Plummer, K. *Documents of Life 2: An Invitation to Critical Humanism*. London: Sage, 2001.

Poovey, M. "Figures of Arithmetic, Figures of Speech: The Discourse of Statistics in the Late 1830s." *Critical Inquiry* 19.2 (1993): 256–76.

———. *A History of the Modern Fact: Problems of Knowledge in the Sciences of Wealth and Society*. Chicago: University of Chicago Press, 1998.

———. *Making a Social Body: British Cultural Formation, 1830–1864*. Chicago: University of Chicago Press, 1995.

Porat, Z. "Who, Me? Evil and the Rhetoric of Interminable Interrogation in Pierre Bayle's Critical and Historical Dictionary." *Literature and Theology* 9.1 (1995): 46–65.

Porter, D., and R. Porter. *Patient's Progress: Doctors and Doctoring in Eighteenth-Century England*. Redwood City, CA: Stanford University Press, 1989.

Porter, R. *The Enlightenment*. Basingstoke: Palgrave, 2001.

———. *The Greatest Benefit to Mankind: A Medical History of Humanity from Antiquity to the Present*. London: HarperCollins, 1997.

———. *Patients and Practitioners: Lay Perceptions of Medicine in Pre- Industrial Society*. Cambridge: Cambridge University Press, 1985.

———. "The Patient's View: Doing Medical History from Below." *Theory and Society* 14.2 (1985): 175–98.

———. "The Scientific Revolution: A Spoke in the Wheel?" In *Revolution in History*, ed. R. Porter and M. Teich. Cambridge: Cambridge University Press, 1986.

Porter, R., and M. Teich, eds. *The Scientific Revolution in National Context*. Cambridge: Cambridge University Press, 1992.

Putnam, H. *Pragmatism: An Open Question*. Cambridge: Blackwell, 1995.

Quennell, P. *Mayhew's London: Being Selections from "London Labour and the London Poor."* London: Pilot Press, 1949.

Quesada, J. "Suffering Child: An Embodiment of War and Its Aftermath in Post-Sandinista Nicaragua." *Medical Anthropology Quarterly* 12.1 (1998): 51–73.

Rai, A. *Rule of Sympathy: Sentiment, Race, and Power, 1750–1850.* New York: Palgrave, 2002.

Randall, D. "Providence, Fortune, and the Experience of Combat: English Printed Battlefield Reports, Circa 1570–1637." *Sixteenth Century Journal* 35.4 (2004): 1053–77.

Rapp, R. *Testing Women, Testing the Fetus: The Social Impact of Amniocentesis in America.* New York: Psychology Press, 1999.

Rauschenbusch, W. *Christianity and the Social Crisis,* London: Macmillan & Co., 1908.

Recchiuti, J. L. *Civic Engagement: Social Science and Progressive Era Reform in New York City.* Philadelphia: University of Pennsylvania Press, 2007.

Reddy, W. M. *The Navigation of Feeling: A Framework for the History of Emotions.* Cambridge: Cambridge University Press, 2001.

———. "Sentimentalism and Its Erasure: The Role of Emotions in the Era of the French Revolution." *Journal of Modern History* 72.1 (2000): 109–52.

Redfield, P. *Life in Crisis: The Ethical Journey of Doctors Without Borders.* Berkeley: University of California Press, 2013.

Redmon, D. *Beads, Bodies and Trash: Public Sex, Global Labor and the Disposability of Mardi Gras.* New York: Routledge, 2015.

Renault, E. *Souffrances sociales.* Paris: La Découverte, 2008.

Residents of Hull-House. *Hull-House Maps and Papers.* Urbana: University of Illinois Press, [1895] 2007.

Rhodes, S. D., E. Eng, K. C. Hergenrather, I. M. Remnitz, R. Arceo, J. Montao, and J. Alegra-Ortega. "Exploring Latino Men's HIV Risk Using Community-Based Participatory Research." *American Journal of Health Behavior* 31.2 (2007): 146–58.

Rhodes, T., M. Singer, P. Bourgois, S. R. Friedman, and S. A. Strathdee. "The Social Structural Production of HIV Risk among Injecting Drug Users." *Social Science & Medicine* 61.5 (2005): 1026–44.

Richardson, R. D. *William James in the Maelstrom of American Modernism.* Boston: Mariner Books, 2006.

Riesebrodt, M. "Charisma in Max Weber's *Sociology of Religion.*" *Religion* 29.1 (1999): 1–14.

Rifkin, J. *The Empathic Civilization: The Race to Global Consciousness in a World in Crisis.* Cambridge: Polity Press, 2009.

Riskin, J. *Science in the Age of Sensibility: The Sentimental Empiricists of the French Enlightenment.* Chicago: University of Chicago Press, 2002.

Roberts, F. D. *The Social Conscience of the Early Victorians*. Stanford, CA: Stanford University Press, 2002.

Roberts, J. "Structural Violence and Emotional Health: A Message from Easington, a Former Mining Community in Northern England." *Anthropology & Medicine* 16.1 (2009): 37–48.

Roberts, M. J. D. "Charity Disestablished? The Origins of the Charity Organisation Society Revisited, 1868–1871." *Journal of Ecclesiastical History* 54.1 (2003): 40–61.

Roberts, N. "Character in the Mind: Citizenship, Education and Psychology in Britain, 1880–1914." *History of Education: Journal of the History of Education Society* 33.2 (2004): 177–97.

Rock, M. "Sweet Blood and Social Suffering: Rethinking Cause-Effect Relationships in Diabetes, Distress, and Duress." *Medical Anthropology* 22.2 (2003): 131–74.

Rorty, R. "Is Truth a Goal of Enquiry? Davidson vs. Wright." *Philosophical Quarterly* 45.180 (1995): 281–300.

———. *The Linguistic Turn: Recent Essays in Philosophical Method*. Chicago: University of Chicago Press, 1967.

Rose, G. *Mourning Becomes the Law: Philosophy and Representation*. Cambridge: Cambridge University Press, 1996.

Rosenwein, B. H. "Worrying about Emotions in History." *American Historical Review* 107.3 (2002): 821–45.

Rummel, R. J. *Death by Government*. New Brunswick, NJ: Transaction Publishers, 1994.

Rylko-Bauer, B., M. Singer, and J. V. Willigen. "Reclaiming Applied Anthropology: Its Past, Present, and Future." *American Anthropologist* 108.1 (2006): 178–90.

Sandel, M. J. *Justice: What's The Right Thing To Do?* New York: Farrar, Straus and Giroux, 2009.

———. *What Money Can't Buy: The Moral Limits of Markets*. New York: Farrar, Straus and Giroux, 2012.

Saum, L. O. *The Popular Mood of America, 1860–1890*. Lincoln: University of Nebraska Press, 1990.

Sawchuk, K. "The Cultural Apparatus: C. Wright Mills' Unfinished Work." *American Sociologist* 32.1 (2001): 27–49.

Sayad, A. *The Suffering of the Immigrant*. Cambridge: Polity Press, 2004.

Scaff, L. A. *Fleeing the Iron Cage: Culture, Politics, and Modernity in the Thought of Max Weber*. Berkeley: University of California Press, 1991.

———. *Max Weber in America*. Princeton, NJ: Princeton University Press, 2011.

Schensul, J. J., J. Robison, C. Reyes, K. Radda, S. Gaztambide, and W. Disch. "Building Interdisciplinary/Intersectoral Research Partnerships for Community-Based Mental Health Research with Older Minority Adults." *American Journal of Community Psychology* 38.1–2 (2006): 79–93.

Scheper-Hughes, N. *Death without Weeping: The Violence of Everyday Life in Brazil.* Berkeley: University of California Press, 1992.

———. "Making Anthropology Public." *Anthropology Today* 25.4 (2009): 1–3.

———. "Three Propositions for a Critically Applied Medical Anthropology." *Social Science & Medicine* 30.2 (1990): 189–97.

———. "Undoing: Social Suffering and the Politics of Remorse in the New South Africa." *Social Justice* 24.4 (1998): 114–42.

Schilder, P. "The Social Neurosis." *Psychoanalytic Review* 25 (1938): 1–19.

Schluchter, W. *Rationalism, Religion, and Domination: A Weberian Perspective.* Berkeley: University of California Press, 1989.

Schneiderhan, E. "Pragmatism and Empirical Sociology: The Case of Jane Addams and Hull-House, 1889–1895." *Theory and Society* 40.6 (2011): 589–617.

Schopenhauer, A. "On the Suffering of the World." In *Essays and Aphorisms.* Harmondsworth: Penguin, 1970.

Schroeder, R. "Nietzsche and Weber: Two 'Prophets' of the Modern World." In *Max Weber, Rationality and Modernity,* ed. S. Whimster and S. Lash. London: Routledge, 1987.

Scuzzarello, S., and C. Kinnvall. "Rebordering France and Denmark Narratives and Practices of Border-Construction in Two European Countries." *Mobilities* 8.1 (2013): 90–106.

Seidman, S. "The Main Aims and Thematic Structures of Max Weber's Sociology." *Canadian Journal of Sociology* 9.4 (1984): 381–404.

———. "Modernity, Meaning, and Cultural Pessimism in Max Weber." *Sociology of Religion* 44.4 (1983): 267–78.

Seigfried, C. H. "Introduction to the Illinois Edition." In J. Addams, *Democracy and Social Ethics.* Urbana: University of Illinois Press, 2002.

———. "Socializing Democracy: Jane Addams and John Dewey." *Philosophy of the Social Sciences* 29.2 (1999): 207–30.

Sen, A. *The Idea of Justice,* Cambridge, MA: Belknap Press, 2009.

Shafir, G. "The Incongruity between Destiny and Merit: Max Weber on Meaningful Existence and Modernity." *British Journal of Sociology* 36.4 (1985): 516–530.

Sharp, D. "Thomas Wakley (1795–1862): A Biographical Sketch." *Lancet* 379.9829 (2012): 1914–21.

Shields, P. M. "Classical Pragmatism: Engaging Practitioner Experience." *Administration & Society* 36.3 (2004): 351–61.

Simich, J. L., and R. Tilman. "Radicalism vs. Liberalism: C. Wright Mills' Critique of John Dewey's Ideas." *American Journal of Economics and Sociology* 37.4 (1978): 413–30.

Singer, M., and S. Clair. "Syndemics and Public Health: Reconceptualizing Disease in Bio-Social Context." *Medical Anthropology Quarterly* 17.4 (2003): 423–41.

Skultans, V. *The Testimony of Lives: Narrative and Memory in Post-Soviet Latvia.* London: Routledge, 1998.

Slack, P. *The Impact of Plague in Tudor and Stuart England.* London: Routledge & Kegan Paul, 1985.

Smith, A. *The Theory of Moral Sentiments.* Mineola: Dover Publications, [1759] 2006.

Smith, M. J. *Professional Education for Social Work in Britain: An Historical Account.* London: Allen & Unwin, 1965.

Smith, P. D. *City: A Guidebook for the Urban Age.* London: Bloomsbury Press, 2012.

Sniadecki, J. P. *Digital Jianghu: Independent Documentary in a Beijing Art Village.* 2013. Available at http://dash.harvard.edu/handle/1/11064403.

Solicari, S. "Selling Sentiment: The Commodification of Emotion in Victorian Visual Culture." *19: Interdisciplinary Studies in the Long Nineteenth Century* 4 (2007). www.19.bbk.ac.uk

Solomon, R. C. *The Passions: Emotions and the Meaning of Life.* Indianapolis, IN: Hackett, 1993.

Sontag, S. *Regarding the Pain of Others.* London: Hamish Hamilton, 2003.

Sorisio, C. "The Spectacle of the Body: Torture in the Antislavery Writing of Lydia Maria Child and Frances E. W. Harper." *Modern Language Studies* 30.1 (2000): 45–66.

Specht, H., and M. E. Courtney. *Unfaithful Angels: How Social Work Has Abandoned Its Mission.* New York: Free Press, 1995.

Spelman, E. V. *Fruits of Sorrow: Framing Our Attention to Suffering.* Boston: Beacon Press, 1997.

Spencer, H. "The New Toryism." *Contemporary Review* 45 (1884): 153–67.

Spierenburg, P. *The Spectacle of Suffering: Executions and the Evolution of Oppression: From a Pre-Industrial Metropolis to the European Experience.* Cambridge: Cambridge University Press, 1984.

———. *Violence & Punishment: Civilizing the Body through Time.* Cambridge: Polity Press, 2013.

Spinrad, W. "Charisma: A Blighted Concept and an Alternative Formula." *Political Science Quarterly* 106.2 (1991): 295–311.

Sprague, E. "Francis Hutcheson and the Moral Sense." *Journal of Philosophy* 51.24 (1954): 794–800.

Stamatov, P. *The Origins of Global Humanitarianism: Religion, Empires and Advocacy.* Cambridge: Cambridge University Press, 2013.

Steiner, G. *Language and Silence.* London: Faber & Faber, 1967.

Stoecker, R., and E. Bonacich. "Why Participatory Research? Guest Editors' Introduction." *American Sociologist* 23.4 (1992): 5–14.

Stowe, H. B. *Uncle Tom's Cabin or Negro Life in the Slave States of America.* Ware: Wordsworth Classics, [1852] 1999.

Strand, K.J., N. Cutforth, R. Stoecker, S. Marullo, and P. Donohue. *Commu-nity-Based Research and Higher Education: Principles and Practices*. New York: John Wiley & Sons, 2003.

Strong, T. B. "What Have We to Do with Morals? Nietzsche and Weber on History and Ethics." *History of the Human Sciences* 5.3 (1992): 9–18.

Stuhr, J. J. *Genealogical Pragmatism: Philosophy, Experience, and Community*. Albany: State University of New York Press, 1997.

Sturdy, S., and R. Cooter. "Science, Scientific Management and the Transforma-tion of Medicine in Britain c. 1870–1950." *History of Science* 36 (1998): 421–66.

Sumner, A. "Global Poverty and the New Bottom Billion: What If Three Quarters of the World's Poor Live in Middle-Income Countries?" *IDS Working Papers, 2010* 349 (2010): 1–43.

Sumner, A., and M. Tiwari. "Global Poverty Reduction to 2015 and Beyond: What Has Been the Impact of the MDGs and What Are the Options for a Post-2015 Global Framework?" *IDS Working Papers 2010* 348 (2010): 1–31.

Swatos, W. H. "The Disenchantment of Charisma: A Weberian Assessment of Revolution in a Rationalized World." *Sociological Analysis* 42.2 (1981): 119–36.

Sznaider, N. *The Compassionate Temperament: Care and Cruelty in Modern Society*. Lanham, MD: Rowman & Littlefield, 2001.

Tapias, M. "Emotions and the Intergenerational Embodiment of Social Suffer-ing in Rural Bolivia." *Medical Anthropology Quarterly* 20.3 (2006): 399–415.

Taussig, M. T. *Shamanism, Colonialism, and the Wild Man: A Study in Terror and Healing*. Chicago: University of Chicago Press, 1987.

Taylor, C. *Modern Social Imaginaries*. Durham, NC: Duke University Press, 2004.

Tenbruck, F. "The Problem of the Thematic Unity in the Works of Max Weber." *British Journal of Sociology* 31.3 (1980): 316–51.

———. "The Problem of the Thematic Unity in the Works of Max Weber (with Prefatory Remarks)." In *Reading Weber*, ed. K. Tribe. London: Routledge, 1989.

Tester, K. *Compassion, Morality, and the Media*. Buckingham: Open Univer-sity, 2001.

Therborn, G. *The World: A Beginner's Guide*. Cambridge: Polity Press, 2011.

Thomas, K. *Man and the Natural World: Changing Attitudes in England, 1500–1800*. London: Penguin, 1983.

———. *Religion and the Decline of Magic: Studies in Popular Beliefs in Six-teenth and Seventeenth Century England*. London: Penguin, 1971.

Thompson, A. *The Art of Suffering and the Impact of Seventeenth-Century Anti-Providential Thought*. Aldershot: Ashgate, 2003.

Thompson, B., M.J. Cohen, and J. Meerman. "World Food Insecurity and Malnutrition: Scope, Trends, Causes and Consequences." In *The Impact of Climate Change and Bioenergy on Nutrition,* ed. B. Thompson and M.J. Cohen. Dordrecht: Springer, 2012.

Thompson, E.P. (1971) "Mayhew and the *Morning Chronicle.*" In *The Unknown Mayhew: Selections from the "Morning Chronicle,"* ed. E.P. Thompson and E. Yeo. London: Merlin Press, 1971.

Thompson, E.P., and E. Yeo, eds. *The Unknown Mayhew: Selections from the "Morning Chronicle."* London: Merlin Press, 1971.

Thompson, J.B. *The Media and Modernity: A Social Theory of the Media.* Cambridge: Polity Press, 1995.

Tinsley, D.F. *The Scourge of the Cross: Ascetic Mentalities of the Later Middle Ages.* Walpole: Peeters, 2010.

Tiryakian, E.A. "Collective Effervescence, Social Change and Charisma: Durkheim, Weber and 1989." *International Sociology* 10.3 (1995): 269–81.

Todd, A.J. "Sentimentality and Social Reform." *American Journal of Sociology* 22.2 (1916): 159–76.

Todeschini, M. "The Bomb's Womb? Women and the Atom Bomb." In *Remaking a World: Violence, Social Suffering, and Recovery,* ed. V. Das, A. Kleinman, M. Lock, M. Ramphele, and P. Reynolds. Berkeley: University of California Press, 2001.

Todorov, T. *The Conquest of America: The Question of the Other.* Norman: University of Oklahoma Press, 1984.

Tomalin, C. *Charles Dickens: A Life.* London: Penguin, 2011.

Tomkins, J. *Sensational Designs: The Cultural Work of American Fiction, 1790–1860.* New York: Oxford University Press, 1985.

Toy, C.H. "On the Asaph-Psalms." *Journal of the Society of Biblical Literature and Exegesis* 6.1 (1886): 73–85.

Tribe, K., ed. *Reading Weber.* London: Routledge, 1989.

Tronto, J.C. "Care as a Basis for Radical Political Judgments." *Hypatia* 10.2 (1995): 141–49.

———. *Caring Democracy: Markets, Equality and Social Justice.* New York: New York University Press, 2013.

———. *Moral Boundaries: A Political Argument for an Ethic of Care.* New York: Routledge, 1993.

Turco, L. "Sympathy and Moral Sense: 1725–1740." *British Journal for the History of Philosophy* 7.1 (1999): 79–101.

Turner, B.S. *The Body and Society: Explorations in Social Theory.* London: Sage, 2008.

———. *Classical Sociology.* London: Sage, 1999.

———. "The History of the Changing Concepts of Health and Illness: Outline of a General Model of Illness Categories." In *The Handbook of Social Studies in*

Health and Medicine, ed. G.L. Albrecht, R. Fitzpatrick, and S.C. Scrimshaw. London: Sage, 2000.

———. "Introduction: Marx and Nietzsche." In *For Weber: Essays on the Sociology of Fate*. London: Sage, 1996.

———. *Max Weber: From History to Modernity*. London: Routledge, 1992.

———. *Vulnerability and Human Rights*. University Park: Pennsylvania State University Press, 2006.

Turner, S. "Charisma Reconsidered." *Journal of Classical Sociology* 3.1 (2003): 5–26.

Turner, S.P., and J.H. Turner. *The Impossible Science: An Institutional Analysis of American Sociology*. New York: Sage, 1990.

United Nations Childrens Fund (UNICEF). *Levels and Trends in Child Mortality: Report 2010*. New York: UNICEF, 2010.

United Nations Development Programme (UNDP). *Human Development Report 2006. Beyond Scarcity: Power, Poverty and the Global Water Crisis*. New York: UNDP, 2006.

Valli, L., ed. *Reflective Teacher Education: Cases and Critiques*. Albany: State University of New York Press, 1992.

Vidich, A.J., and S.J. Lyman. *American Sociology: Worldly Rejections of Religions and Their Directions*. New Haven, CT: Yale University Press, 1985.

Vincent-Buffault, A. *The History of Tears: Sensibility and Sentimentality in France*. Basingstoke: Macmillan, 1986.

Vitz, R. "Sympathy and Benevolence in Hume's Moral Psychology." *Journal of the History of Philosophy* 42.3 (2004): 261–75.

Voltaire. *Candide, or Optimism*. Harmondsworth: Penguin, [1759] 1947.

———. "The Lisbon Earthquake." In *The Portable Voltaire*, ed. B.R. Redman. Harmondsworth: Penguin, [1756] 1949.

Wacquant, L. *Punishing the Poor: The Neoliberal Government of Social Insecurity*. Durham, NC: Duke University Press, 2009.

Wallerstein, N., and B. Duran. "Community-Based Participatory Research Contributions to Intervention Research: The Intersection of Science and Practice to Improve Health Equity." *American Journal of Public Health* 100.1 (2010): 40–46.

———. "Using Community-Based Participatory Research to Address Health Disparities." *Health Promotion Practice* 7.3 (2006): 312–23.

Walsham, A. *Providence in Early Modern England*. Oxford: Oxford University Press, 1999.

Ward, B. *Miracles and the Medieval Mind: Theory, Record, and Event, 1000–1215*. Philadelphia: University of Pennsylvania Press, 1982.

Ward, L.F. "Mind as a Social Factor." *Mind* 9.36 (1884): 563–73.

Ward, W.G. *On Nature and Grace*. London: G. Barkley, 1859.

Warren, M. "The Politics of Nietzsche's Philosophy: Nihilism, Culture and Power." *Political Studies* 33.3 (1985): 418–38.

Wasielewski, P. L. "The Emotional Basis of Charisma." *Symbolic Interaction* 8.2 (1985): 207–22.

Wear, A., ed. *Medicine in Society: Historical Essays.* Cambridge: Cambridge University Press, 1992.

Weber, Marianne. *Max Weber: A Biography.* New York: John Wiley & Sons, 1975.

Weber, M. *Economy and Society: An Outline of Interpretive Sociology.* Berkeley: University of California Press, 1978.

———. "The Nature of Charismatic Authority and Its Routinization." In *Max Weber on Charisma and Institution Building,* ed. S. N. Eisenstadt. Chicago: University of Chicago Press, 1968.

———. "Politics as a Vocation." In *From Max Weber,* ed. H. H. Gerth and C. W. Mills. London: Routledge, 1948.

———. *The Protestant Ethic and the Spirit of Capitalism.* New York: Charles Scribner's Sons, 1958.

———. "Religious Rejections of the World and Their Directions." In *From Max Weber,* ed. H. H. Gerth and C. W. Mills. London: Routledge, 1948.

———. "The Routinization of Charisma." In *Max Weber: The Theory of Social and Economic Organization,* ed. T. Parsons. New York: Free Press, 1947.

———. "Science as a Vocation." In *From Max Weber,* ed. H. H. Gerth and C. W. Mills. London: Routledge, 1948.

———. "The Social Psychology of the World Religions." In *From Max Weber,* ed. H. H. Gerth and C. W. Mills. London: Routledge, 1948.

———. *The Sociology of Religion.* London: Methuen, 1966.

Weiss, J. "On the Irreversibility of Western Rationalization and Max Weber's Alleged Fatalism." In *Max Weber, Rationality and Modernity,* ed. S. Whimster and S. Lash. London: Allen & Unwin, 1987.

West, C. *The American Evasion of Philosophy: A Genealogy of Pragmatism.* Basingstoke: Macmillan, 1989.

Whimster, S. *Understanding Weber.* London: Routledge, 2007.

Wickberg, D. "What Is the History of Sensibilities? On Cultural Histories, Old and New." *American Historical Review* 112.3 (2007): 661–84.

Wilkinson, I. *Risk Vulnerability and Everyday Life.* London: Routledge, 2010.

———. *Suffering: A Sociological Introduction.* Cambridge: Polity Press, 2005.

Williams, J. *Wordsworth: Romantic Poetry and Revolution Politics.* Manchester: Manchester University Press, 1989.

Williams, J. E., and V. M. MacLean. "Studying Ourselves: Sociology Discipline-Building in the United States." *American Sociologist* 36.1 (2005): 111–33.

Williams, R. *The Country and the City.* London: Chatto & Windus, 1973.

———. *Keywords: A Vocabulary of Culture and Society.* Glasgow: Fontana, 1976.

———. *Marxism and Literature.* Oxford: Oxford University Press, 1977.

Williams, S. J. *Medicine and the Body.* London: Sage, 2003.

Wilson, E. *Patriotic Gore: Studies in the Literature of the American Civil War.* New York: Oxford University Press, 1966.

Wines, F. H. "Sociology and Philanthropy." *Annals of the American Academy of Political and Social Science* 12 (July 1898): 49–57.

Winship, M. "Prodigies, Puritanism, and the Perils of Natural Theology: The Example of Cotton Mather." *William and Mary Quarterly* 51.1 (1994): 92–105.

———. *Seers of God: Puritan Providentialism in the Restoration and Early Modern Enlightenment.* Baltimore, MD: Johns Hopkins University Press, 1996.

Wolin, S. S. "Max Weber: Legitimation, Method, and the Politics of Theory." *Political Theory* 9.3 (1981): 401–24.

Wollstonecraft, M. *A Vindication of the Rights of Woman and A Vindication of the Rights of Man.* Oxford: Oxford University Press, [1792] 1994.

Wong, D. F. K. Wong, Y. L. Chang, and X. S. He. "Rural Migrant Workers in Urban China: Living a Marginalised Life." *International Journal of Social Welfare* 16.1 (2007): 32–40.

Woodcock, G. "Henry Mayhew and the Undiscovered Country of the Poor." *Sewanee Review* 92.4 (1984): 556–73.

Woodham-Smith, C. *The Great Hunger: Ireland, 1845-9.* London: Penguin, 1962.

Worboys, M. *Spreading Germs: Disease Theories and Medical Practice in Britain, 1865-1900.* Cambridge: Cambridge University Press, 2006.

Worden, B. "Providence and Politics in Cromwellian England." *Past and Present* 109.1 (1985): 55–99.

Wordsworth, W. "Descriptive Sketches." In *The Poetical Works of William Wordsworth,* ed. E. de Selincourt. Oxford: Clarendon Press, [1793] 1952-59.

———. "Preface to *Lyrical Ballads.*" In *Wordsworth and Coleridge: Lyrical Ballads and Other Poems.* Ware: Wordsworth Editions, [1802] 2003.

World Bank. *World Development Report 2011: Conflict, Security, and Development.* Washington, DC: World Bank, 2011.

Wright-Carozza, P. "From Conquest to Constitutions: Retrieving a Latin American Tradition of the Idea of Human Rights." *Human Rights Quarterly* 25.2 (2003): 281–313.

Yang, K. S. "Chinese Social Orientation: An integrative Analysis." In *Chinese Societies and Mental Health,* ed. T. Y. Lin, W. S. Tseng, and Y. Ye. Oxford: Oxford University Press, 1995.

Yang, L. H., A. Kleinman, B. G. Link, J. C. Phelan, S. Lee, and B. Good. "Culture and Stigma: Adding Moral Experience to Stigma Theory." *Social Science & Medicine* 64.7 (2007): 1524–35.

Yeo, E. *The Contest for Social Science: Relations and Representations of Gender and Class.* London: Rivers Oram Press, 1996.

Zarowsky, C. "Writing Trauma: Emotion, Ethnography, and the Politics of Suffering among Somali Returnees in Ethiopia." *Culture, Medicine and Psychiatry* 28.2 (2004): 189–209.

Zhao, C. M., and G. D. Kuh. "Adding Value: Learning Communities and Student Engagement." *Research in Higher Education* 45.2 (2004): 115–38.

Žižek, S. *Violence.* London: Picador, 2008.

Index

Addams, Jane, ix–x, 22; and academic recognition, rejection of, 108–109, 167, 173, 192; biographical information, 164–166; and caregiving as "doing sociology," 163, 166, 167, 169–173, 184–185, 198; and "charity organization" approach to poor relief, 172, 177; and childcare, 169; class and cultural prejudices, strategies designed to expose and unsettle, 167–168, 177–178; and collaborative/cooperative culture, 87, 168–169, 173, 177–178; and community-based participatory research, 174–175, 184–185; and controversy, 170–173; and democracy, socializing of, 168, 174, 186, 246–247n17; egalitarianism of, 166; Nobel Peace Prize (1931), 166; and pragmatism, 84, 89–90, 167, 178, 246–247n17; sanitation campaign of, 169–170; sentimentally disposed sociology of, 76; and social suffering as goad to action, 178–179; as sociologist, marginalization of, 76–77, 163–164, 166–167, 171–173; as sociologist, rehabilitation of, 164, 166–167, 184–185, 187, 246n16; workplace organizing of, 169, 170–172. Works: *Democracy and Social Ethics*, 89; *Hull-House Maps and Papers*, 170; "The Subjective Necessity for Social Settlements," 168; *Twenty*

Years at Hull-House, 168, 169, 171, 178–179
Adorno, Theodore, 122
African Americans: excluded from professionalization of social science, 77, 166–167. *See also* slavery, abolition of
Agamben, Giorgio, 153
AIDS, viii–ix, 106, 182, 240n16
Aldersgate-Street Dispensary, 61–62
amelioration and prevention, 110–111. *See also* interventions in social suffering
American Civil War, 55, 56–57, 88, 190, 191
American Journal of Sociology, 167
American Sociological Association, 76, 167
Amerindians, Spanish conquistadors and, 141–144, 238–239n9, 240n18
animal suffering/animal rights, 39, 42
anthropology: amenability to research and writing on social suffering, 109–110; critique of medicalization, 135; and public health, 181–182; scientistic vision sought for, 59. *See also* ethnography; medical anthropology; social science
anticolonial movement, 190
antinomies of existence, 112, 113, 118, 131–132, 138
Antonio, Robert, 119

CALIFORNIA SERIES IN PUBLIC ANTHROPOLOGY